Management of Training Programs

Management of Training Programs

By

FRANK A. DePHILLIPS, Ph.D.

*Professor of Management and
Industrial Relations*

WILLIAM M. BERLINER, Ph.D.

*Associate Professor of Management and
Industrial Relations*

JAMES J. CRIBBIN, Ph.D.

*Associate Professor of Management and
Industrial Relations*

ALL OF NEW YORK UNIVERSITY

1960

RICHARD D. IRWIN, INC.

HOMEWOOD, ILLINOIS

Library of Congress Catalogue Card No. 60–14053

PRINTED IN THE UNITED STATES OF AMERICA

PREFACE

A CYNIC has remarked that when the world comes to an end it will be neither by fire nor by water, but rather from the sheer weight of books which will crush it into oblivion. Despite the sardonic tone of this comment, it contains a germ of truth. In a world in which educated people are subjected to a constant barrage not to lay head to pillow until they have read this or that masterpiece—most of which will be gone and forgotten in two years—any new book must justify its claim to the reader's time and attention. Unless it offers either new ideas or improved procedures, and this is especially true of a book addressed to the busy businessman and student, the prudent reader should seek out more profitable ways of spending his energy.

Today there is clear evidence that American business is maturing at a rapid pace. No longer is the progressive executive content to concentrate solely on the profit motive and self-aggrandisement. More and more attention is being devoted to such questions as the social responsibilities of private capitalism, business and ethics, decision making, long-range planning—the organic functions that are an integral part of any enterprise. Business problems are no longer considered in isolation from the social forces and pressures of the environment, nor apart from their interrelationships within the matrix of the organization. It is the authors' opinion that a similar development should be going on in the field of training. The insular tendency to consider training as merely a discrete staff function, and at that often limited to the lower operating and supervisory levels, working more or less in isolation from the other forces and activities of the company, must yield to a concept of training that makes it an integral phase of the managerial process. The parochial view which begins training with perhaps a "course" in college and end by delegating training responsibilities to an individual or department, and holds that it should be largely concerned with questions of "how" often to the neglect of the more important question of "why," must give way to one that considers the problems of the training profession within the frame of reference of the theory and practice of management. This the present work attempts to do.

v

The four units of this book are organized about seven central themes:

1. The interdependence of management and training—historically, philosophically, and operationally.
2. The interpersonal and human relations problems involved in planning, organizing, and conducting training programs as a management responsibility.
3. The close integration of training methodology and learning theory, with particular emphasis on individual differences, the nature of the instructional-learning process, and training procedures.
4. The managerial aspects of organizing training programs, with special emphasis on the important role played in such programs by the organizational structure and personality.
5. The discussion focused on various types of training programs, organization of training departments, various training techniques, mechanical aids to training, and the other "how-to" devices that are essential for the competent trainer.
6. The detailed consideration of the need and importance of research and evaluation in training. The field of training must devote itself more persistently to these problems than it has done in the past if training is to be a profession rather than a technique, and the trainer a manager rather than a technician.
7. The consideration of the future of training as a profession.

Unit I deals with the problems of training and the history, meaning, and purposes of training in business and industry. Considerable attention is paid to the relationships existent between management and training. Finally, it analyzes the critical importance of the human equation in training.

Unit II is concerned with theories of learning and principles of training, a rather remarkably neglected area when one considers its importance for the trainer. Various learning myths and learning theories are examined and a common body of principles drawn therefrom for the guidance of the trainer. The nature of the instructional-learning process is analyzed, the advantages and limitations of various training techniques are described, and the effective use of mechanical aids to training is considered.

Unit III examines the organizational structure within which training takes place, the establishment of training programs, and their administration. Special emphasis is devoted to job-skill and special training programs and to supervisory and management development procedures.

Unit IV is devoted to an analysis of the problems involved in training research and evaluation, with particular emphasis on the survey, experimental, and philosophical methods of research. Finally, the future of the training profession is scrutinized.

This book is not offered as a cure-all or a panacea for every training situation. The authors have tried, with what success the reader must decide for himself, to avoid certain common errors: (1) over-emphasis on how to train to the neglect of why to train; (2) consideration of training problems apart from their relationships to the company as a whole and to management's role in training; (3) the listing of abstract principles devoid of all practical application; (4) the opposite mistake of concentration on tricks and gimmicks of training without a conceptual frame of reference that makes the formulas and rule-of-thumb procedures meaningful and effective. Through the use of case studies, problems for examination, illustrative materials, and practical suggestions, the authors have endeavored to combine five important questions within the framework of a sound philosophy of management and training. These questions are: (1) why train? (2) how train most effectively? (3) to what end should training be directed? (4) how can training be evaluated? (5) to what extent is training a management function and how can this function be most efficiently executed?

ACKNOWLEDGMENTS

For the stimulation of their ideas and for their co-operation in allowing certain copyright materials to be adapted and reproduced, acknowledgments are gratefully made to the following publishers and authors: The Ronald Press Company: Lester B. Sands, *Audio-Visual Procedures in Teaching;* Earl G. Planty, W. S. McCord, and C. A. Efferson, *Training Employees and Managers for Production and Teamwork;* William B. Cornell, *Organization and Management in Business and Industry.* Prentice-Hall, Inc.: Roger Bellows, *Creative Leadership;* Frederick L. Whitney, *The Elements of Research;* William M. Sattler and N. Edd Miller, *Discussion and Conference.* D. C. Heath Company: John Dewey, *How We Think.* McGraw-Hill Book Company, Inc.: Edwin E. Ghiselli and C. W. Brown, *Personnel and Industrial Psychology.* Bruce Publishing Company: William A. Kelly, *Educational Psychology, 4th Edition.* Barnes & Noble, Inc.: James D. Weinland, *How to Improve Your Memory.* Harcourt, Brace and Company: Ernest R. Hilgard, *Introduction to Psychology.* Alfred A.

Knopf, Inc.: David Krech and Richard S. Crutchfield, *Elements of Psychology*. Princeton University Press: Stanley L. Payne, *The Art of Asking Questions*. New York University Press: Sir Noel Frederick Hall, *The Making of Higher Executives; The Modern Challenge;* Stuart Chase, *The Social Responsibility of Management*. Richard D. Irwin, Inc.: William Foote Whyte, *Man and Organization*. The Macmillan Company: M. Richardson, *Fundamentals of Mathematics*, rev. ed.; T. L. Kelley, *Scientific Method: Its Functions in Research and Education*. University of Pittsburgh Press: William McGehee, *Persistent Problems in Training*. Dryden Press: Nathaniel Cantor, *The Teaching-Learning Process*. Houghton Mifflin Company: Norman R. F. Maier, *Psychology in Industry*. John Wiley & Sons: *Learning Theory, Personality Theory, and Clinical Research*. Harper & Brothers: Douglas H. Fryer, M. R. Feinberg, and S. S. Zalkind, *Developing People in Industry*. Simon and Schuster, Inc.: Bertrand Russell, *Authority and the Individual*. American Management Association: Lyndall F. Urwick, *Management Education in American Business;* Joseph M. Trickett, *A Survey of Management Development. Advanced Management:* Perrin Stryker, "The Growing Pains of Executive Development." *Management Record:* "Management Development Today." *Business Week:* "A Vital Topic—Business Vitality." *Saturday Evening Post:* C. F. Kettering, "More Music Please, Composer." *The New York Times:* "Manpower Challenge of the 1960's." National Industrial Conference Board: *The Conference Board Record,* "Allocation and Control of Research Expenditures."

Acknowledgment is also due Marc J. Paterson for his advice and critical reading of the manuscript; to Yolanda Leale of the Department of Management and Industrial Relations of New York University, for her invaluable typing assistance; and, most of all, to the wives of the authors who daily put into practice with an admirable elan and finesse the ideas that are merely discussed in this book.

FRANK A. DePHILLIPS

NEW YORK, N.Y.   WILLIAM M. BERLINER
July, 1960   JAMES J. CRIBBIN

TABLE OF CONTENTS

Analytic or Inductive Method. The Synthetic or Deductive Method. The Analytico-synthetic Method. The Need for Stong Leadership. Philosophical Research—the Road to the Professionalization of Training.

BIBLIOGRAPHY

INDEX

Unit I

MANAGEMENT FUNCTIONS
AND TRAINING PROBLEMS

1. MANAGEMENT PRINCIPLES CREATE TRAINING PROBLEMS

Purpose of the Chapter

THIS CHAPTER seeks to do five things: (1) to indicate the importance and the need for training in American business and industry, (2) to define the nature and objectives of training, (3) to describe various current views of the role of the trainer and the training director, (4) to illustrate by brief cases some of the important problems that confront the trainer and which will be dealt with in detail throughout the remainder of the book, and (5) to show how intimately management theory and practice are related to the theory and practice of training. The chapter endeavors to present training not as mere theoretical procedures or as a series of "gimmicks" to be applied mechanically according to a rule of thumb but rather as a dynamic process which takes place within the frame of reference of an ongoing business operation.

The Opportunity and the Challenge

It is commonplace these days to justify the importance of any pet undertaking or interest by bringing communism into the picture. The following excerpt from the 1958 Collective Agreement between management and the workers of the Kiev Machine Tool Works, one of the very few such contracts that have come to the attention of the West, spells out the opportunity and the challenge that face management in the democratic countries with respect to its responsibility for training:

In order to carry out successfully the majestic program for the fastest possible solution of the basic economic task of the USSR . . . namely, to overtake and outstrip the biggest capitalistic countries in the production output per capita in order to strengthen the defensive capacity and might of our Homeland, . . . the workers undertake to amplify Socialistic obligations for

3

the fulfillment and overfulfillment of the production plan of 1958. . . .

This Collective Agreement between the Directorate of the Kiev Machine Tool Works . . . and the workers, engineers, technicians, and clerical employees, represented by the Plant Committee of the Trade Union of Machine Tool Workers . . . makes as its goal the fulfillment and overfulfillment of the state plan for turning out production in specific categories of high quality, further growth in the productivity of labor, the lowering of the cost of production, the raising of the profitableness of the enterprise, the introduction of new technique and progressive technology of production, the dissemination of the advanced methods of work, the further improvement of organization and standardization of labor, the increase in the qualifications of the cadres. . . .

Lenin once stated that in the final analysis the productivity of labor would be the most important single factor for the victory of communism. If management needed any reminder of the importance of training at all levels, from apprenticeship to top executive, surely the purposes of this agreement should serve that end. Training all personnel to peak efficiency is not only a key factor in the struggle between East and West, but it is a task that management in the United States can do extremely well, if it but bend its back to the job.

Meeting the Challenge of Changing Social Conditions

The training challenge and opportunity for management arise not merely from the struggle between democracy and communism. In large measure, they stem from the economic and social changes which are taking place in America regardless of any totalitarian state. So radical are the scientific and technological advances that are taking place that a spokesman for the United States Department of Labor has said, "The transformation we're now seeing will make the 18th century Industrial Revolution look like a pink tea." If this is true, then management will require highly trained and skilled people to carry on ever-increasing and complex business and industrial operations. And these people must be trained if they are to keep pace with technological progress. Mechanization and automation not only have tended to reduce the number of dull and repetitive jobs but have also tended to eliminate the number of dull, repetitive workers. The responsibility of management is to select and train the best possible corps of employees.

At the higher levels, there is an increasing need for what might be termed a new class in American society, the professional manager. This is the executive, who through a process of formal education and long experience on the job has become an expert in the organization and administration of complex business enterprises that he does not own. The discovery and development of executive potential is one of the most pressing problems of industry today.

At times in the past, management has been inclined to engage in many activities without taking time out to evaluate their real worth and effectiveness. Today there seems to be a greater concern for measuring, even in an approximate way, the worthwhileness of some of the things which are done in a given organization. Consider, for example, the following comment of Whyte concerning the merit of one of the most popular types of training:

> Countless thousands of supervisory training programs have been carried on. In nearly every case, you will find that the participants enjoy the programs and say they get a good deal out of them. However, if you wish to be more tough-minded and seek to test a human relations training program through research, then you find that the values of such programs are indeed still to be demonstrated.
>
> The only systematic research studies we have fail to show any significant improvement in supervisor-worker relations, following a human relations training program.[1]

Nature and Objectives of Training

1. *The Riddle of Training in Business and Industry*. Few organizations would admit that they can survive without it—yet some act as though they could.

Everyone knows what it is—yet management, unions, and workers often interpret it in light of their own job conditions.

It is going on all the time—yet much of it is done haphazardly.

It is futile to attempt it without the needed time and facilities—yet often those responsible for it lack either or both.

It costs money—yet at times there is no adequate budgetary appropriation for it.

It should take place at all levels—yet sometimes it is limited to the lowest operating levels.

It can help everyone do a better job—yet those selected for it often fear it.

It is foolish to start it without clearly defined objectives—yet this is occasionally done.

---

[1] William Foote Whyte, *Man and Organization* (Homewood, Ill.: Richard D. Irwin, Inc., 1959), pp. 4–5.

It cannot be ignored without costing the company money—yet some managers seem blind to this reality.

It should permeate the entire organization and be derived from the firm's theory and practice of management—yet sometimes it is shunted off to one department that operates more or less in isolation from the rest of the business.

What is it? The answer to this question and to the paradoxes presented is *training*.

2. *Nature and Objectives of Training.* Training, or an even better term would be "education," can be defined in the following way:

That process which, under company auspices, seeks in a planned, co-ordinated and continuous manner to develop in all employees those understandings, skills, and attitudes, which will maximize individual present and future efficiency and the effectiveness of the over-all company operation.

The scope of training is as broad as the needs and philosophy of a given organization. It may include orientation training for new employees, retraining of older employees caused by changes in procedures or by the introduction of new machines and techniques, brush-up courses for experienced personnel to sharpen their efficiency, job skills training at any given level, human relations training, technical and professional training, supervisory and executive development, general education within the company, and organization-sponsored education in neighboring colleges. Regardless of the type of training involved, however, the objectives remain the same, namely, increased personal efficiency, professional growth, and more effective company-wide operations.

Different Things to Different People

The definition of training is an ideal. The manner in which different trainers view their job is far from ideal or even identical. One trainer has been with the company for twenty years. His concept of his job may have changed very little in that time with respect to basic essentials. He may consider himself as a "how-to-do" expert, writing manuals, organizing courses, and conducting training sessions often at the lower operational levels. At the other extreme may be the "expert," often a former college professor with or without a Ph.D. in psychology. He may specialize in executive development, human relations, and group dynamics. He may rarely, if ever, be greatly concerned with training at the lower operational levels. Then, again, the trainer or training director may be an "organizer." Doing little of the actual training personally, he may organize, co-ordinate, and supervise a variety of programs as demanded to meet the needs of the company. As likely as not, he serves at times as a consultant to management and is responsible for structuring training programs of every type to increase organizational efficiency. One trainer may have come up through the ranks with little or no formal training in the field; another may have entered the company already trained academically for his job but lacking any long-term familiarity with company problems; still another may have begun with experience and then have secured formal education in the field to supplement his practical "know-how." Finally, some trainers and training directors enjoy a status and prestige that enable them to make their influence felt company-wide in the formulation and implementation of policy and practice; others simply lack such status and content themselves with carrying into execution decisions and policies formulated by management.

The different ways in which different trainers and training directors conceptualize their work are not merely the result of personal preference or idiosyncrasy. To a great extent, they are determined by certain organizational factors. A few companies have neglected training until the dismal statistics covering rejects, reworks, turnover, grievances, poor morale, and the lack of a pool of executive potential proved to be painful reminders of their oversight. Other firms have approached the problem more realistically and have recognized the need for training but have given the idea only half-hearted support by restricting training programs to a particular department or level. A few organizations have recognized the importance of training, have carefully defined its aims, scope, and emphases, have evolved a co-ordinated system of programs, and have appreciated the fact that management theory and practice are reflected in training theory and practice. They have rid themselves of much of the riddle of training in business and industry.

Some Practical Training Problems

In any scientific undertaking it is essential to consider at the outset the practical problems that must be analyzed. Any attempt to present prematurely answers to problems that have never really been understood renders even the most perfect solutions meaningless. The following case studies are given in order that the student and practitioner of training may think about some of its ramifications and give his own solutions to the problems proposed. They also represent some of the important ideas which are discussed in the remainder of the book.

ELECTRONICS, INC.

Electronics, Inc., is a young company, which has grown in ten years from one small building and five employees to three buildings, seven hundred employees, and an annual business of over $10,000,-000. The director of personnel and industrial relations has just finished presenting a plan for the introduction of a supervisory development program at the weekly staff meeting. The immediate, unspoken reactions of the other participants are the following:

PRESIDENT: How come we need training? The place for a man to be trained is next to his boss. We've gotten along pretty well so far. I wish Bob would remember that we're running a company for profit's sake, not a school for charity's sake.

TREASURER: Here we go pampering them again. In all my forty years in business no one ever had a "development program" for me. The place to develop yourself is in the school of hard knocks. If these supervisors are no good, then get some who are. I'll bet the next thing he'll try to sell us is some "human relations" boondoggling.

DIRECTOR OF ENGINEERING: Count me out. All of my people are trained.

SALES MANAGER: Why waste time on trifles? I've got a sales meeting to go to. I thought these meetings were for important problems.

QUALITY CONTROL DIRECTOR: This is a good idea. So many of my people are inspection-minded instead of being conscious of preventive quality control.

PLANT MANAGER: My boys really could use this. If it would only get them off my back by running to me whenever something goes wrong and teach them how to handle some of their own problems, it would be worth its weight in gold.

GENERAL MANAGER: Sounds like a good idea. But where will we start? How much will it cost? Who will do it? How much time will it take? Who will be involved? How do we get the stuff out the door while these people are running off to school? We'll have to take a hard look at this before we buy it.

The most crucial problem facing any training director is that of selling top management on its value. How might the personnel director go about selling his program to each of the people described above?

METECTIC COMPANY

Another important problem facing anyone interested in training is that of defining training needs, objectives, and organization of the program. Top management of Metectic Company, a laboratory engaged in the manufacture of small electrical gauges and temperature regulators, has given a go-ahead for a supervisory development program for twelve foremen in the shop. Since much of the work done is concerned with small and highly intricate components, a high degree of skill is required. Each foreman is responsible for about ten assemblers, men and women, ranging from twenty-three to sixty-three years of age and including both the newcomer and the old hand.

After two hours of discussion, the personnel director, the production superintendent, and the general foreman, to whom all foremen report, have listed the following possible topics for inclusion in the ten-week program. The program is to be conducted once each week, in two-hour sessions, one hour on company time and the other on the participants' time at the end of each Wednesday.

Safety
Company policies and rules
Discipline
Giving orders
Self-improvement
Recent changes in the field
Cost control and reduction
Fighting the grapevine
Handling people
Job organization
Building morale
Writing reports
Instruction and training
Company plans and prospects
Competitors' products
Special problems: the new worker, supervision of women, supervising
    the older worker
Getting along with the union

"Well, fellows," the personnel director remarks, "We've got about twenty items which might be considered, but we have only ten meetings. What do we include and what do we leave out?" The general foreman replies: "How do we really know, Fred, what they need? Why don't we try and find out from the men themselves what they think they need?" "Oh, I don't know," chimes in the production superintendent; "if we don't know what they need to do a good job, maybe we need the training more than they do. If we go along with this suggestion, then perhaps we should ask the assemblers themselves and top management as well. I just can't see this at all."

This discussion indicates that the problem of determining training needs and organizing a program to meet them within a definite time limit is not an academic question. How would you go about discovering the way in which the ten weeks might be best used for the benefit of both the foremen and the company as a whole?

NOW YOU'VE GOT IT . . .

Walt, the assistant training director, is fingering a memo from the manager of office services:

DEAR WALT:
In line with our recent meeting with Irv [the training director] and yourself, it has been decided to institute a training program for office supervisors. At your convenience, I should like to consider this matter in greater detail with you regarding the mechanics of the program. We are especially interested in the finances and facilities required.

DON

Walt, since he is to be responsible for the program, is now faced with the practical problems of determining the cost of the program, the kind of room and equipment needed, the time at which each session will meet, the course outline, and other necessary details. Although in the over-all training picture such minutiae are not of crucial importance, they have much to do with the success of any program. Some trainers have discovered to their regret that failure to plan adequately for these minor items has hindered their efforts seriously.

A TRAINER AND HIS THOUGHTS

The office is dark except for one desk lamp in a corner of the room. The workday has ended, and the normal noise level has given way to that subdued quiet which descends upon every office when the people who give it life have departed. Deep in thought sits Jerry Coyne, assistant training director for Ulic Textiles. Several hours before, he had completed the seventh of a fifteen-session training course for salesmen.

The first two or three sessions had worked out very well. The last two had been so-so. Today's meeting had been a real dud. The trainees seemed to just drift away from him, doodling, yawning, looking out the windows, and indulging in mild horseplay. To make matters worse, he overheard several of the participants talking in the men's room during a "break" in the session. "What do you think of all this?" one had asked the group. "At first he was pretty good," one replied, "but now all he does is talk, talk, talk." "You've got something there," another voice said, "I'm fed up listening to him already, and we still have eight meetings to go."

This brief scene highlights the importance of the trainer's mastery of his art. It is not too difficult for anyone to be interesting once or twice. The trainer who conducts a series of sessions, however, is faced with an entirely different situation. He must answer for himself such questions as the following: How can you motivate people and hold their attention? What instructional approaches are available to any trainer? What techniques can he use? What principles of training and learning should he be mindful of? How can he vary his methods of conducting a training session? What audio-visual and mechanical aids can be used? How should they be employed to derive the most from them?

SIDDER ENGINEERING

Behind the trainer stands the man. When people are involved in a training program, it is too late to change their psychological histories. Some trainees will gladly overlook certain personality limitations if the trainer proves that he is a master of his craft. Others, however, will allow their resentment of the man to blind them to his excellence as a trainer. If a trainer is to succeed, he must be adept at establishing a warm and friendly relationship with most, if not all, of the trainees. If both competence and cordiality are required, which is more important in general? Which might be more important in training young machinists? Older workers? Women workers? Management trainees? Technicians? What personality traits are most likely to be resented by various kinds of trainees? What personality traits make for the "good trainer"? It might be well to answer these questions for the scene presented below and then to do the same for other possible training situations.

The third meeting of a training program for model shop and laboratory personnel of Sidder Engineering has just ended, and five of the group are going home in the car pool.

SAM: What do you think of George, fellows?

ED: He's first-rate. He's probably the best all-round engineer in the company. What a man!

BART: Oh, he's good, all right. But why does he have to act so superior? Sometimes he makes me feel as though I were a moron. Just because we're not engineers, he acts as though we were dirt.

ED: Bart, you're too sensitive. He's not in there to hold our hands and make us feel good. His job is to get something in our heads. If he does that, he's OK with me.

JACK: I'm inclined to agree with Bart. George sometimes acts as though he were casting pearls. More than once I've been mad enough to tell him off.

SAM: Maybe you people are too sensitive. Anyway, let's forget George until tomorrow. Who's free for bowling tonight?

ONE THING AT A TIME—BUT WHICH ONE FIRST?

A group of employees are on their way to lunch when one of them happens to glance at the bulletin board. "Wait a minute, fellows," he cries, "there's a new notice on the board." All stop and read the following:

Commencing on Monday, March 2nd, a six-session training program will be conducted for personnel of the Accounting Department. Each session will begin at 8:30 and end at 10:30. The purpose of the program is to increase over-all departmental efficiency and to promote the development of the staff.

WILLIAM BLIGHTE
Director of Training

"I always knew you fellows in accounting couldn't add," comments one of the group. "What do you mean add?" says another; "I'll bet they count the money while Mark and the rest are in those sessions. Did you see the new car Mark got the other day?" Mark grins and replies, "The fact of the matter is that every other department in the company needs training more than we do. They just want to begin with the best."

The notice and the byplay it caused bring up certain important questions for the trainer and training director. When there are several departments that either need or can profit from a training program, how does one go about establishing a priority? If the trainer or training department has a limited budget, in what areas should he concentrate? What criteria should guide him in his efforts to get the most from the time and money and personnel devoted to training?

THUS FAR, AND NO FARTHER?

Many organizations have at one time or another considered the possibility of inviting an "outside" university or management consultant to conduct a series of conferences on leadership and human relations for executives. Even more send key personnel to seminars which are arranged by various associations. Two quite different points of view are possible with respect to such practices. The first maintains that they are good, since an expert, who is not involved in the daily operations of the firm, can provide a fresh point of view and new insights with a minimum of bias and preconceived ideas. The second position holds that any expert, however wise, is so unfamiliar with day-to-day company problems that he can do little more than present his personal experiences and/or glittering generalities that may or may not apply to the particular company concerned. This gives rise to certain interesting questions. What can an "outside" expert contribute to the training programs of a company? What should the company do for itself? How can one establish a balance between external seminars and internal corporate effort so as to derive a maximum advantage from each? Has the typical training director or trainer the necessary experience, preparation, and status to attempt to develop top management? What risks does the trainer run who confines his plans and efforts to skill training and the lower levels of supervision? How can a trainer increase his status and prestige without indulging in empire-building?

ANABCO INSURANCE

Anabco is a large insurance company. In one department there are approximately 110 women clerical workers. For many the work is repetitious and monotonous, requiring little formal education and less initiative or ingenuity. A majority of the workers are young and single, although many are married and about a third are middle-aged. The "old girls" spend quite a bit of time criticizing the "young girls." They complain that the younger employees waste time, gossip, talk about nothing but men, and think about nothing but the weekend date. In the eyes of the younger group the more mature women are "old maids," who are jealous. Both groups complain that the supervisors show favoritism. The younger workers feel that the supervisors "kow-tow" to the older women because of their age. The more mature em-ployees, on the other hand, accuse the supervisors of demanding things of them that they would not ask of the younger women, such as working overtime. The supervisors are weary of the friction and verbal vendettas that are beginning to divide the office into two armed camps. At their request, the office manager has asked the training director to give a human relations workshop or workshops for the leaders of both factions.

Do you think that a human relations workshop(s) is the answer to this problem, or should the office manager and the supervisors settle it as a disciplinary matter? If you were to conduct the work-shop(s), would you put the leaders of both groups in the same train-ing section or have a separate section for each? What might the con-tent of such a workshop include? How would you conduct it? How might you motivate the women to change their outlook? What motives seem to be more effective with women than with men? What motives do you think might work better with the younger women than with the older group, and vice versa?

WHAT WENT WRONG?

"People sure are funny," Bob mutters to himself, "I thought that both Marge and Tom would be glad about this secretarial training program, but they acted as though I were threatening them." The background for this remark was a new secretarial training program that was going to be instituted in order to provide a pool of secre-taries within the company. Only the best typists were to be selected, and Marge was in this group. Tom was Marge's boss.

What thoughts are running through the minds of Marge and Tom?

MARGE: I wonder why they picked me? Maybe they're planning to promote me. But then again, maybe my work hasn't been as good as I thought. At first I kind of liked the idea of being educated "on company time." Now I'm not so sure. If I'm a good worker, why do they have to train me? Besides, I mentioned this to Peg, and she said that in her old company she had been through a program like this, only to find herself back in the same old job. She said it was a big buildup for an awful letdown. I am going to ask Tom about this.

Tom: Why do they have to take Marge, my best worker? I thought it was a boss's job to train his subordinates. I wonder if they are as satisfied with this aspect of my work as I thought? After they put Marge through this program, I'll probably lose her and have to start all over again with someone new and inexperienced. Besides, why was Bob so vague about what would happen after the end of the program? I'm going to speak to him and clear this matter up.

It is interesting that being selected for a training program can at times cause a certain amount of uneasiness, if not actual fear, on the part of the trainees. People being what they are, some superiors may be somewhat defensive with respect to certain types of training programs either because they misinterpret them as a criticism of their work or because they run the risk of losing their best workers. How important is it to create a state of psychological readiness for any training program? How can this be done most effectively? What can be done to prevent misunderstanding of the purposes of a training program? What might Bob do to clear up the questions that Marge and Tom have about the training program?

DIALOGUE IN THE EXECUTIVE DINING ROOM

One of the most difficult tasks confronting the trainer and management is that of determining the real worth of any training program. Listen to the president and the general manager as they discuss the problem of evaluating training programs.

President: Pete, I'm beginning to wonder whether we haven't gone overboard on this idea of training. We're giving quite a bit of time, money, and personnel to it. How will we ever know whether it is paying off?

General Manager: We'll evaluate it, of course. There are lots of ways of discovering whether training is worth its salt.

President: Such as?

General Manager: The main one is the profit and loss column. This is the sixty-four dollar question. Besides, better morale, greater efficiency, fewer boners, reduced friction and turnover, better communications and co-operation are all signs of the value of training.

PRESIDENT: Sounds wonderful. But how are we going to measure these things; and, even if we do, how can we be sure that they are the results of training?

This brief conversation before dessert brings up some difficult questions. How necessary is it to evaluate the effectiveness of a training program? What should the criteria be? How does one go about such an evaluation? What use can be made of the results of such an appraisal?

Questions, Questions, Questions . . .

The preceding cases have been presented to stimulate the student and practitioner of training to reflect on some of the important problems in the field, which will be considered in the following chapters. They have highlighted problems concerned with (1) selling training to top management; (2) the organization of a program; (3) principles of learning and the methodology of the trainer; (4) the personality of the trainer; (5) motivation and human relations; (6) practical questions dealing with establishing a priority for training programs, audio-visual aids, course content, physical facilities, and budgetary allotments for training; (7) relative values of in-company and extra-company programs; and (8) evaluation of training. It is the responsibility of the reader to formulate his own answers to these problems. The book can do no more than stimulate him and offer suggestions to help him do so more effectively.

Management and Training Theory

Now that a few of the specific problems which the trainer must cope with have been described, it is important that the relationship between management theory and practice and training theory and practice be kept in focus. Failure to do so can easily result in the trainer's being reduced to the level of a functionary whose sole responsibility is for short-term training programs at the skill and lower supervisory levels in terms of "how-to-do-it."

The primary purpose of any company is to satisfy the legitimate needs and desires of its customers, stockholders, employees, and the community at large with optimum efficiency, minimum cost, and maximum profit. This, too, is the ultimate aim of all training. The functions of an executive are to plan, organize, delegate, control, coordinate, energize, and supervise company operations. As an executive, the director of training has similar duties in his own area of activity. In his efforts to perform his functions the executive must steer a cautious course between fascination for mere theory and pre-occupation with day-to-day details to the neglect of his over-all objectives. The training director must be on his guard against similar dangers.

The interrelationships that exist between management and training, moreover, go far beyond a parallelism between the executive and the training director. It would be a lethal error to consider the problems of training apart from the framework of the company in which it takes place. Company philosophy, objectives, structure, climate, and conditions influence training programs from the moment of their conception to the evaluation of their results. If organizational and departmental objectives and policies are clearly defined, then those that pertain to training can be readily conceptualized. If personnel are well suited and prepared for their jobs, the task of the trainer is facilitated. If good human relations exist in the firm, the advantages of co-operation will benefit the training programs. If these desirable organizational factors are lacking, however, even the best training program is almost foredoomed to failure from its inception.

Finally, the interdependence of management and training can be illustrated by listing several commonly accepted management principles and then examining the training questions that stem from them.[2]

1. *Definite Clear-Cut Policies Are Essential to Effective Management.* How will such policies affect any training department or program? Is it necessary for the training department to have similar policies? Who should formulate them? How can they be translated into workable procedures?

2. *To Be Successful, a Business Must Advance; It Cannot Remain Dormant.* Is this also true of training programs? How does one determine the nature and extent of modification required in a training organization? The timing of such changes? The manner of their introduction? What demands on training do such developments as automation and data-processing techniques make?

3. *To Insure Proper Development of a Business and Efficiency of Operation, a Company Must Be Well-Balanced Internally.* How would you apply this principle in determining where the emphasis on training should be within a given organization?

---

[2] These principles have been adapted from William B. Cornell, *Organization and Management in Industry and Business* (New York: Ronald Press Co., 1947), pp. 51–60.

For example, should training be concentrated on new employees? Retraining experienced workers? Front-line supervisors? Middle management? Top management? Do the same training principles apply to each of these kinds of training programs? Are the training procedures identical, similar, or different? Since no specific training program can do all things equally well at once, what criteria might guide the trainer in judging the area in which he might spend his time and energy most profitably?

4. *All Elements Which Are Not Essential to Successful Operation Should Be Eliminated, and All Those Retained Should Be Reduced to Their Simplest Form.* How would you reply to the statement that training is a "frill"? To the belief that, when business is poor, training programs should be trimmed or eliminated entirely? How can you tell when a particular training course has outlived its usefulness? How do you determine what is essential, what is important, and what is incidental in a training program?

5. *Scientific Distribution of Work Results in Specialization of Effort and Specialization of Task with the Resultant Advantages Derived from Concentration.* Should trainers be specialists or generalists? Is it better to obtain trainers from within the organization and then help them secure the necessary formal education, or is it better to employ trainers who already have formal education in the field and then let them become familiar with company problems through experience? To whom should the training director report? How do you prevent clashes between specialists? How do you preserve a broad, company-wide viewpoint while concentrating on specific, individual problems?

6. *Whenever Practicable, Best Practice Should Be Determined, Expressed in Terms of Definite Units or Standards and Adopted as a Pattern for Use in Operation or Performance, Planning, and Control.* Can there be a standard training program or programs? How might different so-called standard programs vary? Can there be a standard content for any training program? A standard time duration for a training course? A standard method for evaluating results?

7. *Management Succeeds or Fails as Human Relations in Business Are Intelligently or Unintelligently Handled.* What can the trainer do to improve his own interpersonal relationships? Can a training program succeed if human relations within the organi-

zation are very poor? What effects may insecurity and rivalry have on even the best training program?

8. ***In Order to Accomplish Satisfactorily Anything of Importance, There Must Be Planning in Advance of Doing.*** How do you ascertain whether or not a training department is needed? A particular type of training program? What is involved in planning a training program? What company factors must be taken into account in preparing for the introduction of a training program? What is involved in organizing and structuring a program? Who should plan a training program? What information should be included in the program?

9. ***Planning Is of Little Value Unless There is Subsequent Control to Make Certain That the Plans Are Carried Out.*** When one speaks of "control of the training program," what exactly is involved? Who should head up training in large organizations? In medium-sized companies? In small businesses?

10. ***The Effort of Two or More Individuals Working as a Unit toward a Common Goal Is Greater than the Sum of the Efforts of the Individuals Working as Individuals.*** How does one go about developing support for training at the top-management level? The departmental level? What, if anything, can be done to gain acceptance for training on the part of individual supervisors and employees? Should the content and methodology of a training program be decided by the one who knows most about it or cooperatively by all who are affected by it?

11. ***A Person Exercising Authority Should Be Held Responsible for the Carrying-On of All Activities within the Scope of His Authority.*** As a staff service, what are the limits of authority possessed by the director of training? The individual trainer? Who should have the right of decision regarding such specifics as the number of programs to be offered, selection of the trainees, content of the training programs, and so on?

12. ***Wise Leadership Is the Most Important Single Factor in Successful Operation.*** Is the trainer or training director's leadership one of ideas or action? In what ways is his leadership authoritative? Persuasive? Consultative? Inspirational? Is it a major responsibility for the trainer or training department to act as a research and resource agency within the organization?

These dozen universally accepted managerial principles, together with their derivative training questions, indicate how intimately one's concept of management and his interpretation of the function of training are interwoven. This truth is so fundamental that, at the risk of being unduly repetitious, it is reiterated throughout the remainder of the book.

What Is the Return on the Investment?

Any rational undertaking is based on the premise that the people involved have calculated both its advantages and disadvantages. Management would be wise to do likewise. The fact is that embarking on a training program is not wholly a matter of milk and honey. In the first place, training is almost certain to be opposed by some supervisors who see their men taken off the job in order "to go to school." It at times may be resented by those who are selected for the program, because of doubts and fears as to precisely why they have been asked to participate. Jealousy may prompt those who have not been chosen to criticize the program. Organized labor may sometimes look on training with a jaundiced eye. As a result, human relations in the department or plant may at first be worsened rather than improved. Production, too, may at least initially show a noticeable decrement as trainees substitute new but unfamiliar methods for those that are almost a matter of habit, although less efficient. Since every company suffers from some turnover, it must more or less devote itself to what amounts to an almost continuous training policy. Finally, training requires a considerable expenditure of personnel, time, energy, and money. The planning, organizing, administering, and evaluating of a program, not to mention a series of different programs, is a demanding managerial task which perforce must take at least part of the twenty-four hours that are allotted to every executive, however talented he may be. No guaranteed results, moreover, can be promised from any training program. Although research is eloquent as to the beneficial results of a well-organized training program, the saying, "Man proposes but God disposes" applies with special emphasis. Many a program has been undone by factors which no one could completely foresee in the planning and organizing stages. This possibility, of course, makes the trainer vulnerable in the eyes of those who "are looking for results."

In view of these very real disadvantages, management has a right to inquire, "What return can I normally expect on the personnel, time, energy, and money invested in training?" The following results represent the benefits that management can usually expect to reap, in whole or in part, from an efficient training setup.

1. More and higher quality of production once training is accepted and workers master new and more efficient procedures. Management will secure more than a fair return on its investment as rejects, reworks, waste, spoilage, lost time, and costly errors are minimized.
2. Better customer relations with fewer complaints, a natural result of more efficient and better quality production.
3. Lower operating costs with a consequent reduction of need for expensive overtime work and "emergency production."
4. Dollar savings with respect to company equipment. The unit cost of modern machinery tends to be quite high. When employees learn not only how to use it in the most efficient manner but also to take care of it properly, the chances of losing on this financial investment are reduced greatly.
5. "Breaking a new man in" at any level tends to be rather time-consuming and may be rather expensive. Training accelerates his efforts to become competent.
6. Training can bring about the desired results of having fewer misfits on the job, with a resultant reduction in absenteeism and turnover.
7. A greater pool of trained personnel is provided for promotional possibilities. In addition, the company enjoys the situation of having people available who can substitute for others on an emergency or permanent basis when needed.
8. Training can help reduce accident rates.
9. Fewer grievances and less labor trouble.
10. Freedom for supervisors to concentrate on the real problems of supervision and over-all improved administration, systems, and procedures.
11. Better understanding of company aims, policies, and methods, coupled with better adherence to company rules and regulations.
12. Improved attitudes toward the company and better communications.
13. Increased company flexibility to adapt to new business conditions, enter new fields of endeavor, take advantage of new industrial opportunities, and so on.
14. More and better employee suggestions for increasing the efficiency of the department, plant, or business.

If the organization manages to secure even some of these potential training results, the effort spent on setting up an effective program will have been more than worth the while. Training, however, also serves the best interests of the worker in the following ways:

1. Improved skills and/or the acquisition of new skills.
2. Increased earning power and a better chance of promotion.
3. Decreased fatigue and fewer mistakes.
4. Increased self-respect as a competent worker.

5. Expanded trade, supervisory, or executive knowledge.
6. Better understanding of the job and of related jobs.
7. Greater motivation to do a better job.
8. Increased job satisfaction and higher morale.
9. More effective and systematic work habits.
10. Reduction in tensions due to lack of competence and difficulties with supervisors and other workers.

Surely, very few employees would have any objection to training if they appreciated that these benefits might accrue to them as a result of it.

What Does It Include?

It would be unwise to conclude this introductory chapter without at least outlining the potential scope of training. Planty, McCord, and Efferson[3] have given the following outline of the scope of training.

Examples of Knowledge to Be Developed
1. Company products.
2. Company policies.
3. Company history.
4. Company rules and regulations.
5. Company problems.
6. Company plans.
7. Raw materials.
8. Waste control facts.
9. Cost reduction facts.
10. Safety facts.
11. Economics of industry.
12. The American system of free enterprise—rights, privileges, and duties.
13. Technical knowledge of machines, mechanical theory, strength of materials, etc.
14. Competitors.
15. Knowledge of social skills and co-operation.
16. Motion study and wage systems.
17. Knowledge of one's own strengths, weaknesses, and needs.
18. Principles of management.

Examples of Skills to Be Developed
1. Basic job operation skills.
2. Punching time clock.
3. Disciplining.
4. Giving orders.
5. Receiving orders.

---

[3] Earl G. Planty, William S. McCord, and Carlos A. Efferson, *Training Employees and Managers* (New York: Ronald Press, 1948), pp. 21–22.

6. Winning friends.
7. Self-analysis, direction, and improvement.
8. Waste control.
9. Cost control.
10. Cutting waste motion.
11. Conference participation.
12. Writing notices.
13. Speaking clearly and persuasively.
14. Job organization, time budgeting.
15. Conference leading.
16. Co-operative development of policy.
17. How to write up suggestions.
18. Reporting absences.
19. Making job breakdowns.
20. Administrative skills—planning, organizing, commanding, controlling, and improving.

Examples of Attitudes to Be Developed
1. Appreciation of company policy and procedure.
2. Sympathy with company problems and desire to help.
3. Willingness to work.
4. Understanding and co-operation with supervisors.
5. Understanding and appreciation of employee position and problems.
6. Group spirit.
7. Feeling of responsibility for waste, cost, and welfare of company.
8. Feeling of satisfaction, security, belonging, togetherness, individual and group importance.
9. Feeling of participation in management.
10. Appreciation and feeling of interdependence of employee and company.
11. Desire to have high record of attendance, production, and safety.
12. Appreciation of rules and regulations and desire to comply with them.
13. Feeling of friendliness and ease in work environment.
14. Department spirit—pride in work, product, and workers.
15. Identification of employee with company.
16. Feeling of pride in company.
17. Feeling or worthwhileness of work and position.
18. Interest in welfare, success, and satisfaction of all employees.

Summary

To orient both the student and the practitioner of training to problems in the field, this chapter has sought to do five things. First, the need for training arises from many factors, not the least of which is the determined effort that Russia is at present making to overtake the so-called capitalistic nations in man-hour production output. In addition, radical changes in the technique and technology of business and industry in the United States require intensive consideration of ways and means of increasing efficiency at all levels from orientation training to executive development. This need is heightened by the realization that in many training areas, such as that of human relations, there is little conclusive evidence that the time and energy expended are paying off.

Training has been defined as the process by which an organization seeks, in a planned, co-ordinated, and continuous manner, to develop in all employees those understandings, skills, and attitudes that will maximize individual present and future efficiency and the effectiveness of the over-all company operation. Regardless of the level at which it takes place or of the name which may be given it, training always seeks to achieve these aims. Because of personal experience and training or company factors beyond the control of an individual, different trainers may tend to interpret their jobs in a markedly different manner. At one extreme, one training director may have the training, status, and prestige which enable him to engage in executive development and policy formulation activities; another may be a specialist in "how-to-do" techniques at the lower operational levels.

Typical case problems have been presented to help the reader secure an overview of some of the questions which anyone interested in training must think about and to orient him to the material that will be considered in subsequent chapters. Finally, an effort has been made to indicate how intimately one's concept of management theory and practice is related to his view of training theory and practice, a major theme of this book.

THINGS TO DISCUSS AND TO DO

1. How would you reply to the objection, "We do not need training. Soon mechanization and automation will transfer most of the responsibility to the machines and a few highly skilled workers"?
2. Interview several training directors in order to ascertain just how they view their jobs. In what ways are they similar? Identical? Different?
3. Discuss with the class exactly how you would attempt to solve each of the case problems presented in this chapter.
4. Does anyone know how training directors spend their time? Go to the library and try to find out by reviewing the literature in the field.
5. Find out as much as you can about the ASTD (the American Society of Training Directors). What type of organization is it? Who may join? In what activities does it engage? How can it help anyone who is interested in the training field?

2. HISTORY OF TRAINING—FROM HOW? TO WHY?

Purpose of the Chapter

EVERY FUNCTION performed by man has a history. The training and development of people in business organizations is no exception. This chapter is designed to give the reader some perspective and a frame of reference so that he will have some understanding of the reasons for present-day problems in this field. It has often been said that we can learn from history. Certainly the history of training and education in business and industry can give us only little to go on. Much of its impact is still to be felt. If we need reasons and background for the development of sound training programs and methods in business, this chapter should help guide the way.

The casual observer may look upon the American economy in wonderment or take it for granted. We use the products of its factories, do business with its banks and insurance companies, and have relations with a myriad of other organizations without giving too much thought to their complexity. Rarely do we reflect on the varied knowledge, talents, and experience possessed by the individuals who are responsible for the success of these organizations. If this casual observer were to ask, "How did all this happen?" he would not be able to receive a simple answer.

Many factors have contributed to the growth of our country, not the least of which has been the skilled individual performing the daily tasks that keep the industrial machine functioning. These skills are many and varied, ranging from simple hand operations to programing for giant computers. Included among these skills are those exercised by all levels of management in their efforts to plan, coordinate, and control the various aspects of the business organization. One of the most important aspects is training. Employees did not learn all the needed skills, nor did they acquire all the knowledge necessary for their jobs, by themselves. Trial and error, formal education, training programs, and absorption on the job have all made their contributions to the development of employees in business and industry.

Although familiarity may lead us to take many of today's products and services for granted, they represent the cumulative result of millions of man-hours devoted to increasing the efficiency of American business and raising the standard of living of the American people. Not even the stoutest defender of "the good old days" would want to return to the inconveniences of yesteryear, and few companies would want to return to the business methodology of a former time. In order to understand more fully the importance of training in modern business enterprise, it is necessary to examine at least the important developments that have contributed to the growth of the American economy.

Early Developments

The typical business at the beginning of the twentieth century was a relatively small, simple operation utilizing few methods which are familiar today. Little attention was paid to management problems as we know them today. The factory and its growing need for machinery was pre-eminent in the minds of businessmen. One of the dominant characteristics of the era was the prevalence of the owner-manager. This individual was usually a self-made man who had started his own business and personally nursed its early growth. His thoughts were largely directed toward his machines and the processes they made possible. Men to run these machines were necessary but incidental. Though necessary, they were relatively easy to obtain, and the wages that had to be paid were the lowest possible for the maximum hours possible. There was little or no governmental regulation or interference from other outside agencies, so that the businessman was left to make his own rules. Among other things, this led to a work orientation with an emphasis on production. The newly found usefulness of machines and their dependability in turning out uniform products at relatively lower prices were of prime importance and interest to the owner. The resultant division of labor made it possible to hire people who had little of the artisan skill of their predecessor journeymen. The machine did the skillful operations, and the man became merely an extension of the machine.

Industrial Growth

The transfer of skill from man to machine had been developing for some time in the world. Now it was rapidly taking hold in the United States. As in other countries, the attendant social and moral problems of this transfer were given but little attention here. The development was looked upon as an industrial one, and the social problems were not considered to be the concern of the entrepreneur. His efforts were directed toward production and profit. Because the community at large viewed industrial growth in this manner, these companies were left free to develop as they saw fit.

Coupled with this industrial growth was the concurrent growth of the country. Railroads spanned the country, and the population began to disperse geographically in increasing numbers. The relative ease of travel and transportation enabled some of the populace to see more of the country and how people in other sections lived. This created a demand for the products from the growing factories. News was also able to travel further and more rapidly. More and more people wanted to enjoy the fruits of American industry, and the factory owner was pleased to fill this desire. Markets were developed for a greater variety of products than had ever before existed on a wide scale in this country. The needs of consumers on the retail level were reflected in the growth of heavy industry. Even the farms of the country were becoming larger and increasingly mechanized. This meant more steel and more steel mills. Mining and heavy industry grew with the rest of industry, and, with the exception of depression years, the economic curve moved ever upward. More and more workers were needed to fill the jobs created by this growth. The increasingly important engineers and innovators created more technological marvels. The substitution of natural energy for human effort grew in all types of endeavor. The mortality rate declined continuously after the Civil War as the result of medical advances, and this was coupled with an increasing birth rate. Population growth served the country well. Not only did this mean more customers for the goods produced, but it also meant an increasing labor supply for the growing factories. As long as mechanization of industry was not too common, machines for factories as well as consumer goods were custom-made. As mechanization increased and factories grew and the demands of the growing population became greater, mass production of machinery as well as consumer goods became a more prevalent reality. There was an abundant supply of raw materials, power facilities, and skilled labor. As a result, business continually moved to adopt mass production, specialization, and division of labor. This required standardization, interchangeable parts, precision tools, and a larger labor supply.

Division of Labor

When mass production first became feasible in this country, manufacturers found a ready supply of skilled labor from among the various groups of artisans that had been making products on a made-to-order basis. These individuals readily adapted their skills to the factory, since the transition was relatively simple. It was merely one of using someone else's equipment to perform the same tasks that had been done before. Machines were handmade, and so were many of the parts that went into a finished product. The early emphasis in mass production was to replace hand labor with machines as rapidly as possible. The embryonic factory did not have too many high-speed processes, and the machines were relatively uncomplicated. The artisans that made these machines did not have sufficient knowledge as yet to develop intricate machinery, nor was there any great amount of pressure on them to intensify their effort. The know-how that was now being applied to industry came from those machinists that had worked in United States government arsenals and in the growing textile industry. The first successful efforts in mass production came in consumer-goods industries, since it was here that the demand was the greatest.

As the mass-production concept became more prevalent and economically possible, the factory itself developed more intensively. As each industry moved toward mass production, the intensity of mechanization became greater. No longer was it a simple situation of replacement of hand labor with machinery. Now the emphasis was being placed on more intricate machinery, high-speed processes, and larger machines. Increasingly greater amounts of hand operations were being shifted to machines. The factories needed larger work forces, and the owner-managers turned to sources of labor supply that had not as yet been tapped. Farm mechanization had decreased the need for farm labor, and the growing cities attracted the youth that would formerly have earned his living on a farm. These people were used to hard work and long hours, so this aspect of working in a factory held no problem for them. Specialization had increased to the point where these relatively unskilled laborers could be brought into the factory and shown their tasks in a short period of time. It was possible to utilize this source of labor supply along with the population of the cities.

Specialization and division of labor could now be practiced with efficiency because the operations were broken down so simply that novices could become efficient in a short time. The labor market was filled with people who were anxious to take the jobs offered in these factories. Many of them had never earned as much money before, and they did not consider the higher cost of living in the city. In addition to the readily available labor supply in this country, waves of immigrants came from abroad. Most of these people settled in the cities, and they too were used to long hours and hard work. The entrepreneur was in a good position to staff his growing factory with eager hands at a relatively low cost. The machines performed the intricate work, and all that the man was needed for was to feed the machine and take off the finished work. The skills required were easily taught, and if a new worker did not learn his job in short order, he was fired and replaced by a worker who could. This large labor market enabled the manufacturer to utilize the technological developments that were rapidly becoming typical in industrial plants. In such an atmosphere formal training programs were practically nonexistent. Trial-and-error methods were common, and the worker learned his job by observation and absorption.

Independence of Management

Mass production requires larger factories with greater investment in capital equipment. It also requires mass consumption. The fact that American markets were growing at the turn of the century gave impetus to the technological growth of the country. The businessman soon recognized this idea of selling at a lower price to many people rather than at a high price to a relative few. The United States was going through industrial growth along with an economic philosophy based on Adam Smith's concept of laissez-faire. The need and demand for merchandise prompted the innovator and the financier to team up and develop the large-scale factory. The society that existed in the latter part of the nineteenth century created the ideal climate for this team. Government generally felt that business should develop unhampered by regulation. The population was largely uneducated, and there were no strong union movements. Actually, economic and social pressures for growth were all on the side of any aspiring entrepreneur.

The United States had a great potential waiting to be tapped by any diligent businessman. The Puritan philosophy of Colonial times which frowned on leisure and treated work and productive effort almost like a religion created the framework for the industrial growth of the country. Very frequently the owner of a business got his start by developing a process, and by working in his home he refined it. He worked long hours with great enthusiasm. He may have sought financial help from bankers, or he may have saved his own money for a start. In his new business venture he worked extremely hard, with no time out for relaxation. He felt that what he did was his own business and that his success was in direct ratio to the amount of effort he put forth. Because of this effort, he was a respected man in his community, since the widely accepted credo was an Horatio Alger concept which, put simply, meant hard work equals success. As his business grew and he found an increasing market for the products he manufactured, his workday became longer, and he worked harder to reap the harvest of growing profits. These profits he quickly plowed back into the business for new machinery and larger plants.

Obviously, as his business grew, he needed more employees. When he hired them, his expectations of their effort were as high as those he had for his own effort. He felt that he was complete master in his own domain, and this view was shared by society. He set the working hours and the pay scale with little or no outside influence other than competitive conditions in the community where his factory was located. In the beginning he was able to hire skilled workers, so that he had no training problem other than to give orders and to see that they were carried out. In fact, many of the men he hired were inspired by the same ambitions as those of the owner, and they felt that they too could own a business if they worked hard and saved their money. The owner-manager was largely self-taught, and he saw no reason why his men should not follow his example. When the refinement of mass production reached the point where it became necessary to hire workers in larger numbers who were usually unskilled, he applied the same standards to them. If they did not meet his requirements, he replaced them. In some instances he even replaced older workers with younger, more energetic ones who were willing to work for less money. The apprentice system still supplied the need for skilled machinists, and other technicians were also developed in this manner. In this kind of framework it is little wonder that a need for any kind of training program did not exist. If skill training was not in evidence, then certainly no other kind was even thought of. The business might be passed on to a son or some other relative or sold to a competitor to make a larger company, but no thought was given to management development. Supervisory training was not thought necessary, for the supervisor's job was to set the pace. He was a straw boss who often was chosen because he was the best worker and could force the others to keep his pace. Any excessive attention given to the development of a worker's ability was looked upon as wasteful and time-consuming. In fact, training was often thought of as synonymous with coddling employees, and few, if any, businessmen desired this kind of reputation.

Business Growth Complexities

The growth of business caused many problems for the entrepreneur. From the compact family organization, there evolved the corporation with the specialization of functions that this type of business requires. Ownership and management became separated, and the businessman turned increasingly to the experts for the management of the business. It was no longer possible to run the business in the simple manner that existed when the organization was small. Increasing competition and expanding markets dictated the need for more emphasis on mass production. As the business grew, the owner became aware of the knowledge that he did not possess. He came more and more to rely on experts in such specific fields as production, sales, purchasing, accounting, and personnel. He became dependent on auxiliary institutions, such as banks, insurance companies, lawyers, and consulting agencies, for help in his various business problems. Thus the growth and increasing complexity of business made it necessary to create a management structure. As a result, the chief executive had less contact with the operation of the business, approaching it indirectly through subordinate officers.

The advent of the corporate form of enterprise created the need for a different type of leadership than that which was necessary to start the business. When the business grew in size and turned to outside financing, then ownership and management became separated. Increased emphasis on scientific management developed a need for a so-called professional manager. Once again the businessman turned to the labor market, and, as he had done for skilled workers in the past, he hired experience. Many of the early managers in American business were trained engineers. This was logical because the emphasis was on production and most of the practitioners of scientific management were the products of engineering schools. There was a great need for leadership, and the businessmen turned to the men that had solved the production problems. So the technicians and engineers became executives. Business continued to grow, and the managers followed the practices of the owners who had hired them. Little or no attention was given to formal training of employees. In fact, training was looked upon by many people as employer propaganda. In some instances it was felt that training of employees would only increase the number of skilled people and thus fill the labor market with unwanted workers. Very few employers looked upon training as their responsibility. Self-development furnished enough skilled employees, and the employers thought that this was the best way, even though some of the self-development took place in their own businesses through the trial-and-error learning that was inevitable on any job, regardless of past experience.

World War I brought some of the first changes in the thinking of employers in relation to employee training. The rapid expansion of industry, the siphoning of manpower to the military, and the closing of European supply sources forced many industries to develop people to fill these gaps. Time was not available to allow the self-development process to take place, and businessmen had no choice but to embark on training programs to fill the positions created by the war economy. The postwar recession saw a return to the practices of the past in regard to training, but along came the growth of the twenties, which once again gave an impetus to training. Of course, this growth was largely skill-oriented. Management training was in an embryonic stage. Little was known about management as a separate field of endeavor, even though the practitioners of scientific management had increased in numbers. These individuals were largely engineers, and their efforts were related to production. Finance and accounting were the other major areas of executive practice, and in-company programs for management development were scattered and few. The era from 1900, however, saw the emergence of the business school on the collegiate level. Many of the major universities had undergraduate and graduate business schools, and many of the executives in business received their training in these schools.

The depression years of the thirties again dealt a setback to training in industry. With a labor market that was glutted with people, few business organizations needed to have formal training programs for employees. It was simply a matter of hiring and firing until the right workers were found. People put forth extra effort in order to hold their jobs, and once again the responsibility for development was placed on the shoulders of the individual employee. In 1940, war again served as an accelerator for industrial training in this country. This time the need was much greater than in World War I. World War II was broader in its scope, and industrial operations were far more complex. In addition, the impact on our economy was much greater because we were just emerging from a depression and our work force was not large enough to furnish the necessary war materials for us and our allies. Training received major emphasis, and it became a crash program for our country to develop and train the necessary skilled people, including supervisors and managers, for our rapidly expanding industrial machine.

The Growing Need for Training

Probably the most significant change in industry over the last half-century has been the tremendous growth of the size of business organizations. From the small companies of the late 1800's have grown the present corporate enterprises with branch plants and locations in this country and other countries in the free world. Accompanying this growth in size is an increasingly complex organizational structure. With every success in an organization leading to growth, the "boss" found himself being separated from immediate contact with many of the daily operations by the employment of experts to do this work for him. Each new assistant and staff department increased the gap, and slowly but surely the professional manager began to take over the increasing complexities of running the business. Early scientific management was concerned mainly with problems in the internal management of each industrial concern. The larger and more difficult problem of adjusting an individual business to industrial society as a whole has only recently begun to receive much attention.

Recognition of Training Need

After long years of drought in industrial training, business began to harvest its sparse crop. In the days of Frederick W. Taylor, employee training programs were not developed by management. Helpers and laborers were expected to learn from the skilled workmen with whom they came in contact. Those workers who seemed capable or seemed to know the most about the job were promoted by management. This system was all right as long as the unskilled worker observed and learned from a skilled employee that practiced his skill effectively and efficiently. Unfortunately, this was not always the case, and, as a result, poor methods were perpetuated. This approach to training has been practiced in industry for many years and in fact still exists in many companies. Excessive amounts of time are the hallmark of learning when this method is used.

During World War II the United States Department of Education sponsored two programs that were to have far-reaching effect on industrial training. These were the Training-Within-Industry (TWI) and the Engineering, Science and Management War Training (ESMWT) programs. These programs developed under an emergency situation contributed to the training of millions of people in industry during the war. More than this, however, they formed the basis for industry training in the immediate postwar years, and they and modifications of them are still in use today. Industry grew quite large as a result of the war, and the pent-up demand after the war added to this growth. American industry embarked on an unprecedented expansion program. New plants were built all over the country, and many new materials developed during the war created enterprises that had not existed before. Plastics and electronics unfolded marvels for the American public, and still more businesses started and expanded.

Among the problems that this growth created was the need for highly trained personnel. Raiding of competitors' staffs was no longer possible on a wide scale, since many of the skills required were new ones. In addition, a problem which industry did not even notice had developed. The long years of depression coupled with the war years had caused an unusual situation. A good portion of the top management in American business was approaching the retirement age, and there were no younger executives to fill their shoes. No management training had been carried on during the depression, and World War II had taken many younger people who might have gained experience by the trial-and-error method in industry. The need for skilled labor and management personnel had never before been greater. If expansion was to be carried on, then accelerated training programs were the only answer. No longer could industry depend on the long process of learning by many years of experience. Many of the skills had to be developed from no previous pattern. Training was necessary on all levels in many business organizations. Methods had to be developed to impart this training in as rapid a manner as possible.

The Purpose of Training

With the growth of business in the postwar years came the introduction of new methods and processes. Many wartime developments were adapted to civilian use. Machinery which had never been used before became standard in many companies. Industry began to recognize a responsibility that they had never recognized before—the training of employees. Its purpose was to prepare people to function as efficiently as possible in the corporate framework. This recognition included the fact that vocational training in schools and colleges could not completely fill the needs that existed in the business organization. Training in a specific company must be fitted to the needs of that company, and business was at last recognizing this.

This change in thinking was evolutionary. No major change comes about in a short period of time, and formal training in industry was no exception. Many events contributed to this development, but perhaps the most important was the very apparent need that existed after World War II. This need, coupled with the tangible experience that was gained from wartime training programs, gave business the impetus it needed. They found that, by systematic methodology, novices could be trained to perform skills quite efficiently in a short period of time. Given sufficient information about simple human relations theory, men and women filled the many wartime supervisory positions quite adequately. So TWI was applied to the problem of training in the postwar world. As formal training grew, another factor led to even greater emphasis on formal industrial training. This was the widespread adoption of promotion-from-within policies.

The long years of depression and war seemed to create a strong desire for security in the minds of employees. Business found that promotion from within enhanced the morale of employees already working for the company and enabled them to attract qualified people for development. It also lowered labor turnover and reduced operating costs. Since many of the positions that developed after the war were quite complex in nature, it behooved management to train employees and keep them. Businesses were getting larger and still more complicated. Companies found it necessary to decentralize their organizational structures so that they could continue to operate effectively. This meant an even greater need for well-trained management personnel. Machinery was being developed that still further lessened the need for unskilled labor, and the inflationary spirals that became standard raised labor costs to a point where efficiency became necessary for survival. In order fully to utilize the potential of the work force and the techniques and tools they used, formal training in efficient methods became an absolute necessity.

Training and Education

In addition to the wartime training programs, another educational phenomenon had taken place in America. Millions of returning servicemen took advantage of the offer of free schooling that a grateful country made. Those that successfully completed their course of study found a ready market for their newly acquired knowledge. Another factor added to the change that was taking place in industry. During the war many women entered the workforce. Many of these women had never worked before, and industry found that they could be trained rapidly for many skilled jobs. They were also quite efficient, and thus another barrier of tradition was falling. These women did not want to leave their jobs, and the rapidly expanding economy welcomed them. The result was a better-educated pool of labor, with a large percentage of these people desiring a higher standard of living. The fact that an increasing number of women were entering the labor market also contributed to the changes in the nature of the labor market.

The educational level of the postwar work force contributed greatly to the growth of training programs in industry. Better communications and greater understanding of the usefulness of learning made the average employee more receptive to training. He recognized that he could become more useful and earn more money if he acquired the necessary knowledge and skill demanded by business. The growth of industry and the shortage of skilled supervisory, technical, and management employees made formal training programs a matter of necessity for the business firms that desired to grow as rapidly as they could. They readily saw that expansion was based on the development of competent people. Of course, not all companies could embark on fully integrated training programs, but those that could did so rapidly. Skill training was still the most heavily emphasized type of training, but many companies saw the need for other programs as well. As stated earlier, the age level of management in many companies was nearing retirement. Replacement for these people was a pressing need. Executive training programs became the order of the day in many businesses. Colleges graduates were recruited to fill these programs, and, after a period of training varying from six months to four and five years, they were assigned to junior executive positions for the seasoning necessary to fill the higher-management positions that were going to become vacant.

The skill programs that were developed were needed to fill the gap that was also created by the war years. Many new techniques and machines made it necessary to build a work force that could cope with the increasingly complex technology. Electronic data-processing in the office and automation in the factory created the need for highly trained technicians. Many jobs that had never existed before were created by the scientists and innovators, and some of them were so unique that a company had no choice but to train its own people because there was no other alternative available to them.

Increasing emphasis was given to positive human relations in industry, owing to the many lessons that had been learned the hard way in labor strife before the war and the job relations training during the war. Supervision was now being recognized as a distinctly separate function. The first-line supervisor, perhaps the most neglected member of management, at last began to receive the recognition that his job deserved. The many supervisory programs that evolved in companies all over the country placed emphasis on the skills and attitudes necessary for good supervision. Supervisors were trained to be people-oriented rather than work-oriented, and the human relations era in industrial training was begun. After some years of experience with supervisory training and junior executive training programs, attention began to be focused on another pressing training need. This was the development of people for higher-management positions from among those middle managers that had shown growth potential. This problem was attacked with enthusiasm by corporations, colleges, universities, and other outside agencies, such as the American Management Association. In many companies, executives who had not seen the inside of a classroom for decades returned to school to learn the art of being a better executive.

Much of the training that was started after World War II still goes on in American industry. In fact, it is being expanded in many areas.

This is particularly true of management development and such skill programs as are concerned with training people to utilize the newer technological developments. A more incisive and penetrating analysis of these programs and their future implications will be taken up in later chapters. Suffice it to say here that training has been accepted as a necessary and useful factor in business growth.

Training as an Integrating Device or Mechanism

Very often when going to the dictionary to look up the meaning of a word, a person will have a hazy idea of the definition he seeks. After searching for the word, finding it, and reading its meaning, the individual will be frustrated because the definition he has found does not seem to fill the need as he has expected. Such is the case with the word "training" as applied to business situations. *Webster's Collegiate Dictionary* states that training means to educate narrowly. It then goes further to describe education as the general and formal word for schooling, especially in an institution of learning. Going on, it states that training suggests exercise or practice to gain skill, endurance, or facility. Needless to say, this definition, while correct, is certainly not broad enough to cover the multitudinous aspects of training in business and industry. If we consider training in the narrow sense of developing an understanding of an organized group of facts and methods involving familiarization with manual skills that are necessary for the performance of some specific job, then much of the training in industry today would come under the broader area known as "education." There are very few jobs left in business that require the development of manual skills alone. Practically all of them require mental skill as well. Certainly, management and supervisory development could be called "professional education," since many writers in the field of business management consider their field a profession. Actually, education and training are very closely related, tending to merge with one another.

The training of employees has broad implications for any company that undertakes such a task on a wide scale. First of all, management has to recognize that training is a continuous process. It is not something given to a new or transferred or promoted employee in some capsule form and then forgotten. Neither is it the observation of an experienced worker by a new employee, with haphazard directions given to the new employee verbally and in rapid sequence. Training is the continuous systematic development of all employees in a company. This means on all levels of management, supervisory and nonsupervisory positions, and in all the skills, knowledge, and attitudes necessary for the optimum performance of these positions. The continuous systematic development of employees implies a formal program utilizing expert knowledge, competent teachers, suitable educational facilities, and the necessary controls and follow-up to determine the acceptance and use of the information and skills imparted in the company programs. In addition, the success of any training plan hinges upon the proper selection of individuals for training. Haphazard selection, coupled with company politics, can cause failure in the best training plan.

A primary concern of professional management should be the development of employee interest in job assignments. An employee that is highly motivated and interested in his job will probably take pride in his task accomplishment and most likely be more productive. It is not implied here that proper selection and training of employees will act as a panacea for this complex task, but the development of scientific selection and sound, well-planned training programs will certainly aid materially in the achievement of this goal.

The Over-All Company Viewpoint

An area that is largely neglected in many industrial firms is the development of a company viewpoint. Many factors contribute to the daily efforts of human beings in business enterprises, and they are difficult to isolate and define clearly. Certainly one of these is loyalty. The word is a simple one, but it has many meanings. In the typical factory there are two apparent factors that cause conflict in the development of a single loyalty to a company. One is the labor union, and the other is the management of the company. The average worker has to divide his loyalty between the two or adhere to one camp. In many instances the labor union to which he belongs prepares a constant stream of information pointing up the role of the union and its place in achieving economic goals for the employee. Management is given little credit for its part, and in most companies nothing is done to convince both union and nonunion employees that management is also playing a part in the successful development of beneficial factors for employees. Many spokesmen have said that business is much too timid in stating its viewpoint and defining its contribution to the welfare of our country. A definitely worthwhile goal of industrial training should be the systematic and continuous development of the necessary knowledge, skills, and attitudes designed to enhance the welfare of the individual employees, the company as a whole, and the nation. Company goals and individual goals are not so far apart as many think. Certainly, an employee that received his livelihood from a corporate venture has a stake in that venture's success. Likewise, the company has to maintain an efficient work force if it is to achieve enduring success in the economy.

Unfortunately, much of the training that has been and still is given emphasis in business organizations is skill-oriented. The important areas of social attitudes and emotional factors that contribute to achievement in industry have been largely neglected. Much of this is intangible and difficult to measure and therefore is hard to justify from a cost basis. But it does not take too much thought to recognize that manipulative skill alone does not run a machine or complete clerical tasks. The human being is a mysterious entity, and muscular skills are just one facet contributing to the successful achievement of job performance. The emotional, economic, and social aspects of industrial life need emphasis in training programs along with the skills necessary for job accomplishment. Training that encompasses these areas will help develop a company viewpoint that should make for a more cohesive work force.

In large, multiplant operations it is necessary to maintain uniformity in many of the operations that are essential in the daily running of these plants. Training programs designed to promote an over-all company viewpoint will certainly help. Even methodology developed on a uniform basis can aid in this goal. Uniform procedure is necessary when standardized operations exist, and any management control is based on such standards. The philosophy that the company presents to its public should also be consistent. Hence the necessity for some orientation of employees as to this philosophy. In order to obtain optimum benefit from any training program, it should be developed by a training specialist. The concept of specialization is widely accepted in industry and certainly should apply in the important field of training. Expert knowledge of the training function is necessary if a suitable program is to be designed to fill company needs. Sound management principles dictate the need for planning systematically the many phases that would be included in any company-wide training program. This would be especially true in the larger company with branch plants. If training is to be effective and the results of such training are to be measured with any accuracy, then there must be a well-developed plan that is followed by all the people that are responsible for training.

One of the primary questions that must be answered when considering formal training programs is whether or not the cost of such programs is justified. It may be difficult to understand, but training goes on whether there is a formal program or not. Hence training costs exist and represent overhead cost to the company even if most of the learning takes place by trial-and-error methods. One of the greatest myths that the American businessman is taken in by is the experience myth. He feels that if he hires experienced help, he does not need a training program. A few moments' deliberation and observation will show him that a new employee often does not know all that he claims to know and therefore has to learn on the job. In addition, few new employees are acquainted with company policies, procedures, and practices when they are hired. Certainly, they have to learn this, and they do after a time-consuming ordeal of trial and error when material is scrapped and machines are broken and avoidable errors take place. This is the learning process that goes on without a formal training program. It is costly, and the businessman has to pay these costs, but they are not so apparent. Because of this lack of appearance of training cost, the businessman believes that he does not have any training expense, even though his machines and materials are used while the employee is learning his job.

The Individual Viewpoint

Since most human beings are interested in their individual welfare, the natural desire of an employee for self-improvement is understandable. As mentioned earlier, the level of education in this country has risen considerably in the past fifty years. This naturally leads to a greater appreciation of what education can do for an individual. Couple this with the desire for job security which is so evident in industry, and you see one of the most powerful arguments for employee training programs. From the employee's viewpoint, training makes him a more valuable worker and therefore makes him less vulnerable to economic fluctuation. It also enables him to become a more skillful employee and earn more money. He may be able to advance to a new job that is rated higher or that has greater opportunity for advancement. As jobs become more complex, the employee may feel insecure. In the face of rapid technological change, the uninformed employee may become despondent and resentful of a management that he feels may cast him aside. Here skill training coupled with human relations programs can satisfy the employee's desire for information along with skill improvement to enable him to assume greater responsibilities which may be imposed by the technological advance.

For the many employees that learned their jobs by the trial-and-error method, a training program can teach them to do their jobs with greater efficiency and less effort. Training that is general in nature rather than designed for a specific job can give the employee greater understanding of the meaning of his job in the over-all company operation. Such subjects as company organizational structure, management principles, and simple economic theory may help the employee see that he has a place in the company and that he is not merely a payroll number. Human relations training that is properly developed and presented may help the employee understand himself and his fellow employees with a greater degree of insight. All in all, the employee may become a more useful individual through the correct use of formal training programs. This means an employee whose morale and productivity will be higher, but more important to his own welfare and the welfare of the company is the fact that this employee will probably represent greater potential for advancement and therefore be more valuable to the company.

The Problem of Training Utilization

Perhaps the foregoing presentation of the individual's viewpoint in relation to training seems oversimplified. Certainly, only the positive aspects were mentioned. There is a negative side, and all too frequently this side prevails.

Whenever a person buys a new gadget, he is usually quite anxious to try it out and see whether it works. This is a perfect description of the employee that has just gone through a training program. He is anxious to find out whether all the information he has gathered as a result of the program can be put to use. If he is not able to utilize his newly acquired knowledge and skill, then much of the effort that was put into the training program will be wasted. This is the side of training that can be very frustrating to the employee. If he cannot use his training, he may become dejected and regress to a level of performance that is less efficient than his achievement was before he was exposed to training. Questions as to the desirability of the training program will arise in his mind. Quite naturally, he will reason that if the company will not give him the opportunity to utilize the training, then it must not be very worthwhile. Any benefit that might have been possible will rapidly disappear, and the employee might very well quit so that he may find another position where his effort will be appreciated. While skill training may be more rapidly utilized by the company, it is possible that an employee trained in a new technique will not be given the opportunity to use these skills. Frustrations are more apparent, however, when the employee has been given supervisory or management training which he successfully completes and then he is not given responsibilities that are commensurate with his training.

One might ask the question that if training can benefit the industrial concern so greatly, why is it allowed to degenerate into a frustration mechanism that can cause lower morale, lower productivity, and higher labor turnover. No company likes to have the reputation of being a good school that trains employees for its competitors. In fact, many companies hesitate to start comprehensive training programs for this very reason. Yet each year many hundreds of employees are given various kinds of formal training, and soon after completion of this training they seek opportunity in another company. The management that has given the training may consider these employees ungrateful and impatient, but this does not alter the fact that they have quit their jobs without giving the company that trained them the benefit of their new knowledge. This adds a large cost to the training department overhead, and all of it is not justified. Certainly, some of the labor turnover that results in this manner is unavoidable; but the bulk of it is avoidable.

First of all, training programs should not be started without careful planning. A company should not institute an elaborate training department just because another company in the same industry has one. This means that a definite need must exist before a formal program to fill this need is developed. There should be nothing haphazard about the program's development. Training that was successful for another company should not be bought sight unseen, because many types of training have to be highly individualized to suit a specific company's needs. Before the program begins, planning by management should attempt to determine what will be done with the employees that finish the program successfully. If there is no apparent need for the skills that the program will develop, then the program should be shelved. This is particularly true when training skilled employees for new skills and when training lower-level or first-line supervisors. Obviously, a growing organization has to have long-range plans also. This means the development of supervisory and management personnel for the long-term growth of the company. These people have to be given training which may not be used in the immediate future. This fact should be carefully explained to the trainees, so that no false hopes are built up. The staffing problems that a company has in a dynamic economy tend to mitigate the possibility of developing definite plans for trainee utilization. Nevertheless, the attempt should be made to render these plans as definitive as possible, for, without them, training will not return the optimum benefit on the investment that the company makes.

Planning for short-term needs is naturally easier than planning for the long-range possibilities. If a company is going to switch from hand bookkeeping to machines, then they know that they will need a certain number of skilled machine operators. They can attempt to hire experienced people, or they can train current employees for the positions that will open when the machines are installed. As the company grows, their paper work grows also. They may want to utilize electronic data-processing, complete with computers. This presents a different problem because the time lag between training and job efficiency is much greater for a computer programer than it is for a bookkeeping machine operator. Training may have to start as much as two years before the integrated data-processing system is installed. Another facet to a problem of this kind is the fact that experienced people are difficult and expensive to obtain, so that training becomes a necessity if the new electronic machines are to be properly utilized. Supervisors and managers will also have to be trained to use this equipment, as well as the information that the machines will record. This also takes a considerable period of time, because it means breaking old habits and developing new ones and because instituting any radical change in a company's methodology is a difficult task at best. These problems will be discussed in greater detail in later chapters, but it is necessary to state here that probably the most important aspect of planning in relation to training is the human aspect.

It must always be remembered that education opens locked doors for people. The reactions to training are many and varied. This means that the trainees must be carefully chosen, using psychological tests, aptitude tests, and multiple interviewing, as well as careful evaluation of past performance and present desires. An employee from one department should not be chosen simply because one has been chosen from another department. Company politics should not dictate choice. Neither should an employee be chosen in order to fill a quota of a specific number of employees for a program. In other words, great effort should be expended to correlate the individual's goals with the corporate goals because, where this is done, training has a much greater chance for success.

If training programs are properly planned and organized and the trainees are properly instructed and then placed in jobs where they can use their knowledge, then a positive impact on the company will result. To derive the greatest benefit, however, the program has to be understood by all levels in the company. For training to act as an integrating mechanism, it must be utilized and understood by the people who are exposed to it, as well as by the people who will work with these trainees after the program is completed. Careful communication to all employees concerned is necessary. The information given should include why the program is in existence, how people are chosen for training, and what results are expected. It must have the unqualified approval and backing of top management, and they must in turn follow through to see that this same approval is given right down the line. Rumors should not be allowed to start, and the people chosen for training should be told exactly what their contribution is going to be. There should be no implication that they are being chosen because they do not know their jobs, and they should be given sufficient notice as to the starting date for the training. Their superiors should be fully informed as to their progress and the role they will play in the follow-up that is necessary after every training program. Only in this manner can training be utilized effectively. Any company that attempts to accomplish effective employee education with anything less should be prepared to cope with failure in their efforts. High labor cost certainly dictates the need for efficient performance. Effective training programs can help a business organization attain this goal. The reward to the company that undertakes such an effort is well worth the cost.

Summary

Industrial growth and the accompanying division of labor caused many problems in American business. One of these was the great need for skilled workers. Individuals who had no previous experience in manufacturing had to be trained in a variety of skills in a relatively short period of time. Most of the early learning took place on the job rather than by the use of any formalized training program. Not much was done to develop formalized training methods until World War II. The high cost of previous trial-and-error methods finally made an impression and formalized training programs for skilled jobs started to become widespread. The war experience helped to show businessmen the value of training and development on a formalized basis. A growing recognition of a variety of training possibilities took place. It was discovered that training could reduce labor turnover and develop higher morale. The introduction of training programs in a company helped individuals to increase their value and earn more money. Promotion from within became a common company policy and as a result supervisory and management development programs began to become popular. Top management recognized the value of training as an integrating mechanism having an impact on all levels of a company. The need for better short- and long-range planning also became apparent so that a company was able to make optimum use of the employees trained for job skills as well as supervisory and management responsibility.

THINGS TO DISCUSS AND TO DO

1. Discuss the many ways that formalized training programs may act as an integrating device for the company undertaking such programs.
2. Do some library research on the growth of American business and try to determine the role training and education have played in this growth.
3. Discuss various reasons why you think it took a relatively long period of time for the need for formalized training in industry to become apparent.
4. Prepare an outline of the reasons for the rapid acceleration and growth of skill training, supervisory training, and management development since 1940.
5. Discuss the relationship of short- and long-range planning in a business organization to the training and development programs a company undertakes.

3. HUMAN RELATIONS IN TRAINING—
STRENGTH OR CLICHÉ?

Purpose of the Chapter

TRAINING PROGRAMS flourish better in a favorable human relations climate. Therefore, the purpose of this chapter is to present those factors that are basic to the cultivation of the kind of human relations climate conducive to successful training. These factors include co-operation, leadership, and integration. Accordingly, the responsibilities for dealing with the human equation in training of top management, staff, line management, and trainees will be discussed.

Training and Co-operation

Training is a co-operative enterprise. Its success depends upon the extent to which all members of the management team possess and apply the proper knowledge, skills, attitudes, and acts essential to the generation and continuation of co-operation among the many varied human elements of a business organization. Co-operation is essentially a "people's proposition," it stems from mutual respect and understanding. Co-operation refers to unity of human effort, participation, and action. Co-operation may be defined as a kind of human activity that is characterized by the co-ordination of human energies for the purpose of attaining common objectives. The attainment of objectives through co-operative effort requires that all the individuals or parts involved need to be integrated into an efficient, organized whole. To integrate human energies requires more than co-operation. In addition, it demands that all the parts that comprise the whole must be properly related and balanced. In essence, integration depends upon careful planning, organizing, and executing. Co-operation is the human quality that provides the motivating power necessary for integration to take place. Getting people to co-operate is the prerequisite necessary to the problem of integrating their capacities and abilities into an efficiently related and balanced team.

As a means of illustrating the relationship between co-operation and integration, let us analyze the case of a man who seeks to build a house with the help of four of his neighbors. His first problem is to motivate and interest his friends so that they will co-operate with him. Assuming that he secures their co-operation, he is now faced with the problem of planning, organizing, and putting into action the abilities of his partners. To accomplish this purpose he needs to understand the capacities and abilities of the people he is to use in his venture. Thus he requires some understanding of human behavior. Now suppose he must train each of the partners to accomplish specialized jobs, such as bricklayer, carpenter, electrician, plumber, and the like. The most basic requirement he must meet is that of securing a co-operative and integrated utilization of all the men. Accordingly, he achieves co-operation by combining and uniting all his training needs into a related and balanced whole. The success of his venture also depends upon his acceptance and understanding that training is truly a dynamic, continuing, and co-operative activity. Training can never be static, since training needs change, new innovations in construction may require more instruction, new employees must be trained, supervisors and other management personnel will require development and training. Training never stops, and it needs constant co-operation and integration.

Leadership: The Motive-Power for Co-operation

Further analysis of the hypothetical problem described reveals that a most necessary and vital need of an effective training program is leadership. Some person must become the prime mover who generates co-operation and who plans, organizes, and acts to secure effective integration of the various phases of training. In the operation of a business, co-operation is necessary among all the functions of the organization. Such functions as sales, finance, and manufacturing must co-operate if a company is to operate efficiently. In effect, there must be a uniting of functions, characterized by agreement to participate with each other, an understanding of the problems of each, and a combining of all, in order to pull together in attaining a common objective—success of the business.

Training is a vital and dynamic function and must also be recognized and included, along with all the other functions of a business, in a co-operative manner. It is significant to understand that such functions as sales, manufacturing, finance, and training do not inherently cause co-operation to take place. They require some motive power that is controlled and directed, in order for them to become united and fused as a team. A football team is composed of eleven players, each having individual and different functions to perform. However, for a team to perform successfully, it is necessary that the functions of each of the players be united for co-operative action. The causative agent or the catalyst responsible for generating the motive power with proper control and direction is a human being. In the case of a business, top-management people are the causative agents or leaders, while the football team requires a coach. Things do not co-operate, people co-operate. The success or failure of any co-operative movement, therefore, is primarily dependent upon the qualities that make up the leadership personalities of the people who plan, direct, and control the actions of others.

Co-operation and Human Relations

Training is a systematic, organized, and planned procedure directed at changing the behavior of people in some desired manner. In a business, training is used to change the behavior of new and old employees so that they may perform their jobs more efficiently.

The extent to which behavior can be changed so that co-operation can take place depends upon the human equation. Accordingly, it is necessary to know what responsibilities and human characteristics are required to facilitate co-operative action in carrying out the training function in any business. In order to explain the human characteristics and responsibilities necessary for conducting an effective training program in business, it is important to label and identify the individuals who are the leaders or motivators of a training program. For purposes of convenience, such leaders or individuals will be referred to in the following manner; first, that part of the management team known as top management; second, those who have advisory responsibilities to the company, generally known as staff management; third, those who actually carry out the policies of the company, usually called line management; and, fourth, the participants in the training program often referred to as the trainees.

In a more specific sense, top management will include such persons as the chairman of the Board of Directors, the president, and certain vice-presidents. Staff management refers to the assistants and advisers to the top-management group. Department heads, supervisors, and trainers will identify those known as line management. Finally, the term "trainee" will include both new and old employees on various organizational levels who are to be trained.

In summary, it is important to recognize and accept the following key points as essential to the conducting of a successful training program in business:

1. That training is a co-operative activity and that co-operation is a human activity.

2. That willingness to co-operate is the motive power required to plan, organize, and put into action a well-integrated training program.

3. That integration or the proper relationship and balance of all the parts of a training program into an efficient whole is fundamental.

4. That co-operation and integration depend upon good leadership and that such leadership must possess the proper knowledge, skills, and attitudes as well as the understanding of the dynamics of human behavior.

THE RESPONSIBILITY OF TOP MANAGEMENT FOR DEALING WITH THE HUMAN EQUATION IN TRAINING

Top management is responsible for the planning, organizing, executing, and evaluating of a training program, since training is predicated upon the co-operation and integration of human capacities and abilities. In general, such psychological equipment covers the broad areas of knowledge of human behavior, the skills necessary for efficient action, and the attitudes of people.

Knowledge Requirements of Top Management

Knowledge of human behavior includes the studies of psychology, sociology, philosophy, and, to some extent, anthropology. All these areas of knowledge are interrelated and are usually classified as a part of the social sciences. Furthermore, they are concerned with the actions of people as individuals, as well as the actions of groups of people. From the viewpoint of individual behavior, top management must understand the nature of individual differences, the psychology of adjustment, of motives and motivation, of conflict and frustration, of emotions and feelings, and the nature of the psychology of learning and of leadership.

Knowledge of group behavior is emphasized in the studies of sociology and anthropology. An understanding of the manner in which groups of people behave, including the motives of group dynamics, the problem of informal grouping of people, informal leadership, status, and acceptance of members of a group are important areas of knowledge required by top management.

Skill Requirements of Top Management

Skills in dealing with the human equation in training are also important to a successful training program. Management leaders use skills as tools or techniques in order to utilize their knowledge of human behavior effectively. Ability to use human relations skills involves the areas of logical thinking, organizing, planning, motivating people by directing and controlling behavior toward clear-cut goals, the use of effective communicating media, and skills in generating co-ordinated and co-operative action.

Attitude Requirements of Top Management

Attitudes may be referred to as a predisposition to form opinions in certain ways. They are sometimes thought of as mental sets or as fixed habits of reacting to different situations, since they are learned over a long period of time. Attitudes are learned from experience and are mixed with feelings and emotions which cause the individual to formulate opinions about people, ideas, and things. They also possess a qualitative character, in that they may be favorable or unfavorable, strong or weak, short or long in duration, and they are built into our personalities. Top-management people have attitudes toward training that may be either favorable or unfavorable. For example, a leader who has learned from "the school of hard knocks" may feel that all learning and training should take place in the same way for all people. His attitude toward a training program in his company may be unfavorable, and his opinions will not permit him to endorse a sound procedure to train others.

With this general background of the knowledge, skills, and attitudes required by top management to deal with the human equation in training, it is important to apply them in a more specific manner because the personality of the top-management leader can effect the success or failure of a training program. The extent to which such leaders understand the nature of their own actions and the effects of their actions on others can determine how co-operative and integrated a training program will be. Therefore, the kind of personality the leader possesses will have an impact upon the effectiveness of the training program. Thus one of the most basic factors to be understood by members of top management is the nature of their own individual personalities.

Management Self-Understanding

Initially, the leader must understand his own attitudes. In general, does he have favorable attitudes toward training? In other words, have his experience and background provided him with a frame of reference that is conducive to the acceptance of a training program? For acceptance of a training program means more than words. It requires a sincere belief in the value of a training program as a means of making his business successful. Surface acceptance is not enough, for in a more significant sense it is necessary to give to the training function the proper respect and position that it rightfully deserves. Such prestige can be achieved only when the attitudes of top management are such that training is recognized as one of the major functions of the business and not as a supplement or appendage. When training is accepted in this way, it should then be integrated and built into the organization so that it operates co-operatively to serve the training needs of all parts of the business.

A company in the oil-refining business had experienced a series of disastrous accidents involving considerable property damage and resulting in several incapacitating injuries to a number of employees. The company had an extensive safety program headed by a safety engineer with a large staff of assistants who were responsible for insuring safety in all the operations of the oil refinery. As was expected, an intensive investigation of the causes of the accidents was undertaken. After many months of investigation, the safety engineers made recommendations that resulted in certain changes in equipment, controls, and other physical factors that would insure safe practices.

It is important to note that, in the treatment of the problem, little, if any, attention was given to the human equation as a possible contributing cause for the accidents. From a human relations viewpoint, the search for causation would have been pursued beyond the physical conditions and would have attempted to penetrate into the human causes for the accidents. At a later date, when the number of accidents had not been reduced sufficiently, an investigation was ordered by top management from the viewpoint of the human causes that might be responsible. The most significant factor revealed by the study was that the company "climate" or the attitudes and mental set of top management was orientated and directed toward materalistic values. It was discovered that the personality of the top executive had a direct effect upon the generation of such a climate. He was a man who had a highly specialized engineering background, coming from a family of engineers and brought up in a culture of materialistic values. His approach to safety, as it was to most business problems, was based on formulas, statistics, engineering improvements, and physical maintenance. This attitude filtered downward and affected the attitudes of the entire management team, resulting in a "climate" of materialism. His personality did not permit him to recognize that human factors could be important in safety, and, more important, he was unable to see how training of human behavior is related to safe practices and improvement in efficiency.

In summary, it should be noted that top management in this case failed to understand that training is a co-operative activity involving changes in human behavior and that it requires acceptance by top management, with the resultant prestige that this acceptance will give it. Furthermore, an effective training program requires properly oriented leadership that possesses the knowledge, skills, and attitudes necessary for the establishment of a co-operative and well-integrated utilization of human effort. Specifically, it is well to recognize that training should do more than teach knowledge and skills, for attitudes toward work and safe practices are just as important. In addition, training must be co-ordinated with the needs of all the functions of a business, whether they are safety, production, sales, or any other business activity.

It is obvious from the foregoing that top-management leaders not only must understand the nature of their own behavior but also must understand the behavior of others. Top management can do a great deal in shaping favorable attitudes in subordinates who are responsible for carrying out training programs and for improving co-operation in all phases of the business. In this respect, these leaders can select and train subordinates and motivate and stimulate their interest and desire so that a training program that is truly co-operative and integrative will result. In this connection Stuart Chase points out:

"The real solution is for managers, generally, to acquire a better understanding of modern social science and the way in which a scientist arrays facts and logic to reach conclusions. The manager himself needs to become something of a social scientist to get the most out of the findings pouring in. He especially needs to know more about checking his intuition against the growing body of dependable knowledge about human behavior."[1] This growing body of dependable knowledge concerning human behavior covers such broad areas as the following: causation of human behavior, the psychology of attitudes, the nature of frustration in people, morale, the nature and role of leadership in business, the psychology of individual differences, the principles of human motivation, and the dynamics of group behavior.

Top managers can effectively deal with the human equation in training by remembering the following key points:

1. Training is a co-operative enterprise.
2. Co-operation takes place between people, not things.
3. Good leadership generates co-operation.
4. Leadership is dependent upon an understanding of human behavior.
5. The leader recognizes that his biases, prejudices, conflicts, frustrations, and attitudes can affect training and the general climate of the company.
6. Proper acceptance and prestige for training are essential.
7. Training is related to the effecting of changes in human behavior.
8. Training is a unifying force which requires integration of all company activities.

THE RESPONSIBILITY OF STAFF MANAGEMENT FOR DEALING WITH THE HUMAN EQUATION IN TRAINING

Staff management will herein refer to those members of the management organization that aid and advise top management. This classification will include all assistants without line or operational control who are engaged in the various staff functions in the business organization.

---

[1] Stuart Chase, *The Social Responsibility of Management* (The Edward L. Bernoys Foundation Lectures) (New York: New York University, School of Commerce, Accounts, and Finance, 1950), p. 24.

Staff Assistants as Co-ordinators, Advisers, and Integrators

In general, the function of staff management is to gather information and evidence which is refined and analyzed and from which advice, counsel, and recommendations result. These are then presented to top management for evaluation and action. Since no single individual can be an expert in all functions of a business, including human behavior, staff assistants become those partners on the management team who assist top management and line management in dealing with the human equation in training. For staff managers to render effective help to management, it is vital that they be aware of the fact that training should be one of the functions for which they are responsible. This elementary fact is not always grasped and understood by such people, and often top management is responsible for this attitude. The staff assistant is in a very fortunate position in the company organization, since he is the recipient of much information and evidence from above and below. His role as related to the human equation in training is vital because he can analyze and evaluate the progress of training and thus can discern the needs and improvements that may be recommended. For example, he can determine how well integrated the training program actually is, whether effective co-operation is taking place, whether the training is really effective and, if not, what possible courses of action might be pursued.

Staff Management and Human Relations

Working in concert with other staff members, are individuals who are human relations specialists. These people develop recommendations on how to understand and deal with the human requirements in jobs. They help prepare for a wholesome climate and acceptance of training by motivating and stimulating an interest in all departments to co-operate with the training department and by suggesting methods to facilitate co-operation, evaluation, and employee improvement. Although they usually do not have line authority, they can affect the attitudes and actions of top management and thereby cause improvements to take place. Furthermore, they can directly and indirectly influence other members of the management team by stressing the human factors involved in training. In general, the role of the staff assistant is to motivate, foster, and encourage co-operation, co-ordination, and integration of training by utilizing the many known facts concerning human behavior.

Staff assistants can be most helpful if they remember, in addition to the key points already mentioned for top management, the following guides to action:

That they are partners on the management team and, as such, they have responsibilities for insuring the success of a training program.

That they are in an enviable position to analyze, evaluate, and recommend improvements in the training procedure.

That they can motivate people and stimulate co-operation.

That they can be a potent force in fostering better integration of all training required in a company.

THE RESPONSIBILITY OF LINE MANAGEMENT FOR DEALING WITH THE HUMAN EQUATION IN TRAINING

The line management in a company refers to those employees generally known as department heads, section managers, supervisors, foremen, and trainers. In a broad sense, their responsibilities are to carry out company policies and to see that the necessary activities for efficient production are accomplished. Top managers and staff management were largely concerned with the problem of the human equation and the establishment of co-operation and integration of training for the entire company. Line management, on the other hand, has a primary obligation of placing emphasis on one of the segments or functions of the business. For example, the various department heads are concerned mainly with the training needs within each of their own activities. Production is interested in training insofar as manufacturing is concerned; sales wants sales and advertising training programs; and finance is interested in training in relation to its needs. Consequently, the delegation of such training responsibilities to the line managers results in emphasis being placed upon the encouragement and establishment of co-operation of the people within each department.

Knowledge, Skill, and Attitude Requirements of the Department Head

The department head must also realize that training is essential to effective operations, and his attitudes must likewise produce a climate that is conducive to the acceptance and application of training. Part of his function is to motivate and stimulate co-operative participation by section managers, supervisors, and foremen in carrying out a training program. His personality becomes the motive power in organizing, planning, and carrying out the training plan. He requires a knowledge of the areas of training needs essential to his specialized functions, as well as a knowledge of human behavior. Although he may not be a training expert himself, he should understand the broad nature of training as it relates to his departmental requirements. As a co-ordinator of the activities of people in his department, he must integrate the training function with all the sections for which he is responsible. Of prime importance to him is the selection and training of the supervisors and trainers who will become the individuals through whom he can develop aptitudes and abilities of employees most effectively. The line manager is in an excellent position to carry on and encourage research, analysis, and evaluation of the training program in his department. Discovering needs and changing conditions requiring training and understanding whether the right knowledge, skills, and attitudes are developed in the training program are part of his problem. To accomplish his objectives, he must be more than a technical expert, he must also know a great deal about human behavior, especially with regard to attitudes, conflict or frustration, morale, leadership, and group dynamics. Line managers must also be aware that they must communicate with top and staff management if training is to be a truly co-operative activity.

Knowledge, Skills, and Attitudes of Trainers

Other members of the management "partnership" involved in a co-operative training program are supervisors, foremen, and trainers. Depending upon any number of factors, such as the size of the company, the number of employees, and the nature of the business, the actual training process may be delegated to various people. In some cases the personnel department may perform training services for the entire company, while in other instances the supervisors and foremen do the training. For purposes of this discussion, all such individuals will be classified as teachers or trainers, since they are the people who will do all the necessary training, whether the training is for executive development, supervisory improvement, or special job training. In many of the larger companies a personnel director is usually in charge of training, or someone generally titled "training director" has the responsibility. In either case, the director is responsible for determining the needs of training in conjunction with all the members of the management team from top management to supervisors and foremen. His role extends to the planning, organizing, administering, controlling, and evaluation of all training activities. Specifically, he must determine what training is needed, who should be trained, how such training should take place, when it is required, by whom it ought to be carried out, and under what conditions it should occur. To carry on such an activity, he needs to know a great deal about human behavior.

Basically, the director must generate co-operation within the training division and with all departments in the company. He must be a motivator, co-ordinator, and integrator of all human activities related to training. Since he is on "the firing line" of all training, his personality, his attitudes, his interest, drive, and enthusiasm toward training will have an important effect on the climate in which training will be conducted. The director should understand the technical and human requirements of jobs in order to determine the content of training programs. He has the problem of selecting the people who will do the training, and he requires an understanding of the human qualities of a good teacher. He needs an understanding of the psychology of motivation, of individual differences, of attitudes, and of learning. With respect to the psychology of learning, he should be equipped with knowledge of the nature, laws, conditions, and methods of effective learning.

A Negative and Positive Approach to Training

In smaller companies the training function is often delegated to the foremen and supervisors or some employee selected by them. Where this occurs, the importance of preparing the trainer with the proper knowledge, skills, and attitudes to train others is more outstanding.

In a small company of approximately 75 employees manufacturing gas stoves, the foremen do all the training. The usual method is to ask the new employee to watch and observe the work of others. If the foreman is not too busy, he tries to tell the trainee what to do. Often he may pass the learner on to some worker to do the instructing. In this very informal method of training, the trainee learns the skills of his job by himself through a trial-and-error method. This method of learning is characterized by a process of trying out the many movements needed to perform the job and determining, while doing, which of the movements satisfy him in order to do the job. Such methods of training fail to take into consideration the psychological implications in the learning process. A training method of this kind is wasteful in terms of time, effort, and energy expended and serves only to increase the cost of operating the business. More important is the fact that such training overlooks the psychological damage that can result, such as frustration, unfavorable attitudes toward the company, fellow workers, and foremen, accidents, and the possibility of learning wrong habits.

In another small company of approximately the same size as the one previously referred to, the products manufactured are special-purpose hoses, such as gas-pump hoses and hoses for the transporting of chemicals that are destructive and volatile.

In this company, training is recognized as a major function of the business, and its relation to effective management practices is understood. Top management's attitude and acceptance of training are indicated by the care with which it has studied and analyzed its training needs, by calling in a consultant. Some of the recommendations made by the consultant included a systematic organization of training, and under each foreman in the ten different sections of the company an employee was carefully selected who possessed the human qualities for teaching others. This was done mainly by the use of psychological tests and interviews. Selection of the trainers was based on such human qualities as mental capacity or ability to learn, interest in people and the company, patience, tact, communicating ability, emotional maturity, and potential to motivate people favorably. Furthermore, the ten trainers were given an intensive training program in the methods of training and in the nature of human behavior, with special emphasis on the psychology of learning. To provide for a continuing interest and for further development and improvement of training, conferences were scheduled on a monthly basis. These conferences also included top management and at times the line foremen, which resulted in a co-operative enterprise aimed at continually evaluating and improving and integrating all training functions into the company organization. At a later date, top management encouraged the trainers to attend courses given at a local college at company expense.

These contrasting descriptions of how two small companies deal with training highlight the points made throughout this chapter, namely, that training is a co-operative venture that requires effective leadership, which is properly integrated and accorded the acceptance and prestige it deserves. Of most importance is the high regard given to the fact that training is vitally dependent upon the human equation.

It is significant to note that the trainer is a most important link in the chain of any co-operative training program; for the trainer, in the last analysis, becomes the responsible agent for carrying out the actual training and the knowledge, skill, and attitudes that he possesses and uses in the discharge of his function will directly effect the success or failure of the business.

Human Relations Requirements of the Trainer

To train others efficiently, the trainer should be equipped with proper knowledge, skills, and attitudes. With regard to the knowledge he should possess, it is helpful to classify this area into job knowledge and psychological knowledge. For purposes of this chapter, job knowledge will be treated lightly and refers to a thorough understanding of the nature and breakdown of the job into its logical arrangement of steps and also includes skill in performing the task. Of more importance to the trainer are the human requirements necessary for the performance of the job. In this category are such human qualities as mental capacity, motor co-ordinations, physical and postural factors, visual acuity, temperament, and attitudes. A knowledge of these requirements, as well as many others, will serve to help the trainer to perform his training function in a more meaningful framework. His knowledge of the psychological nature of the learning process is also important. This body of knowledge includes individual differences, theories of learning, methods of teaching, motivation, attitudes, communications, visual aids, and lesson plans.

With regard to skills, the trainer should be adept in performing the job, should be skilled in logical thinking so as to arrange the content of his lessons, should be a good demonstrator, a clear, concise, and skillful speaker, and should have skills in human relations.

Finally, the trainer's attitudes must be favorable, so as to produce a wholesome climate for learning to take place. He should be well motivated himself, enthusiastic, interested, and co-operative and must give acceptance, prestige, and loyalty to training. His attitudes then should be implanted in the learners as he proceeds to teach; for, as previously indicated, technical skill is not enough to give to the trainee or learner, it is equally important to instill favorable attitudes toward the company, the job, fellow workers, supervisors, and satisfactions and advancements that may be achieved through training.

THE RESPONSIBILITY OF THE TRAINEE FOR DEALING WITH THE HUMAN EQUATION IN TRAINING

In the final analysis, the test of a training program resides in the trainee or the learner. The extent to which he has acquired the knowledge, skills, and attitudes which his training experience has given him must result in improvement in production and in job loyalty and satisfaction if training is to be successful. All the human effort and energy expended by top management, staff management, and line management, including trainers, in achieving a co-operative, integrated training program are wasted if the trainee does not make his contribution as a member of the training team.

Self-Motivation Is the Keynote to Effective Learning

The trainee is responsible for absorbing the knowledge that management had determined as necessary for him to do his job for himself and the company in the interest of efficiency. This means that the trainee must apply his effort and energy in a directed manner so as to learn all the knowledge of the specific job he is to do. Such knowledge includes an understanding of the purpose of the work he is to perform in relation to the products produced or the services rendered by the company, the steps or sequence of the operations involved in doing the job, the materials, the equipment, and the terms necessary to its use. Furthermore, the trainee should know how his job is integrated with other jobs and how it can affect other jobs in the company, and he is also responsible for learning the many personnel rules and regulations concerning absences, illnesses, vacations, promotions, and the like.

Knowledge is usually a prerequisite to the acquisition of a skill. The trainee is responsible for learning the skills needed to do the job effectively, including such skills as the motor co-ordinations required, the arrangement of his work, the speed and accuracy necessary, the safety skills, and the human relations skills needed to get along with fellow workers and management.

Self-Motivation Leads to Job Satisfaction

Without proper motivation and favorable attitudes, the trainee can do little to acquire the knowledge and skills needed for his work. Although management is usually held responsible for motivating and developing wholesome attitudes in the trainee, it is unwise to conclude that the trainee cannot and should not make a direct contribution himself. The trainee can do this if he realizes that he is being educated and trained at considerable expense by the company and that he represents a sizable investment to management. Anyone aware of the costs involved in getting an education in a college or trade school should be better motivated to learn in a training program. Furthermore, the trainee should recognize that his training is a steppingstone to further training and advancement. By accepting the attitude and viewpoint that training is mutually beneficial both to management and to the learner, the latter is in a better mental and psychological state of readiness to absorb the knowledge and skills of the job. The trainee who views training with bias, prejudice, and suspicion, believing that it serves only management's purposes, cannot learn effectively. In a word, the trainee should be self-motivating and should develop wholesome attitudes because they can help him to satisfy his own needs and ambitions.

Summary

Training is truly a co-operative venture. From top management to staff, line management, and the trainee, the co-operation of all the members of the team is required if training is to be successful. Leadership that is aware of the importance of the human equation in training is a prerequisite, but there must also be a unified and integrated utilization of the members of the management team. As previously stated, co-operation does not take place between things, but between people; therefore, to the extent that management understands, acquires, and uses the knowledge, skills, and attitudes concerning human behavior, training will be either successful or unsuccessful.

THINGS TO DISCUSS AND TO DO

1. How would you attempt to secure the co-operation of several supervisors who view training as "none of our business"?
2. As a staff assistant, how would you "sell" the disinterested president of the company to support the training program?
3. Prepare a statement from the president of a large company that is to be communicated to all department heads, titled, "Support Our Training Program."
4. What would you tell an employee who felt that the training he was receiving was a waste of time?

5. Assume that you are a training director and have discovered the following problems:

   a) A department head refuses to permit several of his subordinates to attend supervisory development conferences because they take up too much time.

   b) A supervisor who feels that it is not his responsibility to induct new workers as part of the training program.

   c) A trainer who is doing his job of instructing poorly.

   In each of the problems explain how you would generate co-operation.

6. Discuss the steps that might be taken in order to secure the co-operation of all department heads in a company.

7. Why should the training program be integrated with the functions of the safety director?

8. Do a survey among the members of your class in order to determine their attitudes toward the course.

9. Visit a company that has a training program and observe the degree of co-operation you find among the supervisors and others involved.

Unit II

TRAINING-LEARNING PROCEDURES

4. PRINCIPLES OF LEARNING AND TRAINING—MORE THAN TELLING AND SHOWING

Purpose of the Chapter

THIS CHAPTER is concerned with five problems: (1) the definition and nature of learning; (2) the four types of learning; (3) modern learning theories; (4) the methods that three different theorists might use in solving the same instructional problem; (5) the learning principles that most psychologists find acceptable.

LEARNING AND THE TRAINER

Learning is the most universal and important occupation of mankind. It is the major task of the young, the never-ending duty of the adult. Learning is the means of progress. The ability to learn is man's distinctive characteristic. Every human achievement is the result of this ability. Learning is the means whereby the trainer justifies his existence. Learning seems to be such a commonplace activity that only when one begins to ask questions about it, does it become apparent that learning is a complex process.

1. What is meant by learning and knowledge?
2. Is there more than one type of learning? If so, how many different kinds are there?
3. What are the major aspects or stages of each type of learning?
4. Are psychologists agreed on what learning is *not?*
5. Do they agree on what takes place when an individual learns something?
6. Are there principles of learning that most psychologists, regardless of their theoretical orientation, accept as true?
7. What factors help or hinder the learning process?
8. What technique is best adapted to each type of learning?

9. How can the trainer put learning principles into practice with reference to each instructional technique?

10. What is the role of the instructor in the teaching-learning process?

Questions like these require answers. It is only the most naïve of trainers who fancy that the ritualistic application of a mechanical procedure is an adequate substitute for genuine insight into the nature of the learning process. The present chapter seeks to present simple, perhaps oversimplified, answers to the first six questions. Chapter 5 is devoted to answering question 7. The remaining questions are considered in Chapter 6.

Most trainers usually utilize enlightened principles of learning in their work. It is not clear, however, that in all cases, they realize why these procedures work as well as they do; nor is it evident that the psychological principles on which an effective instructional-learning relationship is based are always clearly understood. The four-step method of instruction, for instance, is little more than an adaptation of the old Herbartian steps of the nineteenth century.

Why does this process of preparation, presentation, application, and follow-up succeed? Might there actually be a better method of instructing trainees? Every text, including this one, offers the trainer a plethora of approaches to supervisory development. No one knows for sure, however, whether the case study, role-playing, conference, or lecture-discussion method is best for supervisory development. Nor is there any sizable body of evidence that any one procedure is the best for dealing with a particular phase of a supervisory development program, such as discipline, morale building, communications, or giving orders. Perforce, trainers are eclectics, utilizing a variety of methods for the attainment of their objectives.

The second phenomenon of training in industry has to do with the great emphasis that is placed on "know-how" and "how-to-do" and the relatively small interest shown in the theories and principles of learning that are basic to these mechanics. Textbooks abound with techniques, rules of thumb, and "gimmicks" for "getting across" to trainees. At times such procedures are not justified on the basis of what is known about the learning process. While this may appear to be an abstract consideration, it is difficult to see how a profession of training can be established unless it gives greater thought than it has in the past to the problem of developing a known body of principles, based on research in industry, that is related to its central task, the teaching-learning process.

MEANING OF LEARNING AND KNOWLEDGE

Learning is the mental activity by means of which skills, habits, ideas, attitudes, and ideals are acquired, retained, and utilized, resulting in the progressive adaptation and modification of behavior.[1]

Learning, therefore, is self-development through self-activity. It involves the development of an individual's capacities, the actualization of his potentialities, and the reorganization of his experiences in the direction of what is wiser and better. It is characterized by a passage through four stages: (1) the individual is at first in a state of *unconscious incompetence*, in which he is not even aware of his lack of knowledge; (2) when he becomes aware of his ignorance and the need to do something about it, he enters the stage of *conscious incompetence*; (3) with effort, he succeeds in reaching the third stage, *conscious competence*, in which his knowledge is deliberately and often woodenly applied; (4) continued effort may bring him to the level of *unconscious competence*, in which he utilizes his knowledge easily and gracefully as though it were second nature to him. The purpose for which the individual struggles through these four stages is to acquire some type of *knowledge*. Knowledge, therefore, is the objective or the end point of the learning process. This is true whether one is speaking of the mastery of a skill, such as operating a lathe; the development of an attitude, such as building good will toward a company; or the promotion of clear understanding, such as comprehension of the organizational structure of a company.

FOUR BASIC KINDS OF LEARNING

The nexus between the learning process, knowledge, and principles of learning can best be understood by a discussion of four basic kinds of learning and the kind of knowledge which each seeks to foster.

Sensori-Motor Learning

Mary Smith is starting to learn to type. She wants to learn because it will mean a better job. In the beginning, her movements are uncertain and unco-ordinated. She gets the paper in wrong. She has difficulty setting the margins. She makes many mistakes. She knows that she wants to write "Now is the time for all good men to come

---

[1] William A. Kelly, *Educational Psychology* (4th ed.; Milwaukee: Bruce Publishing Co., 1956), p. 238.

to the aid of their country." When she tries to type this sentence, however, she types one letter at a time. "Now is" becomes "Nowis." "The" comes out "hte." After several unsuccessful tries, she complains, "I know what I want to do, but I just can't make my fingers do it." She wants to look at the keys but is reminded that she is not supposed to do so. After a short practice time, she feels quite tired and a little frustrated.

Now everyone knows that, with time and practice, Mary will learn to type. Why is she having so much difficulty? The fact is that Mary is trying to learn a skill. All sensori-motor learning is skill learning, whether it involves mechanical drawing, playing a musical instrument, or operating a drill press. Mary's experience illustrates the five stages into which skill learning may be divided. *First,* Mary wants to learn how to type; she is motivated. *Second,* her beginning attempts to master the skill have the following characteristics: (1) incomplete understanding and inaccurate perception of the elements involved in the task, their interrelationships, and the relationship of each element to the skill as a whole; (2) poor muscular co-ordination, futile movements, and random and trial-and-error effort; (3) an expenditure of energy that is out of proportion to the difficulty of the task involved.

As Mary practices in the right manner, she will enter the *third stage.* Characteristics of this stage are (1) a clearer understanding of the requirements of the total task and how the separate elements contribute to its accomplishment; (2) better muscular co-ordination of the different movements into a single pattern; (3) a reduction of "mistakes" and the gradual elimination of mere trial-and-error learning; (4) the satisfaction that comes from the realization that one is "getting the knack of it." *Stage four* is reached when an individual realizes what constitutes the nature of a good performance. This is accompanied by the adoption of good form and repetition of the correct movements with some degree of co-ordination. The *final stage* is devoted to practice in the right manner under the guidance of a clear understanding of every aspect of the task, the development of rhythmical co-ordination with a minimum of fatigue, concentration on particularly difficult aspects of the course, and a sense of accomplishment at a job well done. The objective of skill learning is not mastery of the separate elements of a job but rather the smooth, co-ordinated mastery of these elements so that the task may be performed easily, intelligently, accurately, and rapidly with a maximum of efficiency and a minimum of fatigue. It is left to the reader to test these stages for himself by learning to tie a Spanish bowline, to drive a tractor-trailer, to operate a planer, a milling machine, or similar equipment.

Conceptual Learning

All purposive learning involves some intellectual content; all such learning requires some trial and error. When the term "conceptual" is used, therefore, it refers to the relative importance of abstract cognitive factors in the learning process. The aim of "conceptual learning" is the mental assimilation of some fact, principle, law, or generalization and its integration with that which is already known. In general, such learning emphasizes the understanding of abstract terms, inferences, hypotheses, and theories; it is concerned with inductive and deductive thinking; it involves reflective thinking, judgment, and reasoning with respect to the definition, analysis, and solution of problems. It is clear, for instance, that there is a vast difference between the degree of understanding required for a missile nose-cone engineering proposal and that needed to operate a shaper.

1. *An Illustration of Conceptual Learning: Inductive Reasoning.* In World War II the Air Force was faced with the problem of selecting those cadet pilots who would justify the time and expense involved in their training, not to mention the matter of preventing unnecessary deaths, by becoming successful airmen. A battery of tests, which was assumed to have a certain validity, was administered to student pilots. However, all candidates who had passed other screening procedures were allowed to enter the training program, regardless of their scores on the test battery. The progress in training of all the candidates was carefully checked. Finally, the successful and non-successful pilots' test battery scores were compared, with a view to discovering whether these scores would have been helpful in screening out those who ultimately proved inadequate and in selecting those who "made the grade."

Approximately fifty thousand pilots were processed in this manner by the AAF aviation psychology program. What were some of the results? Sample findings included the following: (1) 81 per cent of those who were allowed to enter training despite a stanine score of 1 (the lowest possible) "washed out"; (2) at the other extreme, only about 13 per cent of those with a stanine score of 9 (the highest) failed to complete their training. A detailed summary of the results would be inappropriate. Suffice it to say that the test battery proved to be a useful screening device.

This illustration indicates that, as there is an advisable technique for mastering a skill, so there is one for intellectual or rational training. It is called *the scientific method*, although in actual practice there are many "scientific methods," and is ordinarily applied to the process of *inductive reasoning*. As is well known, inductive reasoning describes a conceptual process wherein one proceeds from an accumulation of facts, all or most of which point in a given direction, to a conclusion, generalization, law, or principle that explains this phenomenon. Using the AAF experiment, the steps in the scientific method may be described as follows:

1. A problem is encountered or creatively contrived, giving rise to a "felt need" for a solution. The AAF had a need for some procedures for distinguishing between successful and nonsuccessful cadet pilots—before entering training.

2. A clear statement of the problem, subsidiary problems, and the variables involved is formulated. The problem is defined. The problem of the AAF was defined in terms of identifying and measuring those characteristics that predicted success in pilot training. Job analyses, rational analyses, and other procedures indicated that such factors as intelligence, spatial visualization, mathematical achievement, perceptual speed, reaction time, and so on were essential in pilot success.

3. A critical evaluation of possible solutions is made on the basis of logic and the evidence already on hand. The most reasonable solution is selected. This proposed solution is called a *hypothesis:* a statement tentatively assumed to be true, which is to be evaluated by gathering pertinent evidence. For the AAF it was assumed that a carefully tailored test battery would help solve its problem.

4. Evidence that is germane to the problem is collected, usually under controlled conditions. Fifty thousand cadet pilots entered training, regardless of their test battery scores. Data were then gathered on those pilot cadets who had completed training and those who had failed to do so. A comparison was made of the data on success or failure and the corresponding test battery scores.

5. The hypothesis is tested to discover whether it "stands up" under the new information and explains the data. The AAF found that the test battery proved helpful in screening out ultimately unsuccessful cadet pilots.

6. Verification of the study is often made. It is "replicated" with different subjects to see whether it holds up. The AAF replicated this study with a second group of one thousand cadet pilots.

7. A solution to the problem is reached, decisions are made, and generalizations may also be reached. The AAF solved, at least to a degree, its original problem, and it was determined to use the test battery as a screening device. Applications of the same procedure to other, related, AAF problems might be made by a process of *deductive reasoning*.

2. *A Second Illustration of Conceptual Learning: Deductive Reasoning*. Inductive reasoning involves going from the particular to the general; deductive reasoning refers to the cognitive process whereby an idea, law, principle, generalization, or theory is applied to a specific situation or set of circumstances. In business the implementation of policy is often an excellent example of deductive reasoning. The policy serves as a general guide to action. It is the responsibility of the manager to put the policy into practice largely on the basis of his familiarity with his particular department. Since the entire field of policy formulation and implementation is something of a semantic swamp, a simpler example may be more useful.

On the basis of observation, research studies, and other techniques, the following conclusions have been reached with regard to women workers:

Women have less muscular strength, smaller legs, and stomachs than men. They are about as intelligent as men but less apt mechanically and usually less well technically trained. They have superior finger dexterity and tend to be superior at detailed and routine work. They are absent from work more often, are more reliant on group support, are more sensitive to the physical environment, and are more responsive to praise and blame. They show their emotions more readily than men, usually make a greater effort to please, and often would rather work for a man than another woman. Women tend to be more people-oriented than men and rarely devote their energies to the job to the exclusion of off-the-job interests, to the degree that is characteristic of a man who is ambitious for success.

Assuming that these generalizations are true, it is the responsibility of the supervisor to apply them to his own particular work group with respect to hiring men or women for particular jobs, assignment of work, giving praise, blame, and recognition, dealing with cliques, discipline, rest periods, building morale, human relations, and similar problems.

3. *A Third Illustration of Conceptual Learning: Problem-Solving.* Try to solve the following problems. As you attempt each problem, be sensitive to your own thought processes, to what you are doing in an attempt to arrive at the solution.

1. Nine match sticks are arranged in a three-by-three pattern of rows and columns. You have three additional match sticks in your hand. Place the additional sticks in the pattern in such a way that there will now be four match sticks in each row and four in each column.[2]
2. A man sells 60 pieces of candy at 3 for 1 cent and another 60 pieces at 2 for 1 cent. Would his income be more, less, or the same if he sold the 120 pieces at 5 for 2 cents?
3. A telephone dial has 10 holes. How many signals, each consisting of 7 impulses in succession, can be formed: (*a*) if no impulse is to be repeated in any given signal; (*b*) if repetitions are permitted?[3]

If you solved all three problems correctly—congratulations! Regardless of your success or failure, however, solving problems like these is a far cry from the requirements for operating a machine. The three problems illustrate what is meant by conceptual, intellectual, and rational learning. If you were conscious of your own efforts to solve these problems, you probably found that, like Mary Smith's efforts at skill learning (p. 69), certain distinguishable elements in your problem-solving approach(es) formed more or less a pattern.

1. You had to read the problems. All learning of any type begins with direct experience, *sensation*, a process of collecting data as a necessary prerequisite for the solutions. Often this involves a "translation" of the data into a more appropriate form. For instance, you may have drawn a picture of the data in problems 1 and 3. You may have written the numbers inherent in problem 2.

2. In *perception* the information provided by the sense organs is unified and interpreted, giving knowledge of reality. You may have read the problem, drawn a picture of it, and even read it aloud to yourself.

3. *Memory* makes available what you have learned and retained in the past—experience with similar problems and related problem-solving techniques. If you were familiar with permutations and com-

[2] David Kretch and Richard S. Crutchfield, *Elements of Psychology* (New York: Alfred A. Knopf, Inc., 1958), p. 390.

[3] M. Richardson, *Fundamentals of Mathematics* (rev. ed.; New York: Macmillan Co., 1958), pp. 8, 203.

binations, then problem 3 was easily solved; the same applies to problem 2 and, to a markedly lesser extent, to problem 1.

4. *Imagination,* especially creative imagination, makes it possible for you to consider the problem from many angles, avoiding the continued repetition of inappropriate procedures. "Imagining" problem 1 is almost a necessity to arrive at the correct solution.

5. *Attention and concentration* enable you to focus your energies on the problem at hand with a minimum of distraction and interference.

6. *Interest, goal motivation, and an attitude of confidence* help you to persist in your efforts to solve the problems in spite of failure and temporary setbacks.

7. *Creative thinking and a sound problem-solving technique* eventually bring about the correct solutions. You secured a clear understanding of the known factors in the problem—*ideas*—as well as the "unknowns." You then made *judgments* between and among these ideas. Using the original data, the ideas, and the judgments, you *reasoned* to the correct answer. The solution may have come quickly as a result of a rapid insight into the problem, or slowly by conceptual trial and error, eliminating plausible but erroneous solutions until the correct one was reached.

Conceptual learning is typical of many, if not most, business situations. Engineering proposals, plant layouts, planning, policy formulation, evolution of organizational charts, decisions concerning product lines, allocation of salesmen, drawing up the budget, selection of personnel, and so on demand this kind of learning.

Associational Learning

All learning involves some process of association. By *associational learning* is meant that type in which facts and ideas are linked largely by a process of conditioning, so that one serves as a stimulus for recalling the other(s). Associational learning is basic to safety training, in which red is associated with danger, green with safe conditions, and yellow for caution. Airline pilot checks are largely a matter of associational learning. Associational learning is fundamental to differently colored carbons and wires, diversely shaped controls, spelling, number, and code combinations, simple mathematics, dates, events, memory of dates and events, formulas in science, and a host of other phenomena. It is a major component in sensori-motor or skill learning. It is important to note that, although in this case conditioning plays an important role, it is rarely sufficient in itself for optimum performance. The knobs, dials, movements, and sequence of operations should have significance for the learner. They should be meaningful. Given this condition, associational learning is a matter of drill, repetition, and review, based on the ideas of contiguity, contrast, and similarity.

Attitudinal Learning

Of all the so-called kinds of learning, attitudinal or appreciational learning is least understood. How are attitudes, ideals, satisfactions, and values built up? No one really knows, although this is most significant for such problems as job satisfaction, morale, motivation, interest, and human relations. All that is known is that certain factors, such as enlightened supervision, are associated with job satisfaction. How these factors are interrelated and what particular pattern of them is most conducive to a desired result—for instance, morale— is an X. The relative importance of conditioning, early childhood, personal ambitions, the demands of society, the expectations of fellow workers and supervisors, value systems, and so on is a mystery. It is perhaps for this reason—people have a tendency to conceal lack of knowledge with a cliché—that it is said, "Attitudes are more caught than taught."

MYTHS ABOUT LEARNING[4]

It has been claimed that each of the following statements represents a so-called "myth of learning":

1. That learning is an independent process that takes place apart from the learner's and instructor's past experiences, perceptions, needs, expectations, and self-concepts.
2. That the instructor's task is to set forth what is to be learned; the student's task is to learn it.
3. That knowledge accepted on authority is learning itself.
4. That the subject matter has the same meaning for the instructor as it has for the learner.
5. That the instructor is responsible for the learner's acquisition of knowledge.

---

[4] Nathaniel Cantor, *The Teaching-Learning Process* (New York: Dryden Press, Inc., 1953). These "myths" have been adapted from chapter iii, "The Assumptions of Orthodox Teaching."

6. That education is solely a verbal process.
7. That the instructor's task is to equip the learner with a repertoire of skills and techniques to meet specific situations.
8. That the learner can solve problems which he does not experience or has not experienced.
9. That the presentation of subject matter affects all learners in about the same way and that all facts and ideas have approximately the same significance for all learners.
10. That the values which prompt the instructor to pursue his goals are the same as those which stimulate the student.
11. That learning is for later living and responsibilities and not for present living and the solution of problems.
12. That repetition alone is a cause of learning.
13. That habit alone is a cause of learning.
14. That, because psychologically the mental processes involved in learning are relatively the same for all learners, it follows that all techniques which are utilized to stimulate learners will serve all of them equally well.
15. That the only way to evaluate learning is from the outside perspective of the instructor.
16. That one learns best by having something told him, shown him, or explained to him.
    Are all these statements myths?
    Are they all equally "mythical"?
    If some of them are not myths, why not?
    What ill effects is an assumption that they are valid and true likely to have on a training session?

LEARNING THEORIES AND TRAINING

If you had difficulty answering the above questions or were unsure of your responses, the following sections may prove of some help. Many statements have thus far been made in this chapter concerning the definition, types, and so-called myths of learning. The reader may justly ask, "On what basis have they been made?" To do so is to place the trainer, be he in industry or in college, in a somewhat awkward position.

One reason why books on training at times avoid the problem of learning theory is the simple fact that there is no *one* theory that can explain the process completely and satisfactorily. Instead of an approach that can prove either that it contains the whole truth or at least that it is demonstrably superior to its competing theories of learning, we have different and sometimes opposed conceptual viewpoints. Each of the major theories explains some aspects of learning better than its competitors, only to "fall down" when it comes to explaining other aspects of the process. This situation is the more annoying because the trainer is primarily a teacher and, as such, needs a sure theory of learning by which to live. Yet the theorist, to his own humiliation, must admit that he has no certain solution to the trainer's dilemma. The findings of learning experiments are enlightening and stimulating because of the discoveries made. At the same time, they are frustrating because such findings are usually incomplete. The humbled theorist, therefore, is compelled to admit that he has no one best road to learning but rather many frames of reference, each of which is superior in some ways and inferior in others.

Snygg has well expressed this problem. "Most psychologists are paid to help people to learn. This is very embarrassing because the truth is that nobody knows very much about learning."[5] He also concluded that after fifty years the ones who have benefited most from learning theory are the theorists themselves. The conflicting results of some of their experiences have kept them in business, much like the two shipwrecked sailors who made a living by taking in each other's washing. This situation has at times been worsened by a human tendency to take one's stand beneath the banner of one or another theory and "take on all comers." Because of this, it is important that the trainer be familiar, at least in broad outline, which is all that the present book can hope to accomplish, with the viewpoints of the major theories. Failure to do so involves a risk of clinging tenaciously in blind faith to a technique or at least of not understanding why a given technique is as effective as it is.

SOME MODERN LEARNING THEORIES

Oscar Wilde once remarked that history was an account of things that never should have happened in the first place. The history of modern learning theory is perhaps an example of this. One way of avoiding an abstract explanation of the theories is to see how hypo-

---

[5] Donald Snygg, "Learning: An Aspect of Personality Development," in *Learning Theory, Personality Theory and Clinical Research* (New York: John Wiley & Sons, Inc., 1954), pp. 129–30.

thetical trainers might *theoretically* go about instructing trainees in solving an entirely fictitious problem. We say "theoretically," because no trainer worth his salt allows a theory to dictate to his hard-earned instructional experience. The problem is for illustrative purposes to point out certain key ideas in each theory, rather than attempt an exhaustive analysis. Trainer A is a behaviorist; Trainer C is a connectionist; Trainer B is a Gestaltist.

THREE SOLUTIONS TO THE SAME PROBLEM

A trainer is responsible for instructing a small group of electricians with respect to how to "wire" a new and fairly complicated board. The board has many terminals. Some are round, others are diamond-shaped, still others rectangular. They are also of different sizes. Each terminal has a number printed above it. A group of about forty wires enters the board at the right bottom corner. For each wire two connections are to be made, one to each of two terminals. The wires are colored differently and have number tags that correspond to the numbers above the terminals. The job of the trainees is to learn how to wire the board. How might trainers with different theoretical orientations go about helping them?

Trainer A

Trainer A probably would not spend any great amount of time explaining the over-all purpose of the board, what function it served in the total communications system, what had preceded the wiring of the board, and what would follow operationally. He would likely spend little time on explaining the interrelationships of the wires and how each and all contributed to the proper functioning of the board. He might "get right down to cases" by picking up a wire and showing how its number corresponded to the appropriate number on each terminal, pointing out that the proper wire could easily be identified by its color. He would make sure that each trainee noted the importance of the shape of the particular terminals concerned. He would try to get the trainees to associate the numbers, color, and shape of the corresponding terminals and wires. He would show the trainees how to perform the operation of linking this one wire with its proper terminals. He would have the trainees do it for themselves. He would insist on "learning by doing." The pairing of the wire with the correct terminals would be done over and over, practiced and drilled in, until the trainees could make this connection almost unconsciously. When one such connection was mastered, the trainer would consider a second, and then another, until the entire board was wired. In like manner, the trainees would learn each connection separately by a process of painstaking instruction, practice, drill, and review until all were learned. During the learning process the trainer would be patient until the trainee "got it right." He might even use music to help the trainees learn the right connections. He would praise each perfect connection but not give the trainee a steady diet of praise. Wrong connections he would either not reward at all or punish. He might have the trainees repeat out loud, or to themselves, the color, number, and shape of the wire and terminals as they performed the operation. At times he might indicate how similarly colored and/or numbered wires went to similarly shaped and numbered terminals, but he would make certain that the trainees did not apply this notion of similarity where it did not work, by making them discriminate between different connections.

Thus, in this oversimplified presentation, the instruction-learning process would consist of a demonstration of each wire connection separately by the trainer, practice by the trainees, one wire connection at a time, praise, correction or simply ignoring a connection, depending on whether it was correct or incorrect, continued practice to the point of mastery so that the trainees performed the operation as a matter of almost "second nature," generalization and discrimination. In a gradual additive way, going from one wire connection to the next, the trainees would learn to wire the board until they could do so almost unconsciously.

Trainer B

The approach of Trainer B would, at least in certain respects, be quite different from that of Trainer A. He would probably take great pains to explain the over-all purpose of the board, the function it served in the total communications system, where the wires came from, what had preceded the wiring of the board, what would follow operationally after it was wired. He would make a great effort to help the trainees to get an idea of the entire board as a unit. He would insist that wiring the board involved much more than merely making the separate connections. He would stress the fact that the wires and terminals constituted not single links that were additive, but rather a pattern of electrical interrelationships organized for a specific purpose. He would work in such a way, explaining, describing, and so on, as to engender in the trainees a clear understanding of the workings of the board as a totality, indicating how each wire contributed to this whole. While not neglecting the individual connections, he would urge the trainees to think of them not as separate linkages but as interdependent aspects of a functioning board.

He would not have the trainees learn each wire connection in a piecemeal, one-by-one, additive fashion. He would not "get down to cases," as did Trainer A, by demonstrating the first connection right away. Rather, when he felt that the trainees had a fairly accurate notion of the board and of the relationships of the wires to each other and to the boards as a unit, he would demonstrate the proper method for linking wire to terminals, emphasizing the color, number, and shape characteristics. Practice and drill would not serve as the basic learning techniques but rather as a means for giving trainees direct experience in attaching the wires to the terminals, so that they might further clarify their understanding of the board and its workings, as well as master the particular skill involved. He would emphasize how similarly colored and/or numbered wires served similar purposes, seeking to have the trainees generalize and apply this knowledge in learning to make the separate connections. He would try to motivate the trainees by pointing out the importance of the board and the need for wiring it correctly as part of the total communications system. He would stress that the goal is not to make a series of more or less separate connections properly but rather to wire the entire board correctly. He would praise and blame as he felt it to be necessary.

Trainer C

Trainer C's approach might be rather similar to that of Trainer A and, in some respects, similar to that of Trainer B. He would first attempt to create a state of psychological readiness to learn on the part of the trainees by trying to motivate them and arouse their interest. He would not force them to learn until he felt that the trainees were "ready" to do so. On the other hand, once they indicated that they were "ready" and wanted to learn the board, he would not prevent them from doing so. He might try to show the trainees how the wires and terminals "belonged" together because of their similar numbers, colors, and/or shapes. Yet he would make sure that the trainees saw the problem as one of connecting all the wires to the correct terminals and the importance of doing so perfectly. He would make sure that the trainees learned how to wire this particular board, utilizing their experience with similar boards only when the connections to be made were identical. He might begin by demonstrating the simplest connection between a wire and its terminals.

Like Trainer A, he would rely on "learning by doing," drill, practice, and review, until the trainees could perform each wiring connection almost unconsciously. Much like Trainer A, he would proceed from one connection to the next in an additive manner until all were mastered. Unlike Trainer B, he would spend little or no time explaining the over-all purpose of the board, the function it served in the total communications system, what had preceded the wiring of the board, what would follow operationally, the interrelationships of the wires to each other and to the total task of wiring the board. He might combine similarly colored, numbered, and/or shaped wires and terminals in order to facilitate the learning process. He would emphasize that the trainees be alert to colors, numbers, and shapes and not merely to one or another of these characteristics. He would praise every successful movement of the trainees, much more so than Trainer A. Incorrect movements would be followed by correction and/or rebuke. He might teach the trainees not merely to wire the connections but also to unwire them. The basic learning process would consist of (1) arousing a readiness to learn; (2) continuous practice in making single connections, involving drill and review; (3) giving the trainees rewards for success.

It is clear from this contrived and oversimplified example that trainers with a bias in favor of one or another of the major learning theories may tend to perform the same instructional task rather differently. Let us attempt to pick out a few of the salient ideas of each theory from our fictitious illustrative example.

Behaviorism

Influenced largely by Pavlov's dog experiments, J. B. Watson proclaimed that, given a baby early enough in life, he could condition him to be a doctor, lawyer, or Indian chief. Conditioning is a process of learning that consists in acquiring new ways of reacting to stimuli, developed through attaching new stimuli to established modes of behavior. Thus, in the classical experiments, the dog was "taught" to salivate (conditioned response) at the sight of light (conditioned stimulus) by first turning on the light for several seconds before giving him his food (unconditioned stimulus), which, of course, usually made him salivate (unconditioned response).

Anyone who fancies that this experiment (and many others that have been made) has no application should do three things: (1) observe himself and others and discover how many of their acts, attitudes, skills, fears, and ideas are largely the result of conditioning; (2) reflect on the extent to which Russia relies on conditioning in its propaganda warfare outside the mother country and in its educational system inside; (3) think of the reactions of different people in business to such words as, "strike," "speed-up," "automation," "shape-up," "check-off," "efficiency expert," "unions," "strikebreaking," and so on. A person who, because of some methods change, has in the past been fired with a reaction of distrust, fear, and resentment may now attach these same emotions to the mere words "time study," "efficiency expert," and "methods change"—words which, before his unhappy experience, may very well have brought no emotional reaction at all.

All conditioning, in essence, is mechanistic and seeks to interpret learning on a physiological basis, the heart of which is the conditioned reflex. Pavlov's experiment is a form of simple conditioning. In a higher form—instrumental conditioning—the subject is forced to do something to receive a reward or to avoid a rebuke (shock). Thus a rat might be forced to press a bar (conditioned response) to get food (unconditioned stimulus) so as to enjoy eating (unconditioned response). In the problem the trainees had to make the correct connection in order to receive praise from Trainer A. Moreover, it would be entirely possible, theoretically, for Trainer A to teach the trainees the proper connections by a process of conditioning, without their knowing anything about why or what they were really doing. Many assemblers are conditioned to perform a given series of operations according to a specific sequence without having a clear idea as to why they must do so in a particular manner. As has been mentioned, workers are conditioned to react differently to red and green lights or controls. In fact, most people are color-conditioned in one way or another. It is principally by a process of conditioning that a typing skill is mastered. Music tends to give a "lift" to workers engaged in repetitive and monotonous work by conditioning. Finally, it is common knowledge that many emotional reactions are conditioned responses, as when an individual tends "instinctively" to fear or rebel against authority.

Apart from these general observations, what ideas of behaviorism are of practical use to the trainer?

1. Acquisition. (Trainer A patiently waited until the trainees had mastered one connection before going on to the other. He took up each connection in turn, feeling no great need for an explanation of the purpose of the board, its function in the total communications system, the interrelationships of the wires, etc.) Conditioned responses are acquired slowly and gradually. The trainer who starts a session with a burst of speed or who tries to cover too much in too short a time soon discovers that he is in outer space alone.

2. Successive Approximation. (Trainer A broke the total task into subunits. When the trainees had mastered each unit, he rewarded them. This proceeded until they had wired the entire board.) This concept is well illustrated in an experiment by Skinner, who taught a rat to pull a string—to get a marble from a rack—pick up the marble—and carry it to a tube projecting two inches above the ground—lift the marble up—and drop it down the tube, by rewarding each major step in the process. For the trainer this suggests the need for breaking down a complicated task into subunits, based on job analysis or some similar procedure. As each subunit is mastered, the trainees should be rewarded. Not a few technical, supervisory, and management development programs fail to do this. They consist of what may appear to the trainers to be simply a listing of topics, each of which is considered in order.

3. Generalization. (Trainer A explained how similarly colored and/or numbered wires were attached to similarly shaped and/or numbered terminals.) Conditioned responses which initially are set up in relation to specific stimuli have a tendency to "generalize" to similar stimuli. An office machine operator, according to the behaviorists, who has been conditioned to one model may more readily learn to operate a new model on the basis of this principle.

4. Discrimination. (Trainer A was careful not to allow the trainees to proceed in wiring the board on the basis of their past familiarity with similar boards only or to assume that all connections were made exactly alike.) Generalization may be either positive, as above, or negative. It is important to teach the trainees to discriminate between stimuli. For instance, negative employee attitudes to a particular supervisor may at times "generalize" to include the entire management or company. Naïve attempts to apply human relations principles, without due consideration of the particular characteristics of the people involved and of the situation, has caused some supervisors to "go sour" on them. They "generalized" that what would work well with the reasonably conscientious and well-adjusted worker would work equally well with the malcontent, lazy, or emotionally disturbed employees. They failed to "discriminate."

5. Secondary Reinforcement. (The trainees responded not only to the reward of making the connections successfully but also to the praise and/or correction of Trainer A.) Stimuli associated with the primary rewards tend to acquire secondary reinforcing properties themselves. A chimpanzee was conditioned to get a chip which he used to obtain food. Eventually the chips, which he collected, served as rewards in themselves. Individuals work for many different primary objectives. It is fairly obvious that they do not do so merely to secure praise from the boss or to get a title or to have a secretary. Nonetheless, praise and/or blame and status symbols have powerful secondary reinforcement properties.

6. Experimental Extinction. (Trainer A never rewarded a wrong connection.) If one wishes to eliminate a response, he sees to it that the unwanted behavior is never rewarded. Many an employee has voiced the idea of this principle negatively by saying, "You can break your back around this place, and no one gives a damn. The hell with it. I'll do just as much as I have to." Trainers must be careful to reward the responses they wish to develop and no others.

7. Timing of Reward. (Trainer A praised the trainees as soon as they had completed a subunit of the total task.) Evidence indicates that rewards and punishments should be as close as possible to the response. Teaching machines that inform the learner of his errors immediately are superior to delayed correction. Test results and examination papers should be returned as speedily as possible. Mistakes should be corrected when made. Discipline should follow as closely as possible on the heels of the offending act; the same applies to praise. A man has a right to know where he stands.

8. Partial Reinforcement. (Trainer A did not praise every single successful movement or subject the trainees to a steady diet of praise.) Often a supervisor asks, "How often should I praise my men?" Considerable research evidence indicates that subjects who were rewarded only half the time showed no more diminution of effort than did those who were rewarded every time. What is more significant is that, when the rewards were stopped altogether, the "half-rewarded" group continued making appropriate responses (resistance to extinction) for a much longer time than did those who had previously been rewarded all the time. Occasional rewards do not seem to lessen effort but establish more strongly the desired behavior than do rewards that are given every time.

Gestalt or Field Theories

Most of the ideas of behaviorism and connectionism were originally based on experimental evidence derived from animals. There are advantages in working with animals. They are more prolific than men, easier to get along with, cheaper to house and feed, more willing to work for room and board. Moreover, many things learned from animal experimentation apply to people. On the other hand, it is as dangerous to assume that rats are just like people as it is to assume that people are just like rats. The field theories of learning, therefore, represent a reaction to interpreting learning simply in terms of conditioned responses or in terms of the formation of connections or stimulus-response (S-R) bonds. This reaction has stemmed from the experiences of clinical and social psychologists, the perceptual research of the Gestaltists, the work of psychoanalysts, and the modern educational emphasis on the "whole man." The Gestaltists have attacked nearly every behavioristic interpretation of learning theory. On the other hand, they have contributed some significant concepts of their own, which are considered below.

1. *Figure and Ground*. (Trainer B took great pains to make certain that the trainees knew the function of the board in the communications system, what had preceded, and what followed operationally.) Every organismic theory of learning views it *not* as a mere matter of conditioning or connecting S-R bonds but largely as a matter of the interaction of the figure (the board) and the ground (the communications system of which it is a part). All insist that behavior (figure) is meaningless unless interpreted in light of the surroundings (field) in which it takes place. In fact, the same behavior may take on different meanings in different surroundings. An excellent example of this idea of figure and ground is the little experiment in which one sees now a picture of a young woman, now a picture of an old woman, while looking at exactly the same, identical picture. A silhouette is another example of the same idea.

This concept is so obvious—now that we have experimental evidence for it—that reflection on the following questions should clarify its application to training situations. What significance does this idea have for the adoption of a packaged training program or one that has worked well in another company? A situation in which the trainer is enthusiastic and tries his very best, whereas the trainees know that the company looks on training as something akin to a super-fluous luxury? Emphasis on the formal organization of a company to the neglect of its informal organization? Giving trainees a list of rules of thumb for dealing with grievances, discipline, and so on? Sending executives to A.M.A. seminars rather than training them on company premises?

2. Wholes. (Trainer B stressed the importance of seeing the interrelationships of the wires to each other and to the board as a unit.) Field theories of learning emphasize the importance of gestalts, patterns, and wholes, on the premise that the whole is always more than the mere sum of its parts. Learning for them involves the inter-action of the whole individual with his total situation. This difference between the Gestalt approach and that of a theoretically naïve behaviorist can be illustrated with a problem in time-and-motion study. In this procedure a breakdown of the necessary movements, together with the time required for each, is secured. Superfluous movements are eliminated, and the worker is instructed in the "best" method of per-forming his job. Suppose that a job consisted of five operations, A, B, C, D, E, which require 2, 3, 5, 1, 6 minutes to perform. Now suppose that B and D are eliminated. One might expect (assuming that in each case the worker was given enough practice to reach maximum effi-ciency) that the new total time would be 13 minutes (17 minus 4). This rarely happens. The new time will usually be greater than a mere subtraction process would indicate.[6]

Why is this so? According to the Gestaltist idea that the whole is always more than the sum of its parts, the worker does not learn a series of discrete movements which he adds together—A, B, C, D, E—but rather a pattern of interrelated movements within a functional unit. Destroy the pattern, as by removing operations B and D, and he must learn a new movement pattern. This accounts for the fact that the new time total is rarely that which would be obtained if the time required for the eliminated movements were simply subtracted from the old total time. Much the same idea applies to Mary Smith (p. 69) and her learning to type. She will never be an efficient typist so long as she persists in thinking of the skill as a sequence of sepa-

---

[6] Edwin E. Ghiselli and Clarence W. Brown, *Personnel and Industrial Psychology* (New York: McGraw-Hill Book Co., 1948), pp. 268–69.

rate operations that are cumulative rather than as a pattern of movements which are given "sense" and interdependent meaning because of the fact that they constitute aspects of a given whole and coordinately contribute to its achievement. This idea is of crucial importance in the learning of any skill.

3. Insight. (Trainer B made every effort to see that the trainees had a clear idea of the nature of the task in which they were engaged.) Solve the following problems, and you will see almost at once what is meant by "insight":

A. Connect all the dots by drawing four straight lines, being sure not to raise your pencil from the paper and not to go through any dot more than once.[7]

```
.  .  .

.  .  .

.  .  .
```

B. Give the next two numbers in the following series:
8 6 9 5 11 3 12 . . . . . .

C. A scientist has a jar with two germs in it. The number of germs doubles every second. At the end of a minute the jar is full of germs. After how many seconds was it half full?

If you solved these problems correctly (and problem 1, p. 74), you probably did so "in a flash" after considerable mental trial and error. You had a "click" or "Aha" or "I've got it" reaction. You had gained insight into the problem, and the solution followed quickly. Insight may come rapidly or slowly, but it always signifies that the learner has "seen the point" of the problem or even a joke in terms of the meaningful relationships that exist between the variables involved. This question of insight has been one which behavioristic and connectionistic theories are hard put to explain completely and adequately.

Some degree of insight is essential to almost every business situation and to every type of learning. Learning a skill obviously is made easier if the trainee has a clear understanding of the purpose of the skill and how the various movements combine in an interrelated manner for the attainment of that purpose. Conceptual or intellectual learning is impossible without insight, whether it deals with problem-solving, the inductive, or the deductive method of thinking. The attitudes of workers toward their job are largely influenced by their ability to see how it fits in with the work of the department as a

---

[7] Kretch and Crutchfield, *op. cit.*, p. 362.

whole and that of the company; much the same thing applies to the individual's attitude toward his role in the department and organization. Associational learning is made much easier if based on insight into what is to be associated. For instance, try to memorize the following sequence of numbers:

68111316182123262831

It is rather difficult to do so, unless one realizes that the numbers increase first by 2 and then by 3. Then the process is easy.

4. Perception. (Trainer B sought to have the trainees see not only how each connection was to be made but also how they were related to each other and to the board as a whole.) Perception, strictly speaking, is the act by which data received via the senses are unified and interpreted, giving knowledge of reality. In a broader sense, it refers to the way in which an individual "views" or perceives reality. "The optimist sees the glass as half-full, the pessimist as half-empty," is a good example. In all learning it is essential that the trainee perceive all the data that are required for the mastery of the skill or the grasping of an idea or solution. In wiring the board, he must perceive just what is involved and how to make the necessary connections; in learning to type, he must perceive how each movement is related to every other movement; in problem-solving he must be certain that he perceives all the data, explicit or implicit, that are given in the statement of the problem. Take the following example as an illustration: "A 20×20 inch piece of tin is to be shaped into a box having a height of 4 inches by folding the sides upward. Find the volume of the box." It is impossible to solve this problem, unless it is "perceived" that a 4-inch square must be cut out of each corner, thus reducing each side to 12 inches. Once this is "seen," the solution is obvious.

While this principle has evident applications to the work of the employee, supervisor, or manager, it has wider significance as well. How do trainees, especially older workers, perceive the training program when they feel that they have been selected for it because someone doubts their competence? How might the effectiveness of two trainers be influenced, if one perceived his superiors as "backing him to the limit," whereas the other perceived them as giving him only "lip service"? How might older and new workers perceive methods changes? How might an old family company perceive the introduction of the teamsters union?

5. Closure and Pregnanz. (Trainer B explained the entire board and insisted that the trainees learn to wire it with an ease and rhythm of movement.) In one experiment it was shown that when two sets of subjects were engaged in identical tasks and one group was interrupted near the end of the task, whereas the other was forced to stop much earlier in the process, the first group later remembered much more of the task and completed it much more quickly when it was resumed. People like a completed picture (closure). They dislike loose ends that cause confusion. They like what they are doing to make sense and be finished. The trainer who organizes his material poorly, the one who fails to see that his presentation constitutes a rationally unified unity, and the one who fails to cover adequately in the time allowed the material that the trainees expected to learn—all are violating the principle of closure. At a higher level, failure to communicate completely with employees and merit ratings about which the subordinates never hear, once they are made, are other examples of violations of this concept.

Pregnanz has reference to the fact that the learner will tend to perceive and understand more readily that which presents the clearest and best "figure" for him. Intelligent policies consistently applied do this. In training, the proper use of audio-visual aids is partly based on this idea. The trainer who merely scrawls haphazardly over the blackboard and the one who is careless in drawing his illustrations thereon violate this principle. Pregnanz is had when the salient features of any illustration or presentation are so clear that they readily make sense to the trainee.

6. *Maturation.* (Trainers A, B, and C would not even have started training unless the trainees were capable of learning to wire the board.) According to this principle, to attempt to train anyone before he is capable of understanding it is futile. Does this explain why some programs of multiple management have failed? Might it be one reason why so many short courses in human relations with old-time supervisors have been less than perfect successes? "Management all the way down the line" is an enlightened idea. What must be done antecedently before it has any chance of becoming a reality in a given company?

7. *Integration and Differentiation.* (Trainer B tried to [1] have the trainees get a clear idea of the job as a whole; [2] have them see how each connection was related to the total job; [3] have them learn to make each connection perfectly; [4] have them integrate each connection as an aspect of the total task.) If an oversimplified illustration is permissible, a behaviorist would go about building a house by laying the foundation, then the first floor, then the second, then the plumbing would be added, and so on until the roof was put on. A field theorist would begin by getting a very clear idea of what a house is. Once this was understood, by a process of *differentiation*, the relationships of the various parts of the house would be understood. Each section of the house would then be built, bearing in mind its relationship to every other aspect of the process, until all were *integrated* into one house. How would you go about helping Mary Smith (p. 69) to learn to type, using this principle of procedure?

8. Goals and Motivation. (All the trainers tried to motivate their trainees toward a given goal. Trainer B would stress the importance, not of making single connections properly, but of the goal, wiring the entire board efficiently.) All learning theories stress goal behavior and motivation. The field theorists greatly emphasize them. They are of the opinion that all behavior is purposive, even when it may not appear to be so to the outside observer. Therefore, they are likely to reject the concept of trial-and-error learning.

Connectionism

Perhaps no man has had more influence on American teachers and trainers than Thorndike, the father of connectionism. His two major tenets were (1) whatever exists at all, exists in some amount; (2) learning is connecting, and man is the great learner primarily because he forms so many connections. The magic words, therefore, are "S-R bond." Learning consists basically in the formation or strengthening of a connection between a specific situation or stimulus and a specific response. A stimulus may be "any state of affairs or event which influences a person"; a response, "any state of affairs or condition within the organism"; a connection, "the fact or probability that a given stimulus will evoke a certain response." Like behaviorism, connectionism is a kind of conditioned-response approach to learning. Thorndike, however, was a realist as well as a theorist. Under the assaults of the field theories and as a result of his own experiments, he modified some of his original laws and added others. Some of the more important connectionist laws of learning are the following:

1. Law of Readiness. (Trainer C tried to create in the trainees a psychological state of readiness to learn.) The law of readiness claims that (1) when a connection is ready to function, to do so is satisfying; (2) to be forced to do so when not ready is frustrating; (3) to be prevented from so doing when ready is annoying. Obviously, this principle highlights the importance of motivating trainees before teaching them. Among its other practical applications, which are left to the reflection of the reader, it cautions the trainer to adapt his methodology to the "personality" of the group. To expect inexperienced employees who have had no exposure to role-playing to do a satisfactory job of it right off the bat is a violation of this concept. On the other hand, to lecture to experienced workers, who have many stimulating ideas and suggestions to offer and are eager to do so, is also a violation of this principle.

2. Law of Exercise.   (Trainer C had the trainees make the necessary connections themselves.) "Learning by doing" is the emphasis here. This law consists of two parts. The *law of use* claims that the more a connection is exercised, the more securely it will be "stamped in." As stated, the law is not true. Practice of itself is no guarantee that the desired learning will take place. In fact, it has been shown that one can correct biting his fingernails by deliberately biting them, and correct typing "the" as "hte" by consciously doing so. In skill training, therefore, mere repetition is useless unless the trainee understands its purpose and discovers the consequences of each response. The *law of disuse* says that failure to exercise a connection results in a lessened ability to do so.

3. Law of Effect.   (Trainer C praised the trainees every time they made a correct connection.) When a response is accompanied by or followed by a satisfying state of affairs, the connection is strengthened. This is a roundabout way of saying, "Nothing succeeds like success." This law seems obvious, yet it is not so simple as it appears. As was mentioned under *partial reinforcement,* occasional reward is no less effective in producing the desired behavior than every-time reward and produces greater resistance to extinction of the behavior, should the rewards be stopped. Certainly the idea of partial reinforcement is more consistent with what happens in life. As the fun of gambling or fishing lies largely in the fact that no one expects to win all the time or catch a fish at every cast, so employees are probably more pleased with occasional earned rewards than a steady diet of them. The law of effect may apply to improved *performance;* it is not at all clear that it applies equally well to the improvement of *learning.* The obverse side of this law states that behavior that is not rewarded tends to be discontinued. Certainly there is a grain of truth here as it applies to industry. It might be wise for the trainer to insert the word "seems" before those of "rewarded" and "not rewarded," since it is difficult in specific instances to judge what constitutes reward. One man's reward may be another's lack of reward.

4. *Mind-Set.* (Trainer C tried to get the trainees to see the problem in the right light.) Mind-set is closely related to the broad interpretation of perception (p. 89). Mind-set has to do with the way in which a person views or approaches a problem or situation. It determines to a considerable degree how he will react to it. If you had difficulty solving the dot problem (p. 88), it was probably because your mind-set made you think of a rectangular solution rather than the true one. Gary Moore had an excellent example of the importance of mind-set on his television program. A well-known comedian made the audience rock with laughter. Then the part of the show which is called "The Hidden Camera" showed a film depicting the same comedian telling the same jokes to customers in a pet shop in which he was acting as a clerk. What greatly amused the television audience caused the customers to think of the comedian acting as a clerk as either not funny or slightly unbalanced mentally. They had a different mind-set. What differences in mind-set might you expect from trainees who feel forced to attend a training program and those who saw in it a giant step toward advancement? Give other examples of your own.

5. *Belongingness.* (Trainer C tried to show the trainees how a particular wire, or set of wires, "belonged" with specific terminals.) Learning is accelerated when the trainee sees a "fitness" in connecting two or more movements, events, or stimulus-response patterns. Examine the following figures, and you will see how important this principle may at times be. Is it easier to solve for the area of the square by using Figure 4–1 or by using Figure 4–2?[8]

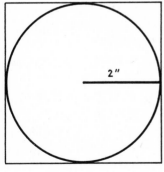

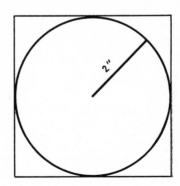

FIG. 4–1.   FIG. 4–2.

[8] Kretch and Crutchfield, *op. cit.*, p. 382.

6. Identifiability. (Trainer C began with the simplest connections.) Trainees tend to learn more quickly those connections that can be most readily identified. This is one reason why the trainer should proceed from the simple to the complex and from the known to the unknown. It underlies the importance of job analysis as a first step in training. It is the reason why the aims of the program must be clearly understood by the trainees. Make other applications of your own. Compare your efforts involved in solving the following two problems and you will realize the importance of this idea:[9]

A. Two civil service jobs have the same starting salary ($4,000) and the same maximum ($7,000). One involves a semiannual increase of $150; the other, an annual increase of $300. Which job would you take if both were offered to you, other things being equal?

B. All men are mortal.
All wolves are mortal.
Some men are carnivorous.
THEREFORE—which of the following is true?
a) Some wolves are carnivorous.
b) Some men are wolves.
c) Some mortals are carnivorous.
d) No men are wolves.
e) Some men are not wolves.
f) All men are wolves.

7. Analogy. (Trainer C made the trainees learn how to wire this particular board, rather than relying on their familiarity with similar boards only.) When a situation is such that the learner has no native or acquired responses for it, he tends to react by interpreting the situation in light of his similar past experiences. This, of course, is partly a function of mind-set and habit. It explains why retraining is necessary when changes in procedures are introduced. It is well illustrated by the person who is inclined to "do everything himself." As he moves up the promotional ladder, he continues this behavior until he is overwhelmed by work. He must be trained to delegate authority. What other illustrations of this concept can you recall?

8. Partial Activity. (Trainer C was careful that the trainees took into account the colors, numbers, and shapes of the wires and terminals.) Partial activity refers to the fact that one element in a situation or problem may at times be "prepotent" in causing the

---

[9] Richardson, *op. cit.*, pp. 8, 14.

response. Trainers who are prone to overdo the personality angle, who are as dull as sawdust, who overindulge in humor or sarcasm, or who "run to death" such techniques as the case study, role-playing, and so on, should bear this principle in mind.

9. *Polarity.* (Trainer C taught the trainees both to wire the connections and also to unwire them.) There is a tendency for a stimulus-response sequence to operate more readily in the order in which it was learned and practiced than in the opposite order. Try reciting the alphabet backward, and you will see what is meant. Because a person knows that 7×6 equals 42 is no guarantee that he knows that 6×7 also equals 42. Does this explain why at times the best worker does not make the best trainer?

10. *Availability.* (Trainer C began with the connection which was easiest to learn.) The more ready a response is to function, the easier it can be called into play. It is for this reason that trainers wisely begin not by lecturing but by orienting what is to be presented around the experiences of the trainees. Provocative questions which challenge long-standing or prejudiced beliefs rely on this principle. The trainer who has lectured for two or three sessions and then tries to switch to a discussion method soon discovers the importance of this idea. Add other instances of your own.

11. *Associative Shifting.* (Trainer C taught the trainees to group similar wires and terminals according to similarities of colors, numbers, and/or shapes.) When stimuli occur together, the response elicited by one tends to be associated with the other(s). When such responses occur frequently together, the stimulus for one tends to suggest the others as well. This idea is basic to the use of illustrations, examples, audio-visual aids, and so on. Does it have any reference to the climate of the training session—permissive, chaotic, democratic, or authoritarian—and the effectiveness of the trainer's efforts?

12. *Multiple-Response.* (Trainer C insisted that the trainees learn by doing, correcting their mistakes when they occurred.) When a person is faced with a new situation, he will react first in one way. If this proves unsatisfying, he will try one and then another type of response until he succeeds. Being satisfying, this response will be "stamped in." Review the problems given in this chapter and see whether this is not exactly what you did. It is important to note, however, that a human being should not go through this process mechanically, but intelligently. There should be no place for blind trial and error in training. Trainers who have difficulty "reaching" their trainees, in keeping order and discipline, in gaining and keeping attention, should vary their methodology and approach in line with this principle. How does this apply to the trainee's efforts to cope with a new situation or problem?

SOME IMPORTANT LEARNING PRINCIPLES

It might appear that very little is known concerning the learning process. Quite the opposite is true. Theorists may give different names and diverse accounts to explain what takes place when a person learns something. To a considerable extent they agree on the importance of certain principles for the learning process. The following ideas, most of which nearly all theorists would accept, are presented by way of a summary. In the next chapter an attempt will be made to apply these principles to the instructional processes involved in skill and conceptual learning.

1. Each individual is the psychological center of his changing world of experience. Therefore, to learn anything, he must first experience some unfulfilled need. This need, which may represent either an externally imposed or a self-initiated problem, must be sufficiently strong to arouse him to action.

2. All learning is a form of self-active adaptive behavior aimed at (1) the satisfaction of needs; (2) the more complete enhancement of these needs; or (3) the prevention of a decrease in their satisfaction.

3. The learner must perceive some goal or reward that is related to the satisfaction of his need and worth the effort involved in attaining it.

4. The learner must have some motivation, intrinsic or extrinsic, which causes him to become involved with the problem and which enables him to focus his interest and attention on and channel his resources for its solution. Motivation that is either too strong or too weak is harmful to the learning process.

5. The learner must have some experience of success while, at the same time, learning to increase his frustration tolerance of ambiguity and failure until such time as success is forthcoming. He must learn to analyze failures in order to attain success.

6. The learner should be rewarded as soon as possible after the success. He need not be rewarded for every small bit of progress but only after a major step is successfully completed, since occasional reward is just as effective as every-time reward.

7. The sense organs must operate efficiently so as to be accurate avenues of data regarding reality.

8. The perceptual processes that give knowledge of reality involve perceptions of similarities among the data presented by the senses and perceptions of differences. The learner must discriminate between relevant and irrelevant data for the solution of his problem.

9. The learner's perceptions are a function of his involvement with the problem, his past experiences, his habits, needs, emotions, goals, and values.

10. The learner's interpretation of the data and his efforts to resolve his problems are a function of his frame of reference, his mind-set, and his drive strength.

11. Individuals vary widely with respect to their physical, intellectual, emotional, and social resources for learning.

12. Data received via the sense organs must be assimilated and integrated with that which the learner already knows. The learner, however, must not permit past experiences and habits to lessen his flexibility in adapting to the requirements of the new problem.

13. The aim of learning is not merely the acquisition of knowledge but its retention, application, and transfer to other problem situations. The learner should master both content and an effective problem-solving technique.

14. Learning is easier when the data are meaningful, when they "belong" together in a significant whole or pattern, when their interrelationships and their relations to the total task are meaningfully organized.

15. The learner is helped if he can perceive his specific difficulty against the background of its antecedent or concomitant circumstances and conditions.

16. Learning is made easier if the learner can gain insight into the nature of his problem and into the precise relationships that exist between the problem conditions or variables.

17. Learning cannot be forced. Unless the requisite degree of maturation and psychological readiness to learn is present, learning is either difficult or impossible.

18. Learning is facilitated if the specific aspects of the problem-solving process are differentiated from the total task, mastered within the frame of reference of this task, and then integrated within this framework.

19. The learner not only must learn abstractly what is to be mastered but must also apply it.

20. The goals of learning must be attainable, and the learner must approach his task with a spirit of confidence and optimism.

21. The learner should proceed from the known to the unknown, from the data that are most readily understood to those that are less easily grasped, without permitting the former to blind him to the importance of the latter.

22. The learner should make use of every possible aid to learning —his memory and imagination, illustrations, drawings, and other forms of mechanical aids.

23. The learner should build up patterns of thinking conducive to effective problem-solving. He should have a technique for testing the most plausible solution. If it fails, he must be adaptable enough to view the problem from a different angle, testing each solution until the correct one is found.

24. The learner never learns generally but in specific situations. He should, however, generalize his method and/or solution to other similar difficulties and problems.

25. The learner makes fastest progress when the problems to be solved are commensurate with his past experience, knowledge, and spirit of confidence.

26. Learning is accelerated when the learner has some understandable criterion by which he can judge his own progress.

27. The criterion of learning is not what the instructor thinks, grades, or the ability to use a given technique at the request of the instructor, but rather the extent to which the learner utilizes what he has learned voluntarily from day to day.

28. The beginning of learning is a need which must be satisfied, the procedure is self-activity, the immediate aim is the satisfaction of the need, the intermediate objective is the use of what is known in one's daily behavior, the final end is a reorganization of behavior in the direction of what is wiser and better.[10]

SUMMARY

This chapter has sought to answer six basic questions. A definition of learning and knowledge was given. A description of four so-called types of learning—sensori-motor or skill, intellectual, conceptual or

---

[10] These principles have been derived from a variety of sources, but chiefly from Kelly, *op. cit.*; Kretch and Crutchfield, *op. cit.*; Cantor, *op. cit.*; Snygg, *op. cit.*; and Carl R. Rogers, *Client-Centered Therapy* (New York: Houghton Mifflin Co., 1951).

rational, associational, and attitudinal—was presented. Sixteen so-called myths of learning were outlined for the reader's consideration, to judge the extent to which each was "mythical." The theoretical approaches that three trainers, schooled in different theories of learning, might adopt in instructing trainees with respect to the same problem of wiring a board was described by means of a totally fictitious problem. A brief explanation of a few of the major concepts basic to the behavioristic, the Gestalt, and the connectionist theories of learning was presented. Finally, some twenty-eight principles of learning, acceptable to proponents of most learning theories, were detailed. In the following chapter these principles will be applied to (1) the teaching-learning process; (2) factors that condition the learning process; (3) the role and task of the trainer-instructor.

THINGS TO DISCUSS AND TO DO

1. Using the material of this chapter, and especially the twenty-eight principles of learning, outline a training procedure to teach Mary Smith (p. 69) how to type.

2. Most books describe the so-called scientific method; few teachers insist that students practice it; even fewer students do so on their own. Take a problem and show how you would go about solving it by using the scientific method of inductive thinking.

3. Compare the so-called "myths of learning" with the principles of learning given at the end of the chapter. If you were a trainer, what use would you make of both "lists."

4. Take any problem of your own and indicate how you would go about training another, using the three learning theories explained in the chapter.

5. What reply would you make to (1) the trainer who has come up from the ranks and says, "This is all a lot of words. What we really need are a group of fool-proof techniques of training"; (2) to the trainer who says, "This is nothing but 'polished-up common sense'"; (3) to the young trainer who says, "What I need are not theories and all that nonsense but good lesson plans and mechanical aids"?

5. TRAINEE DIFFERENCES DEMAND TRAINER FLEXIBILITY

Purpose of the Chapter

THE PRECEDING chapter was devoted to a discussion of the meaning, types, myths, theories, and principles of learning. An attempt was made to indicate that techniques that are not rooted in a clearly understood learning frame of reference are like the Biblical status—made of gold and silver but having feet of clay. The present chapter seeks to continue this discussion by indicating the practical significance of certain factors that condition the trainee's efforts to learn. It is the whole man who learns, and he is a very complex being. The factors that are considered in this chapter include the following: individual differences, motivation, interest and attention, memory, overlearning, whole versus part learning, transfer of training, learning set, habits, and reading skills.

INDIVIDUAL DIFFERENCES

Training is based on the premise that persons are more alike than different. Every trainer, however, realizes that people are diverse with respect to almost every human attribute. *Physically,* they vary in heredity, health, height, weight, body structure, tempo of living, energy level, need for activity and rest. There are wide divergences in the ability to react to visual, auditory, taste, tactile, odor, movement, depth, space, size, color, time, and shape stimuli. *Mentally,* no two individuals are alike in their keenness of perception, vividness of imagination, accuracy of memory, general intelligence, common sense, ability to handle ideas, or special aptitudes. They differ with respect to educational level, achievement, job experience and skill, and life history. There is a range of interests and ability to concentrate. *Socially,* people differ with respect to their maturity, sophis-

100

tication, and the extent to which they either accept or resist the mores of the groups to which they belong. They differ in the amount of recognition, acceptance, patience, praise, or firmness they require. They come from different cultures, nationalities, religions, and social classes, each of which has had some effects on the trainees. Each has a different *personality*. Some are lighthearted and optimistic, others moody and pessimistic, still others slow and lethargic, a few are "short-fused" and irascible. They have different *value systems and goals*. Some are hyperconscientious, others almost devoid of a sense of duty. They vary in terms of loyalty, ideals, moral principles, and a sense of what is right and fair. In addition, no two trainees are likely to have exactly the same *perceptions of the company*, their jobs, their boss, the trainer, and the training program. Finally, trainees differ in their own *self-concepts*. One may see himself as self-confident, sociable, aggressive, friendly, emotionally stable, co-operative, persevering, and determined to learn. Another may be self-doubting, seclusive, submissive, resentful, and hypercritical. A third is likely to be impetuous, impulsive, unreflective, easily discouraged, and subjective. The vast majority will probably think of themselves in terms of various combinations of these extremes.

What does all this signify for the trainer? While it is impossible for him to be constantly mindful of these differences, he should be aware not only that the trainees differ among themselves but that each one is different from him.

From these ideas the trainer can make the following applications:

1. The trainer's goals and level of aspiration are not likely to be exactly the same as those of the trainees. His motives and interests are not apt to be the same as stimulate them. His enthusiasm and drive are rarely matched by those of the trainees. It would be well for the trainer to spend some time, unless he knows the trainees well, in discovering *their objectives and expectations* of both the program and him. Presumably he knows what he wants to accomplish. To complete the picture he must learn what they expect to get from the program.

2. The trainer probably feels comfortable and at ease. Among the trainees he is likely to find a range of attitudes and emotional reactions, including those of fear, resistance, superiority, interest, uncertainty, and friendliness. The trainer should get the feel of the group. Any effort expended in creating a permissive, democratic atmosphere, rather than one that is authoritarian or laissez-faire,

will be time well spent. At the outset each trainee has his own idea of the "rules of the game." The trainer should check to see whether they see eye-to-eye.

3. It is too late for the trainer and the trainees to change their personalities. It behooves the trainer, however, to be cognizant of any differences that may exist. Humor, irony, and even a bit of sarcasm may be entirely acceptable to one group and annoying to another. Some groups take naturally to an informal procedure, while others prefer a more structured and logical approach. Trainees also differ with respect to the amount of firmness, friendliness, independence, support, challenge, and discipline that they require. At one extreme, the trainer must beware of the individual who accepts every word as gospel truth; at the other, of the pugnacious person who has a compulsive "itch" to argue and disagree.

4. The trainer must adapt his methodology to the experiences of the group. Lectures, lecture-discussions, panels, role-playing, "buzz groups," and case studies are not always equally acceptable to all trainees. Preferences range from carefully tailored talks, followed by a question and answer period, to demonstrations and "learning by doing," in which the trainees manipulate equipment, to the free and easy give-and-take of group discussions. His pacing, too, must be governed by trainee range of intelligence or experience. The brightest person can do from two to five times as much work as the dullest or the same amount in one half to one fifth the time. It is necessary to make certain that neither end of this ability continuum is lost or bored in the training process. This can be done by means of the use of differentiated materials according to ability, individual projects and reports, a tutoring system that utilizes the abilities of the superior trainees, and small-group discussions consisting of a mixture of average, superior, and below-average individuals.

5. Above-average trainees not only learn faster but also have greater attention span and powers of concentration and self-motivation. They like to deal with ideas, are more easily challenged, and are likely to be "self-starters" and "self-finishers." Slower learners require more detailed instructions, concrete illustrations, specific details, factual examples, frequent repetition and review, more motivation and recognition. Each, however, needs the satisfaction of success, and it is the trainer's job to see to it that each enjoys it.

6. Individual differences being what they are, no trainer should be so naïve as to expect that he will be able to relate equally well to

all trainees. Some will take to him naturally, enjoy his approach, and think him "the most." It is quite possible, however, that at least a few may think him something less than a substitute for Einstein. If the trainer gets along reasonably well with most people in most of life's social situations, it is likely that he will be acceptable to most trainees.

MOTIVATION[1]

A *motive* is anything that induces the trainee to learn. It has the capacity to arouse and sustain activity. Sometimes a distinction is made between motives and incentives. *Incentives* are extrinsic to the learning situation. They represent some type of goal for the attainment of which learning is a necessary means in a given situation. They are devices which initiate action where interest and participation might otherwise not develop. They are the "carrot" that one holds in front of the burro to get him to move. Motives, on the other hand, are more fundamental and vital than incentives and go beyond them, supplying larger and more worthy purposes for learning. Motives tend to be internal to the person and the learning situation. Thus personal ambition, a desire to excel or to do a good job, and curiosity might be termed "motives." Recognition, social approval, status symbols, and praise or blame are incentives. If the reader finds this distinction of little use, it will be sufficient to think in terms of intrinsic motives and extrinsic motives.

Motivation is the process of utilizing intrinsic and extrinsic motives to energize learning. Its purpose is threefold: (1) to arouse interest, (2) to stimulate a desire to learn, and (3) to direct the aroused interest and effort toward the attainment of a training goal. The ability to motivate trainees is one of the touchstones of the expert trainer. Since learning is not a process of passive absorption, the trainee's task is to be active in the proper manner; that of the trainer, to motivate him to do so.

Intrinsic Motives

1. *Disturbances and Deficiencies.* The trainer can often make great use of the disturbances and deficiences of the trainee.

---

[1] Much of the material dealing with the effectiveness of various types of incentives has been adapted from William A. Kelly, *Educational Psychology* (4th ed.; Milwaukee: Bruce Publishing Co., 1955), chap. xvii.

Undue fatigue at work, dissatisfaction with results, annoyance at failure, inability to solve day-to-day problems, a reasonable degree of fear, a felt need for greater efficiency or education, a desire to avoid frustration, a sense of inferiority which stirs a man to overcome it without overwhelming him—all these are motivational levers which the trainer can utilize.

2. *Satisfaction of Needs.* Since the trainee is consciously or unconsciously trying to satisfy his needs, the trainer should capitalize on this fact as much as he can. To do so, he must be aware of the variety of human needs. A simple outline of some of those that are more important for the training situation is given below:

Physical
    Satisfaction of economic needs
    Balance of rest and activity
    Relief from monotony
    Opportunity for physical movement
    Good training environment—adequate facilities
    Safe training conditions
    Need for change of activity
    Need for variety of activities
    Desire for novelty

Intellectual
    Satisfaction of curiosity and interests
    Learning about one's self
    Learning about others
    Learning about the environment and the job
    Level of aspiration
    Knowing the goals and purposes of the program
    Knowing one's relationships to other trainees and the trainer
    Knowing the relationship between the program and future jobs
    Understanding what is expected
    Development of abilities and aptitudes
    Expert guidance in learning
    Humane supervision of the learning process
    Overcoming remediable limitations
    Criteria for evaluating progress
    Understanding of personal plans and ambitions

Psychological
    Sense of personal worth as an individual
    Self-acceptance, self-esteem, and self-confidence
    Opportunity for self-expression and self-assertion
    Experience of achievement and success
    Desire for distinction and the urge to excel
    Impartial treatment
    Freedom from arbitrary coercion

Respect for personal abilities, ideas, convictions, ideals, and feelings
Reasonable independence
Desire for advancement and increased status
Feeling of importance
Social
Acceptance as an equal by the group
Group approval and a sense of belonging
Identification with the aims, standards, and methods of the group
Sense of contributing to the group
Ability to participate as an equal in the group
Recognition for a job well done
Sympathy and help in time of need
Opportunity to help others and to be consulted
Appreciation of the contributions and achievements of others
Freedom to disagree with the group without fear of being rejected
Opportunity to communicate with the group

Extrinsic Motives

Extrinsic motives are generally thought of as being either financial or nonfinancial. Any standard text on wage incentives will provide information concerning the former type. This section is limited to a consideration of some of the nonfinancial incentives that the trainer can use.

1. *Praise and Reproof.* Unfortunately, much more research has been carried on in education than in industry concerning this problem. Fortunately, there are no startling differences in the conclusions drawn from research in both fields.

COMPARISON OF POSITIVE AND NEGATIVE INCENTIVES

INCENTIVE	ORDER OF MERIT	BETTER RESULTS	PERCENTAGE SHOWING	
			Same Results	Poorer Results
Public praise	1	87.5	12.0	0.5
Private reprimand	2	66.3	23.0	10.7
Public reprimand	3	34.7	26.7	38.7
Private ridicule	4	32.5	33.0	34.5
Public ridicule	6	17.0	35.7	47.3
Private sarcasm	5	27.9	27.5	44.7
Public sarcasm	7	11.9	23.0	65.1

The accompanying table, which has been adapted from Maier,[2] speaks for itself. It is evident from this summary of the research

---

[2] Norman R. F. Maier, *Psychology in Industry* (New York: Houghton Mifflin Co., 1955), p. 401.

studies that "you get further with honey than with vinegar." There is a definite trend of "better results" as one goes from "public sarcasm" to "public praise" and a corresponding movement of "poorer results" from "public praise" to "public sarcasm." Only one form of disapproval, "private reprimand," improved results rather than worsened them. On the other hand, notice that every form of reproof, positive or negative, resulted in improvement on the part of some people. What this table tells the trainer is not to follow some generalized cliché to praise publicly only, but rather to "emphasize the positive," if possible, while remembering to take into account individual differences in administering praise and blame.

Other studies have revealed the following results for the guidance of the trainer:

1. Individuals of inferior mental capacity tend to respond better to praise.

2. In one study, *extroverted* subjects improved more when blamed. *Introverted* subjects showed greater improvement if praised.

3. Three groups were used in a study. One was praised, the second rebuked, and a third ignored, being given neither praise nor reproof. The praised group showed the most improvement, The criticized group also improved but to a lesser degree. The ignored group improved little, if at all. These findings agree with the Irish saying, "Love me if you will. Hate me if you must. But, for God's sake, don't ignore me."

4. Praise given immediately after performance is more effective than delayed praise.

5. Females are likely to be more influenced by praise than by rebuke. While the same is true of men, the degree is different.

6. In administering either praise or blame, the personality of the supervisor is a decisive factor.

2. Rewards and Punishments. Nearly every worker is, to at least some degree, a status seeker. Titles, office quarters, desks of a certain type, one's own secretary, method of pay, profit-sharing plans, credit cards, expense accounts, freedom from punching the clock, executive dining rooms, and the right to make decisions, to be consulted, and to be invited to conferences are all a kind of "golden fleece" that every company holds out to the ambitious employee. The trainer should make the most of this reality. Punishment, too, can often help the trainer. In one eastern brewery a condition of the executive development program was that no one should be absent from any session. The son of the owner missed a meeting and was excluded from the rest of the sessions. When it was explained to him why this disciplinary measure was necessary to insure that all the participants received all the benefits of the program, he not only agreed but also was the first volunteer and the strongest proponent of the regulation when the program was offered a second time. When the reason for punishment is justified and understood by all concerned, when the punishment "fits the crime" and is proportionate to the offense, when it is administered impartially and constructively, and when there are no aftereffects of prejudice against the malefactor, punishment can accelerate the learning process, and no trainer should be fearful of using it. It would be well to bear in mind, however, that women may be either more openly emotional in terms of crying and so on or inclined to sulk and pout in a subdued manner, whereas men are likely to be more openly antagonistic to punishment.

3. *Knowledge of Results*.   As might be supposed, research evidence confirms the popular view that "a man likes to know where he stands." One experiment indicates this very well. One group was informed of its results, received records of scores made, and was encouraged to improve. A second group was not so informed. The informed group improved much more rapidly. When the experiment was about two thirds completed, the conditions were reversed. Learning thereupon decreased for the group that had previously been informed and increased for the groups that had before this been unaware of the results. The trainer should make every effort to let the trainees know, to answer their expressed or unexpressed question, "How am I doing?"

4. *Experience of Progress*.   Experience of progress is an extension of the idea of knowledge of results. In addition to receiving scores, grades, and comments from the trainer, trainees often need a more comprehensive picture of achievement. Records of quality, quantity, and service are an excellent way of having the trainee keep his own box score. In learning a skill, for instance, the trainee can make excellent use of *learning curves*. Learning curves are a graphic picture of progress. They are usually of two types: (1) the amount of work done is plotted against the time taken to do the work, and (2) the amount of time is plotted in relation to the job which has been done. In typing, one might plot the time taken for successive typing exercises, the number of errors made on these trials, the number of letters completed within a given time period, and so on.

Learning curves have other advantages beyond merely giving a picture of progress. Nearly all skill curves have the following characteristics: (1) initial spurt, when the subject "starts with a bang"; (2) fluctuations or unevenness of achievement; (3) negative acceleration, when for many possible reasons progress slows down; (4) plateaus, periods in which no improvement seems to be made; (5) limits of improvement, when apparently the trainee has "reached his limit." Analysis of the curves motivates the trainee to improve. Fluctuations, negative acceleration, and especially plateaus are warning signs for the trainer and trainee to check on the latter's understanding of the task, his motivation, and his methodology of performing it. Plateaus often mean either that the trainee is using the time really to understand what he is doing or that his method of doing it needs checking and improvement. In using learning curves, however, it is well to remember that improving typing skill, to continue our example, from 120 to 130 words per minute is quite a different task from improving it from 50 to 60 words per minute.

5. *Competition and Rivalry*. In an interesting study with college students, one group was divided into two subgroups, which competed with each other as groups. In a second group, each person was paired off with another, so that individual competition resulted. The third or control group received no incentive beyond what it provided for itself. When the results were in, it was found that the control group improved slightly. The group competition in the first group produced a larger gain. The group that had individuals competing against one another, however, show a gain that was almost six times as great as that for group competition. Other experiments not only have confirmed this finding but have shown that, if given a choice, three out of four people tend to prefer to compete for an individual prize rather than a group prize. While these results speak for themselves, two other ideas must be kept in mind: (1) competition must not be permitted to destroy other important social values in terms of morale, group co-operation, and cohesiveness; (2) there is evidence that when a group problem-solving approach was adopted, subjects attained more correct answers than were achieved when individuals worked alone.

6. *Participation*. In view of the social human needs that have been pointed out (p. 104), it would be surprising if research did not confirm the idea that a person likes to "have a say" or be represented in planning and doing the work for which he is responsible. Maier[3] reports an experience of his own with reference to telephone repairmen. Company procedure was to send a different repairman to a given station if it broke down twice or more a month. The men felt that the same man ought to make all the repairs on a given station and that at times the foreman should accompany him. When this system was adopted, "repeat" calls dropped from 17 to 4 per cent and remained at this or a lower figure. Numerous other studies have given rise to the following conclusions:

1. When people participate in decision making and work planning, they tend to be less aggressive toward one another.

2. They show less dependence on the leader.

3. They spend more time on productive work.

4. There is more group initiative for initiating and starting new work.

5. They more readily accept change.

6. They have a greater feeling of acceptance and belonging.

7. They are easier to direct as subordinates, the work efficiency increases, and the quality of decisions often increases.

8. Participation tends not only to increase improvement but also to make it relatively more permanent.

7. *Relating Training to the Job.* It is not the responsibility of the trainer, nor would it be wise for him, to try to change a man's personality. The one common denominator that they share is the man's performance on the job. Since *the job* looms so large on the typical trainee's horizon, it is an excellent source of motivation. Every effort should be made to indicate the importance of the particular job, its relation to the work of the department and to the company as a whole, the job requirements, and the most effective methods for doing it well both as a present task and as a means of mounting the promotional ladder.

MAINTAINING INTEREST AND ATTENTION

Mention has been made of how the trainer can capitalize on the trainee's disturbances, deficiencies, and needs to arouse and sustain activity on his part. Ways of using praise and reproof, rewards and punishment, knowledge of results and experience of progress, com-

---

[3] *Ibid.*

petition and rivalry, and participation have been stressed. Closely related to the problem of motivation are questions of how one arouses and keeps interest and attention.

Interest is the pleasurable or painful feeling produced by an idea, object, person, or activity which has the power of attracting and holding attention. *Attention,* in turn, is the focusing of consciousness on a specific idea, object, person, activity, or situation to the more or less exclusion of all others, for the purpose of understanding its nature or of knowing its qualities. Interests are either *native* or *acquired.* Attention is either *involuntary* or *voluntary.* Native interests and involuntary attention are almost spontaneous and demand little or no effort. Most of us are interested and attend to bright lights or colors and loud noises or sounds. Acquired interests and voluntary attention are the fruit of effort, education, and deliberate purpose. Whereas a person is more or less a "pawn" of external forces with respect to native interests and involuntary attention, acquired interests and voluntary attention are largely controlled from within the individual. He acquires an interest in the process of decision making and concentrates on solving a problem that is difficult.

Research has shown that interest and attention are almost spontaneously aroused by certain types of stimuli. The trainer should be aware of the following characteristics of these stimuli and make the most of them in his training sessions:

1. *Intensity.* Seriousness or loudness of voice tone, dramatic gestures, or a dramatic experiment tend to catch interest and attention.

2. *Movement and Change.* The flashing lights of a neon sign caution the trainer that he will be likely to keep the attention and interest of the group if he moves about, manipulates equipment, writes on the blackboard, varies his tone of voice and his pace of speaking, and so on.

3. *Isolation.* The IBM word, "THINK" catches the eye. A large $ written all across the blackboard may get across to sales trainees the importance of learning to sell far better than an hour's lecture.

4. *Contrast.* The use of colored chalk, to give a simple example, can often clarify for trainees different types of ideas or procedures.

5. *Novelty.* The trainer who has mastered the knack of changing his instructional method from time to time is well aware of the advantages of novelty.

6. *Unexpectedness.* It is a good principle to follow that one should not begin three consecutive training sessions in the same way. An unexpected statement, quiz, and so on tend to "keep trainees on their toes," provided that it is not overdone.

7. *Size.* Every trainee can make good use of this newspaper headline technique in writing on the board, the use of gestures, and so on.

8. *Social Suggestion.* A trainee's question or disagreement can be used to stir up questions and comments from other trainees.

9. *Repetition.* Since repetition is the mother of learning, the trainer who is resourceful in making his point over and over in different meaningful ways will tend to insure learning on the part of the trainees.

10. *Attack.* Trainee reaction is almost guaranteed if the trainer occasionally attacks some traditional method of procedure or some unexamined belief of the trainees, provided that this is done in such a manner as not to hurt their feelings or alienate them.

11. *Question.* Clever use of the overhead, directed, reverse, and relay questions (p. 142) nearly always arouses interest and attention.

12. *Organization.* Organizing materials on the blackboard, illustrations, or equipment in a particular manner tends not only to arouse interest but also to make it easy for the trainee to focus his attention on what the trainer wishes him to attend.

Apart from the dozen means of attracting attention which have been outlined, the trainer should also be familiar with certain characteristics of attention and interest. People vary widely in their *attention span.* Test this for yourself by asking some friends to repeat individually the following sequences of numbers and letters, which you say to them, allowing one second between each number or letter:

1 6 4 7 3 1 9 5 8 2

L T Q A P E K S M C

The experienced trainer makes certain that he does not tax the trainee's span of comprehension by trying to cover too much material at a given time or by "jumping around" from idea to idea so that some of the trainees become confused.

Individuals also differ with respect to the *shifting or fluctuation of attention.* The trainer should be on the lookout for telltale signs of fluctuating attention as evidenced by boredom, yawning, doodling, small talk between trainees, and watch-checking, especially if he is explaining a rather abstruse point or has been using the same instructional approach for any length of time. Trainee attention often fluctuates because of distractions. A *distraction* occurs when two stimuli conflict and compete for the trainee's attention and interest. Distractions arise from three main sources. First, there is the trainer. Poor organization of materials, monotonous tone of voice, lack of enthusiasm, inappropriate mechanical aids to instruction, ineffective teaching procedures, inability to maintain discipline, lack of variety, and personal mannerisms all tend to make the trainer his own worst enemy. The second major source of distractions is the environment. Glare from unshielded windows, screeching chalk, poorly equipped training rooms, inadequate ventilation, unnecessary interruptions, and unwanted external noise all work against the trainer. Finally, the trainee may cause his own distractions. Lack of sleep, fear, absence of motivation, an uninquisitive and unquestioning mind, and an absence of purpose are fruitful sources of distraction. Some trainees have never learned *habits of attention* through self-discipline. No surgeon bears up under a six-hour operation simply out of the joy and interest in it. He concentrates on his task because he has taught himself to do so in light of its importance. If the trainee expects to learn anything, rather than merely be amused or entertained, he will have to imitate the surgeon.

Acquired interest and voluntary attention are the result of trainee effort. The trainer can help by pointing out the usefulness of the program, its relationship to the job and trainee needs, how it can be profitable even off the job. He can keep training down to earth and in line with the expectations of the trainees. If he succeeds, learning will be quicker and more palatable. It will be retained longer. Boredom and distractions will be minimized. What is learned will stand out, be intensified, and better unified in the mind of the trainee.

MEMORY AND FORGETTING

Memory is a process of *retaining, recalling,* and *recognizing* some past experience. It is often divided into (1) rote or mechanical memory and (2) logical or meaningful memory. Rote memory is "learning by heart." Since the heart is a noncognitive organ, it usually results in the use of clichés, principles, and procedures without real understanding of what is involved. Mere memory of a manual of operations and the utilization of rules of thumb produce a mechanical man. Logical memory is the memory of ideas and relationships based on understanding. It is the memory of meaning. Rote memory is really a process of conditioning and is most useful in such situations as spelling, number combinations, and the instruction of individuals who lack the capacity to understand why they are to perform an operation in a given manner. It is useful for the person who is content with knowing merely how to do something. Logical memory is for the individual who wants to know both how and why.

Forgetting starts as soon as learning begins. It is not a passive process of loss, like melting snow, but a highly selective process of consciousness. Since no one can remember everything, it is important to select the important things that one wants to recall and concentrate on them. Rotely memorized material quickly vanishes. Using nonsense syllables, Ebbinhaus found that he forgot 41.8 per cent within twenty minutes after the first learning; 55.8 per cent after one hour; 66.3 per cent after one day. Other experiments with "meaningful materials" have shown that they are much more easily retained and recalled. Since forgetting is a kind of unconscious distraction which plays havoc with rote memory, the trainer would be wise to stress the logical aspects and the meaningfulness of anything he wants trainees to remember.

Improving One's Memory[4]

The statements "I forget" and "I can't remember" are a challenge to the trainer. True learning has not taken place unless the trainee remembers what he has been taught. There are no tricks to improving one's memory. There are clear-cut principles that must be practiced day in and day out.

1. Go about Initial Learning in the Correct Manner. A vivid initial learning experience will greatly aid the process of retention. Make your first impressions as exact, definite, and vivid as possible. Distinguish clearly between what you want to remember and what is relatively unimportant. Organize your original learning so that it makes a sensible unit that is readily recalled. Many people

---

[4] These suggestions have been adapted from James D. Weinland, *How to Improve Your Memory* (New York: Barnes & Noble, Inc., 1957), chap. 5; and Kelly, *op. cit.,* chap. viii.

forget because they think that they have learned something when they have merely reduced it to the level of rote recitation without any degree of insight or understanding of what they are about.

2. Use the Four "R's"—Recite, Repeat, Review, and 'Rite it Down. Frequency of exposure to an experience helps to stamp it in. Reciting and repeating what you wish to remember, periodic reviews, and writing it down on paper all contribute to the process of retention.

3. Apply It in Action. Putting what you wish to remember into action not only helps you to remember it but also gives you a better understanding of the matter as a whole and of the crucial aspects of it that you simply cannot afford to forget.

4. Develop an Interest in What You Want to Remember. One man's forgetful nonsense is another man's interest. Since memory is highly selective, an intensive interest in what you want to remember gives it more meaning and provides you with a convincing reason for remembering it.

5. Become Emotionally Involved. To any individual the most important words in the English language are "I, Mine, and Me." Insults are remembered for years without any effort. If you can make what is to be remembered part of your emotional makeup, you will recall it with ease. Pride at having mastered it or shame at having muffed it at first are extreme examples of the power of self-involvement in the matter of memory.

6. Learn "All Around" the Material. Trying to remember something in isolation is about as difficult as trying to judge distance without visual cues. Remembering is a response to a stimulus. The more one knows about the general area of information of which what he wants to remember is a part, the more likely he is to find a cue that will bring it back to the level of consciousness. The more you know about baseball, the easier it is to recall a given player or team.

7. Distinguish between the Important and Unimportant. Memory is not a matter of cluttering your head with odds and ends of intellectual lumber. Erasmus said that a good memory is like a good fish net. It retains the big fishes and lets the little ones get away. Before starting to learn, ask yourself the following questions: How much? and Why?

8. Make a Firm Resolution to Remember. Anything you expect to remember must first "register" with you. If you were led into a dead-end cave and knew that when you reached the end your guide was going to leave you to find your own way out, you would pay a great deal more attention to cues and check-points for turns, and so on, on the way in than you would if you were going on a guided tour of the cave.

9. Have Confidence in Your Ability to Remember. If you begin by accusing yourself of having a "terrible memory," you will recall very little. De Quincey once stated, "The memory strengthens as you lay burdens on it, and becomes trustworthy as you trust it."

10. Develop Habits of Attention and Concentration. With respect to memory, most people can be divided into four groups: (1) like wax to receive and like wax to retain; (2) like wax to receive and like marble to retain; (3) like marble to receive and like wax to retain; (4) like marble to receive and like marble to retain. Developing a good memory is not a matter of tricks but of considerable effort of the proper kind. Habits of initial attention and concentration will pay off in the end.

11. Over-Learn What You Wish to Remember. Many people make the mistake of ceasing to learn about something when they have "barely mastered" it. This is fatal for memory. The whole idea of the four "R's" (item 2) is to help you to overlearn the material and to drive it home until you have complete mastery. Overlearning is discussed more fully on page 116.

12. Make the Appropriate Connections between Aspects of What Is to Be Recalled. What has been said thus far applies largely to the memory process of *retention*. You should also master the technique of *recall*. The following ideas may help:

a) Use the Principle of Similarity. It is easy to recall Judas, Iago, and Booth because all three were traitors; to recall an ellipse because it is like a circle. Group what you wish to remember by similarities, as a salesman might do with his customers.

b) Use the Principle of Contrast. The salesman might also learn to remember his customers by their contrasting orders, personality traits, and so on. If you recall that Rommel was a German general, it is easy to recall Montgomery as the British general who opposed him.

c) Use the Principle of Contiguity. If you see Sicily as the boot of Italy, it is difficult to forget it. A man who is promoted can readily recall the reasons given for his promotion.

d) Use Artificial Connections. Making artificial connections between colors, sizes, or sequences of operations by a process of conditioning can help memory. For instance, it is possible to sing a foreign song in this manner without knowing the language, or to assemble a machine in the same manner.

e) Use Ingenious Connections. Mnemonic devices and cues can be helpful. "VIGORBY" is an easy way to recall the colors of the spectrum, since the word is made up of the initial letter of each color.

f) Use Logical and Meaningful Connections. This method is obviously the most efficient. If you can relate ideas, operations, or events together in terms of their meaning or relationships, you will recall them rather readily. One can group fascism, nazism, and communism as related to state supremacy, whereas democracy is based on the supremacy of the people. Algebra and computers are an extension of an arithmetical number system. A salesman may remember his customers according to their sex, age, locations, and so on. A course on human relations might be recalled under the followings: (1) misconceptions of human relations; (2) history, nature, meaning, and importance of human relations; (3) human relations and human needs. Using additional ideas and concepts, one might recall the important aspects of a twenty-four-session program on the subject.

g) Use Organization. Material that is organized into compact, meaningful units can be more readily recalled. In physics, for instance, one might think in terms of heat, light, electricity, gravity, etc.; in statistics, of measures of central tendency, measures of variability, measures of relationship, and so on.

OVERLEARNING

Why is it that some things are so easily remembered, such as how to skate, while others are readily forgotten, such as how to speak a foreign language? One answer lies in the word *overlearning*. Overlearning refers to that learning that takes place after what is necessary for one correct repetition or perfect reproduction. The results of but one experiment are given to indicate how important this concept is for both the trainer and the trainee. The application of its results are left to them.

One group was asked to memorize twelve nouns until it was able to give one perfect repetition (for example, after 10 trials). A second group overlearned the material by 50 per cent (that is, 5 trials after the bare mastery point of 10 trials); a third group overlearned by

100 per cent (10 additional trials). After two weeks, how much did each group remember? Group 1 recalled 15 per cent of the nouns; Group 2, 65 per cent; Group 3, 90 per cent. The evidence speaks for itself.

WHOLE VERSUS PART LEARNING

In Chapter 4 (p. 79) the question was raised as to whether it was better to begin wiring the board by teaching each connection separately or whether it would be more efficient to give the trainees an over-all understanding of the board and teach it as a unit. Actually, this is more than a theoretical question. It is related to such similar problems as these: How long should each training session last? How much material should be covered in a given session? Are several short sessions better than one long meeting?

Although there is no simple answer to these questions, research evidence provides the following guides:

1. Distributed practice tends to produce more effective results than massed, concentrated practice or cramming. Often we learn between practice periods (*reminiscence*); or, as William James used to say, we learn to ice-skate in summer and to swim in winter. Practice periods should be long enough to accomplish a meaningful unit and should be followed by periods of rest and change of activity.

2. The whole method of instructing, learning, and memorizing should be utilized whenever possible, but never if the unit is so large as to overwhelm or confuse the trainees.

3. The whole method is superior if the task involves a few operations of approximately equal difficulty.

4. The whole method is better if the material can be logically organized into meaningful, related units. For the mastery of ideas and principles, the whole method is superior.

5. The greater the intelligence of the trainees, the safer it is to use the whole method.

6. If the trainees are expected to use what is learned in a logically related way, rather than by following a set procedure or unvarying routine, the whole method is better for initial learning.

7. When the trainees are expected to organize, outline, and interpret the learned material as a unit, the whole approach is superior, since associations among the parts are more readily perceived as well as their relationship to the task as a whole.

8. When the matter to be mastered is long, abstruse, or complicated, it is wise to break it down into *natural, logical* subdivisions, after giving trainees an idea of the entire task as a whole. Each unit should be logical, complete in itself, and capable of being mastered in the time allotted. The whole method may be used to unify each subunit into the total task.

9. When the whole method is employed, it often happens that trainees have difficulty with this or that aspect of it. The part method should be used to learn the more difficult operations or ideas within the frame of reference of the over-all task.

These concepts are basic to the formulation of a training syllabus or manual, with its provisions for (1) a logical breakdown of topics; (2) spaced learning and distributed practice; (3) relating new material to old and to the purpose of the program as a whole; (4) checkups to see that old matter has been mastered before proceeding to new; (5) periodic reviews at the end of natural units.

TRANSFER OF TRAINING

Transfer of training refers to the application of ideals, ideas, values, habits, attitudes, and methods that have been learned in one situation to another similar situation or problem. It is *positive,* if the old learning speeds up the new; *negative,* if it interferes with it; and *zero,* if it has no evident effect. Thus a radio expert might make good use of his knowledge in learning about television, a baseball star be hurt by his tendency to swing a golf club as though it were a baseball bat, and a machinist neither helped nor hindered in his efforts to play the piano.

Obviously, the question of transfer of training is crucial for learning. If the trainee can "use what he has already learned," then the trainer's task is facilitated. From the trainee's point of view, also, this is a key question. Promotions, transfers, methods changes, changeovers in equipment or procedures, adjusting to new organizational setups, all depend on his ability to transfer his knowledge to the new arrangements. Without going into a detailed analysis of the various theories that have been conjured up to account for transfer, it is sufficient to consider two questions: (1) Does transfer take place? (2) How does it take place?

After reviewing all the studies performed since 1890, Orata concluded that nearly 80 per cent showed transfer to be a fact. He also determined that such transfer did not occur automatically but was the result of certain identifiable characteristics of (1) the situation; (2) the instructor and instructional method; (3) the mental ability of the learner; (4) the attitude of the learner.[5]

1. The Situation. Few would deny that transfer takes place when the two learning situations are identical or similar. Second, it appears that transfer involves a *generalization or transposition* of ideas, methods, and attitudes from one learning situation to another. The trainer's job and that of the trainee are made easier if a new machine is similar to that with which the trainee has been working for years. It is the responsibility of the trainer to point out these similarities.

2. The Instructor and the Instructional Method. The trainer who teaches merely the specifics of an operation or procedure is getting a poor return on his invested time and energy. The trainee, it is true, must learn specifically, not generally. But a narrow approach to training and mechanical drill coops up the mind. The trainer should point out the particular ways in which the methods, habits, ideas, insights, and attitudes learned with one piece of equipment can be helpful in other work and life situations. No one is really interested in solving a particular case study or role-playing situation. What is desired are general principles, understandings, and techniques for dealing with many similar problems of which a given case study or role-playing is an example. Much the same idea applies to supervisory, human relations, and executive development programs. It is the job of the trainer to teach specifically for a given job, while, at the same time, showing how what is learned can be applied to other, related problems and situations.

3. The Mental Ability of the Learner. Bright people often see similarities where duller individuals perceive only differences, and see differences where the duller ones perceive only similarities. If it is the task of the trainer to use analogies, to point out a wide range of applications, and to relate his specific instruction to other applicable areas, it is the job of the trainee to make his own applications to his work and life. The logical process involved in analyzing a complex managerial case, the need for care in machining a tool,

---

[5] *Ibid.*, p. 337.

principles of health and safety learned in a course, respect for one's subordinates, and similar ideas can be generalized to many activities in life.

4. The Attitude of the Learner. Mechanical drill, routine "learning by doing" in the form of dull repetition, rote memory, and the aimless following of a set series of steps or operations have little positive transfer value. The trainee must learn with transfer possibilities in mind. He must be curious about both the how and the why of what he does. He must constantly be on the lookout for other applications of what he learns. Every invention and every good suggestion are the result of transfer of training. In fact, modern business organization in terms of line and staff and organic functions is a "transfer" from the army and church organizations. The trainee who has had good experiences with training programs, who has developed habits of logical thinking, attention, and concentration, and who is inquisitive and curious will tend to transfer them to any training program. Unfortunately, the trainee who has had opposite experiences will tend to do the opposite.

It is important that *negative transfer* be prevented. If a procedure is revised, specifications changed, or a supervisor faced with a new situation, there may be a negative transfer factor present. Old habits have a tendency to interfere with new ways of doing things. One might very easily decimate the population of a large city merely by reversing the gas and brake pedals. In like manner, a man who has worked for many years in one department may, if transferred to another, unconsciously act as he did formerly. Negative transfer can be prevented by (1) making sure that trainees understand that, because two things are similar in some ways, they are not necessarily identical; (2) helping them to understand the differences by use of the principle of contrast; (3) pointing out the ways in which new procedures demand new adjustments; (4) explaining and discussing the differences, as well as the similarities; (5) assisting the trainees in gaining insight into the reasons for the changes and differences.

LEARNING SET

Anyone who has seen a ball player strike out because he expected a fast ball but was fooled by a change of pace pitch, or anyone who has witnessed runners as they hear the words, "On your mark—Get set . . . ," knows what is meant by the word "set." *Set* refers to the anticipatory readiness of a person to behave in a given manner or to make a particular response. The illustrations given above refer to *motor set*. A *perceptual set* exists when one is predisposed to perceive stimuli or behavior as organized in a particular way. Americans, for instance, see the man in the moon; Chinese see a rabbit in the moon. A *mental set* is a readiness to engage in a specific kind of intellectual behavior. When the president delivers his State of the Union Message to Congress, Democrats and Republicans are likely to have different mental sets concerning its contents. The set which trainees have toward the training program and everything connected with it is extremely important. This is indicated by three experiments, which speak for themselves.

Siipola divided 160 subjects into two groups. Group B was told that she was going to show them on a tachistoscope words having to do with travel and transportation. Group A was informed that the words would be related to animals and birds. Thereupon she showed both groups a list of words that included six nonsense syllables. For these syllables, Group A gave 63 per cent animal or bird responses, and Group B 74 per cent travel responses. They saw what they expected to see![6]

Bellows reports two studies on the problem of set. In the first, two groups were formed, each consisting of half management people and half labor representatives. A picture of a man was shown them, and a brief description of him was given. He was at one time described as a manager and at another as a union man. Management personnel, when informed that he was a member of management, saw him as "honest, conscientious, and adaptable." When told that he was a union member, they saw the same man as "alert, determined, and aggressive." Conversely, union people saw what they were told was one of their own as "active, alert, and capable." But when described as a manager, he suddenly became "active, aggressive, and alert."[7]

Many years ago Luchins, of New York University, introduced an excellent experiment to demonstrate the importance of learning set. There have been many adaptations of this experiment, one of which is given below. You may wish to try it out on some friends for yourself.

---

[6] Ernest R. Hilgard, *Introduction to Psychology* (New York: Harcourt, Brace & Co., 1953), p. 297.

[7] Roger Bellows, *Creative Leadership* (Englewood Cliffs, N.J.: Prentice-Hall, Inc., 1959), p. 136.

Take two groups, the experimental and control. Ask the control group to go into another room where it cannot observe what the experimental group is doing. Now have the experimental group solve the following five problems, using all *three containers*. Problem 1 is a practice problem. It is solved by filling the 127-pint container, then pouring out water to fill the 21-pint container, and then filling the 3-pint container twice, leaving 100 pints in the 127-pint container, the amount desired $(127 - 21 - 3 - 3 = 100)$.

PROBLEM	CONTAINER CAPACITY			AMOUNT DESIRED
	A	B	C	
I..............	21	127	3	100
II..............	14	163	25	99
III.............	18	43	10	5
IV............	9	42	6	21
V..............	20	59	4	31

Now have both groups solve the following problems, telling them to do so in any way they can:

VI................	23	49	3	20
VII................	15	39	3	18
VIII..............	28	76	3	25

Each of the above problems can be solved by using only *two* containers (VI— $23 - 3$). Results of innumerable repetitions show that the number of "experimentals" who miss the obvious solutions ranges from 70 to 100 per cent. In fact, at times some experimentals fail to solve the problems at all because they insist on using all three containers! The number of "controls" who miss the easier method is much lower, at times approaching zero. Such is the power of habit and mind-set in problem-solving![8]

These three experiments are evidence of the importance of learning set on the part of the trainees. It affects all aspects of the program— the reaction to the trainer, his methodology, program content, usefulness of the course, and the amount of work and co-operation that trainees are prepared to proffer. Learning set also has reference to the trainer. Does he see his task as just another job to be done? The trainees as just another group that is to be instructed according to a dull routine? His method unvarying and inflexible? Does he see in each group a challenge? Does he try his level best to make the program profitable, interesting, and stimulating? Answers to these

---

[8] Adapted from David Kretch and Richard S. Crutchfield, *Elements of Psychology* (New York: Alfred A. Knopf, Inc., 1957), p. 384.

questions stem primarily from the set that the trainer brings to his work. The French have a pithy saying, "The eye sees what it looks for. But what the eye looks for already exists in the mind of the viewer." There is no better summary of the importance of "set" for both the trainer and the trainee.

HABITS

Man is a walking bundle of habits, for better or for worse. This is a fact that the trainer should always keep in mind. *Habit* is a relatively permanent acquired mode of behavior that involves a tendency to repeat certain actions in the same general way under similar or identical conditions. Habit is the great "economizer" in training. The more the trainee can reduce to the effortless level of habit, the more his energies and efforts can be directed to learning something new. Habit renders activity more rapid, easy, precise, and perfect. It makes action almost automatic, resulting in lessened fatigue, simplified movements, and more uniform action. The trainee with good habits of attention, of logical thinking, of careful workmanship, of speaking, writing, reading, and self-discipline is fortunate. Trainees, however, often suffer from poor and inefficient habits. It is important for the trainer to know, therefore, not only how to help trainees build proper habits but also how to break ineffective habits.

Habits that one wishes to build, whether they be safety, work, or politeness habits, should be sought for according to the following principles:

1. *As Quickly as Possible Make Automatic and Habitual as Many Useful Actions and Procedures as Possible.* This is a key to developing either a skill or the ability to think logically.

2. *Seize Every Opportunity to Practice the Habit You Wish to Develop.* Habits are not made by thinking about them but by doing something about them.

3. *Only Perfect Practice Makes Perfect.* Proper habits are built up, not by unthinking repetition of what is done, but rather by regular repetition accompanied by close and sustained attention to what one is doing in order to insure that he is doing it in the best possible way.

4. *Habit Building Is Facilitated by a Sense of Satisfaction and Achievement.* Repetition of the desired act will not produce a habit unless it is accompanied by a sense of success and a feeling of satisfaction. Success and satisfaction stimulate interest and effort, thus making it easier to acquire the wanted habit.

5. *Develop as Strong a Motivation as Possible to Acquire the Habit.* The greater the momentum and initiative one can develop when he begins to acquire the habit, the longer will be postponed feelings of discouragement and failure.

6. *Never Allow an Exception to Occur until the Habit Is Securely Rooted in Your Life.* As William James, whose laws these really are, says, "Each lapse is like the letting fall of a ball of string which one is carefully winding up: a single slip undoes more than a great many turns will wind again." Continuity of training is the great means of making the nervous system act infallibly right.

7. *If You Should Fail and Break Your Resolution to Build the Desired Habit, Do Not Become Discouraged but Start Again.* As Alcoholics Anonymous knows well, the work done in building the habit before the time of failure is not lost, unless one becomes discouraged and gives up. If he starts again, the progress previously made stands to help his new beginning.

8. *Keep the Faculty of Effort Alive in You by a Little Gratuitous Exercise Every Day.* In other words, make a habit of building the right kind of habits.

There are two major methods for breaking an undesirable habit. First, any habit will begin to disappear if a negative approach is taken toward it and one abstains from indulging in it. From sheer disuse it will eventually die. The second and far superior method is to develop an antagonistic habit which counteracts the habit one wishes to be rid of. A careless workman might, for instance, try to take pride in his tools, his equipment, his level of skill, or the neatness and cleanliness of his work area. Obviously, in attempting to rid one's self of an ineffective habit, one should put into practice the eight principles given above.

READING SKILLS

At first, it may seem strange to find any consideration of reading habits in a book on training in industry. The fact is, however, that it is difficult to conduct any but the most simple type of training program without relying, to some extent, on the trainee's ability to read effectively. Moreover, research indicates that far too many people in business are reading less efficiently than should be the case. Reading is certainly a factor that influences the efforts of both trainer and trainee. It will be sufficient here to review a few of the key ideas with reference to reading skills. Anyone who is interested in pursuing this matter further should consult the reading references in the Bibliography.

There are five major types of reading skills: (1) reading to grasp the main idea; (2) skimming; (3) reading for details; (4) reading to understand directions; (5) reading in order to evaluate, criticize, or apply what is read. When one reads for the main idea, he is usually interested in the meaning of each paragraph and how they combine to achieve the author's over-all purpose. A paragraph is concerned with one central idea that is often the answer to either What? Why? or How? This idea is generally condensed into one sentence, which is known as the *topic sentence*. It is good to practice finding or making up a topic sentence for the paragraph. Try also the idea of giving your paragraph a title and then discover how each sentence is related to this central idea. Is the sentence the topic sentence? Does it fill in major details? Minor details? Does it provide a useful explanation or application of the main idea? If some sentences seem to have no relation to the main idea, you have probably failed to analyze the paragraph correctly or completely. Until you see how the sentences in a paragraph are related to one another, you will have difficulty understanding it as a whole.

Skimming is used when the trainee wishes (1) to discover a particular fact or idea without wasting time, as you might "skim" over a crowd to pick out a friend; (2) to get a general impression of what the writer says; this is often called "skim-reading" or "skipping appropriately," since you wish not detailed information but a general comprehension of what the author is saying. A trainee might skim a service manual to find out how to repair a temperature indicator, or he might do so to get a general knowledge of what is covered in the manual as a whole.

When a trainee *reads for details*, he reads first for general comprehension and then for specific meaning. He must first get the main idea and an over-all familiarity with what is written. He must then master the specific details that are important. He must see how each detail is important in itself and how it is related to the other details in what is written. Thus the sequence is main idea, major details, minor details. This type of reading is usually fairly slow and painstaking because no major detail can be omitted if the reader is to understand what he has read. *Reading to understand directions* is a form of reading for details which also relies heavily on understanding the main idea. A serviceman must first comprehend the main idea of the service manual which he is using. He must then master each step of the instructions that it provides. Finally, he must see how each step is related to the other and how all of them are related to servicing a particular type of equipment as a whole.

Reading to interpret, evaluate, or apply what is read is much like a juggler who must keep his eye on each ball as it is in the air while, at the same time, understanding the total task in which he is engaged. When doing this type of reading, it is important to ask yourself questions such as the following: What is the principal contention or position of the author? What facts does he produce in evidence? Are the facts reasonable, true, and verifiable? What conclusions does he draw from the facts? Are his conclusions too narrow, too broad, inconsistent with the data? Are the data or the conclusions distorted by bias? Have important facts been consciously or unwittingly omitted? Is the writer in a position to know the real facts and to interpret them?

How does one go about reading a book, manual, or report so as to understand it? The following suggestions may help, although the references in the Bibliography will provide much more assistance.

1. Before reading, ask yourself how much you already know about the subject, what you would like to learn, etc. Marshaling what you already know and do not know will get you in a state of readiness to profit from reading.

2. Skim for general comprehension, noting carefully introductory statements, summaries, the major problems or questions considered by the author, the principal divisions and subdivisions of the book, report, or manual. Be sure to keep an eye open for unexpected omissions on the part of the writer, which you thought would be considered.

3. When you have a rather clear idea of the book, report, or manual as a unit, now consider the first major division. First, ask yourself what you already know, what you do not know, and what you want to learn about it. Ask yourself or put the major heading in the form of a question. Then read, in order to get an answer to your question. Be careful to note all topic sentences, definitions, technical terms, directions, italicized statements, examples, illustrations, facts, dates, procedures, etc., introductory and concluding comments.

4. Now *recite*. See if you can not only mentally give an outline of what the writer has said but also answer the question with which you began. If you cannot do both, then reread until you can.

5. Now *review* the matter for yourself, asking yourself questions that may not have been considered by the author and making up your own questions to see how well you have grasped, interpreted, and applied what he has said. Make certain that your questions deal with important details, the main idea, and the implications of both.

6. Go through the same process until you have finished each major division and subdivision of what you read.

7. When you have completed your reading, now see if you can mentally outline what you have read, ask yourself key questions, answer any questions the writer may have given, and try to apply what you have read to your own work situation in your own way. If this self-testing process indicates that you have a good understanding of what you have read, go on to the next unit, chapter, or report.

SUMMARY

This chapter has been devoted to a consideration of some of the trainee factors that can help or hinder the training process. The trainer must be aware of and take into account the wide range of trainee differences—physical, mental, social, personality, goals, values, perceptions of the company, and self-concepts. He should learn how to capitalize on such intrinsic motives as trainee disturbances, deficiencies, and needs—physical, intellectual, psychological, and social. Extrinsic motives or incentives can also help the trainer. Accordingly, he should know how to make the most of praise and reproof, rewards and punishments, knowledge of results and experience of progress, competition and rivalry, participation, and relating training to the job. The trainer can use the twelve means of arousing native interest and involuntary attention to his advantage, while at the same time helping the trainees to cultivate acquired interests and voluntary attention habits. He should understand both the sources of distraction and how to cope with them. Since training assumes memory, the trainer ought to know how to help trainees to develop a retentive memory, so as to forestall forgetting. The merits of overlearning and those of part versus whole learning should be clear. Two of the most important ideas for the trainer are a clear insight into the nature and characteristics of transfer of training and the importance of building the correct learning set on the part of the trainees. Since his task is to develop efficient work habits and to assist trainees in overcoming those that are ineffective, a knowledge of habit is essential for the trainer. Finally, since little training can be done without some reading skill, a simple outline of the various kinds of reading skills and a general reading technique have been presented.

THINGS TO DISCUSS AND TO DO

1. *Can it be done?* Consider a group of employees or trainees with which you are familiar. What outstanding individual differences exist in the group? Would it be possible for a supervisor or trainer to meet all of them? The most important ones? How might he go about doing this?

2. *Are you like other people?* First ask yourself what would be likely to get you to do a good job (for instance, money, recognition, advancement, etc.). Then ask a representative group of people at different job levels the same question. Finally, examine a book on industrial psychology and see how your answers and those of your friends compare with those on reported research. What does it all mean, if anything, from the trainer's point of view?

3. *Put it into practice.* Try to teach someone a skill, idea, or procedure. In your instruction include as many of the dozen means for arousing interest and attention as you can.

4. *Can you help?* A friend asks you to help him improve his memory. What suggestions might you give him? Another friend is trying to learn a skill, such as working a lathe. What might you suggest with respect to the part versus whole method of learning?

5. *A problem in transfer.* A group of field service engineers are being trained to become sales engineers for a company that makes military aircraft parts. How would you try to help the trainees to transfer what they had learned as field service engineers to the sales situation? What new training would they need as salesmen?

6. FACT AND FICTION ABOUT THE INSTRUCTIONAL PROCESS

Purpose of the Chapter

THIS CHAPTER is concerned with five practical aspects of the instructional process: (1) the nature of teaching, including the role of the instructor, training, and other requirements; (2) methods of dealing with some practical problems in teaching, such as speaking, asking questions, handling situational and personality problems; (3) discovering training needs and the formulation of lesson plans; (4) the four-step method of instruction; (5) a self-evaluation check list for the trainer.

THE TRAINER AS A TEACHER

When one hears of the wonders of the new so-called teaching machines that promise almost to eliminate the instructor, he is reminded of the cartoon showing two ladies of the evening standing beneath a lamp post as they discuss the wonders of automation. One says to the other, "Automation may be marvelous, dearie, but it will never replace us." Much the same is true of training. The heart of the training program is instruction, and the trainer is, first and foremost, a teacher. As such, he will never be replaced by machines, television, training aids, lesson plans, or the other paraphernalia that one associates with effective training.

Training is both an *art* and a *science*. The trainer must therefore be master of the scientific knowledge he wishes to impart and an artist in deftly putting it across. By its very nature, training is a *relationship* between the trainer and the members of the training group. This relationship is not sustained by glib clichés, canned lectures, or stereotyped routines. It is capitalized on by the dynamic impact of one human being on another. Training is a *process of communication* by which the instructor helps the trainee to acquire knowledge or skill. Training is a *complex* process in which no one can anticipate every question, emotional reaction, or eccentricity of the trainees. The successful trainer is resourceful. He must literally try to be all things to all men. Training is a *highly individualistic process*, and no two trainers can possibly teach in exactly the same manner. The trainer must be true to his own personality rather than ape someone else. Training is a demanding exercise in applied psychology, since only the expert can create a climate that is conducive to learning, motivate the trainees, arouse their interest, hold their attention, cope with the human relations problems that arise, and help the trainees enjoy the satisfaction of genuine accomplishment. Training is a difficult *problem in management,* for the trainer must organize his content and methodology so that the trainees may make maximum progress with a minimum of wasted time and effort. Finally, training is a *humbling process*, since the teacher realizes that his main aim is trainee learning and not merely to put on a good show.

THE NATURE OF TEACHING

What is it to teach? Can anyone really teach another anything? These are interesting questions. To teach is to help an individual, in every reasonable way, to pass, by use of his own resources, from a state of ignorance to that of knowledge. Since a person *learns what he lives,* teaching can never be reduced to the level of formulas, pat procedures, or stylized methods. The trainee must experience the right thing in order to learn the right thing. Second, since one *learns by doing,* trainees must be allowed to use their own ideas rather than be forced to submit to the precooked pabulum of mimeographed notes. Finally, one *must apply what he has learned.* This means that the trainer must often yield the center of the stage so that trainees may test their learning. These three principles are at the heart of good training.

The trainer's role is sixfold. He teaches by presenting material that is *meaningful* to the trainees which they can accept intellectually as making sense. He also presents material that is *important* to the trainees. Otherwise, it is impossible to secure their fully willed cooperation. The trainer should present subject matter that gives the trainee a clear idea of what it is possible for him *to do and to become,* else motivating him is almost impossible. The trainer must *bring this idea down to the realities of day-to-day work and life,* if the trainee is to consider it realistic and attainable. The trainer must not dictate to or lecture the trainees but rather *work co-operatively* with them for one primary purpose—their improvement. Finally, trainer and trainee *must recognize and accept their respective roles* in this process. That of the trainer is to be a competent guide and helper; that of the trainee is to be responsive to direction, active in learning, and diligent in relating what is presented to the actualities of his work situation.

REQUIREMENTS FOR INSTRUCTION

Effective instruction is a function of seven factors.

1. Job Knowledge

You cannot give what you do not possess. This adage is especially true in training. The trainer must be a master of what he is presenting to the group. He must, however, know much more than the specific operations involved. In addition, he must be familiar with such items as the following: the operations that preceded those which he is teaching, those that will follow, the interrelationships among the various jobs; the formal and informal organization of the departments; the unwritten mores and taboos of the employees with whom the trainees work; the attitudes and idiosyncrasies of the supervisors; the morale and climate of the department in which trainees are working; the human relations that exist therein; the policies, rules, and standard operating procedures; the limitations of the equipment; the peculiarities of day-to-day working conditions; and the kinds of on-the-job emergencies that arise from time to time. Unless he either knows or takes the trouble to find out about these things, his instruction runs the risk of being more theoretical than practical.

2. Teaching Skills

In the past, one of the greatest difficulties of instruction in industry has been the lack of teaching experience or knowledge on the part of those responsible for this function. Many a trainer has been "ordained" an instructor and then has been left to sink or swim on his own. Another mistaken notion is that the best worker makes the best trainer. The simple fact is that occasionally the best worker makes almost the worst trainer simply because he is so expert that he fails to understand or sympathize with the learning problems that trainees encounter. Moreover, reading some manuals on how to train tends, now and then, to give the erroneous impression that, to be a successful trainer, all one has to know are the laws of readiness, exercise, and effect and the four-step method of instruction.

If the trainer's job knowledge is not matched by equal competence in the art of instruction, then his effectiveness will be severely limited. This fact has been recognized by numerous organizations that have excellent training programs and specialists equal to any to be found in any college. The real difficulty lies in the fact that superior instructors are a rare quantity both in schools and in industry.

The trainer should certainly be skilled in the various instructional approaches that are discussed in this chapter and Chapter 7. He should be well grounded in the material considered in Chapters 4, 5, 7, 9, and 14–17. It is impossible to formulate an "ideal" background for the specialist from the point of view of formal education. Training directors, however, might reasonably be expected to have acquired, formally or informally, knowledge of most of the areas in Section A, many of those in Section B, and a cross-section of those in Section C below. Personnel with less experience in the field might be expected to possess similar, but more circumscribed, familiarity and to plan to fill in the gaps in their background.

SECTION A
Necessary Knowledge

Educational Psychology	Differential Psychology
Psychology of Learning	Supervisory and Employee Training
Visual Aids to Instruction	Effective Business Writing
Public Speaking	Conference Methods
Methods of Teaching	Human Relations in Industry
Industrial Psychology	Vocational Education
Tests and Measurements	

SECTION B
Helpful Knowledge

General Psychology	Social Psychology
Psychology of Personality	Curriculum Development
Personnel Interviewing	Counseling Techniques
Group Dynamics	Methods of Research
Educational Administration and Supervision	Sociology
	Report Writing

SECTION C
Useful Background Knowledge

Business Organization and Management

Policy Formulation

Safety and Accident Prevention

Office Management

Development of American Industries

Economic History of the United States

Systems Analysis

Personnel Management

Business Statistics

Job Evaluation

Motion Economy and Work Measurement

Labor History

Labor Problems and Industrial Relations

Production Planning and Control

Decision-Making

3. Experience

Can a specialist train for a job that he has never performed? Should the specialist be selected from outside? The effective trainer blends theory with practice. He must have some business experience, preferably in the area in which he is instructing or in related fields. He must be familiar with the structure and functioning of a modern business concern. Over and above this, he must understand the peculiarities of the various jobs that exist in a given plant or office. He may secure this knowledge by performing the jobs, by observing others do them, and by talking with the supervisors and the workers. Granted that the instructor must have firsthand information concerning the jobs and operations involved, it must be remembered that he is a trainer *not* because he can do the job better than the worker but because he is a specialist in the teaching-learning process. Since his forte is teaching, it is just as important that he have this type of experience as it is for him to have business experience.

There is no clear-cut answer to the second question asked above. At times so-called "natural teachers" can be found in the organization. With some direction and perhaps with a few courses at local universities, they can be developed into first-rate trainers. Unfortunately, such men are almost always excellent workers, and it is difficult to pry them loose from their "bosses," who wish either to keep them or to give them a line promotion. Often it is easier to secure a professionally educated teacher, who has had several years of classroom experience, and orient him to the day-to-day work situation. The specialist's role is to instruct foremen and supervisors in the art of teaching. It is then their responsibility to train their own subordinates. Many organizations follow this system. Such a plan for "instructing through others" is in many ways superior to a highly centralized system. It allows for a division of labor, since the specialist and the supervisor do what each is best qualified to do. It also involves the supervisor and constantly reminds him of the need to train his subordinates. Human nature being what it is, however, it is necessary to give the supervisors brush-up courses from time to time and check up to see that they carry out their training responsibilities. A variation of this approach gives the responsibility for on-the-job training to the supervisors. Supervisory and management development programs are administered by the specialist, often with the collaboration of executives of the company. Finally, there exist highly centralized training organizations in which all training is done by representatives of the training department. This allows for better co-ordination and control but may tend to isolate the department from the rest of the company. In general, it is best first to look for the training specialist within the organization. If he cannot be found, then there is no recourse but to secure him elsewhere.

4. Personality

"Personality" is one of those deceptively simple words that everyone understands, yet no one can define to the satisfaction of all. Personality may be defined as the pattern of all of a person's capacities, activities, and habits—physical, mental, emotional, social, and ethical—which he has organized in his own particular way, within the limits of influences beyond his control, and which he consistently reveals in his behavior. At the risk of ignoring the fact that it is the *pattern* and *organization* of the individual's characteristics rather than the possession of mere abstract traits that constitutes personality, it may help to indicate certain factors that tend to make for an acceptable trainer personality.

A. Mental.   The trainer should obviously be above average mentally, although he need not be exceptionally so. He should be flexible in his outlook, adaptable to various trainee differences, and ingenious in creating more effective methods for putting across what he intends to teach. Shrewdness in sizing up the group, sensitivity to their changing moods and reactions, and resourcefulness in adjusting his training procedures to trainee needs are also desirable qualities. He must know how to pace his presentation so as neither to bore the bright nor frustrate the dull. Skill in asking thought-provoking questions and an adeptness in thinking on one's feet are most important.

While immersed in details, he must be mindful of the objectives of the program and of the interrelated aspects thereof, so as to insure steady trainee progress. The trainer should have a good memory, lest he become overdependent on notes, to the distraction of the group. Among the most important characteristics of the trainer are good judgment, so that he distinguishes between what is important and what is irrelevant; orderliness, so that he does not confuse the trainees; sense of timing, so that he does not try to force too much on them too soon. Above all, he should understand both his assets and his limitations as a person and as a technician.

B. *Physical.* Training and teaching are hard work. Trainees tend to think of the specialist as a man who is never absent, late, tired, or "down in the dumps." Moods, irritability, and "getting out of the wrong side of the bed" are luxuries that the trainer must "check at the door" before entering the training room. The trainer's alertness, energy, and enthusiasm often have much to do with his success in arousing interest and attention. Two additional facts are significant for the trainer: first, he should be very careful of his personal appearance; second, while he should make his language suit the level of the group, he should avoid the vulgar and the profane in a foolish attempt to curry favor with trainees.

C. *Emotional.* It is assumed that the instructor is reasonably stable emotionally, keeps a checkrein on his instinctive reactions, and has a high degree of frustration tolerance. If he is to succeed as a trainer, he must be understanding, sympathetic, and patient. He must, at least to a degree, be forceful, sociable, friendly, and cooperative rather than fearful, submissive, seclusive, hypercritical, and resentful. He can ill afford to indulge in temper, sarcasm, or the defense mechanisms of rationalization, projection, "sour grapes," and negativism by blaming the trainees for his own deficiencies. An undue tendency to be moody, nervous, or high-strung disqualifies anyone from being a trainer. The trainer should be sufficiently self-confident and poised as to be able to allow the trainees to be themselves without fear of coercion or retaliation. He should not feel so insecure or inadequate that he demands that they bend to his every whim or insists on mere conformity rather than true learning. He should be mature enough to admit his mistakes rather than try to bluff, to discuss rather than argue, to instruct rather than criticize or belittle. If he is to succeed, he must enjoy his work and help the trainees to derive satisfaction from the learning process.

D. *Social.* The specialist should never make the mistake of running a popularity contest on company time. It is much more important that the trainees respect him as an individual and as an instructor than that they like him as a person. On the other hand, he should be adroit at establishing good human relations with the group. The instructor who creates a cordial atmosphere has little to fear from the point of view of his ability to establish rapport. If he treats the trainees as equals, helps them to feel at ease, and is courteous, rapport will tend to take care of itself. It will also help to be tactful while refusing to play favorites. A sense of the humorous, especially when it applies to yourself, is one of the best social lubricants. The trainer who takes himself too seriously, tries to dominate the group, or acts as though he were vastly superior to them is courting failure. Nervous mannerisms also tend to hinder good social relations because they distract the trainees from their primary task. The trainer who normally gets along reasonably well with most people in a majority of his social relationships need have little fear concerning his acceptance by the trainees, especially if he keeps in mind the trainee needs discussed on pages 104–5.

E. *Ethical.* Nothing alienates trainees more quickly than unfairness. The trainer must be rigidly just in dealing with his group. He should give credit where credit is due and inform the trainees how they are doing. Few things contribute more to interpersonal relations than friendliness and fairness; few things destroy them faster than favoritism and unfairness. Finally, it is lethal for the trainer to speak with a "double tongue" or to say one thing and then contradict himself by doing the opposite.

5. Trainer Attitudes

There is an old saying that "character is more caught than taught." The importance of the trainer's attitude toward his job and toward the trainees can hardly be overemphasized. One specialist may be lethargic, apathetic, and resentful of his job, his position on the status totem pole, and the trainees. He may see his task as merely the presentation of predigested notes in a routine, monotonous fashion. His instruction lacks all semblance of spark, enthusiasm, and sense of achievement or satisfaction. Another sees each group and session as a new challenge. He is enthusiastic and alert to better ways of doing things. He derives great satisfaction from the progress of the trainees and stimulates them to do even better. Small wonder that the two trainers produce widely divergent results. This matter of trainer attitudes has a wider application in terms of trainee relationships. Democratic procedures are not taught by autocratic methods; nor executives developed by training them as sheep; nor powers of creative thinking increased by conditioning trainees; nor independent thinking promoted by fostering dependence; nor reflective thinking stimulated by emphasizing mere indoctrination in traditional ways of doing things. Finally, the trainer must beware of overdoing the perpendicular pronoun by indulging in rambling reminiscences of personal experiences. The five important "I's" that he should concentrate on are Intelligence, Information, Initiative, Integrity, and Ingenuity.

6. Communications

Training is basically a problem in communications. Communications involves four basic aspects: (1) the conception and organization of what is to be communicated; (2) its adequate expression in terms of correctness, clarity, completeness, and cogency; (3) an awareness of the importance of the connotation, as well as the denotation, of what is communicated; (4) insight into the psychological factors that underlie all communication, such as the mind-set of the listener. These ideas can be illustrated by a simple example. Mr. A is telling Mr. B something. What are the factors that Mr. A had better keep in mind if he expects to get through to Mr. B? First, he had better think of *what he really wants to say*. Is he clear in his own mind as to precisely what he intends to communicate? Second, Mr. A should consider how he can *best state* what he has to say in terms of unity, coherence, and emphasis, so that *he* does not give grounds for misinterpretation. Next, he might consider what Mr. B *expects to hear* and how he will *probably react* to what is said, in order to forestall any misunderstanding on Mr. B's part as far as this is possible. After Mr. A has told Mr. B, he should examine whether what he actually said was what he intended to say. Finally, he should be aware of Mr. B's *reaction to what he has heard* (which may be something quite different from what Mr. A said) and *what he thinks of it*, so as to be ready to clarify any misunderstanding.

The trainer attempts to deal with the first aspect of the communcation process by having clearly defined objectives and effective lesson plans. With these as a basis, he should be in a position to know precisely what he wants to cover in any given session and how he wishes to do so. His next task is to organize the presentation of his material into three major sections: (1) what the trainee must do; (2) how he can best do it; (3) what he must know to do it perfectly. It is important that technical terms be defined exactly, without indulging in either pretentious vocabulary or "jargonese." The more simply the material can be presented, the easier it will be for the trainee to understand it. Step 3 involves an awareness of the connotation of what is said by the trainer. Terms such as "management," "labor," "fringe benefits," "socialized medicine," "aggressiveness," and so on, even when defined exactly, have a connotation in the minds of the hearers that may be quite different from that of the trainer. The word "computer" may refer to a laborsaving device to the trainer but a job threat to the trainee. The term "member of the management team" may mean one thing to the trainer and quite a different thing to the foreman, who feels that management neither understands nor cares about his problems. Finally, the specialist must be sensitive to the attitudes of the trainees toward the company, the program, and himself. He should constantly seek for "feedback," to check whether he is getting through to the group and whether it understands what he is trying to explain. Rushing forward while the trainees are left far behind is a travesty on training.

7. Management

One of the difficulties in the past with some trainers has been their tendency to regard themselves almost exclusively as technical specialists. Gradually this self-concept has been widened to include the fact that, to a large extent, they are also managers. A manager's responsibility is to plan, organize, control, decide, lead, co-ordinate, represent, supervise, and evaluate the operation of a business activity. This definition applies to the training director and, to a lesser degree, to the training specialist. In fact, the effectiveness of the six abilities that have already been discussed depends on his skill in managing the training program efficiently. He must know how to discover the need for various training programs and represent these unmet needs persuasively to the management so as to gain its support. He must then be competent in planning the program, taking into account the manifold minutiae involved therein, ranging from the development of a training manual to making certain that the training room is available when required. He must be able to organize the "men, machines, and money" aspects of the program so that the objectives of the program will be attained maximally. Not only must he be able to make the numerous decisions that are necessary, but he must also be competent to co-ordinate, control, and supervise the different phases of the program. Finally, he must be adept at evaluating its results and reporting them to management, in order to justify its initial vote of confidence. Managing several training programs, in short, demands executive skill of a high order.

SOME PRACTICAL PROBLEMS IN INSTRUCTION

1. Problems of Speaking

Industrial trainers differ from college professors in that they rarely give long lectures. On the other hand, the trainer spends considerable time in exercising his vocal cords. If he is to hold the attention of the trainees, he must be expert in speaking interestingly. The following questions may help the instructor to check on the effectiveness of his speaking habits.

1. Was the subject matter well organized logically and psychologically? Did the introduction challenge, motivate, interest, provoke, or cause the trainees to think? Did it tend to produce apathetic or negative responses from the group?

2. Were the central ideas clearly explained, illustrated by examples, and summarized into a cohesive whole? Were the transitions from one main idea to the next carefully handled?

3. Were the main ideas illustrated by examples, statistics, contrast, comparison, stories, questions, problems, visual aids, understatements, slogans, and proverbs?

4. Did the trainer use his body to emphasize the points made? Were his gestures appropriate, natural, and co-ordinated? Did his bodily movement show vitality, good timing, variety, and appropriateness?

5. Did he speak in a natural, relaxed manner? Did his voice convey meaning, feeling, and expressiveness?

6. Was his speaking characterized by appropriate enthusiasm, forcefulness, grammatical correctness, clear articulation, simplicity, and variety?

7. Did he use proper technical terms while avoiding "fancy language"? Was effective use made of humor, figurative language, and colorful words?

8. Did he indulge in distracting speech mannerisms, such as "er-er" or "let us say, for instance"?

9. Did he speak with the proper volume, or was his volume too loud or too low? Did he vary his volume to suit his ideas?

10. Did he speak at a suitable rate, or did he speak too slowly or too rapidly?

11. Did he speak to the point or wander aimlessly?

12. Did he use short sentences, vivid verbs, and concrete nouns, or did he indulge in complex sentences, vague adjectives, and "loaded" terms?

13. Did he gauge his manner of speaking to the intelligence, experience, interests, and mood of the group?

14. Did he co-ordinate his speaking with his gestures and use of visual aids?

15. Did he use his voice to keep contact with the trainees, asking questions, throwing out challenges, and presenting problems or anecdotes for their consideration?

16. Did he make good use of pauses, silence, trainee questions, and so on?

17. Did he monopolize training time with a monologue, or did he give the group ample opportunity to participate?

18. Did he budget his time so as to say what he set out to say within the time allotted with due regard to the importance of the skills or ideas considered?

2. Problems of Asking Questions[1]

Asking the right questions in the proper manner is an art that every effective trainer has mastered. Good questions not only provide for a change of pace but also accelerate the learning process. Questions can be used (1) to discover how much the trainees already know about the manner; (2) to identify objectives; (3) to check understanding; (4) to introduce the subject matter of the training session; (5) to ascertain the ability of the group to solve its own difficulties; (6) to determine the willingness of the group to participate; (7) to discover the range of talents, experience, and abilities within the group; (8) to guide the discussion; (9) to underline the important ideas to be developed; (10) to make transitions from one topic to another; (11) to summarize what has been considered; (12) to stimulate reflective thinking; (13) to get a reaction from the "quiet members"; (14) to control the overtalkative; (15) to test the logic of the trainee's thought processes; (16) to force the group to apply abstract ideas to the day-to-day job; (17) to arouse and sustain interest; (18) to secure "feedback" from the trainees; (19) to evaluate the training session; (20) to focus the attention of the group on the important points that the trainer wishes to get across; (21) to emphasize and drive home important points.

There is almost no end to the types of questions that the trainer can use in the course of a session. Some of the more common are given below.

---

[1] Some of this material has been adapted from Stanley L. Payne, *The Art of Asking Questions* (Princeton, N.J.: Princeton University Press, 1951), *passim.*

1. *Introductory Questions.* "What do you think are the objectives of this training program?"
2. *Suggestion Questions.* "How might the company go about building better morale in the plant?"
3. *Follow-Up Questions.* "What were the results of this systems change?" "What positive effects resulted?" "Were there any negative results?" "Could you give me some examples of each?"
4. *Evaluative Questions.* "What were the good points in this demonstration?" "How did the trainee fail to make his subject clear and interesting?"
5. *Reason-Why Questions.* "Why don't we get more suggestions from our secretaries?"
6. *Debate-Type Questions.* "Is management gradually losing its right to manage because of union and governmental pressures?"
7. *Distinction-Type Questions.* "What is the precise difference between the terms "policy," "rule," and "procedure"?
8. *Knowledge Questions.* "Do you know how to operate this lathe?"
9. *Information Questions.* "How much do you know about our inventory-control precedures?"
10. *Memory Questions.* "What were the main points that we covered in our last meeting?"
11. *Probing Questions.* "Now you said that the company did not give its supervisors enough freedom in determining how their jobs should be performed. Could you tell us a little more about this?"
12. *Source Questions.* "Someone has stated that the foremen think that higher management does not care about the problems they face. Where or how has this idea developed?"
13. *How-Do-You-Feel Questions.* "How do you feel about the recent changes that have been made in the profit-sharing plan?"
14. *What-Do-You-Think Questions.* "If the company begins to automate in the plant to any considerable extent, what do you think will be the reactions of the employees? Will efficiency go up? Will we have trouble with the union? How will it affect morale?"
15. *Opinion Questions.* "What is your opinion of the new executive appraisal program that has been introduced?"
16. *How Questions.* "If I want to cut a stencil, just how do I go about it? What steps should I follow?"
17. *Intensity Questions.* "How strongly do you feel about the new procedure that centralizes all purchasing and denies Engineering the right to make its own purchases of technical equipment?"
18. *What-Would-You-Do Questions.* "What would you do if a woman employee was late two or three times a week?"
19. *Should Questions.* "Should a supervisor take time out to listen to the personal or family problems of his subordinates?"
20. *Ethical Questions.* "Has the company the right to ask personal questions on an employment form or application?"

21. *Hypothetical Questions.* "If you were the head of your department, what changes would you make?"
22. *What-Do-You-Mean Questions.* "What do you mean when you say that the company trains its supervisors and then nothing happens?"

QUESTIONS IN ACTION

It is not sufficient for the trainer to know *what* kinds of questions to ask, he must also know *how* to ask them. There are several techniques for getting the most out of trainer-initiated questions. The *overhead question* is one that is not directed to any particular member of the group but which is "thrown out" to the group as a whole. It is excellent for starting a general discussion, arousing interest, keeping the trainees on their toes, getting them to think, and ascertaining agreement or disagreement in the group, getting trainees to summarize what has been learned, and so on. This form of questioning is often called *open-ended,* because it serves as a stimulus for trainees to respond as they think best. Often one finds in the open-end question such cue words as *how, why, should, how do you feel, what do you think, what do you mean, what is your opinion,* and so on. One difficulty with the overhead question is that it allows the more confident and vocal to monopolize the discussion.

The *directed* question is one that is aimed at a particular individual. It is often used to control overtalkative members by giving others a chance to "get into the act," to break up private conversations, to stimulate the silent trainees, to provide the reticent with an opportunity to "show off" in an area with which the trainer knows they are familiar, to challenge the competent but apathetic, and similar uses. The *redirected* question is used when the trainer wishes to involve the group in finding a solution to a query made by a trainee, or when he feels that the trainee who originally asked the question really knows the answer or can arrive at it with some assistance. The *rhetorical question* is one that the trainer asks without expecting the trainees to answer it. This technique is used for dramatic effect, to arouse interest, to catch attention, to challenge, or to provoke the group.

1. Hints on Asking Questions

A question on the tongue of the trainer is much like a scalpel in the hand of a surgeon. It can be used to help or to hurt. These suggestions may be useful in mastering the art of asking questions.

1. Don't talk down to the trainees by asking questions that insult their intelligence.

2. Don't ask questions with a double meaning.

3. Don't ask questions that are "emotionally loaded," likely to arouse resentment or to give rise to negative reactions.

4. Don't ask sarcastic questions.

5. Don't ask long, involved questions that only confuse the trainees.

6. Don't use double negatives in questions.

7. Don't use highly abstract words or foreign-language terms.

8. Don't ask questions that may embarrass some members of the group.

9. Don't ask complex, double-barreled questions.

10. Ask pertinent questions simply and clearly.

11. Ask a variety of questions so that all, from the dullest to the brightest, can answer at least some of them.

12. Ask questions that emphasize how, why, what, where, when, information, opinion, feeling, thinking, meaning, purpose, judgment, memory, suggestion, evaluation, reasons why, etc.

13. Phrase questions in language that the trainees can readily comprehend.

14. Aim directed questions at individuals who are capable of answering them.

15. Use questions to test knowledge and to give the trainees a chance to show off what they know, not to humiliate them.

16. Know the specific reason why you are asking a particular person, or the group, a specific type of question and then use the answer to attain that purpose.

17. Time questions so as to give a change of pace in your training.

18. Acknowledge the trainee's response and co-operation either openly or indirectly.

19. When several trainees volunteer answers, make a mental note of the order in which their hands were raised and recognize them in that order. If time does not permit you to hear all of them, explain this to the group.

20. Help trainees to answer the questions and build as best you can on the answers given, however incomplete. Do not proceed from trainee to trainee, securing answers without comment.

21. When trainees ask questions, assume that each is sincerely asked. Avoid belittling remarks, feeble attempts at humor, and sarcasm.

22. If a "wise guy" asks awkward or embarrassing questions, calmly tell him that he is out of order.

23. When you do not know the answer to a trainee's question, simply admit it. Then be sure to have the answer for the next meeting.

2. Common Classroom Problems

Every trainer must be ready to cope with a host of problems that arise from time to time in a training program. In this section consideration will be given to certain situational difficulties. The following section is devoted to ways to deal with various personality problems.

A. *Restlessness at the Beginning of the Session.* When trainees are restless or talkative at the outset of a session, remind them of the need for order. A good preventive measure is to start work immediately. They may be restive because you waste time getting started or come late. If these measures do not produce the desired results, give a five-minute quiz at the outset of each session until things quiet down.

B. *Boredom.* Boredom usually arises from three sources: (1) the nature of the subject matter; (2) teacher method; (3) trainee mind-set and motivation. If the topic tends to be dull, vary your approach to liven it up. Use cases, anecdotes, problems, discussion, role-playing, and other techniques. If the subject has some inherent interest, then evaluate your instructional procedures. You may be talking too much, too vaguely, or too ramblingly. Try starting off each session with a different method until interest is aroused. Let the trainees carry the ball at least some of the time. Let them have some say as to how the course might best be conducted. When boredom stems from the trainees' mind-set or lack of motivation, take out time to discuss with them the objectives and benefits of the program *for them*. Gear instructions to their immediate, urgent needs and their jobs. Try to make the most of the incentives discussed on pages 105–9. Give them an opportunity to verbalize what their real feelings are. When boredom is extreme, it may be useful to set aside ten minutes or so at the end of the meeting for a "gripe session." Speak to the informal leaders outside the training session to discover their needs, motivations, and reactions to you and to the program.

C. *Lateness.* When trainees "dribble in" to the session late, make it obvious that you are taking note of this fact. If it continues, tell the group of the need for being on time, regardless of their other duties. If it is persistent, exclude the worst offenders from a given session. The same procedure applies to those who leave early.

D. *Side Conversation.* When private conversations take place, use your eyes and the directed-question technique to control them. Other means of "breaking it up" include assigning the individuals to role-playing situations, asking them to summarize what has been covered, sending them to the chalkboard, giving them special assignments, relaying the questions of other trainees to them, and so on. If such conversations still continue, then simply tell the individuals that they are interfering with the other trainees and you will not permit it. Also check your instructional methodology. You may be the source of their lack of attention.

E. *Inappropriate Humor.* When trainee humor is appropriate, enjoy it and use it. When it is inappropriate or borders on the "wise-guy" approach, try to ignore it. If you are adept at repartee, a quick "comeback" usually takes care of this problem. When certain individuals persist in this behavior, put them to work, give them difficult problems to solve, and otherwise deprive them of the time needed to think of the so-called jokes or wise cracks. Often they will see the connection and quiet down. If they do not, call them to order.

F. *Sleep.* A tired trainee may at times doze. If done but rarely, you may wish to overlook it. Should it happen with undue frequency, remind the individual that he is learning on company time and should see to it that he comes to the session in fit shape to pay attention. Check your teaching method. You may be as dull as sawdust, so that only the most polite and controlled are able to put up with you.

G. *Emotional Antagonism.* Now and then some of the trainees use the session as an opportunity to give vent to their dislike for other trainees by showing them up, making sarcastic comments, laughing unduly at their mistakes, and so on. They may tend to waste precious time in emotional arguments merely to put those whom they dislike in a bad light. Be alert to catch this as soon as possible. If it goes beyond bounds, frankly tell the class that you will not tolerate it. Treat each clique with impartiality. Mix the two "sides" in training projects and otherwise help to minimize the friction between them.

H. *Unofficial Session Endings.* It sometimes happens that, as the end of the session approaches, trainees disturb the group by shuffling papers, moving about, talking, etc. Remind them that the session ends when you are finished. If this does not work, then save something important to them for the end of the session—a quiz, description of an assignment, an interesting case, announcement of a test for the next meeting, and so on. This will usually attract their attention.

I. *Inattention.* No one can pay strict attention all the time. Inattention may be shown by yawning, doodling, talking, sleep, restlessness, and in many other ways. Analyze when trainees tend to be inattentive. You may be overdoing one instructional technique. You may not be getting through to them because of an ineffective teaching procedure. You may be too abstract, monotonous, unrealistic, or serious in your approach. You may be too dependent on notes. Your voice may be colorless. Whatever the reason, use directed questions and relay questions, vary your techniques, try to keep them on their toes by springing surprises, make use of visual aids, move about the room, be forceful, capitalize on humor, vary the volume, rate, and tone of your speaking. At times the novelty of instructing from the back of the room may be very effective.

J. *Boisterousness.*   Some trainee groups are "loud." Smart remarks crackle across the room, laughter is prolonged far beyond the humor of the situation, additional comments are made, and the noise level of the room disrupts the session. If you enjoy and can cope with this rough-and-tumble arrangement, make the most of it, since it gives a healthy informality to the meeting. If it gets out of bounds, however, remind the trainees that "enough is enough" and that, while you do not object to pertinent remarks and laughter, you do not intend to abdicate to them or to waste time.

K. *Coping with Delicate Topics.*   From time to time controversial, embarrassing, or confidential subjects may arise during a training session. Obviously, the handling of such topics requires considerable prudence and tact. If the information is confidential, then merely state that you are not free to disclose the material. Trainees will respect you if you get across to them the fact that you would treat any similar matter concerning them in the same way. Try to plan your presentation so as to avoid controversial issues. Should they arise in spite of this, however, do not try to "flimflam" the trainees. State as objectively as you can both sides of the issue and then drop the matter. In cases of "divided loyalties" or resentment against a particular supervisor, etc., try to defend the supervisor, if possible, without seeming to accuse the trainee who feels resentful. Do not allow any prolonged discussion, be as neutral as possible, and make it clear that the training session is not a gripe forum by moving on to more pertinent subject matter. It may happen that trainees may begin to complain about some company policy, rule, or procedure which you are powerless to alter. In such cases it might be wise to remind them that the best way of dealing with the matter is to take up with their immediate supervisors. At the same time, you should defend the company, if possible, by reminding them that there may be good and sufficient reasons for the policy, rule, or procedure of which they are unaware. Do not run down the company or management merely to curry favor with the group.

L. *Keeping the Discussion Moving.* A good case study, difficulty, or problematic situation usually suffices to get a discussion started. If trainees are slow in responding, do not panic at the silence. Let it work for you. They may only be thinking of something to say. If nothing happens, look directly at one or two of your most vocal members. If still nothing happens, use an overhead question, while looking directly at one of your best trainees. Should this fail, ask a direct question related to the past experience of the individuals. Call for ideas, opinions, experiences, and reactions. After the session, analyze just how you went about introducing the case. Your approach may have been largely responsible for the lack of response.

A second problem has to do with keeping the discussion on the problems at issue. Highlight the main features of the problem so that trainees know what to concentrate on. Encourage possible solutions and reasoned opinions. Control irrelevant contributions, tangents, long explanations of personal experiences, and monologues by asking a specific question or by bringing the group back to the point at issue. Recognize everyone who wishes to speak, so that all get a chance to do so. Repeat significant contributions to focus the attention of the group on them. Clarify and enlarge on incomplete contributions to produce better trainee understanding. Draw the silent ones into the discussion. Ask for examples and "for instances." Don't take sides, but do check the overly talkative or belligerent. Try to secure as many practical solutions as possible and then have the group analyze them in terms of their merit, "the pros and cons." Do not allow the majority to "steam-roller" the minority. Do not spend more time on any given phase of the problem than it deserves.

If a discussion is to serve its purpose, it must be concluded expertly. Ask an individual or the group to summarize (1) the problem and its principal facets; (2) the possible solutions considered; (3) the solution that the group thought best; (4) the reasons for its selection; (5) the practical applications of the solution. Then spend a few minutes to help the group reflect on what they learned from the discussion and how they can utilize it on the job or elsewhere.

M. *Passivity.* Some trainees "let the trainer do all the work." It is difficult to get them to participate or to contribute. They see their role as that of "note-takers." When this happens, it may be due to the tone which you originally set for the program, failure to explain their roles, going too fast or too slow, dominating the group, coldness, sarcasm, or poor teaching methods. Most groups will not be too passive if the subject matter is geared to their needs and interests, if the instructor allows room for trainee participation, and if he utilizes effective teaching techniques. Plan your session so as to allow time for group discussion. It is wise to start the very first meeting with at least a few minutes of discussion, so that the group realizes that it will be expected to contribute. If they are extremely passive, you may wish to remain silent either at the outset of a meeting or during it, explaining that you have no intention of saying anything until they do. They will always say something under the stress of silence.

N. *Wide Range of Ability or Experience.*   Instructing trainees who differ widely in ability or experience is very difficult, since there is a risk of losing either the brightest or the dullest, no matter what you do. It may help to plan so as to teach at different levels in terms of "minimum essentials" and "optimum achievement," to have the better trainees act as tutors to those who are slower, to mix them on committees and projects, to give them differentiated assignments, to have the superior ones work on their own while you help the less capable, and occasionally to have the best take over a part of the session or do individual work, reports, readings, or projects.

3. Common Personality Problems

Individual differences being what they are and training being an exercise in human relations, the trainer can expect to encounter certain personality frictions with which he must be able to cope. A brief description of some of the more bothersome types of trainees is given below, together with a few suggestions as to how to manage the situation.

A. *Mr. Opinionated.*[2]   This individual feels superior in some way to the trainer. He tries to "catch" or put him on the spot. He may disagree openly, even impolitely, and may try to convince the group that his way is better than that suggested by the trainer. Test his knowledge. If he really is as good as he thinks, then make use of his ability for the benefit of the group. If he is not, pass over the first assault with some comment like "We do not wish to waste time debating this, but here is the evidence for my position (or method)." Then see him in private and explain the facts of training life to him. If he persists, then try subtly to get the group to exert its influence

---

[2] The titles, but not the treatment, have been adapted from William M. Sattler and N. Edd. Miller, *Discussion and Conference* (Englewood Cliffs, N.J.: Prentice-Hall, Inc., 1954), pp. 223 *et seq.*

to keep him in line. Should this fail, then prove that he is wrong but do so in such a way as not to crush or lose him. Control him by your question technique. Protect the group from being overwhelmed by him and allow them to evaluate his contributions.

B. *Mr. Timid.* This trainee sees the training situation as a threat with the probability of failure. Therefore, set a friendly, relaxed atmosphere at the beginning. Try to get him to participate by looking at him. Ask him simple questions that can be answered briefly and then praise his response regardless of its quality. Call on him to help you with the visual aids, etc. Appoint him to a small buzz group, where he can work with but a few people. Defend him if others criticize his comments. Give him some special work to do in advance of the meeting, then help him to do it well so that he may excel before the class. If he is extremely reticent, see him before the session and tell him that you are going to call on him for a specific question, thus giving him time to prepare his answer. If you are qualified and have the time, you may wish to talk the whole problem out with him.

C. *Mr. Loquacious.* Some trainees suffer from diarrhea of the larynx. They talk on and on, usually in a confusing and irrelevant manner. Arrange the seating plan so as to box him in. Do not embarrass or hurt him, but *privately* tell him that, while you appreciate his contributions, others deserve an opportunity to speak. Remind him that talking is only half of the communication process. It is also necessary to listen attentively and to think. Occasionally call on trainees in a designated sequence, do not permit someone who has spoken to speak again until all have been heard, and fix a strict time limit for any single contribution. Tell him, again privately, that his statements would be more effective if he thought them through more thoroughly so that he might make them briefly, forcefully, and pointedly. If he persists, arrange that no one may speak without being recognized and then recognize him only in proportion to the extent that you recognize others in the group. Have a "recorder" for the group who is responsible for noting who has spoken, how often, for how long, and with what effect. Then use a few minutes to discuss the results.

D. *Mr. "Hitler."* When the trainer meets up with a "frustrated executive" who wishes to impose his will on the group, he has a problem. Usually the group will handle him in its own way, but there is a danger of isolating him from it. If he is really competent, make use of his ability without giving him any authority over other members of the group. If he is not, then see him privately and explain that others may have good ideas that deserve consideration. Tell him that he will be more effective if he tries to win the group to his point of view rather than impose his will on it. Protect the group from him. When he is part of a small discussion group, make certain that the other members are strong enough to cope with him. Use many of the suggestions made with reference to Mr. Loquacious.

E. Mr. "No-No." This person is likely to be obstinate, to be "agin the government," and to have a chip on his shoulder. He may resent the program, have a grudge against his fellow trainees or a personal dislike for the trainer. Try to make him feel comfortable in the session. Give him deserved recognition and praise. Try to get him to make suggestions or comments. Point out, and have the group point out, the advantages of training, but do this in a practical way that has meaning for him on his job. Praise something or some procedure in his department. Do the same for what he says or does well. Give him specific and definite responsibility within the training group. If you fail to win him over, limit his opportunities to make remarks.

F. Mr. "Yes-Yes." At the opposite pole is Mr. "Yes-Yes." He agrees with everything and everyone. Call on him first, before he has anything to agree with. Arrange situations in which he must defend an opinion that is opposed to that held by another trainee. Encourage and praise him and try to build up his self-confidence. Ask him questions that require definite convictions and evaluations. Remind him that it is not necessary to agree just to avoid trouble or unpleasantness. Bring up debatable issues and force him to take a stand by calling on him first.

G. Mr. Playboy. There is always one in every crowd—Mr. Clown. If his humor is appropriate and serves to relax the class, make the most of it. But if his humor is out of place, see him in private and explain that, while you appreciate his sense of the comical, it would be more effective if he restricted it to situations when the group would be in a position to enjoy it fully. If this does not succeed, remind him that he is wasting the time of the group.

H. Mr. Lone Wolf. This person is a rugged individualist, or at times he is somewhat eccentric, one who is continually out of step with the group. Unlike Mr. "No-No," the group will probably like him and think him something of a "character." Two things can be done with such people. First, they can be used to prevent the group from adopting a stereotyped solution. The uniqueness of their ideas stimulates the group to reflect more carefully. Second, appointing the lone wolf to small groups can help him to learn how to work more co-operatively with others. Do not permit the group to squelch him. On the other hand, do not allow him to obstruct the group's progress.

I. *Mr. Center of the Stage.* Now and then a trainer is pestered by a trainee who is so eager for recognition that he holds up progress. Tell him privately that the idea is not for any one member to "shine like a star" but for the group to work together. Give him his fair share of recognition when he earns it. Control him by some of the methods suggested for Mr. Loquacious. Use good questioning techniques to keep him in line. Have him work in a small group, but appoint someone else to make the report to the entire group. Do not look at him every time he "has his hand up" but recognize him only as often as everyone else is recognized.

J. *Mr. Resentful.* It sometimes happens that a trainee resents the training program. He feels that it is a reflection on his competence or that you are telling him how to perform his job. Be as tactful as you can. Start with a good problem-discussion. When he finds that others have different ideas, he may begin to see some value in the program. Do not argue with, talk down to, or lecture him. Ask him to contribute his experience for the benefit of the group. Accept his resentment as a fact without showing any emotional reaction of your own. If the course is good, events will probably persuade him to pay at least some attention.

K. *Mr. Mute.* Encourage him to speak but do not *directly* force him to do so. Have the group speak in a given order, starting far enough away from him to give him time to collect his thoughts. Try to catch his eye when you ask a question or seek an opinion in an area in which he is well versed. Let him work in small groups or on a committee. Praise whatever contributions he makes but do not "lay it on too thick." Try privately to discover the reason why he is quiet. Tell him beforehand that you are going to call on him, so that he may come prepared to "shine." Try the suggestions given for Mr. Timid.

4. How to Disagree Agreeably

If trainees are interested in what they are doing, it is inevitable that at times they will disagree, occasionally quite emphatically, with the trainer. The following hints may be of assistance in capitalizing on such disagreement.

1. Do not react impulsively, certainly not with ridicule, sarcasm, or belittling remarks.

2. Pause for a moment and reflect on what was said. You may have misinterpreted the statement.

3. Consider the denotation, connotation, attitude, and circumstances behind the statement.

4. Calmly determine whether the disagreement is basically intellectual or emotional.

5. If the statement is principally emotional, remain calm. Thank the trainee for his interest, answer briefly and objectively, and then make a point of talking it over with the trainee after the session. "Tabling" a comment for a few moments often helps lessen the tension.

6. Never allow yourself to be drawn into an emotional argument which serves only to create antagonism.

7. If the disagreement is intellectual, consider whether you may have caused it because of poor instruction or faulty communication. Make certain that all concerned have a common understanding of the problem, words, terms, and whatever else is involved.

8. If a real disagreement exists, restate the trainee's reasons for his position. Then ask the group for its opinions. This will cue you in on the extent of the misunderstanding. Group correction of the individual stimulates learning and prevents ill feeling.

9. Do not engage in long debates with individual trainees. This only wastes precious time and usually ends up in a battle of wits merely to defend one's ego. The real problem becomes secondary.

DISCOVERING TRAINING NEEDS AND CONTENT

Good training is largely the result of effective planning. Such planning is usually oriented about three problems: (1) discovering areas where training is necessary; (2) determination of training content; (3) efficient instructional procedures. Although there are many methods for establishing training needs and identifying individuals who should be trained, usually some such procedure as the following is adopted.

1. Analyze the Work Force

The first step in getting ready to train is to examine present and future company plans and operational requirements. Questions of production difficulties, methods changes, new techniques, and so on ought be considered. In addition, future company products, changes in personnel, and planned improved work methods must be taken into account. Against this background it is wise to analyze the present work force. Some personnel will soon be retired, and the company would not get a fair return on the time invested in training. A few may be selection mistakes and probably will be soon discharged, while still others are examples of the saying, "You can't teach an old dog new tricks." They perform necessary functions well, are perfectly content where they are, and are not going anywhere in the company. On the other hand, some employees have been identified as "comers" and require promotional training; others are adequate but could use improvement training; still others are efficient but need retraining or a brush-up course to meet new work demands; a few may be somewhat inadequate but show great potential; finally, some are new additions and require extensive training. This first step gives some ideas of the variety and scope of training that may be needed.

2. List the Operations

With the co-operation of supervisors and employees, at times the work in a given area is broken down into more or less discrete tasks or operations. These tasks are listed down the side of a master sheet, while the positions responsible for them are written across the top. It is a simple matter, then, to identify, by placing checks in the appropriate columns, what operations are an essential part of each position's responsibility. Thus, in a machine shop, either the union contract or skill demands may require that different operations be performed by Classes A, B, and C machinists. This operations check list gives a good idea of possible types of needed training, as well as of the areas in which training may be necessary. A *problemaire* which lists a variety of common difficulties is also useful. Supervisors and employees merely check "Yes" or "No" concerning the presence of the problem in their group.

3. Study Available Data

Scattered around any company is much useful information. Statements of company policies, procedures, and rules, operational manuals, test results, exit interview summaries, test results, employee appraisals, job descriptions and specifications, employee files in personnel, job histories, production, inspection, reject, rework, accident, lost time, and turnover records, customer complaints, union grievances, and similar materials at times provide a rich background for going about determining training needs.

4. Observe

The trainer who is anchored to his chair in an office should periodically get around the plant or company. Observing without "snooping" will give him a "feel" for what actually goes on from day to day, as well as help him to determine possible training needs.

5. Talk

The specialist might interview at least three groups of people. He will need the support of supervisors, and he can profitably utilize the information they can give him. They can tell him the areas in which subordinates do a good job and those in which they are more or less deficient. He can also learn just what individual supervisors expect of their workers. If they are in on the program from the outset, it will be much easier to win their co-operation. Workers may also be interviewed formally or informally, to ascertain what they feel are the areas in which they need help. This will not only give the trainer a feel for worker attitudes but also make it easier to gain their interest rather than create fear or resentment of the program. Since ultimately some representative of management must either back up or approve of the program, it is always prudent to try to involve the appropriate department head in the program from the outset. If he is "sold" on it, the trainer's life is made much easier.

6. Evaluate the Personnel

It is not sufficient merely to locate where training is needed, it is also essential to identify individuals who require training, the kind of training they need, and how much is necessary. If the operations check list suggested under item 2 is used, then supervisors can be asked to rate their people on each operation. Previous merit ratings can also be utilized. In one medium-sized company, which planned a gradual changeover from the manufacture of instruments for manned aircraft to components for missiles, adopted this approach. The technical vice-president and his staff drew up a list of fifteen basic factors and then evaluated some sixty engineers. As a result, it was decided to let out seven and to promote five. Fifteen were advised to attend local universities to add to their professional knowledge or to take courses in special fields under the company tuition-remission plan. Eight were given an in-company course in advanced mathematics, while ten took a similar course in advanced physics. The rest of the men were left alone. Plans were made to follow a similar procedure in the model shop, the laboratory, and the plant, in order to train both supervisors and employees for the changing company plans and operational demands.

At times, use may be made of a *worker opinionaire.* A list of operations in terms of machines operated, tasks performed, skills required, responsibilities held, and so on may be drawn up. Then supervisors and/or workers may be asked to check either "Yes" or "No" for each item with respect to the need for additional training. Supervisors and workers may be wrong as to their judgments, but it helps to involve them in training at the outset. Such an approach also helps to make any program more realistic and practical for the trainees.

7. Make a Job Analysis

In general, job analysis is the process of gathering, analyzing, and recording pertinent information about the operations, duties, and organizational aspects of jobs. It is beyond the scope of this book to give a detailed description of the process. Suffice it to say that job analysis is not an end in itself but may be utilized to serve any or all of the following aims: recruitment, selection and placement, organization, transfer and promotion, compensation, improving work methods and working conditions, prevention of grievances, and the formulation of job descriptions and specifications. When used for training purposes, job analysis uses some or all of the following techniques: (1) job questionnaires; (2) interviews; (3) work sampling; (4) job audits by specially trained analysts. This last method is best, since the specialist knows what to look for, how to observe, what questions to ask, how to record in a uniform manner information received, and how to summarize the results meaningfully.

Job analysis is geared largely to training content. It results in a job breakdown. As a result of careful observation, interviews, and perhaps having done the job himself, the analyst lists the major operations or steps that the worker must perform to do the job satisfactorily. If possible, these steps are listed in the order in which they take place and as subtasks of the total operation. When completed, the steps should show the logical advance of the operations from the start of the job to its completion. Second, the *key points* are noted, listed, and described. A key point is any movement, motion, technique, safety precaution, sight, sound, etc., that is so crucial for the perfect performance of the job that it must be done correctly. It can make or break the job. Isolating these key points is extremely important because they represent the heart of how to do the job efficiently. At times, another category of information is added which deals with information that the worker should have in doing the job. Thus the three essential factors are (1) the listing of the operational steps, which tells the worker *what* he is supposed to do; (2) the key points, which tell him *how* to do it perfectly; (3) related information, which tells him *what he ought to know* to do it perfectly. When these data are collected, they are listed in triple columns on a master sheet of paper. The trainer is now in a position to know precisely what he should emphasize in terms of content, the sequence he should follow, and what related information he should include, if learning is to be effective and complete.

8. Make a Lesson Plan

The next task that confronts the trainer is to translate the information that he has thus far collected into an instructional methodology that will result in learning that is efficient and interesting. At times it is either impossible or undesirable to teach the operations involved in the same sequence as that in which they are performed on the job. The lesson plan is a technique for blending knowledge that must be acquired with procedures that take into account trainee individual differences as human beings. In short, the lesson plan represents the psychological organization in terms of instruction and learning of the scientifically analyzed job content. A good lesson plan should contain the following items: (1) essential preliminaries, including the number of the session, its title, name of the trainer, day, date, time, room number, telephone extension of the trainer, arrangements that must be made beforehand, especially if he is not a member of the training staff (to check with him beforehand to make certain that he does not forget to show up), time length of the session, etc.; (2) instructional materials that the trainer will need; (3) materials that the trainees will need or use; (4) mechanical aids to learning; (5) a detailed schedule of points to be emphasized, methods of putting them across (including both trainer and trainees activities), time to be allocated to each section of the plan; (6) trainee projects; (7) suggested readings and activities. A simple example of a lesson plan on "Motivation" in a supervisory development program is given below.

Session Title: The Supervisor and Motivation   *Session Number:* 6

Purpose of the Session: Increased insight into the meaning, nature, and importance of motivation on the job; familiarity with various kinds of incentives; supervisory skill in using incentives.

Day: Tuesday

Date: May 12, 1961

Room Number: 214—Plant

Time: 2:00 P.M.

Length of Session: 2 hours

Trainer: Mr. Brown (Ext. 561)

Arrangements to Be Made:

1. Mimeographed cases by Monday morning, May 11—20 copies.
2. Mimeographed experimental questions by Monday morning, May 11—20 copies.
3. Film, "Motivating Workers" on premises by Friday, May 8.
4. Projector and screen set up by morning, Tuesday, May 12.
5. Arrange for projectionist.
6. Check room after lunch, Tuesday, May 12.

Materials for Instructor: Copies of cases, experimental questions, three psychology texts—Mr. Brown will provide his own.

Materials for Trainees: Duplicated materials will be distributed at the session. Paper and pencils are needed.

Mechanical Aids to Learning: Experimental questions, case studies, film and projector.

Specific Objectives of the Session:

1. Understanding of the importance of motivation on the job.
2. Comprehension of the meaning and nature of motivation.
3. Knowledge of individual differences with respect to motivation.
4. Familiarity with the reasons why people work.
5. Effectiveness with respect to sex, age, job level, marital status, etc., of the workers.
6. Ability to analyze and apply cases involving motivation.

PREPARATION

Key Idea to Be Stressed	Instructional Method	Time
1. Aim of the session; the importance of motivation on the job	Brief introduction; ask for trainee examples of instances in which good or poor motivation affected job performance	5 min.

Time Elapsed—5 minutes

PRESENTATION

1. People are different	Administer experimental questions; summarize results on chalkboard; discuss briefly	10 min.

2. Reasons why people work	Ask trainees: What would be most likely to get you to do a good job? To do a poor job? Summarize answers under appropriate categories	10 min.
3. Definition and importance of different incentives: financial, status, recognition, advancement, privilege, etc.	Give definition with illustrations. Have trainees discuss the various kinds of incentives they have found to be successful. Why? Which ones did not work? Why not? List trainee contributions on the board. Ask for examples.	20 min.
4. Show film, "Motivating Workers"	Give trainees a list of items to be observed during the film. Discuss briefly the highlights of the film.	20 min.

Time Elapsed—65 minutes

APPLICATION

1. Motivating different kinds of workers according to age, sex, education, level of skill, marital status, etc.	General discussion to bring out trainee knowledge, experience, and suggestions. Supplement trainee opinion with research evidence. Summarize results	20 min.
2. Put theory into practice	Have group consider the case of "Sam—Ability High, Ambition Low." Summarize discussion conclusions	20 min.

Time Elapsed—105 minutes

FOLLOW-UP

1. Review	Have group synopsize what they have learned and how they can apply it on the job. Answer questions.	10 min.
2. Need for continuing learning about motivation	Suggest readings. Show the books to the group. Urge trainees to study their people and experiment with different kinds of incentives. Answer any questions.	5 min.

Time Elapsed—120 minutes

THE FOUR-STEP METHOD OF INSTRUCTION

It must be clearly understood that training does not imply the slavish adherence to a teaching package or the stylized utilization of mechanical procedures. The art of instructing really lies in the artfulness of the trainer in following an organized outline while at the same time adapting his presentation to the mood and reactions of the group. Both the lesson-plan idea and the following description of the so-called four-step method of teaching make this assumption. If the lesson-plan and four-step method give logic and consistency to his presentation, it is up to the trainer to make it vital and interesting. The four-step plan, which was evolved in World War II but which is merely Herbart's teaching technique garbed in twentieth-century terminology, consists of the following procedures: (1) preparation; (2) presentation; (3) application; (4) follow-up.

1. *Preparation*

This essential preliminary is concerned with "getting ready" in three major areas. Assuming that the trainer has organized both the content and his method of presentation, the next step is to *prepare the environment*. This consists in taking care of many small things that can help or hinder instruction. Rooms that are locked when trainees arrive; classes that are poorly ventilated; chalkboards that must be erased during session time because they are cluttered with "leftovers" from a previous meeting; chalk, board erasers, and tools that cannot be found when needed; mechanical aids to learning that are not ready to operate or break down during the session; charts that are not prepared in the sequence of their intended use; chairs that are not arranged neatly; and lights that fail to work are examples of the type of items that must be checked beforehand.

The second aspect of this process has to do with *preparation of the trainee*. The aim is to put the learner at ease. He may be fearful, resentful, ill at ease because he is with strangers, apathetic, or merely curious. The trainer's task is to establish a climate that is friendly and cordial. Second, it is necessary to prepare the trainee to learn new facts or ideas and to establish a teaching base. This is done by first discovering what he already knows about the course and then explaining logically its aims, content, and methodology, so that he will know exactly what he may expect of the trainer and what the latter will expect of him. Questions, stories, experiments, demonstrations, job incidents, and the discussion of opportunities for self-improvement are helpful in attaining this objective. Finally, it is needful *to arouse the interest, attention, and motivation of the trainee*. By whatever means possible, the trainer must get the trainee to see "what's in it for him."

2. Presentation

The next step is that of *presentation*. This "showing-how" process is accomplished in four phases:

1. Tell him:
    A. *What* he is to learn or do.
    B. *Why* he is to do it.
    C. *How* he is to do it.
    D. *When* he is to do it.
    E. *Where* he is to do it.
    F. *With What* he is to do it.
    G. *With Whom* or *For Whom* he is to do it.
2. Have him tell you:
    A. This will reveal what he knows, what he thinks he knows but does not, and what he has failed to understand.
    B. It gives you some idea of his attitudes toward you and the training session.
    C. It helps him to clarify for himself what he comprehends and what he has failed to grasp.
3. Show him:
    A. Give a quick demonstration of the total operation or job.
    B. Repeat it slowly, commenting as you do so.
    C. Demonstrate the first key point in the shortest, easiest, and most efficient way. Explain why it can "make or break" the job. Use anecdotes to highlight the importance of doing it well.
    D. Demonstrate one key point at a time. Use simple language and avoid technical terms in the beginning. Illustrate what you are doing with pictures, models, diagrams, or sketches. Explain as you demonstrate.
    E. At first, go slowly, so as to allow time for the ideas to "sink in." Encourage questions and ask questions of the trainees. Do not present too much too soon.
    F. Explain why it is important to perform each operation as you do.
    G. Repeat each demonstration until all understand it.
    H. Emphasize key points. Do not present more than one idea at a time. Do not get off the beam. Do not confuse the trainee with aimless stories, pointless humor, or mixed ideas.
    I. Avoid emphasizing what *not* to do.
    J. Include safety precautions and point out hazards.
    K. When one key point is understood, indicate how it is related to the next one to be considered.
    L. When all key points have been demonstrated, repeat the total operation. Encourage questions and discussion.

3. Application

The trainee is now ready to "try it on his own" and to learn by doing. Bear in mind that he is just beginning to learn. He will probably be clumsy, slow, or awkward. He will certainly make mistakes. He may even become discouraged. Avoid harsh criticisms or comments that may excite or embarrass him. Ask him why he does what he is doing and why he performs the operation as he does. Give close supervision but do not oversupervise. Correct mistakes tactfully and patiently. Coach him on fine points and praise successful performance. Show how to avoid mistakes. Encourage him to continue his efforts despite failure. Aim at mastery initially and not speed. Give public commendation for a job well done. Check his understanding of the job by asking questions. Ask him to draw sketches or diagrams. As he "gets the knack of it," decrease the amount of supervision, while at the same time holding him to high standards of accomplishment.

4. Test and Evaluate

In this step the trainee is "on his own." He must perform the job without any help. The trainer should inspect finished work for quality and quantity. Keep an eye on waste, lost time, and useless movements. Oral or written quizzes may be given. The trainee may be asked to help another who is not doing so well. Keep individual records or performance charts.

CHECK LIST FOR TRAINER SELF-EVALUATION

The trainer is always being evaluated by the trainees. Sometimes it is advisable to have them do so explicitly and anonymously. The suggestion has already been given that the specialist record a few of his training sessions *in toto* and analyze them carefully. The following check list, which is by no means exhaustive, may help him to do so systematically, whether the session dealt with skill training, conference methods, or supervisory or executive development.

I. PREPARATION
   A. *Content:*
      1. Was a lesson plan carefully prepared, covering the objectives of the session, the key points to be covered, and the methods for doing so?
      2. Were the key points or topics sufficiently emphasized and given adequate time allotments?
      3. Were appropriate illustrations, examples, anecdotes, etc., planned and integrated with the major points to be explained.
      4. Were pertinent visual aids selected for their educational impact and dovetailed with the key points?

5. Were trainee activities planned and blended into the lesson plan as a whole?

6. Were crucial questions, case studies, etc., prepared in advance?

B. *The Environment:*

1. Were all necessary trainer and trainee materials, such as charts, posters, chalk, tools, pamphlets, pencils, ashtrays, notebooks, manuals, etc., arranged beforehand?

2. Were adequate lighting, ventilation, heat, and seating arrangements made?

3. Were "good-housekeeping" rules observed? Were the trainees comfortable?

4. Were all mechanical aids to learning prepared in the order of their use and "checked out" before the session began?

C. *The Trainees:*

1. Was the "ice broken" with a cordial greeting, appropriate story, or pertinent question or problem?

2. Were the trainees put at ease and helped to relax?

3. Was an attempt made to arouse trainee interest and attention?

4. Was an effort made to motivate trainees to do their best?

5. Was there any attempt to reduce fear, resentment or tension?

II. Presentation

A. *Introduction:*

1. Was the objective(s) of the session clearly explained?

2. Were the important ideas, issues, or operations clarified?

3. Were facts given, questions encouraged, opinions requested, and examples or past experiences sought?

4. Were technical terms clearly explained with examples and illustrations?

5. Was the introduction geared to the on-the-job realities?

B. *Session Methodology:*

1. Were the main points, ideas, or operations introduced and explained clearly in a logical order?

2. Did the trainer proceed from the simple to the abstract, from the particular to the general? Were complex ideas simplified by use of concrete examples, striking incidents, realistic applications?

3. Did the trainer use a variety of methods to get his points across?

4. Did he encourage trainee participation and contributions?

5. Did he proceed logically from one point to the next without undue haste, yet without loss of time?

6. Did he summarize each point when finished and make an easy transition to the next point, showing the interlock between them?

7. Did he use questions effectively (see p. 140)?

8. Did he vary the speed and volume of his speaking?

9. Did he make the best use of visual aids?

10. Did he make good use of posters, charts, pictures, cases, diagrams, sketches, reports, manuals, etc.?

11. Did he repeat important points over and over in a variety of ways until all understood them?

12. Did he stimulate trainees to answer their own questions, arrive at their own solutions, etc.?
13. Did he control the group effectively? Maintain good discipline? Crystallize thinking? Keep discussions on the beam? Restate and rephrase trainee contributions? Analyze and summarize the progress made?
14. Did he try to give every trainee a measure of success and satisfaction?
15. Did he keep contact with the group by using simple language, dramatic gestures, challenging cases and examples?
16. Did he have the group evaluate ideas or opinions? Get them to pool experiences? Arrive at group solutions or recommendations?
17. Did he get the group to evaluate its own progress? Did he appraise the progress made in an efficient manner?

C. *Conclusion:*
1. Did the trainer leave enough time to bring the session to a gradual, normal ending?
2. Did he summarize the highlights of what had been done?
3. Did he give the group an overview of what would be covered in the next session?
4. Did he end the session on a friendly note, complimenting the trainees and offering to help them with individual problems?
5. Did he evaluate his own performance and make plans for improving it?

SUMMARY

Training is at heart a teaching-learning process. Training has been described as a complex process that makes strict demands on the instructor. The key ideas in teaching are (1) to live what one hopes to learn; (2) to learn by doing; (3) to apply what one has learned; (4) to make what is to be learned meaningful; (5) to present what is important to the trainee; (6) to relate what is taught to the day-to-day job realities. The seven requirements for the competent instructor are (1) job knowledge; (2) teaching skill; (3) experience; (4) personality; (5) proper attitudes; (6) skillful communication; (7) managerial know-how. Among the practical instructional problems considered in this chapter were the following: (1) problems of speaking; (2) problems of asking questions effectively; (3) common impersonal classroom problems; (4) common personality problems that are likely to arise during the session; (5) how to disagree agreeably. Detailed consideration was given the task of establishing and determining training needs. Seven more or less distinct approaches were suggested: (1) analyze the work force; (2) list the operations or use a problemaire; (3) study available data; (4) observe; (5) talk; (6) evaluate personnel; (7) make a job analysis. The technique of formulating a lesson plan was described. The four-step method of teaching was explained as comprising (1) preparation; (2) presentation; (3) application; (4) follow-up. Finally, a self-evaluation check list was presented for the trainer.

THINGS TO DISCUSS AND TO DO

1. *Make a lesson plan.* Take a job or series of operations with which you are familiar. Assuming that you are to teach a group of twenty people who have no experience with the job or operations, outline (1) the key points you will cover; (2) how you will do so; (3) the related information you will try to impart.

2. *What is your opinion?* For each of the following types of training, is it better to have a supervisor who is very familiar with the job but knows little about teaching do the training, or is it wiser to have someone do it who is well versed in teaching but knows only the basics of the job—cutting a stencil—human relations—winding an armature—management development—report writing—communications?

3. *What would you do?* Assuming that you are a trainer, how would you deal with each of the following trainee stereotypes? The trainee who knows more than you about a particular aspect of the session and who makes it clear both to you and to the other trainees? The man who is a quick learner but who has a quick sense of humor and likes to "ham it up" to the distraction of some of the other trainees? The woman who is afraid of the training program? The older worker with many years of experience who feels that you cannot teach him anything he does not already know?

4. *Three different approaches.* Formulate three different teaching methods for presenting the same set of ideas or operations. Assume that for each you have one 2-hour session in which to do so.

5. *What have you observed?* From your own experience since childhood with poor and effective teachers, list the qualities of the good instructor and those of the inadequate teacher.

7. METHODS OF INSTRUCTION—
VARIETY IS THE SPICE OF TRAINING

Purpose of the Chapter

THIS CHAPTER is oriented about the major instructional approaches that the specialist can utilize. Criteria for selecting a given approach are outlined. The nature, advantages, limitations, and suggestions in the use of the lecture, case-study, role-playing, discussion, and conference procedures are presented. Miscellaneous methods, such as panels, use of resource experts, experimentation, question boxes, debates, and brain-storming are also considered.

Definition of a Bore: The Trainer with a Single Method

An explorer need make only one discovery to become famous. An inventor need introduce only one innovation to become rich. The trainer, however, in session after session must interest, motivate, challenge, and instruct efficiently. The fact that the previous meetings have been successful is no guarantee that the present one will not fall as flat as a bride's first cake. In fact, the longer the training program and the greater the number of sessions, the more taxing is the trainer's task of putting his points across with variety, ingenuity, and freshness.

To meet this ever-present problem the trainer can resort to one of three courses of action. First, he can ignore the reactions of the trainees and offer them a "canned" program. Or he can become a magician with a bag of assorted artificial tricks and gimmicks to meet every situation. Finally, he can strive to become master of a variety of instructional approaches, well aware not only of the advantages and limitations of each but also of the types of situations in which each is likely to be most effective. Assuming that the last approach has certain inherent advantages, this chapter seeks to describe the different training methods that are available. In doing so, the meaning, advantages, and weaknesses of each method are indicated. Practical difficulties that may be encountered in utilizing the technique are described. Realistic suggestions for getting the most out of the method are presented. The purpose of the chapter is to enable the trainer to avoid being a bore—a man of one method.

Importance of the Problem

The approach that is used in presenting material to trainees is of crucial significance primarily because a dull, monotonous, ineffective methodology can cancel out job knowledge, experience, painstaking preparation, and individual enthusiasm. Training is fundamentally a problem of communications. The training room is the testing ground in which the trainer must meet this problem. His method is the means whereby he proves his worth as a trainer. Thus the basic question— How much do the trainees learn?—hinges largely on the approach adopted. If the training method, which is the medium of communication, is unequal to the task or mismanaged, then much of the trainer's effort will be negated.

In a two-hour, ten-session training program, there are twenty hours. These hours may be stimulating and challenging or tedious and agonizing, depending upon the trainer's flexibility and resourcefulness in presenting his material. In this sense, a good training meeting is like a good cocktail—a deft mixture of appropriate ingredients in the proper porportion according to the needs of the situation and the taste of the consumers.

Theory and experience give evidence that one of the best ways of catching and holding attention and interest is by change of stimulus. A steady diet of lectures, or group discussions, or role playing, or case studies, or any other training approach soon loses its appeal. In fact, from a methodological point of view, one of the greatest dangers to the trainer is that force of habit will freeze his teaching method into one stereotyped form of presentation. Thus he hamstrings himself and short-changes the group.

Criteria for Selecting Appropriate Training Methods

1. Pertinence. This criterion refers both to the subject matter under consideration and to the group concerned. Although it is possible for a skilled trainer to present his material in many different ways, certain topics lend themselves to one form of presentation rather than to another. For instance, such items as company history, policies, products, organization, and processes are likely to be dealt with most effectively and economically by means of the lecture method, or at least by some combination of methods in which the lecture looms large. Moreover, when precise basic or factual knowledge must be learned, the lecture or lecture combination has certain advantages. Thus new workers—or even experienced ones, for that matter—might be given a lecture on company rules, safety procedures, or just where the products on which they will be working fit into the total company operation. Again, no one would indulge in the hallucinatory process of "discussing" the refraction of light, infrared equipment, hotbox detectors, flowmeters, limit detectors, take-off monitors, or similar technical subjects. From such a pooling of ignorance no one has ever discovered wisdom. On the other hand, in many areas where there is no one, single best answer or technique, case studies, role-playing, and demonstrations may be much more effective than a theoretical lecture. As no one ever learned to be tolerant by hearing a lecture on tolerance, so no supervisor has ever learned to plan his time, solve disciplinary problems, train his replacement, or deal with people merely by listening to lectures on these topics.

The other side of the pertinence coin has to do with the group involved. Some groups are so submissive and fearful that attempts to start discussions, without rather careful preliminary indoctrination, are futile and frustrating. Like a church congregation, they have been conditioned to listen to "words of wisdom" rather than to express their own ideas wisely. Other groups are so accustomed to expressing their point of view that they soon grow restless with any prolonged lecture. Still others find it difficult to learn unless the equipment can be handled and used, while others are either too undisciplined or too illogical to carry on a cumulative, goal-directed discussion. The first job of the trainer is to wed his method to his audience in terms of pertinency.

2. Effectiveness. A trainer is scheduled to discuss the subject of "MOTIVATION" in a supervisory development program. What approaches are open to him?

 a) He can lecture and present, with illustrations, the meaning, importance, and kinds of motivation, giving a summary of the known research evidence regarding their usefulness.

b) He can lecture for half the time and have a general discussion for the other half.

c) He can present a case study to the trainees which involves a problem of motivation and then inculcate his ideas by scrutinizing the case.

d) He can have two or more members of the group role-play a situation, followed by a discussion.

e) He can have a panel of known excellent supervisors analyze how they motivate their people.

f) He can conduct an experiment in motivation with the group, using it as a springboard for a general consideration of the problem.

g) He might simply ask each group member to write down the three things that are most likely to get him to do something, such as money or a feeling of being recognized; and the three that would be most likely to discourage his doing a good job, such as lack of recognition or a boss who plays favorites. He might then use the results as a basis for any form of presentation he might choose to employ.

Which approach do you think would be the most effective with management trainees? With professionally oriented prople such as engineers? With women office supervisors? With older supervisors who have more than fifteen years' experience in the company? With department heads? Do you think that any of the methods might be just as useful as any other with these groups? Whatever you think, no trainer should adopt a method for a training session until he has given serious consideration to its effectiveness with this group, in this company, at this time.

3. Trainer's Familiarity with the Method. As most baseball players feel more comfortable and efficient while playing one position rather than another, so most trainers are more at ease in using one training approach rather than another. Some prepare excellent outlines and can speak fluently and interestingly; others like and are expert in the free-and-easy interchange of ideas that characterizes a discussion; still others excel in their ability to stir up, challenge, and even annoy the trainees into lively debates; some have a flair for the dramatic, while others are skilled in demonstrating while carrying on a running commentary that augments and clarifies the demonstration. Whatever his forte, the good trainer, like a good bridge player, leads from his strong suit without overplaying his hand.

4. *Factors of Time and Physical Facilities.* No company officer would plan and organize his operation without taking into consideration the profit picture and financial status of the organization. So, too, it would be unwise for the trainer to ignore the practical realities of his situation, such as the time and physical facilities available.

Training may be conducted in large, well-equipped quarters or in cramped rooms that have the bare necessities. The type of training resources available obviously conditions the methological approach adopted.

Time, too, is an important factor. If the training program is planned as a quick, slick, slot-machine operation to be completed as speedily as possible, then there will be little opportunity for any thought-provoking discussion. The length of each session must be ample to allow for full consideration of the problem presented. Therefore, in planning the method to be employed, the trainer should always be reality-oriented to the unchangeable circumstances of his situation.

5. *Cost.* The conference, discussion, and lecture methods require little expenditure of money. A mock-up that duplicates actual working conditions, as in the case of training machinists, typists, or naval officers, may involve the outlay of large sums of money. At any rate, the trainer is often forced to compromise between the ideal approach and that which budgetary considerations will allow.

6. *Size of the Trainee Group.* Small groups, ranging from ten to twenty people, naturally lend themselves to group discussions, role-playing, case studies, and laboratory exercises. Larger groups require more organization, which in turn leads to more formality. In fact, it is almost a truism that the larger the group, the more likely the lecture method will be employed, even though at times the trainer may break the group into small "buzz sessions" to achieve variety of presentation.

7. *Type of Training Program.* How might the trainer's approach differ as to method for each of the following programs? Executive development for engineering department heads who now feel a need to get a "company-wide" viewpoint beyond their technical specialties? An apprenticeship program or vestibule school to train recent high-school graduates for factory assembly work? Training college graduates who are to become life insurance salesmen? Safety education for supervisors in a steel mill? Training future airline hostesses? Answering these questions makes it clear that the type of training course envisioned determines to a great extent the training method adopted.

8. *Attitudes of the Training Group.*   Five groups have been chosen for different training programs. Group 1 views training as an invaluable aid for increasing their success of the job. Group 2 considers it a necessary evil. Group 3 is afraid of the program and is hostile to it. Group 4 is convinced that after successfully completing the program the members will be in line for promotion. Group 5 has heard from the "grapevine" that the program does not mean a thing; after it is ended, the people will return to their old jobs and stay there. How will the different attitudes of these five groups affect the methodological approach that each trainer will adopt, provided that he is shrewd enough to sound out these attitudes before starting his first session with each group?

9. *The Trainer's Motivation.*   Trainer A is optimistic, enthusiastic, energetic, dedicated to his job. He is convinced that the wisest way in which management can invest a dollar is to invest it in training. Trainer B is not particularly interested in the training function at all. He has been selected for the job because he was very experienced in the activities of the company. He would be much happier if he could be transferred back into a line position. What effect will the different motivations of these two trainers have on the training methods that they follow?

10. *The Trainer's Personality.*   There is an old saying, "The man is the method." As there is some question as to whether a man chooses his job or whether the job chooses the man, so it might be debated whether a trainer selects his basic approach or whether this question is largely determined by the kind of personality he has. At one extreme there is the trainer who likes the security that careful preparation, detailed outlines, copious notes, and stacks of mimeographed paper give. He controls the training situation quite closely. It is orderly, logical, and disciplined. At the other extreme is the "rough-and-ready" trainer. He is free-wheeling and easygoing. He encourages trainees to disagree with him and argue with one another. He punches holes with great delight in their stereotyped ideas and ways of doing things. He annoys them at times deliberately. His training sessions, to the outsider, may seem noisy, even chaotic. Yet the trainees learn just as much, if not more, than do those in the more formally organized programs. While there are many kinds of trainer behavior that intervene between these two extremes, it is clear that the personality of the trainer has much to do with his choice of instructional method.

11. *Company Climate.* One of the writers of this book once conducted a training program and after the first session discovered that the trainees had been told that they would be rated on the amount of notes they took at each meeting. For this purpose, it was proposed that their notebooks be collected each day and examined. This idiotic proposal was vetoed at once. On another occasion, it was made clear to certain civil service trainees that they would be evaluated on the number of questions that they asked during the training sessions. These two incidents, one in private industry and the other in government service, highlight a fact that has been emphasized throughout this book, namely, that training takes place within the context of the total company milieu and is greatly affected thereby. If the management climate is autocratic, suspicious, authoritative, disinterested, or democratic, it will be reflected in the methods employed by the trainer.

General Training Methods

Assuming that the eleven background factors are borne in mind, it is now possible to discuss the general methodological approaches that are open to the trainer. For reasons of clarity and brevity, each major method will be discussed under four headings: (1) definition and nature of the method, (2) advantages of the method, (3) limitations of the method, (4) suggestions for deriving the most profit from the use of the method.

The Lecture Method

1. *Definition and Nature.* Typically, the instructional method that is most frequently employed with college students and intellectually mature people—the lecture—is a formal, unilateral oral communication between an individual and a group, in which the speaker presents for the group's consideration a series of related ideas that have been carefully organized beforehand as to both content and method of presentation. The lecturer is in complete control. He determines what and how it should be covered, what is to be emphasized, how much time is to be devoted to each idea. It is assumed that, as an expert, he knows what his audience ought to learn. Each lecture is complete, in that it exhausts a given topic or aspect of that topic. The task of the lecturer is to know, to organize what he knows, to present it logically and interestingly. The job of the group is to listen and reflect on what is said. To help him, the speaker may distribute outlines, utilize mechanical aids, or ask questions. The audience is expected to ask pertinent questions either during the lecture or near its end. The lecturer is expected to answer them clearly and fully.

2. *Advantages of the Lecture.*   Although overused, misused, and much abused, the lecture has certain obvious advantages.

1. It can speed up the learning process by allowing the expert to offer in capsule form the benefits of his knowledge and experience.

2. It avoids the evils of rambling, undirected so-called "discussions," which at times are no more than the blind leading the blind.

3. In a good lecture there is a logic, unity, and completeness that is lacking in many other instructional approaches. The speaker can give a blueprint of what he is to cover, develop each idea in an orderly manner in terms of its importance, and weave all the ideas into a cohesive whole by way of a terminal summary.

4. It allows for careful preliminary analysis of significant ideas, their organization, and method of presentation so as not to waste precious training time.

5. Since the lecturer is an expert, the chances are good that the audience will secure a clear understanding of key concepts and facts.

6. If done by an experienced speaker, the lecture can be interesting, thought-provoking, and even challenging.

3. *Limitations of the Lecture.*   The lecture approach is especially open to misuse and abuse.

1. It usually involves an imbalance of activity. The speaker is hyperactive, the group hypoactive.

2. It results at time in superficial knowledge. Because at the end of a lecture the audience can use the right terms and say the right things, it is assumed that it really understands what was considered. Not everyone who glibly uses the words "policy formulation and implementation" really knows what he is talking about.

3. There is the danger that, while notebooks may be full, heads may remain empty.

4. It often ignores the principle that learning, to be effective, must involve self-activity on the part of the trainee.

5. Since it is reduced largely to passive listening, the group may speedily lose interest.

6. The lecturer may become rutted and play "the same record over and over" without regard for the real needs of the group.

7. It makes great demands on the speaker, since he carries the ball almost unaided.

8. It often assumes that the listener will make his own applications of what is said to his own situation, something that many just cannot do well.

9. It assumes that what the lecturer says has the same meaning for each of his listeners—an assumption that is as often false as it is true.

10. Unless the lecturer is very skilled, he may ignore individual differences among members of the group in terms of intelligence, experience, motivation, and so on. Thus he may bore the bright and penalize the slow learner.

11. It tends to develop rote memory and theoretical knowledge rather than understanding and mastery.

4. Suggestions for Using the Lecture.   The following hints may help the specialist to secure the advantages of the lecture while avoiding its defects.

1. Restrict this method generally to groups that, because of above-average intelligence or experience with it, take readily to this form of presentation.

2. Minimize its use unless the trainees are rather highly self-motivated and self-involved.

3. Avoid it, unless you are master of your field, fluent, imaginative, free from dependence on notes, and gifted with at least some degree of humor, stage presence, and the ability to think logically and swiftly on your feet. The lecture method is probably the hardest to do well. Thousands of bored trainees are evidence of this fact.

4. It is useful for giving trainees an overview of what is to be covered in the program, for summarizing what has been accomplished, for establishing transitions from topic to topic, for considering basic concepts and broad questions, rather than skills and factual minutiae.

5. It is useful if time limits are stringent.

6. The lecture followed by a question and answer period is helpful but artificial. Most people want to have answers to their questions as they arise. By the end of the lecture they may have forgotten them, or the questions themselves may seem out of place. Pause after each major point has been made and either invite questions or

ask them of the group. Ask trainees to summarize the ideas presented. Such summaries will "cue you in" as to whether or not the trainees are "still with you."

7. If the lecturer is quite skilled, he may ask the group to list the problems and difficulties that are important to them. In his lecture he can then weave into his prepared talk answers to the questions proposed.

8. Use the lecture-discussion technique. There are three forms of this technique. In the first, the lecturer discusses the problem under consideration and then "throws the floor open" for a general discussion. In the second, the discussion precedes the lecture, being used to discover the real needs of the group. The lecture then serves the purpose of meeting these expressed needs. In the third, the speaker presents his point of view and then divides the groups into several small groups or "buzz sessions" of from five to ten people each. Each group discusses the implications and applications of what has been said and then reports back to the large group for a general discussion.

9. To be effective, a lecture must be well planned and organized logically. Trainees must be given an overview of what is to be covered. The logical sequence of topics must be self-evident. Important points must be reiterated over and over, with a variety of practical examples, and then summarized periodically. Transitions from one topic to another must be clear and the relationship between one idea and another pointed out in such a manner as to constitute a unified whole. Abstract concepts must be illustrated by realistic applications.

10. Since no one can devote his entire attention to any speaker for more than ten or fifteen minutes, provide for a change of pace. Humor, a challenging question, requests for trainee ideas and applications, examples from other companies, trainee summaries, the introduction of a controversial issue, trainee questions, use of mechanical aids, and cases related to the content under consideration— all help introduce a variety in the lecture approach.

Case-Study Method

1. *Definition and Nature.* If the lecture can be classified as a "nonparticipating" instructional method, the case study places an emphasis on trainee participation. In this approach a case that is typical of a category of similar problems is presented for analysis by the group. All essential data are included in the writeup; as often as not, irrelevant material is also intermingled with the pertinent information to seduce the unwary and the unthinking. The basic aim is not merely to solve a particular problem but to develop the trainees' powers of analytical, synthetical, and cross-disciplinary thinking. The problem or case merely serves as a medium for so doing.

2. *Advantages of the Case Study.* The case study, although probably overpropagandized, has certain genuinely strong features.

1. It has an element of realism, since the cases are descriptions of practical situations in existing companies. If the cases are chosen to dovetail with the day-to-day problems of the trainees, they have a meaningfulness that few other approaches possess.

2. It is in line with the principle that, to learn, the trainee must be actively engaged in the process. The trainees must come up with a logical solution to the problem proposed.

3. It forces the trainee to see beyond his narrow specialty and to take into account the perspectives of other disciplines. For instance, a given case may have marketing, manufacturing, financial, accounting, and managerial aspects.

4. It is usually interesting. Since a case is quasi-biographical, most people find it attractive.

5. It stimulates the trainee to sift out the facts, to distinguish between the important and unessential, to analyze data, to judge their interrelationships, to synthesize the evidence, to organize his thoughts logically, and to present them coherently—in short, to obtain a "whole view" of the problem to be resolved.

6. Since there is no *single, infallible* solution, it allows for group evaluation of individual or team answers. Habits of opinionated and careless thinking are soon check-reined in the case-study approach.

7. Different solutions afford a springboard for lively discussions of the relative merits of each.

8. It places the responsibility for learning exactly where it belongs, on the shoulders of the trainees. The chairman merely guides the discussion; the trainees must formulate appropriate solutions to the cases.

3. *Limitations of the Case Study.* Like every other approach, the case study has certain weak points.

1. To write a good case study is very taxing and time-consuming. A complete case may run to as many as forty to sixty pages.

2. If short cases are employed, there is the ever-present danger of oversimplification.

3. It is no easy job to include all the facts that are necessary for arriving at a really satisfying solution.

4. Not all cases are equally useful in helping the trainees to generalize to a class of similar situations.

5. It takes a great deal of time for trainees to analyze thoroughly a carefully prepared case.

6. Few training sessions are long enough for a complete discussion of a complex case. An incomplete, hurried solution is always a temptation.

7. Cases of any value often require more knowledge and experience than many trainees can bring to the problem.

8. Trainees are often unaccustomed to this approach, and so waste time getting used to it.

9. Some trainees either lack the intellectual capacity to analyze a complicated problem scientifically or are unable to discuss an involved issue unemotionally.

10. Guiding the discussion of a multivariate case requires a high order of knowledge, experience, and skill on the part of the chairman. He must be familiar with all the disciplines needed to solve the case. Such trainers are not readily found.

4. Suggestions for Using the Case Study. The following remarks may help obtain the most from the case-study approach.

1. As time permits, work up cases from the actual experience of either the trainees or the company. Cases that have a ring of applicability, importance, and meaningfulness help gain trainee interest and co-operation.

2. Have a variety of cases. A problem involving a major management issue may be quite complex and lengthy, whereas one dealing with the alcoholic or problem-drinker employee may be relatively short.

3. Do not "go it alone" in formulating cases. Use the experience of those who are in a position to give constructive advice.

4. Make certain that all data needed for an answer are given in the case. Incomplete cases lead to either frustration or opinionated guesswork.

5. Since wisdom on the spur of the moment is a rare virtue, trainees must have the cases soon enough to allow them to study and digest them before the training session.

6. If the trainee group is rather large—twenty or more—it may help to divide it into four groups of five members each. Competing

teams naturally give rise to spirited discussions; but make certain that each team includes the skills necessary to solve the case.

7. Do not allow individual or team reports to degenerate into monologues. Such presentations of solutions should be in seminar form. The party responsible should be held to give logical reasons, pro and con, for each step in his solution, as well as to defend his reasoning against the objections of the group. Rigid discipline is necessary to prevent heated but pointless arguments, captious objections, and mere personal opinions.

8. Longer case studies should be written up before they are orally presented.

9. Short case studies may be used to stimulate group discussion, to drive home a point that has been made in a lecture, and to force the trainees to apply theoretical knowledge to concrete situations. Even these, however, should not be sprung on the trainees "cold." They should be prepared to discuss the case intelligently. If a trainee acts as chairman, he should have an outline to help him guide the discussion efficiently.

Role-Playing Methods

1. *Definition and Nature.* More an instructional technique than a general methodological approach, role-playing is another participating or experience type of training. In therapy it is called "psychodrama." In schools and vocational guidance it goes by the name of "sociodrama." All three variations involve the dramatization or acting out of some significant incident. The dramatized event is an attention-getter and springboard for discussion. Emphasis is not on solving a given problem but on helping the trainees to increase their understanding of human nature, their appreciation of why people act as they do, and their insight into human relations problems.

2. *Advantages of Role-Playing.* As a form of reality practice, role-playing has evident advantages.

1. It forces individuals to realize that "it is easier said than done," by making them act out what they say they would do in a given situation. Many a supervisor has declared readily what he would do in a given incident. When asked to role-play the event, however, the tape recorder revealed more "er's" and "ah's" and irritation-producing remarks than constructive comments.

2. Role-playing, if well done, helps the trainee to get "under the other fellow's skin" better than reading a book. Actually playing the

other fellow's part increases the trainee's sensitivity to how he thinks and feels. The trainee learns to see a situation through the "other fellow's eyeballs."

3. Even when done amateurishly, role-playing has a way of involving both actors and observers. Both tend to identify with the roles portrayed. It is surprising what stimulating discussions can arise from a simple scene enacted before a group.

4. It emphasizes the importance of self-activity in learning.

5. The controlled conditions of role-playing enable the trainer to get across the precise point that he has in mind, using people rather than words to drive it home.

6. The fact that people serve as actors makes role-playing one of the best attention-getting and interest-holding devices.

7. As an observer watches role-playing and identifies with one or another of the actors, he may come to a better understanding of his own feelings and actions.

3. *Limitations of Role-Playing*.   Most of the disadvantages of role-playing stem not from the technique but from its misuse.

1. Most supervisors and executives are not trained actors. Hence they may be overly self-conscious as role-players or even treat the entire matter as a joke.

2. At times role-playing is done in such an impromptu fashion as to destroy most of its merits. Roles are not always carefully planned and developed.

3. Many business and industrial situations do not lend themselves to role-playing. This technique works best in the general area of human relations.

4. At times, too much emphasis is placed on solving *the* problem revealed rather than on increased comprehension of interpersonal relationships and job behavior.

5. Now and then, a role-player will go out of his way to be difficult or else may "play to the crowd." Such behavior only serves to irritate or frustrate the other actors.

6. Quite unwittingly, either the roles depicted or the subsequent discussion may touch upon psychological or business problems that are far beyond the ability of the trainees to handle.

4. *Suggestions for Using Role-Playing*.   The following hints are presented, in order to make it possible to actualize the potential benefits of role-playing.

1. Most trainees must be thoroughly briefed on the technique and

their roles. Initially, participants must be trained. Roles must be carefully formulated either by actually writing a script or by discussing the main ideas to be gotten across.

2. The observers—those trainees who are not actually acting out the event—must be briefed on what to look for. It must be made clear that they are not passive watchers but keen observers, who are expected to react to what is taking place and later to discuss it intelligently. In the beginning, a list of things to watch for may be given the observers.

3. Use role reversal. When this is done, a supervisor plays the role of an employee, while a worker enacts the role of the boss. This reversal often helps put the individual in "the other fellow's shoes."

4. Use sequential role-playing. For instance, if the group is considering the problem of disciplining an employee who is habitually late for work, have the same individual play the role of the latecomer, while three different trainees act the part of the supervisor in succession. None of the "supervisors" is present while any one of them is interviewing the worker who is out of line. Thus the group sees how three different people would handle the problem. The different approaches are a natural springboard for general discussion of the problem.

5. Use interrupted role-playing. At times, it is helpful to stop the role-playing after a particular comment is made and to ask the group how it might reply to it or what it might do about it. This is especially true when trainees are role-playing interviews. After the discussion, the role-playing can continue.

6. Use open-ended role-playing. This type of role-playing is not meant to solve a problem but to "set the stage" for discussion by ending the acting on a highly dramatic note. For instance, a man who has been "passed over" three times for promotion might be pictured as complaining about this to his boss. The boss then explains the reasons why he has been passed over. Things go from bad to worse, and finally the worker stomps out of the room with a "You can go to hell!" On this note the scene ends dramatically, and the group can then discuss what went wrong and what the supervisor should or should not do about it.

7. Use small-unit role-playing. If the group is large, it may be difficult for the trainees to identify with the actors or to carry on a profitable discussion. In such instances, it might be advisable to divide the audience into several smaller groups; for instance, fifty

people might be divided into five groups of ten each. Each group then independently role-plays and discusses the same incident. The small groups then reconvene into the large group to report the results of its discussion. Obviously each small group must appoint a recorder who will be responsible for keeping a record of the ideas agreed upon in his group so that he may report them to the other groups. A general summary or discussion may then follow.

8. Use role-playing for so-called human relations problems. Such problems as grievances, interviewing, giving orders, discipline, favoritism, and so on can be dramatized by role-playing.

Discussion and Conference Procedures

1. *Definition and Nature.* In general, a discussion involves a small group of people who have met to define, to understand better, or to solve a problem of mutual interest through the free and co-operative oral interchange of information, ideas, and opinions. There are many types of discussions, such as "bull sessions," conferences, panel discussions, round table, sixty-six groups, buzz sessions, and so on. All are based on the same French adage, "Everyone knows better than anyone." Each assumes that by pooling the knowledge and experience of several people it is possible to arrive at a better solution to any problem than each individual could achieve alone. The very concept of discussion requires that the number of participants be small, rarely as large as fifteen, certainly never more than twenty. Lack of time pressure, a certain degree of informality, friendliness, absence of tension, frank and easy exchange of ideas are all connoted by the term "discussion."

2. *Advantages of Discussion and Conference Procedures.* Few training methods have as many advantages and weaknesses as do discussions and conferences.

1. Each participant has an opportunity to present his point of view and to make himself heard without battling to get a word in edgewise.

2. Each member's ideas are subjected to the critical and constructive evaluation of the other people in the group.

3. It is possible to achieve a better solution from co-operative effort than any one individual might attain.

4. Group members have time to reflect not only on their own contributions but also on those of their peers.

5. A discussion group works as a team. The informal atmosphere

and easy relationships can bring the trainees closer together. Group success in solving a problem can at times be more satisfying than an individual tour de force.

6. Usually from a small group there will be more suggestions of higher quality than one could get from adding individual suggestions. The group members stimulate each other.

7. Small groups provide a built-in check against individual prejudice, error, or eccentricity.

8. To the perceptive participant, the discussion or conference group offers an excellent opportunity to observe people in action: their intellectual ability, their emotional resiliency, their frustration tolerance, their rigidity or flexibility, their characteristic style of participation, their strengths and weaknesses.

9. Well-run discussion and conference groups usually increase the morale of the group as well as individual and group efficiency.

3. *Limitations of Discussions and Conference Procedures.* In actual practice, few techniques are subject to so many criticisms as are discussions and conference procedures.

1. Often the leaders are untrained, unskilled, and unsuited to the task. It would hardly be an overstatement to maintain that most discussions and conferences should cease until so-called conference and discussion leaders master their trade. A title or position does not automatically qualify an individual for this duty, despite the fact that many organizations act as though it did.

2. Some people seem to be temperamentally ill-suited to this type of training procedure. Whether as leaders or as participants, they are either too passive or too overly domineering to be productive. In any discussion group it does not take long to discover Mr. Mute, Mr. Loud Mouth, Mr. Monopolist, Mr. Agin-the-Government, Mr. Yes-Man, Mr. Bluenose, Mr. Isolate, Mr. Know-It-All, Mr. Clown, Mr. Sarcastic, and a host of others who can impede or ruin the success of a discussion or conference group.

3. Many individuals lack either the skills or the discipline that are prerequisites for success. They do not listen but merely wait until another has ceased to speak in order that they may talk. They do not try to build on the ideas of others but get off on aimless tangents. They insist on having their own ideas accepted *in toto*, with no thought of reconciling their views with those of the other members. They cannot follow a logical line of thinking, so that their contributions are characterized by verbal diarrhea and mental constipation. They waste

time defending their egos rather than solving the problem at hand.

4. Some leaders cannot or do not define the question at issue in terms of its important variables, so that the participants can discuss it intelligently and efficiently.

5. Other leaders do not know how to guide the discussion without dominating it, to keep the group on the problem, to draw out the "quiet ones," to hold down the talkative ones, to keep track of the main suggestions made, to blend several apparently disparate solutions into one that contains the best features of each, to encourage contributions without passing judgment on them, to minimize irrelevant contributions, to keep the members working toward a satisfactory resolution of the problem in spite of their mutually imposed frustrations.

6. Too many discussions and conferences are circular verbal exercises as the discussants go round and round, getting nowhere. Too often this impasse is resolved by winning on the basis of "the tyranny of one vote" instead of striving to attain consensus.

4. Suggestions for Using Discussion and Conference Procedures.   Like every other instructional method, the various types of discussion techniques work only if certain rules are observed.

1. Make certain that the topic under discussion is within the experience of the trainees. They must at least know what they are talking about.

2. All participants should know well in advance the topic to be discussed, so that they may come prepared to participate intelligently. Any discussion is an interchange of ideas, not a conflict of unsubstantiated personal opinions.

3. Define the issue clearly in terms of its background and pertinent variables.

4. Keep the group relatively small, no more than ten, if this is possible.

5. Break large groups up into manageable smaller groups. Have the small groups report back to the large group, if necessary.

6. Once it is clear that the group knows what it is supposed to do and what it is dealing with, try to get it to list all reasonable solutions, together with their justification.

7. Consider the relative merits of each proposed solution as compared with the others, using this procedure to narrow the number of possible solutions. When the group has succeeded in narrowing the

alternatives to two, have it weigh the advantages and disadvantages of each in terms of its pros and cons.

8. Do not allow the group to wander randomly from suggestion to suggestion. Nothing is more debilitating or frustrating.

9. Encourage participation on the part of all, but do not rush the group. Creative thinking cannot be forced.

10. Accept the fact that a profitable discussion takes time, but keep the group moving in the direction of a self-determined solution.

11. Try to create a climate that is conducive to free, friendly discussion. Permit no cliques, petty bickering, or personal vendettas.

12. Allow every view a full and impartial hearing. Strive for consensus, but when this is impossible, help the group reach the best solution that circumstances permit. Minority views must be persuaded that they have received fair treatment, even though they may not have been able to win the majority to their opinions.

13. Since disagreement is inevitable, try to get the trainees to "disagree agreeably" without a carry-over of hostility.

14. Have the group evaluate its own performance with a view to taking positive steps toward improvement.

Demonstration Methods

1. *Definition and Nature*. A demonstration is a Latin answer to the Yankee comment, "I've got to be shown." Derived from the Latin word "to show," it is based on the principle that "seeing is believing." It is rooted in the assumption that watching an expert perform what is to be learned is better than hearing about it or reading about it. Whether it concerns an electrician showing an apprentice how to follow a wiring diagram in assembling an electronic component, an insurance salesman telling a trainee how to make his sales approach, a store manager instructing a checker in the use of a cash register, or a field service engineer teaching Air Force personnel how to operate a new missile detection system—demonstrations are based on the idea that one must see exactly what takes place if he is ever to learn. Generally combined with the demonstration is firsthand experience in the operation of the equipment under supervision. Thus demonstrations combine the best elements of observation and experience training. This is true in such a simple operation as demonstrating the workings of a micrometer or in a complicated mock-up of a jet airliner cockpit.

2. *Advantages of Demonstrations.* Since perhaps 90 per cent or more of what we learn comes through the sense modalities of sight and touch, demonstrations obviously have marked advantages.

1. To watch an expert show how something is done while working with the equipment that the trainee is later expected to handle has an element of realism that few other instructional procedures can match.

2. The fact that an expert conducts the demonstration gives the trainee a model that he can imitate.

3. Demonstrations attract, hold, and sustain attention and interest.

4. Demonstrations, if followed by supervised practice, are the best type of reality training and practical experience.

5. They allow for the immediate correction of errors.

6. They emphasize learning by observation and doing, resulting in "know-how" rather than mere "know-about."

3. *Limitations of Demonstrations.* Although demonstrations have many advantages, they are often limited by the following deficiencies.

1. Demonstrations, especially if coupled with supervised practice, as in a machine shop or vestibule school, impose relatively heavy burdens in terms of money, instructional personnel required, and necessary physical facilities.

2. They are well suited for job skill training, job instruction, and on-the-job training. They are of limited usefulness in executive development and management trainee education.

3. They are more applicable for the inculcation of technical finesse than for the development of concepts and ideas.

4. They often tend to stress "know-how" at the expense of "know-why" something is done in a particular way.

4. *Suggestions for Using Demonstrations.* It would be well to keep in mind the following precautions in using the demonstration technique.

1. Make certain that all equipment to be used is of the most modern type and in excellent working order.

2. The demonstration must be done by an expert who is also skilled in explaining the sequence of operations and the relationship of each operation to the end product.

3. The demonstrator must be able to explain simply what he is doing without resorting to too much technical jargon. He must also be able to do this while manipulating the equipment.

4. He must be careful to explain not only what he is doing but why he is doing it.

5. Since the typical trainee can absorb only so much at one time, the expert must proceed slowly, repeating and re-explaining until the trainees "catch on."

6. Make certain that the trainees can see clearly what is going on. This is a minor point but one that is often violated.

7. When the trainees try their hand at imitating the demonstrator, he must insist on high performance standards, while correcting with friendliness, pointing out mistakes patiently and encouraging the trainees to continue their efforts in spite of occasional failure.

8. He must make it easy for trainees to ask questions without putting them on the spot or making them feel stupid.

Miscellaneous Instructional Methods

Although the major methodological approaches to training are those which have already been discussed, there are many other techniques that the trainer can use to improve his instructional efforts. Some of these are discussed briefly in the following section.

1. *Panel Discussion.* The panel technique can be used with considerable effectiveness. A group of three to five people may be invited to give their views on a particular problem or question. For instance, known good supervisors might be asked informally to discuss with trainees how they motivate their people. The comments of these supervisors are often much more effective than the words of a trainer. Again, problems of safety might be considered by a panel composed of an industrial engineer, a safety engineer, a doctor, and a foreman. A group of successful salesmen might discuss the practical problems they have met and solved. A panel of managers might explain the whys and wherefores of certain company policies, rules, systems, and procedures. There is almost no limit to the variety of panels that can be arranged. At times a panel of trainees can give its views on a given problem, thus leading to a general discussion.

2. *Resource People.* Occasionally it might be feasible to bring to a training session one or another resource person who is an expert in a given area. Representatives from engineering, manufacturing, the controller's office, marketing, and so on might be invited to explain just what they are trying to do and why they make what may appear to be silly demands. In fact, if there were more cross-fertilization of this type, much of the interdepartmental misunderstandings would be minimized. The resource person may be secured from within or outside the company. For instance, under certain carefully prepared circumstances, a manager might be invited to answer some of the common complaints that are voiced at the lower levels; or an outside psychologist might be asked to answer supervisors' questions on the psychology of human behavior; or the company physician might discuss such topics as first aid and physiological factors in work and fatigue.

3. Committee Reports.   Occasionally a group of trainees can be given a special assignment and asked to report to the entire group. If the report is made as a team, the large group can profit from the specialized work of a few.

4. Question Box.   Since it is a human habit to think of a good question at an inopportune time, even as one may think of a good joke on the way home from a party, it may help to have a "question box" into which trainees can place pertinent queries at any time. Some few minutes can be taken out at the beginning or ending of any session to answer them.

5. Debates.   A training session can often be livened up if a debate is arranged on a controversial topic, such as "Has Management Gone Too Far in Trying to Practice Human Relations?" or "Should Subordinates Rate Their Supervisors?" The first question represents a rather widely held idea; the second is a practice that is carried on at the headquarters plant of Esso Research and Engineering Company. When a good debate is organized, it is almost impossible not to "take sides," a fact that makes for stimulating general discussion.

6. Experimentation.   For anyone who is interested enough to investigate some of the literature on learning, psychology, and social psychology, there are many experiments that can be used in certain types of training. The effect of "mind-set" can be illustrated simply by saying certain words to a group and asking them to note the process by which the mental image changes as words are added. For instance, "polished, long wooden table," "man in white coat behind it," "bottle of alcohol," "woman on other side of table," "Bunsen burner," and so on. There are several experiments reported on the influence that a group has on individual judgment. There are a host of experiments on memory, whole versus part learning, effects of reward and punishment, influence of set on problem-solving, and similar topics. A simple experiment can be carried out by asking each trainee, in a supervisory development course for instance, to state his opinion with reference to such statements as "When all the theory is finished, you can divide people from an everyday point of view into the strong and the weak." Each person notes his agreement or disagreement with each statement on a scale from 3 to —3 in six-interval steps. The results will surprise you.

7. Problem-Solving. Actually, problem-solving is not a unique technique. Any instructional procedure should be oriented about the solution of problems. On the other hand, it is possible to formulate problems that force the trainees to apply the conceptual steps of the scientific method. Such problems can apply to plant layout, market analysis, transportation problems, policy formulation, personnel selection, evolution of manning tables, and a myriad of cognate problems. In fact, an excellent problem at the higher levels is to determine the objectives and means of executive development; operations research and games theory are essentially problem-solving exercises.

8. Brain-Storming. A recently developed technique, which has probably been overpropagandized but is nonetheless extremely useful, is brain-storming. The basic aim of brain-storming is to release those imaginative, free, and creative original ideas that a conforming, status-seeking, and organization-minded society tends to suppress. In a typical brain-storming session, a relatively small group of people is given a problem and is requested to produce as many suggestion or possible solutions as they can within a given time period. There is no general agreement as to just how long a brain-storming session should last. Some authorities claim that the best ideas are gotten at the beginning, whereas others maintain that qualitatively superior suggestions come toward the end of the session. A key idea in brain-storming is freedom to express what may appear to be even a ridiculous idea without being pounced upon critically by one's peers.

Actually, in brain-storming there is both a quantitative and a qualitative aspect. A method that seems to have worked out reasonably well with the safety directors of the Department of the Army was the following: twenty safety directors from all over the world were divided into two groups of ten. They were asked to give as many practical suggestions as they could in twenty minutes on the following question: "How do you get your job done from day to day with the help of, or in spite of, the formal organization, policies, and regulations of the Army?" At the end of the twenty-minute period, one group had accumulated one hundred and sixty-three suggestions, while the other group had offered one hundred and seventy. From a *quantitative* point of view, this was certainly a well-invested twenty minutes. The participants felt that they both stimulated and competed with one another. To cope with the *qualitative* problem, each group was asked for the remaining two hours and a half to evaluate each suggestion under three headings, "Essential," "Important but Not Essential," and "Helpful but Incidental." The group members felt that this had been a most profitable experience. They realized, of course, that brain-storming gave no final solutions but rather an armory of suggestions upon which they might reflect and which they might test in their day-to-day work. Any trainer can adapt this procedure to practically every problem, provided that he bears in mind that the stimulating aspect is the alpha and the reflective process the omega of the procedure.

Summary

The basic premise of this chapter has been that there is no excuse for a boring and tedious training session. The interested trainer has a repertoire of general instructional approaches at his disposal, including the lecture, lecture-discussion, case study, role-playing, discussion and conference procedures, and demonstration methods. The nature, advantages, and limitations of each approach were discussed, and suggestions for deriving the greatest benefit from each method were given. In addition to over-all methodological procedures, the trainer has available a group of techniques. Among these are panel discussions, resource people, committee reports, question box, debates, experimentation, problem-solving, and brain-storming. The trainer would be wise to bear in mind that any or all of these methods and techniques must be utilized within the frame of reference of the eleven conditioning factors that were discussed at the outset of the chapter.

THINGS TO DISCUSS AND TO DO

1. What do you think of the statement "No trainer should begin as many as three successive meetings in the same way." Give reasons for your position.
2. Take any topic you wish and outline how you would present it to a group of trainees by means of (1) the lecture method; (2) case study; (3) role-playing.

3. For each of the following groups: (1) airline reservation clerks, (2) data-processing programers, (3) management trainees, does it appear that one instructional approach might be better than the others? Give reasons for your opinion.

4. Develop an experiment or case study which you might use if you were conducting a training program for office supervisors.

5. Discuss the advantages and limitations of each of the so-called techniques discussed at the end of the chapter.

8. TRAINING AIDS—PUTTING THE SENSE ORGANS TO WORK

Purpose of the Chapter

THE TRAINER needs all the help he can secure. In this chapter the meaning and purpose of various mechanical aids to learning are considered. Criteria for selecting a given training aid are presented. Hints are given on the productive use of chalkboards, leaf-overs, overlays, films, slides, and projectors.

The Problem of Communication

A Japanese consul was giving a talk to the students of a midwestern university. During the question and answer period that followed his prepared address, he noticed that a student in the first row was busily taking notes. Wise to the pitfalls of diplomacy, he gestured to her to come to the platform at the end of the meeting. "Are you on the school newspaper?" he asked. "Oh, yes," the collegian replied, "and we are running a special article on your talk." "May I see your notes just to make sure that there is no mistake?" the consul continued. "By all means," the student replied, handing him her notes.

As he read the notes, the consul noted that one of the group had asked about the religion of his wife. The consul had answered that she was a Buddhist. The embryonic journalist, however, had written down, "His wife is a *nudist.*"

This anecdote illustrates the difficulty of communications for the trainer. Words are never enough. Even when carefully selected, they are open to misinterpretation. It is for this reason, that the Chinese have a proverb, "One picture is worth a thousand words"; and the Russians say, "He who has seen does not have to be told."

If the trainer is to make certain that what he says is understood exactly as he intended, he needs all the help he can get. In a series of training sessions, moreover, trainers are ever faced with the problem of securing sufficient variety in their presentation to guarantee a high level of trainee attention, interest, and understanding. Few are capable of doing so without the help of mechanical aids. On the other

190

hand, some trainers at times are inclined to utilize these aids merely to introduce a change of pace into their approach, forgetful that the primary purpose of any aid is to facilitate the learning process. For these reasons, some attention must be given to the nature of training aids, their place in the training process, the types available, and how to use them.

Meaning and Purpose of Training Aids

The term "mechanical aids" is really a misnomer. There is nothing mechanical about their role in the training process. A much more suitable and apt term is "training aids." By "training aid" is meant any device which, by appealing to one or another of the senses, singly or in combination, facilitates the training process.

The purpose of any training aid is always the same, namely, as a tool which makes it easier both for the trainer to present what is to be learned and for the trainee to master it with a maximum of effectiveness and a minimum of wasted time and effort. These ends training aids accomplish in the following ways:

1. They provide accurate, effective, and vivid images that insure correct perception of what is presented to the trainees.

2. They help provide a common basis for learning on the part of the trainees, which their own individual experience may not provide.

3. They allow for graphic presentation of material in terms of clarity and emphasis.

4. They help to provide for clear understanding, lasting retention, and easy recall of the subject matter.

5. They help to give trainees a common denominator of understood material, which contributes to intelligent discussion after their use.

6. They help simplify and explain complex ideas.

7. They show the sequence of a complicated series of operations, procedures, or ideas.

8. They clarify relationships of the total subject matter under discussion to the parts thereof.

9. They can substitute for actual equipment when such is not available or when it is impracticable to bring the equipment to the training room.

10. They tend to stimulate interest, to arouse and sustain attention, and to contribute to those positive attitudes that are an essential prerequisite for effective learning.

11. They give training a "reality emphasis" by focusing the trainees' attention on materials that they can see, handle, hear, and see in operation. Thus learning aids are calculated to give a sense of realism and practicality to the training process. They are based on the premise that real and direct experience, or the closest approximation thereto, is the best foundation on which to build comprehension and understanding.

Varieties of Learning Aids

The variety of learning aids that are available to the trainer is almost inexhaustible. Some of the more important are the following:
1. Blackboards, chalkboards, leaf-overs, and overlays
2. Motion-picture films
3. Filmstrips and slides
4. Projectors
5. Written materials: textbooks, manuals, pamphlets, mimeographed notes, training-session outlines, and so on
6. Training graphics: sketches, graphs, charts, pictures, cartoons, posters, diagrams, maps, etc.
7. Display boards and flannel boards
8. Cutaways
9. Models and mock-ups
10. Trainers and demonstrators
11. Tape recorders
12. Television

Criteria for Selecting a Given Training Aid

Since learning aids are tools to be utilized by the trainer for the attainment of a specific purpose rather than substitutes for trainer excellence or "gimmicks" for "jazzing up" a training session, it is important that the instructor be guided by certain clearly understood criteria in their selection. The trainer who ignores these criteria runs the risk of wasting the company's money, his own precious time, and the trainees' co-operative interest. What, then, are these criteria?
1. Is the training aid calculated to attain the specific objective of the training session by motivating trainee learning, arousing interest, holding attention, clarifying core ideas, and emphasizing important points while saving time and effort?
2. Is the use of this particular aid the best means for accomplishing this aim, or can it be better achieved by another procedure?

3. Will it really help the trainee to learn, or will it merely "expose" him to the training aid?

4. Can it be readily integrated into the over-all training session by giving an overview of the topic, practical illustrations of what is discussed, detailed analysis of procedural steps, case study, or review of the principal ideas? Or does it merely serve to provide entertainment, temporary relief from the hard work of the training meeting, or some other extraneous purpose?

5. Does it meet a real need on the part of both the trainer and the trainee?

6. Will it stimulate the trainees to think, and does it provide opportunities for the trainer to ask provocative questions?

7. Does it provide the groundwork for a follow-up discussion on the part of the trainees?

8. Does it help to deepen the trainees' insight into the matter under consideration? To sharpen their critical sense? To increase their ability to analyze and solve problems? To make their own applications? To obtain a more detailed, yet better-integrated, knowledge of the subject matter?

9. Does it stir the trainees to increased desire and ability to express themselves? Or does it make them more passive?

10. Does it add to trainee satisfaction with a particular training session and with the program as a whole?

11. Does it broaden their interests and give them a feeling of accomplishment?

12. Is it attractive? Color, movement, humor, and multiple sense appeal help bring out main ideas and important details.

13. Is it simple and easy to understand? Complicated posters, charts, graphs, etc., may defeat their purpose by making the trainee more confused than he was before.

14. Is the aid correct in all details? Training adis should be used to help the learning process; time should not be wasted apologizing for defects or correcting mistakes in them.

15. Is it up-to-date? Films especially can lose much of their impact if such details as styles of clothes, equipment, etc., hopelessly "date" them as being behind the times.

16. Is the aid geared to the intelligence, experience, vocabulary level, and social mores of the group?

17. Can the aid be seen clearly by everyone in the training group when it is in use?

18. Can the training aid be set up quickly and easily, so that it is ready for use and can be used when actually needed without wasting time and running the risk of losing the trainees' attention?

19. Can it be used with various groups and in different training situations, so that the company may get a fair return on the money expended in providing the aid?

20. Is the aid economical to purchase, borrow, or make and to use?

21. Is it easy to keep in good working order? Is it sturdy enough to stand up under normal, or perhaps abnormal, handling?

22. Can it be stored and taken out of storage easily and quickly?

23. Does the aid have a certain natural attraction, so that it arouses interest?

24. Does it allow the trainer opportunities to test the trainees' understanding of what the aid is trying to get across to them? For instance, does a film give a preliminary overview of the main points to be covered? A summary of the main ideas? Natural transitional points when the trainer may stop the film and have the group discuss either what has preceded or how it might handle a problem that has been presented?

25. Can the aid be tied into what has been previously learned, is now being learned, and will be learned at future training sessions?

26. Does the aid stick to one or at most a few principal ideas, or does it wander back and forth from point to point?

27. Does the aid emphasize what should be emphasized, while keeping subordinate what is of secondary importance?

28. Does it measure up to the sixty-four-dollar question, "Does it make it easier for the trainer to instruct and for the trainee to learn?"

GETTING THE MOST FROM TRAINING AIDS[1]

Blackboards and Chalkboards

Perhaps the most frequently used, and often the most abused, training aid is the common blackboard or chalkboard. From the cave writings of prehistoric man to the latest neon billboard, men have used some kind of writing boards or sign boards to get across more effectively what they were trying to communicate. If the true meaning of a word is the picture that it develops in the mind of the listener, then

---

[1] The authors have found some of the material in Lester B. Sands, *Audio-Visual Procedures in Teaching* (New York: Ronald Press Co., 1956) useful in preparing this chapter.

there will always be an important place for the blackboard in a training program. Familiarity, however, often breeds contempt. Many trainers are so familiar with the ever-present blackboard that they fail to realize that they often violate at least some of the following suggestions.

1. *Make Sure That Your Handwriting Is Legible.* Bear down on the chalk; it is not meant to be an experiment in subliminal stimulation. If you cannot write well, then print. Letters to be seen at a distance of thirty feet should be at least $2\frac{1}{2}$ inches high.

2. *Plan How You Will Use Your Space before You Begin to Write.* It is annoying and confusing for the trainee to have to jump from one end of the blackboard to the other because of your poor planning. Good planning of blackboard use will also minimize the need for erasing. When something is erased, there is always the risk that it may also be erased from the trainees' minds.

3. *After You Finish Writing, Get Out of the Way.* Every trainer makes a better door than a window. Pointers and yard-long rulers were invented largely because the trainees cannot see through you.

4. *Talk to the Class, Not to the Blackboard.* Trainees do not want to get things "on the rebound," as though it were a basketball game. Learn to write and speak at the same time, being sure at least to glance at the group frequently while doing so. Never write for any prolonged period, unless you want to lose the attention of the trainees.

5. *If You Have a Great Deal to Put on the Blackboard, Try to Do So before the Session Begins.* If you cannot do this, then use another method of presentation, perhaps a simple duplicating process.

6. *Ignore the Lower Half of the Blackboard.* Trainees at the rear of the room and in the corners probably cannot see it very well anyway.

7. *When You Have Satisfactorily Covered One Idea, Procedure, or Point, Clear the Blackboard Completely.* Do not risk having the trainees confuse new material with unerased scraps of old.

8. *Watch Out for Glare.* Sunlight and some forms of electric light can at times create a very disturbing glare.

9. *Make Certain that Diagrams, Drawings, and So On Are Accurate and Neat.* If you have little talent in this direction, use templates and stencils. If you have an opaque projector and wish to display a diagram, map, or other complicated visual aid on the board, simply project the reflected image of the diagram or picture on the board and then trace its image on the blackboard.

10. *If You Are Constantly Using Statistical Concepts, It May Help to Line One Section of the Board into a Grid.* This has one disadvantage, in that that section of the board is almost made useless for any other purpose.

11. *Use Color and Shading.* Color and shading not only allow you to emphasize major items by contrast but also have an attention-getting aspect to them.

12. *Never Let the Chalk "Screech."* This can be rather annoying to the trainees. If it does screech once, then hold the chalk at an acute angle with the board and in line with the direction of writing, and you will not repeat this mistake.

13. *Make Certain That Everything That Is Written on the Board Is Grammatically Correct.* Errors in spelling and mistakes in English detract from the effectiveness of what you are writing.

14. *Organize What Is Written for Its Total Effect.* Do not scrawl all over the board without recognizable plan or pattern.

Although a blackboard can be made to serve many uses, the most important are generally the following:

1. *Outline What Is to Be Covered in a Training Session.* Even a brief outline of the major topics to be covered or the main problems to be considered, especially if it is not possible to duplicate the session outline, can serve both to give the trainees an overview of the meeting and to know exactly how each part fits into the total plan.

2. *List Trainee Ideas, Suggestions, Questions, Points of View, Reasons for Taking a Given Position, or "Pros and Cons" Concerning a Particular Course of Action.* Seeing ideas spelled out on the board stimulates other trainees to participate, while keeping important previously made statements in the focus of their attention.

3. *Enumerate Steps in a Procedure, Process, or Operation.* This has an advantage over having the steps mimeographed, since the trainees see each step flow into the following step of the operation.

4. *Teach Technical Terms and Their Meaning.* When trainees see a technical term spelled out, they are much more likely not only to remember it but also to spell it correctly.

5. *Summarize Key Points in the Training Session.* This practice tends to give a feeling of completeness to what has been said over an hour or two-hour period.

6. *Sketch the Interior Parts of Equipment without Going to the Trouble of Taking It Apart.* This is particularly true if trainees are having difficulty in understanding a specific section or operation of the equipment.

7. *Build Up Gradually, Instead of Presenting the Entire Whole at Once, a Graph, Table, or Diagram, So that Trainees May Understand Just How the Completed Graphic Came About.*

8. *Give the Correct Solution to Problems Which Have Been Assigned Trainees.*

9. *Allow Trainees to Clarify Their Statements or Arguments.* At times such statements may not be clear to others who merely hear them. Writing them on the board facilitates understanding.

10. *List Review Questions, Assignments, References, Etc.* The trainer should never underestimate the importance or flexibility of the lowly blackboard in his desire to use some of the more sophisticated devices. The chalkboard is more naturally geared to instruction than many other devices. A blackboard can also easily be changed into a *magna-board* by merely affixing wire screening or a sheet of soft iron to it, and then painting it the appropriate color. Magnetized objects can then be moved about with little or no difficulty. Blackboards are also useful for drawings in series that illustrate, for instance, the evolution of a technical process. Covering all but the one drawing that is being considered and, as the discussion proceeds, revealing the rest give an interesting "strip-tease" effect. At any rate, the blackboard affords the trainer more possibilities, with less expense, than any other aid. The modern trend is to use the blackboard in conjunction with many of the other aids which are considered in this chapter.

Should the chalkboard be gray, black, or green? In most cases, for all practical purposes, it does not make much difference, despite what the manufacturers say. What is more important is to get the most use from your chalkboard space. Portable blackboards are sometimes useful, although they are generally too small. Sliding blackboards, in which one board slides behind another much like a storm window, and boards that can be lowered and lifted like curtains multiply the available board space without taking up an undue amount of space.

Chalk Talks, Leaf-Overs, and Overlays

An excellent method for emphasizing principal ideas and for holding the attention of trainees is to give a *chalk talk*. All that is needed for this technique is an easel to hold sheets of cardboard or large-sized papers, a pencil, charcoal or chalk, and material on which to write; the latter should be at least $2\frac{1}{2}$ feet by 20 inches. As each step in an operation or procedure is described or as each section of a diagram is discussed, the trainer draws a picture of it. For the talented this presents no problem. Those lacking in artistic ability can (1) have someone draw the sketches beforehand or (2) have someone draw in lightly what is to be drawn. The speaker then need only trace heavily over this outline. The trainer, as he builds up his lecture, may wish to paste each drawing on the blackboard so as to obtain a cumulative effect. This approach is especially forceful if cartoons or stick-figures are used.

A similar device involves the use of the *leaf-over*. A series of drawings is prepared beforehand. As the speaker develops his talk, he "leafs over" each drawing to illustrate graphically before the eyes of the group each point made.

When the trainer is trying to explain a complicated process or to make clear the workings or structure of a complex machine, it is helpful to use so-called *overlays*. Drawings are made on any suitable transparent material, each drawing illustrating one aspect of the process, operation, or structure. The drawings are arranged so that each adds an element to the one that preceded it. As the trainer speaks, he lays one on top of the other until the total process, operation, or structure is depicted. Thus, if one were interested in explaining the structure of the body to supervisors in a unit on human behavior or fatigue, the first drawing might be an outline of the human figure; the second might add the skeletal structure; the third, the nervous system; the fourth, the vital organs; the fifth, the endocrine glands; and so on. In this way, when the last overlay was in place, the entire human body structure would be clear. This device is also useful in such problems as the gradual building-up of the organizational framework of a company, the comparison of the formal and informal organization, showing the sequence of operations in an involved process, and the clarification of the interrelation of parts in a complicated machine.

Films

1. *Misconceptions Regarding Films.* One of the authors at one time was speaking to the manager of product engineering while a technical-training course for draftsmen and personnel from the model shop was in progress in an adjoining room. The conversation was interrupted by music from a sound film that was being used to illustrate certain principles of physics which are important for people in an aircraft instrumentation company. "Why do they waste company time on movies?" asked the manager. "We never used movies in engineering school."

This remark is indicative of one of the misconceptions of the use of films in industrial training. For some, films represent a waste of time or, at best, a means for sugar-coating the unpalatable pill of learning. Another misconception, sometimes unfortunately held by a few trainers, is that films are useful merely to "put life" into a training session or to give a change of pace, that films are almost a "reward" given to the trainees in return for their paying attention. Occasionally one finds a trainer who tends to look upon films as a surcease from the burden of training, during which he can relax. Finally, not a few people are inclined to think of a film as self-sufficient, almost capable of supplanting the trainer; this conclusion is drawn from the observed fact that now and then a trainer feels free to leave the room during the showing of a film.

2. *Values of Films.* These opinions of films are so erroneous that they require no refutation. Films, especially sound films, have a combination of action, dialogue, sound effects, and background music that absorbs attention, especially if the plot is clear-cut and the acting professional. Unconsciously, there is an emotional identification with the characters that few, if any, other learning aids can match. Since we learn perhaps more than 90 per cent of what we know through the sensory organs of hearing and sight, it is evident that the training values of films can hardly be underestimated.

Comments from trainees confirm these statements. "Some of the things don't register as well when you hear or read about them as when you see them." "While we were watching the film we weren't conscious that we were learning. This came out only in the discussion period that followed." "The whole thing became more realistic after the film. Before it was just a bunch of words." "I felt sorry for the poor supervisor [*The Inner Man Steps Out*] and wondered how I would handle his problems." "I thought conferences were a lot of baloney until I saw this film [*All We Need Is a Conference*]." "I never realized that there was so much to this company [after viewing a film describing the history and workings of a large firm]." Similar reactions can be expected from such films as *Personality Conflict, The Trouble with Women, The Department Manager, Grievance Hearing, Making That Sale, The Grapevine,* or any other films similar to these published by McGraw-Hill Text-Film Department and other distributors.

The results of research substantiate the personal reactions of trainees to films. Among these findings are the following: (1) films speed up training without loss of effectiveness; (2) films make training sessions more interesting and reduce absences; (3) the learning of factual matter is helped by films; (4) with respect to retention, the use of films is superior to the use of verbal material alone or to the unorganized use of other visual aids; (5) the perception of relationships is increased by motion pictures that show the interaction of cause and effect; (6) the ability to think is more marked in student groups that use films than in those that use only textbook matter; (7) students enjoy films and would like to see more of them, but they are highly critical of films in terms of their technical qualities; (8) films help modify beliefs in desirable directions.

3. Using Films Effectively.   If films are to be used with profit, six standard procedures should be followed as a matter of routine. These are (1) prepare yourself; (2) prepare the projection room; (3) prepare the trainees; (4) show the film; (5) summarize and apply the film; and (6) evaluate the film.

a) *Prepare Yourself.*   Certain preliminary steps to showing a film are about as obvious as they are frequently violated. Films should not be shown on the spur of the moment. When the training syllabus is formulated, the schedule of films should be an integral part of the over-all plan. Since it is desirable that the best film for each idea be selected, this may involve examining the catalogue of various distributors to discover several films that deal with the same topic. It is always necessary to preview any film that is to be shown. If there are several films that treat of the same subject matter, then this preview will not only enable the trainer to choose the best for his purposes but also familiarize him with its content and manner of presentation. Assuming that each film has been picked to drive home a given topic, the next step is to study whatever literature, such as a trainer's guide, test questions, and discussion topics, is provided with it. The trainer is then in a position to plan exactly how he will weave the film into his session as a whole.

Some attention must also be given to the mechanics of the film program. These include such matters as arranging to secure the films, either by purchase or loan, in sufficient time; arranging for an operator, a screen, and a machine in good working order; making certain that the operator knows the room in which the film is to be shown and the exact time of the viewing; making sure that he will have time to set up his projector before the start of the training session; making provision for the return of the film to the distributor or to storage, with the film rewound so that it is ready for use if needed again. Each of these factors should be reviewed lest any of them be neglected. Finally, the trainer should formulate the problems, questions, and discussion topics that he intends to bring up in the session either during or after the film showing, making certain that these items are related to the subject matter of the meeting as a whole. He should remember that he will be talking in at least semidarkness. Therefore, what he intends to say he should know "cold."

b) Prepare the Projection Room. It is clear that the film, operator, and projector should be on hand before the training session starts. Few things are more distracting than to have an operator threading film and running electric wires through the room during a training session. Assuming that the film has been inspected, that the operator has threaded it in the proper type of projector, and that the electrical outlet not only is of the right type but is also conveniently situated, it is wise to check the ventilation and temperature of the room, as well as the means for darkening the room during the showing. Most important of all, make certain that all trainees can see and hear the picture clearly and comfortably, so as to get a complete, rather than "cutoff," view of what is shown. Finally, be sure that the sound is properly adjusted in terms of level and clarity.

c) Prepare the Trainees. Too many films are shown without effectuating a psychological state of readiness on the part of the trainees. It is important that they know the exact reasons why they should pay attention to the picture, lest they consider it as a mere interesting interlude in the training process. They should be given a summary of the main points of the film to arouse their curiosity and interest. They should be told precisely what the trainer expects them to derive from the film. They should know why and how the film fits into the training session. It should be made clear to the trainees that they will be responsible for knowing what is discussed in the film and how their knowledge will be appraised.

d) *Show the Film.*   It is wise to remember that no film is an adequate substitute for the trainer. It is a tool to increase his effectiveness. Hence the trainer should not leave the room while a film is being viewed. On the contrary, the trainer should plan carefully what he will do during its presentation. He can observe the reactions of the group. He may wish to stop the film after an important point has been made and ask the trainees to discuss it. He may wish, especially if it is a silent film, to give a running commentary on what is depicted. He may make short comments just before important scenes are shown, to help focus the attention of the trainees on what he wants them to get out of the film. At any rate, during the showing the trainer is never a passive observer; he is active without interfering with the message that the film is trying to get across.

e) *Summarize and Apply the Film.*   There should always be a follow-up after a film has been shown. This may take the form of a general discussion, in order that the trainer may discover exactly what the trainees have learned or failed to learn. Such discussions help both the trainer and the trainees to filter out important and irrelevant ideas. They usually help the group to improve its ability at self-expression. A second approach is to have the trainees apply the ideas presented in the film to their own jobs, testing the extent to which they will work and under what conditions. If the trainer wishes, he may give the trainees a quiz on the picture. He may also have a list of key questions and problems to be presented to the trainees for their evaluation and consideration. The main points are (1) every film should be reviewed and summarized at its end, and (2) every film should lead to something beyond itself. If it does not, then it has failed, and the trainer has also failed.

It should be noted, in passing, that there is nothing sacred about showing a film but once. Few viewers ever extract all that a given film has to offer in one showing. In fact, some films can be shown as many as three times with profit to the viewers. The criteria for multiple showings are (1) the degree of interest on the part of the trainees and (2) how much additional knowledge results from each successive showing. In general, however, there would seem to be a certain loss of effectiveness if a good film is shown but once.

f) Evaluate the Film.   The showing of films always involves a considerable expenditure of time and effort. It is important, therefore, that every film be evaluated not only by the trainer (presumably this was done before selecting it for viewing) but also by the trainees. Questions that should be answered in such an evaluation, which can be done either by drawing up a simple check list or by group discussion, include at least the following: (1) Was the matter covered authentic and accurate, or was it warped by exaggeration, propaganda, and inaccuracies? (2) Was it valuable in terms of its applicability to the job situations of the trainees? (3) Did it hold their interest and attention? (4) What did they learn from it about their jobs that they did not know before? (5) Were the technical characteristics of the films—plot, acting, photography, dialogue, pace, and background music—satisfactory? (6) Would the trainees like to see it again, or would they recommend that it be shown to other similar groups? Answers to these and similar questions will serve as a "feed-back," informing the trainer as to whether or not the time spent on the film has been well invested.

4. *Miscellaneous Problems Concerning Films.*   The trainer should not be swept away by the usefulness of films without appreciating some of their genuine limitations.

a) Limitations of Films.   Films are not without their deficiencies. In the first place, they represent one of the most expensive types of learning aids. A twenty-minute film can rarely be purchased for less than approximately $125. Even if they are rented at a nominal sum, a good deal of time and effort must be expended on finding, previewing, securing, and returning them. Films also require a darkened room, an experienced operator, projection equipment, and the routine work involved in arranging for the showing. If free films are used, they may not be available when needed. A film that arrives the day after it is required might just as well not exist. On the other hand, to build up a complete film library often requires a budget of thousands of dollars, something that only the largest companies can afford.

One of the greatest limitations of films is that group participation is usually obtained only *after* the film has been shown. Moreover, since the film runs at a constant speed, it is not easy for trainees to take notes or for the trainer to emphasize a given point without stopping the machine. It is true that some projectors have a reverse switch which enables the operator to reshow a particular scene. This feature, however, is found only in the most modern and expensive models. Finally, although he can interrupt, the film tends to impose a certain degree of silence on the trainer.

b) Sound versus Silent Films.   There is no question but that the trend today is in the direction of sound and color films. This trend may not be an unmixed blessing. While color, dialogue, and background music certainly hold attention and interest, they increase the purchase and rental cost of the films. In addition, a slick "Hollywood" approach may at times cause trainees to miss the main points of the film. Sound pictures likewise almost preclude any commentary by the trainer. In evaluating the relative merits of sound and silent motion pictures, one should bear in mind the conclusion of extensive U.S. Navy investigations of the teaching value of films: ". . . where instruction is the principal aim . . . training films should present the subject matter in a simple straightforward way, and avoid the use of fancy film techniques."

c) Sources of Films.   The *Educational Film Guide* lists approximately 10,000 titles, with monthly supplements constantly adding to the list, and more than 700 producers and distributors. Even if most of these titles are of little interest to trainers in industry, the remainder is still too great for detailed consideration. It is sufficient to indicate some of the principal sources of films that can be either purchased, rented, or secured on a loan basis.

A. The Federal Government: Various agencies, ranging from the Air Force to the Veterans Administration, have films that can be obtained on a loan basis.

B. The State Government: Many state governments, such as New York, have films that can be borrowed.

C. Universities: Universities, such as Indiana, Pennsylvania State, Iowa, and New York University, distribute films on a rental basis.

D. Industry: Numerous companies, including General Electric, General Motors, United States Steel, Westinghouse, American Telephone and Telegraph, and many others, have produced their own films.

E. Commercial Distributors: McGraw-Hill, Coronet, Jam Handy, and so on, sell and distribute films on a rental basis for use in business and industry.

F. Professional Organizations: Organizations such as the National Association of Manufacturers and the Society for the Advancement of Management have films which are useful.

d) Sources of 16-Mm Sound Projectors. Some of the major manufacturers of sound projectors include Ampro Corporation, Bell and Howell, Eastman Kodak, Radio Corporation of America, Revere Camera, Keystone Camera, and Victor Animatograph Corporation.

e) How Long a Picture Should Be Shown. No one really knows. Most training films are relatively short, five to twenty minutes, in comparison with commercial films. The trainer must determine how much time in a given session he can profitably devote to a film and then select that film which best meets his needs within this time limit. Certainly, one should have good reason to spend as much as fifty-eight minutes (the running time of an excellent, sophisticated film on human relations) to a single film in a two-hour training meeting. Lengthy films are likely to take on the aspect of "the tail wagging the dog" in training. It well may be, however, that a longish picture that considers several interrelated aspects of a given area—supervisory development, for example—might be much more useful than a series of shorter films that "chop up" the topic into several unrelated segments.

Slides

One of the oldest and most popular type of training aids is the slide. The key to its popularity has been the ease of operation and the flexible uses to which slides can be put. Anyone with no more than five minutes' instruction can learn to operate a 2×2 slide projector. In addition, slides may be purchased from commercial distributors or made up by the trainer to meet the specific needs of a particular company or training situation. In terms of adaptability, a slide projector can be moved about with simplicity, since most can be carried under one arm; on the other hand, when the trainer employs slides to illustrate his points, he is in complete control of the situation. Unlike films or filmstrips, he can show the slides in any prearranged order he prefers. The trainer either can show half-a-dozen slides and analyze each thoroughly or can project a great number, in order to present a preliminary survey of the session topic or to summarize and review the session as a whole.

Slides have few, if any, real disadvantages. Care must be taken lest the slides be torn or smudged, but if they are coated and normal care is taken, this is a relatively remote eventuality. Cost may at times be a factor, since commercial slides have a purchase price of from $0.50

to $0.75 each. Hence, if a large slide library is built up, it may run into a fairly sizable sum. Few training situations, however, require any great number of slides. Balancing the few minor deficiencies of slides is the fact that so many of them can be stored in a small space, enabling the trainer to select the exact slides he wishes to use without wasting time.

Companies such as the Society for Visual Education, American Optical Company, Spindler & Sauppe, and Ampro Corporation produce manually operated, semiautomatic, and automatic slide-changer type projectors, thus making the trainer's task somewhat easier. Other companies, such as American Optical Company, produce projectors that can handle slides, filmstrips, and opaque projector materials as needed. This type of equipment has obvious advantages.

Opaque Projector

The opaque projector will simultaneously project and enlarge any desired object from the size of a postage stamp to a quarto page, so that everyone in the room can see it clearly and without distortion. Maps, charts, diagrams, pictures, drawings, photographs, outlines, directions, reports, and designs can all be displayed much more effectively than they can either by "waving them in front of the group" or passing them around among the trainees. This type of projector allows the trainer to show pictures from a book, sections of a corporation report, and so on, merely by slipping the entire work into the machine without resorting to tearing out pages or otherwise mutilating the volume or book as a whole. A variety of opaque projector which enables the trainer to face the group while demonstrating what he is trying to get across is called an "overhead projector." Practically the only real deficiency in the opaque projector is its size and bulk. The typical projector is not easily moved about and should be permanently fixed to a rolling stand designed for that purpose. Projectors such as those produced by Charles Beseler Company and American Optical Company have pointers which enable the trainer to indicate the precise part of what is displayed that he wishes the trainees to concentrate on. One limitation of the opaque projector is that it forces the instructor to stand in the dark in one place, thus running the risk of losing the attention of the trainees who may indulge in surreptitious "horseplay."

Summary

The meaning, purpose, and variety of training aids available to the trainer were examined. Twenty-eight criteria were given for selecting any of twelve mechanical aids to learning. The uses of and hints for attaining best results from chalkboards were analyzed. Misconceptions about films, their practical uses, methods for attaining maximum profit from them, special problems related to films, and sources of films were considered. The practical purposes of slides and projectors were also scrutinized.

THINGS TO DISCUSS AND TO DO

1. Collect as many catalogues of films and filmstrips as you can from the various professional, governmental, and commercial sources and collate them by area of interest and title.
2. Plan a training session, indicating just what visual aids you intend to use, why you will use them, what difficulties you anticipate in their use, and what benefits for the trainees you expect to produce.
3. Preview a few films, filmstrips, and slides and answer the following questions: (a) How accurate is the information presented? (b) How helpful is the learning aid? (c) What defects does it have?
4. Discuss the various mistakes that you have observed over the years with respect to trainer's and/or teacher's use of the blackboard.
5. Learn how to use a film projector, a filmstrip projector, and a slide projector.

9. TRAINING AIDS—FROM TAPES TO TELEVISION

Purpose of the Chapter

CHAPTER 7 PRESENTED some ideas on the nature, usefulness, and limitations of some of the most commonly used training aids, such as blackboards, chalkboards, leaf-overs, overlays, films, filmstrips, slides, and projectors, together with suggestions for utilizing them most effectively in training sessions. The present chapter completes this discussion of the role of learning aids. It considers briefly the utility to the trainer of the following: (1) magnetic tape and wire recordings; (2) display, magnetic, and flannel boards; (3) training graphics, such as pictures, graphs, and posters; (4) written materials, ranging from company manuals to mimeographed notes; (5) models, cutaways, and mock-ups; (6) trainers; (7) demonstrations; (8) laboratory experiences; (9) radio and television.

Magnetic Tape and Wire Recorders

The limits to the adaptability of the tape recorder and wire recorder in training are literally those imposed by the ingenuity of the trainer. Few learning aids are so flexible with respect to the variety of uses to which they can be put. Almost every sound can be reproduced, from routine orientation or holiday greetings from the president to heated, wrangling disputes in a conference or training session. The major uses to which the tape recorder can be put include at least the following:

1. Formal addresses of welcome to new employees, authoritative statements of company philosophy, policies, programs, history, product lines, plans, rules, standard procedures, benefits, and so on, are easily taped so as to be on hand when needed.

2. Prepared talks by various department heads that explain the work of the department and its place in the total corporate opera-

tion are also useful. Such recordings are particularly helpful in supervisory management trainee and middle-management development, especially if the department heads concerned may not be available on the precise day when the trainer may wish to have them participate. In addition, such tapes can be prepared with an accuracy and completeness that may be lacking if the pressure of circumstances compel the busy executive to give an "off-the-cuff" description of his department. Even if the executive prepares his talk well, however, it is often not geared optimally to the purposes of the training session. Taping the talk can serve the excellent purpose of the dovetailing the talk with the aims of the training session. In addition, tapes prevent such talks from degenerating into mere personal reminiscences. Even if a representative from the department is present at the training meeting, recordings can serve the excellent purpose of getting the sessions started, the departmental representative serving as a resource person to carry on the discussion and to answer the questions of the trainees.

3. At times, use is made of prudently edited excerpts of board, stockholder, or staff meetings, of conferences of managers at any level, of conferences of a department head with his front-line supervisors or of a foreman or office supervisor with his subordinates, in order to give trainees a feeling for how the organization actually works at the operating level from day to day. These recordings give a touch of reality to a training session that is difficult to achieve in any other way.

4. Trainee discussions, panels, reports, and even debates are often well worth preserving on tape. The advantage of listening to what one has said and what the group as a whole has stated helps trainees (1) to reflect more objectively on what has taken place in a training session; (2) to appreciate the quantity and quality of individual and group participation in the discussion; (3) to think more carefully about all the contributions made, rather than merely concentrating on one's own individual point of view; (4) to review the discussion as a whole, emphasizing the important points made therein; (5) to identify and clarify the major points at issue in order that a more orderly discussion may be had, something that is very difficult to do when different people present diverse points of view in rapid succession without bothering to think carefully on what others have contributed.

5. Actual conferences are at times recorded in order to teach

proper conference techniques. There are many reasons why conferences often fail, not the least important of which is the fact that those who take part often lack the necessary skills to participate intelligently, co-operatively, and effectively.

Tapes of actual meetings can serve to highlight such conference defects as failure to define essential terms clearly, begging the point at issue, illogical thinking, attempts to dominate the conference, insensitivity to the feelings of others, lack of tact in presenting an argument, sarcasm, getting off the beam, and generalizing from mere personal experience or, at best, beyond the evidence. They can also be used to identify such disruptive conference personalities as the monopolist who speaks unendingly; the mute who rarely, if ever, contributes; the rugged individualist who is always "agin the government"; the special pleader who wants to manipulate the conference for his own benefit rather than arrive at the best solution for all concerned; the sensitive soul who takes every contrary point of view as a personal insult; and the playboy who impedes the work of the other conferees by ill-timed wisecracks and feeble attempts at humor. In addition to evaluating the quantity and quality of conference participation, tape recordings can be very helpful in appraising the manner of participation. Clarity of ideas, choice of words, and suitability of vocabulary are all embarrassingly evident when transposed to tape.

6. Various kinds of interviews should, from time to time, be taped. One of the principal reasons why one is uncertain as to whether an interviewer has had ten years' experience or merely one year repeated nine times is that seldom, if ever, are on-the-job interviews evaluated. Interviewing, by its very nature, is a private process, and it is a rare interviewer who has either the time or the inclination to record and evaluate, under expert supervision, typical interviews which he has conducted. As a result, good and not so good techniques tend to be preserved under that sacred shibboleth "experience."

Recordings of actual interviews, therefore, can be extremely helpful to trainees. They permit the inexperienced to hear in action a master of the art of interviewing, noting what he says or omits. Saying, how he says it, how he times what he says—in short, trainees listen to a model in action. Subsequent discussion, particularly if the interviewer is present to answer questions, almost necessarily is lively and profitable. More clearly than any other technique, with the possible exception of the sound film, the recording of a trained interviewer in action can point out to trainees the procedures that are proper for the employment interview, the planned interview, the nondirective interview, the stress interview, the group interview, the exit interview, and the disciplinary interview.

7. It is obviously helpful to record practice interviews conducted by the trainees and other role-playing situations. If the most effective training is learning by doing, then the use of the recorder must be an integral part of the training program. Any experienced trainer knows how easy it is to secure from an interested trainee group numerous ideas as to how to handle a disciplinary problem, a grievance situation, the giving of orders and instructions, the handling of cliques and friction among employees, the giving of praise and blame, the explanation of a merit rating system, or the conduct of a wage review, interview, a counseling session, a clarification of company rules, and a host of other day-to-day problems faced by the supervisor. When trainees are called upon to role-play such situations in practice interviews, however, as often as not these fine theoretical ideas come out as a mix-mash of "er's," "ah's," and "if I were you" banalities. Taping these practice exercises allows both the individuals concerned and the group as a whole to evaluate performance on the basis of recorded evidence in an analytical manner not possible in any other way. A variation of this technique is to have two or three trainees handle a given problem—for instance, an interview with an employee who has been turned down for a raise. These interviews are taped. Then, after the group has listened to the tape and has made its own suggestions, a recording of an expert handling the same problem is played, in order that the members of the group can compare similarities and differences in the way in which the same difficulty is handled by the beginner and the expert.

8. From time to time, political speeches, talks by outstanding management and labor representatives, radio programs, meeting activities, and similar items, which may be very useful in some future training program, are taped. If the trainer is always on the alert for interesting and provocative addresses that can be incorporated into his training sessions, he will greatly minimize the possibility that they will become dull and flat.

9. One of the most important applications of the recorder is to tape the trainer in action. The trainer who merely assumes that he is excellent or is beguiled into thinking so by the favorable comments of his trainees, without ever taping at least some of his training sessions, is overlooking one of the most effective means for im-

proving his own performance. Listening to a playback of a training meeting can be an exhilarating, or somewhat discouraging, experience. At any rate, it is certain to help the trainer to discover his strong points and those deficiencies that require immediate remediation. Typical things that the trainer can look for are (1) the logical organization of his presentation; (2) change of pace; (3) pitch, resonance, volume, and variation of voice tone; (4) grammatical correctness; (5) sense of humor; (6) ability to answer questions clearly and to the point; (7) use of examples and illustrations; (8) ability to stimulate questions and discussions; (9) tendency to be monotonous, to carry on a monologue, to give a cut-and-dried "hack" talk, to be vulgar, to wisecrack his way through a meeting without accomplishing its objective, to get off the beam, to tell "off-color" jokes, and to be caught short for time because of poor planning.

10. Since the uses of the recorder are almost infinite, it is needful to indicate only a few of the miscellaneous additional ways in which it can be used. Tape recorders are very helpful in public speaking improvement; speech correction; dictation exercises for training in shorthand, especially if managers who dictate in different ways and at diverse speeds are used; in helping to induct and orient new employees by having them listen to older workers state "Why I Like Company X"; and for synchronized comments with the showing of slides, filmstrips, flat pictures, charts, graphs, and so on.

Using Magnetic Tape and Wire Recorders

It is assumed that any serious trainer will follow the five suggestions (pp. 200–203) which were given in Chapter 7 with reference to the presentation of films. These suggestions apply to all training aids and are (1) prepare yourself to present the aid; (2) prepare the necessary equipment so that it will work perfectly when you want it to work; (3) prepare the trainees; (4) use the training aid; (5) summarize and apply the training aid. As for the tape recorder, an elementary-school child can operate one efficiently. A basic familiarity with the various speeds, the mechanism for controlling the tone and volume, methods for erasing, splicing, and cleaning is essential and easily acquired. It is also helpful to know the different types of tapes, plastic base or paper, coated inside or outside, single, double, and multiple track. A portable recorder is not overly expensive and normally weighs less than forty pounds. Wire recorders have been almost entirely displaced by tapes because of certain defects in terms of quality of reproduction and ease of handling that need not be discussed in detail.

Display Boards and Flannel Boards

Two facts should prompt the trainer to think seriously about the possibilities of display, magnetic, and flannel boards. First, advertisers pour millions of dollars into various types of display boards. It can be safely assumed that they do not do so without sufficient reason. Second, some training rooms are rather dull and drab when compared with the inviting, stimulating, and aesthetically pleasing places they might become; even the best rarely make the most of the available facilities.

Display boards range from the fixed bulletin-board type to portable ones on rollers or tripods, suspended boards that can be raised out of the way of blackboards when not in use, sliding boards that can be moved out of the way when not needed, and combination bulletin boards with pinning material on one side and a blackboard, projection screen, or flannel board on the other. Commercial boards are relatively expensive; simpler ones can be made from any material that will take tacks, pins, or adhesives, including cork, celotex, soft wood, linoleum, composition board, cardboard, and so on.

Magnetic or magna-boards enable the trainer to make either two- or three-dimensional demonstrations with small objects on a vertical surface. Essentially, they consist of a sheet of soft iron or wire screening, painted any desired color, to which objects made of cardboard, balsa wood, or metal are affixed by means of small magnets. A spot of glue is usually enough to hold the magnet fast to the object.

Flannel boards, like magna-boards, are easily made or are readily purchased from commercial firms. Any stiff backing material which is covered with flannel, usually black for purposes of contrast, can serve as a board of this type. Objects with a backing that will adhere to flannel, such as rough paper, sandpaper, felt, suede, or flocking, are placed on the board and cling there.

Display, magnetic, and flannel boards should illustrate the following principles:

1. *Principle of Center of Interest.* What is displayed should illustrate one central idea which serves to attain one definite purpose. This idea may be safety on stairways, an organization chart, a flow chart, a job description, a promotion chart, or any other suitable idea.

2. *Principle of Unity and Simplicity.* A single, cumulative impression is desired by means of a simplicity of design that makes all elements in the display contribute to the attainment of its basic purpose. Crowding the board with a hodgepodge of unrelated materials or failure to organize coherently the elements in the display serves only to lessen its impact on the trainees.

3. *Principle of Balance.* Clarity, realism, and symmetry should be attained by the combination of variety, contrast, and complementary relations of colors, lines, and figures, none being allowed to dominate the display, while none is superfluous in the attainment of its objective.

4. *Principle of Communication.* Headlines, legends, and type or lettering styles should be "eye-catching." Attention-getting qualities of color and contrasting lettering should be capitalized on. Care should also be taken with the form of expression: rhetorical questions, plays on words, puns, extremely positive statements, odd comments, unexpected titles, and challenging remarks can all be used with great effectiveness.

Using Display, Magnetic, and Flannel Boards

Any kind of illustration that will adhere to, or can be pinned to, a display board can help the trainer get across the point he wishes to make. Diagrams of processes, sequence of operations, clippings, pie charts, and drawings may be placed on the display board to illustrate what the trainer is saying. Vividness and vitality can be added to the trainer's presentation if major ideas are highlighted on a display board. For instance, the magnetic and flannel boards are extremely useful in comparing different types of layouts that are possible in the same office or machine shop and for picturing diverse ways in which functions can be assigned under various kinds of organizational patterns. Such boards can also be used to give trainees an overview of what the trainer is going to discuss or, better, to illustrate each idea as the trainer discusses it and to summarize what has been said.

Training Graphics

Training graphics include such learning aids as maps, charts, tables, diagrams, figures, graphs, pictures, cartoons, and posters.

Maps can be used to show the location of company plants, warehouses, major offices, and areas of concentration of sales. Electric maps, whose points of interest are illuminated with tiny lights, can be utilized in sales training, as well as in following a complicated operational process. For instance, the route of an order can easily be traced from the time it arrives at an office until the material is shipped to the customer. The steps in a grievance procedure can also be illustrated in a similar manner.

A chart is a type of record showing tabulated information, relationships, or a sequence of operations. For instance, an organizational chart reveals the formal relationships among executives, the main line of communication, the downward flow of authority, and the upward flow of responsibility. A flow chart depicts the sequence of operations or processes, as might be found in an automotive assembly line or the processing of petroleum. Charts are excellent for illustrating manufacturing processes of all types.

Diagrams are line drawings that are used to illustrate such things as a wiring system, the relationships of stationary parts, and the interaction of moving parts in a motor or machine. Blueprints are an obvious example of line drawings. Diagrams are an almost indispensable training device.

There are two major means for presenting statistical data. The first is the table, which is an array of numbers organized for purposes of clarity and easy comprehension. The second method involves the use of a graph, which is a picture of statistical information. Graphs are usually of the following types: (1) *pictorial* or symbol graphs, which communicate complex ideas in simple pictures—for instance, a man for each salesman in the field or a man for each $100,000 sales or a building for each warehouse; (2) *bar* graphs, that represent data in terms of columns or horizontal bars; such graphs may be crosshatched to indicate various proportions of the total number represented by the graph, as when a salesman's total volume is broken down according to the dollar volume of each product sold; (3) *circular* or *pie* graphs, often used to demonstrate how each company dollar is expended, a different-sized wedge being utilized to represent materials, labor, taxes, and other costs; (4) *line* graphs, that can be used to plot trend lines, frequency, polygons, and similar statistical data. It is obvious that graphs serve the excellent purpose of picturing dramatically what might otherwise be deadly-dull statistical information.

Pictures, posters, and cartoons are obviously devices which serve to illustrate, highlight, or dramatize some idea, operation, or process. It would be difficult to imagine how a trainer could for any length of time get along without pictures of some sort or other. They catch the attention, afford a change of pace, and allow the trainer to emphasize salient points. Pictures of offices, machinery, layouts, and equipment give trainees some feeling of realism, although the two-dimensional nature of such items limits their effectiveness. Posters, of course, are much more informal than pictures. They are inexpensive, have an impact on those who see them, and often make an important point with more than a little humor. Anyone who is familiar with the "Sad Sack" cartoons of World War II or with the safety posters that are omnipresent in every factory is well aware of the advantages of posters. In using them, however, one should be careful lest the humor or informality take precedence over the "message" or lesson, with the result that people read them but miss the point.

Written Materials

The range of written materials in this age of the tyranny of the printed word is almost endless. Since this is so, it is necessary only to indicate some of the typical resources available to the trainer, pointing out certain suggestions for their use.

1. Textbooks, Magazines, Pamphlets, and Monographs. Several years ago Adler wrote a "best-seller" on how to read a book that concerned itself largely with hints which nearly every adult should have learned before leaving high school. No trainer, therefore, should take it for granted that the trainees have mastered techniques of reading effectively. Textbooks are, or at least should be, organized syntheses of information, experience, and research. It is hardly sufficient for the trainer to say, "Read the next chapter" or "Study chapter 13 for the next session." Any book begins as a skeleton of ideas on which the author places the flesh and tissue of language. The reader's task is to reverse the process, X-raying through the verbal clothing so as to gain insight into the pattern of thought with which the author began. The trainer would be incredibly naïve to assume that trainees, even college-graduate trainees, can do this without some assistance.

The trainer should explain to his group the frame of reference and background of the author; his philosophy, if any; his pet prejudices; and his tendency to overstate or understate his case. In addition, trainees ought to be made aware of the author's pattern of organization, peculiarities of style, vocabulary level, and method of presenting his ideas. The trainer might well give some thought to helping the trainees to use intelligently both the Table of Contents and the Index, to search out topic and summary sentences, to learn how to skim, to read both for the main idea and for specific details.

It is necessary, if trainees are to derive the maximum of profit from their reading, to give them a preview of what they are expected to read, pointing out the principal ideas, the major points at issue, the difficulties they are likely to encounter in understanding the text, and especially why the trainer expects them to read it well. The reason for this is that any text has failed to serve its full purpose if, in addition to providing information, it does not challenge the trainee to think more deeply and carefully about the subject matter or fails to stimulate discussion when the trainees meet. Books that are little more than a compilation of drill exercises (like most college mathematics texts), a rehash of facts, or manuals of rules of thumb have little or no place in most training programs.

What has been said of textbooks applies to journal articles and pamphlets as well. Journal articles are often useful because they consider one idea in a direct and simple manner; they also have an attractive touch of up-to-dateness. Pamphlets, many of which are free or inexpensively purchased from governmental and professional organizations, have the advantage of being brief, simple, and expendable. They can be carried in one's pocket and read at one's leisure.

2. *Company-Wide Publications.* Most companies have a wide variety of organizational reading matter. Annual reports, policy manuals, employee handbooks, rulebooks, house organs, booklets on insurance, hospitalization, and pension benefits, copies of labor contracts, publicity releases, promotional materials, announcements, memos, and training syllabi all come under this category. Manning tables, promotion tables, and wage and salary structure descriptions may be similarly classified.

3. *Forms.* Trainees can often profit greatly from an analysis of the various forms used within a company. These may include such items as application forms, merit rating forms, interview forms, order and sales forms, complaint forms, and various types of requisition forms.

4. *Reports.* In every company there are numerous reports that must be routinely made. Budgetary, production, progress, grievance, accident, lateness, absence, sales, service, equipment breakdown, medical, and maintenance reports are in this group.

5. Records. Every department keeps records of its activities. At times acquaintance with these records helps familiarize trainees with the day-to-day operations, particularly if the purpose and uses to which such records are put are explained.

6. Blanks. Such items as questionnaire blanks, morale or job satisfaction devices, rating scales, and suggestion blanks usually have an intrinsic interest for trainees and can be used as a subtle form of public relations in convincing them that the company is interested in their welfare.

7. Duplicated Materials. Reprints of pertinent articles from such journals as *Nation's Business* and *Fortune* are obtainable very inexpensively. A file of such reprints can be of inestimable value to the trainer; it has a distinct advantage over telling the trainees to "look up such-and-such an article," a searching process in which few, if any, trainees engage. Such machines as the spirit duplicator, mimeograph machine, and the Thermofax or Verofax make it simple for the trainer to prepare outlines, cases for discussion, and similar reading matter at little cost.

Models, Mock-Ups, and Cutaways

Models are very effective learning aids not only because they appeal to the sense of sight, and sometimes those of touch and sound as well, but also because they capitalize on a universal interest in "seeing how it works." From six to sixty, people are fascinated by models, which reduce a cracking plant, railroad system, or jet airliner to a table top. Models are generally of three types: (1) the exact model or replica; (2) the reduced-scale model; (3) the blown-up model. The parts of the model may be exact duplicates of the sections of the operational equipment or merely approximations. They may be stationary, or they may move. Moving parts both catch the attention of trainees and facilitate learning by giving a clearer understanding of how the equipment operates. Moving parts also add an element of realism to the model.

A mock-up is a realistic model built to actual size and shape, or as nearly so as possible, but in which those details not necessary for training purposes have been omitted. Whereas the scale model stresses detail and design, the mock-up illustrates the actual size and shape of the object under consideration. Thus a mock-up of a combat information center on an aircraft carrier might be used to train Combat Information Officers and Fighter Directors.

One of the difficulties that automobile manufacturers face in trying to persuade the public that their particular motors are superior to those of competitors is the fact that when one looks at a motor, it is impossible, without a high degree of imagination coupled with antecedent knowledge of the motor, to secure a three-dimensional view of the motor. Cutaways are a means for surmounting this obstacle. In a cutaway, as the name implies, sections are removed, to make it possible for trainees to see the actual operation of the machine or object. Cutaways can be made of nearly everything. A factory can be described by removing floor after floor from the cutaway, in order that the work of the total plant may be visualized. An assembly-line process may be illustrated by removing walls or floors in the cutaway as each production step is completed. On the other hand, "built-up" cutaways can be used to explain a complicated operation or object by adding element to element until the unit is completed. Although cutaways are normally used to "see the insides" of an engine or other form of mechanical equipment, it is possible to make them for the ear, an office, or practically anything else.

Using Models, Mock-Ups, and Cutaways Effectively

In order that the trainer may make the most of the natural interest that models, mock-ups, and cutaways have for trainees, the following suggestions are offered.

1. The model, mock-up, or cutaway should be used only to serve a definite purpose in the training session. They should not be used to impress trainees or merely to arouse attention or interest or to act as the "whipped cream on the cake."

2. Trainees must know precisely why the model, mock-up, or cutaway is being used.

3. Whenever possible, trainees should be permitted to handle, take apart, and operate the model, mock-up, or cutaway.

4. If possible, it is better for trainees to build the models, mock-ups, and cutaways. In industry, however, this is not often feasible.

5. All parts of the model, mock-up, or cutaway should be clearly marked.

6. The model, mock-up, or cutaway should be as close to the original equipment as possible and must clarify the function that this equipment serves.

7. Sufficient time should be allowed in the training session for all

the trainees to see, handle, operate, and discuss the model, mock-up, or cutaway.

8. The trainer must be sure that he explains clearly and precisely the model, mock-up, or cutaway as he or the trainees use it.

9. The trainees' knowledge of what the model, mock-up, or cutaway represents should be tested and obscure points clarified.

10. The model, mock-up, or cutaway should meet the criteria presented on page 192 of Chapter 7, which it might be wise to review at this time.

Trainers

Anyone who is familiar with the Link Trainer realizes that any mechanical trainer is intended to serve the purpose of teaching trainees the actual operation of an instrument or equipment by duplicating it as exactly as possible. Trainers have certain advantages, not the least of which are (1) they eliminate the necessity of bringing into the training room equipment that can better be used in production; (2) they substitute for equipment that it would be impossible to bring into the training room—one can hardly imagine a heavy crane in a training room; (3) they are inexpensive when compared with the cost of actual equipment; (4) since they are built for training purposes, they can be manipulated so as to reproduce all operating conditions (many a pilot, destroyer officer, crane operator, or automobile driver has been rather taken aback by the words of an instructor, "You are now dead," when they failed to do what the situation demanded); (5) trainers come about as close to actual conditions as is possible. On the other hand, a trainer must justify its existence by doing the job it is meant to do better than any other available aid. It takes a certain amount of time and effort to make a trainer. If approximately the same results can be obtained by utilizing a simpler training device, it is silly to waste this time and energy.

Demonstrations

For years it was assumed that the best way to master scientific knowledge was by means of laboratory experiences. This assumption, which probably arose via an overextension of the principle of "learning by doing" and the circumscribing of the word "doing" to physical activity, has not always been upheld by the data of research. Good as laboratory work is, it has been shown that students can often learn as much or more from a lecture-demonstration procedure. This is a reassuring finding, since even a simple laboratory requires considerable equipment, expense, and space. Learning in a laboratory, moreover, is a slow method of learning, despite its acknowledged merits. On the other hand, demonstrations are a means of communicating to an entire group at one time.

A demonstration is a public performance in a sense that is matched by few other uses of training aids. As such, the trainer would be wise to follow the hints given by Fryer, Feinberg, and Zalkind:[1]

1. The demonstration should be kept simple. The trainee should not be confused with detailed and unnecessary refinements. As an aid in simplification, the instructor might put the key points on a blackboard or chart.

2. The aid should be placed where every trainee can see the demonstration. A desirable procedure, frequently followed, is to have the trainees gather around the aid.

3. Digressions from the main points of the demonstration should be avoided. The instructor should follow his prepared outline. If a trainee asks a question that is not pertinent, an answer should be postponed, with an explanation that it will be provided at a more appropriate moment.

4. The pace of the demonstration should be at the level of the trainees' ability to comprehend. Continually checking for signs of inattention, lack of understanding, disagreement, or confusion is necessary to determine the pace that the instructor should follow.

5. Constant summarizing of the various points will serve to clarify and give the trainees time to note the important points. At the end of the demonstration, the major points should be restated. This will result in useful discussion, and it will help to weld the demonstration into a meaningful organization.

6. Following the demonstration, an informal examination of an objective nature, i.e., true-false, completion, multiple-choice, or matching items, may be given. The results of a test will help identify the points that were not understood. These may then be reviewed in further demonstration.

All that need be added to these suggestions is to remind the trainer of five things: (1) he should be very careful of his time allotment (unless he does so, he may be "caught short" before completing the demonstration in all details); (2) he may at times find it more useful

---

[1] D. H. Fryer, M. R. Feinberg, and S. S. Zalkind, *Developing People in Industry* (New York: Harper & Bros., 1956), pp. 118–19.

to have trainees give the demonstration; (3) he would be wise to make absolutely certain that everything needed for the demonstration is on hand and arranged in the proper sequence of use (running back and forth only distracts the trainees); (4) the trainees must know the exact purpose that the demonstration is to serve (if they are at all hazy about this, the demonstration is largely a waste of time and becomes more or less a process of mumbo jumbo); (5) finally, the trainer must master the art of speaking while manipulating his materials, something that is more difficult than might at first seem evident.

Fryer, Feinberg, and Zalkind[2] also present a check-out for demonstrations in the form of ten questions:

1. Was the purpose of the demonstration clear?

2. Were the materials and equipment carefully selected, prepared, and arranged for presentation?

3. Were the generalizations and principles emphasized?

4. Was the speed of presentation too fast or too slow?

5. Were new technical terms introduced with a definition and written on the blackboard?

6. Was the trainee's reaction observed for cues as to the progress of learning?

7. Were questions permitted and answered to clarify understanding?

8. Was the demonstration tied in to previous learning?

9. Was the demonstration pointed toward future work?

10. Were the materials and equipment stored so as to be ready for future use?

Laboratory Experiences

Laboratory experiences and demonstrations are not antithetical but complementary. The former is essential for teaching basic techniques and skills, for emphasizing learning by doing, and for "learning on one's own" by means of individual experimentation and manipulation. In fact, it is rare that laboratory exercises are indulged in, except in conjunction with some type of demonstration. Although the term "laboratory experiences" seems rather far-fetched for industrial situations, such is hardly the case, even if it be granted that business applications are limited. The truck driver in a safety pro-

---

[2] *Ibid.*, p. 119.

gram, the apprentice machinist, the typist, and middle-management personnel participating in a junior executive board or multiple management setup are actually having experiences that may be termed "laboratory," if one extends the meaning of the term beyond the confines of the four walls of a room designated as "the laboratory."

As to laboratory experiences in the narrow sense, most of what was said under the section dealing with demonstrations applies with equal force. In addition, the trainer might keep in mind certain other precautions. If laboratory work is to amount to more than high-class doodling and busy work, trainees should be well prepared in terms of ideas, purposes, and information relative to the laboratory exercises. In many instances it is extremely important that the rules for safety be observed to the letter. Cutting tools, machines in operation, and chemicals can cause serious injury. In a laboratory there is sometimes a tendency to "skylark" or to give vent to a rather distorted sense of humor in terms of practical jokes; discipline, while never needlessly harsh, should be firm with respect to such matters, It is important, too, to take care of the equipment. This implies that the equipment is inspected before use to insure its proper functioning when needed, that there is a set available for each trainee, that parts and tools are inventoried, that they are laid out and ready for use without any wasted time and are properly stored until again needed, that sufficient time is allowed toward the end of the session to "clean up," and that a sufficient supply of spare parts are kept against unforeseen emergencies.

The second set of suggestions has to do with the trainer-trainee relationship in the laboratory. The task of the trainer is (1) to give the trainees an expert demonstration as a model of what they are expected to do and how to do it; (2) to observe each trainee carefully, especially at the outset, in order to correct errors and inefficient work habits; (3) to supervise the trainee at work without getting in his way or taking over; (4) to be patient with the trainee until he gets the knack of it, encouraging him while at the same time holding him to high standards; (5) to make certain that each trainee is at work the entire session time; (6) to help the trainee minimize the amount of trial-and-error learning that he does and accelerate the development of insight into the why, the what, and the best way of attaining the skill in question; (7) to help the trainee analyze his own movements, in order to develop a rhythm that is conducive to efficiency with lessened fatigue; (8) to help the trainee keep a record of his own progress; (9) to provide opportunities for less effective trainees to observe those who are more competent and periodically to have group discussions of the various aspects of the skill involved and common difficulties in acquiring it; (10) to test and to assign supplementary readings, in order to increase the trainees' comprehension of what they are doing.

Radio and Television

Although it is not likely that many companies will go in for closed-circuit television in the near future, there are three other ways in which radio and television can be utilized. First, trainees may be asked to listen to or view selected programs which are calculated to improve their technical skills or help them as individuals. Second, they may be asked to enroll in local educational television courses, such as "Sunrise Semester" produced for the Columbia Broadcasting System by New York University. Finally, radio programs may be recorded, and kinescopes of selected TV programs may be secured from the appropriate sources for use in a specific training program. Certainly, educational television is going to increase in importance in the coming years, and industry would be foolhardy not to make the most of its potentialities.

Summary

Chapters 7 and 8 have sought to provide the trainer and would-be trainer with an armory of learning aids to make his work more effective. Few trainers—or college instructors, for that matter—make full use of the tape recorder, which can be used to preserve formal talks and to evaluate individual and group effectiveness. Since most of what is learned reaches the intellect via the sense of sight, display, magnetic, and flannel boards serve to highlight important points in a training session. Training graphics, such as maps, charts, diagrams, tables, graphs, pictures, posters, and cartoons, also add vitality to training sessions because of their attention-getting qualities. Written materials in the form of textbooks, magazines, pamphlets, company publications, forms, reports, records, blanks, and various types of duplicated materials can not only lessen the trainer's work load but also increase the efficiency of the training sessions. They possess a characteristic of interest that is very useful. Models, mock-ups, and cutaways can often come to the rescue of the trainer in trying to "get across" a complicated idea or process, not only because they dramatize what he is trying to teach but also because they have a persuasive reality to them. Mechanical trainers can at times be used instead of the actual equipment, with a saving in time, energy, and money. Demonstrations allow the trainer to teach an entire group simultaneously. They are interest-arousers and attention-holders. Laboratory experiences serve the excellent purpose of putting the responsibility for learning where it belongs—on the shoulders of the trainee. Finally, few companies utilize the resources of educational radio and television to any great degree. In an age in which these media are bound to grow in importance from a training point of view, it behooves the trainer to make every possible use of what they have to offer.

THINGS TO DISCUSS AND TO DO

1. Secure a tape recorder and use it for one of the following purposes: (1) to record dictation given by three executives or supervisors, who dictate at different speeds and with different semantic or vocal mannerisms; (2) to record a conference; (3) to record a training session; (4) to record a practice interview. After you have listened to the tape, note how much more you derived from this procedure than you did as the dictation, conference, training session, or interview took place.

2. List as many uses for display boards of various types as you can. What are the advantages and disadvantages of each type? Study several catalogues of commercial producers of such equipment, to discover the variety available to the trainer.

3. Put on a demonstration, or have someone do this, before a group. Then evaluate your own performance and have the group evaluate it. What things that you thought you did well, did the group consider well done? What defects did you observe in your own performance? What deficiencies did the group observe?

4. Make up, or have a group formulate, a check list of specific items to evaluate the effective use of learning aids.

5. Make a study of the local area to discover the possibilities of using educational radio and television for training purposes. What programs are available? How can your company utilize each of these programs?

Unit III

THE ORGANIZATION AND ADMINISTRATION OF TRAINING PROGRAMS

10. THE ORGANIZATIONAL STRUCTURE—HELP OR HINDRANCE TO TRAINING

Purpose of the Chapter

THIS CHAPTER attempts to define the relationship of the training function to the rest of the organization structure. Any function of a business has to be based on sound principles of management and it is necessary to consider the training of employees in the same manner that all other business activities are considered. Since proper planning and organization precede successful accomplishment of goals, this chapter makes the plea for careful evaluation of training goals before undertaking a program. It is widely recognized that the adequate training of employees is a definite responsibility of the management of any company regardless of its size. There are certain practical considerations related to company size, however, and this chapter attempts to explain them. A number of actual experiences are offered to highlight the ideas presented in the hope that they will serve to demonstrate the usefulness of following good management principles for the accomplishment of training goals.

Any business activity that is to have more than chance success must be based on sound principles. This is especially true of training, since it is a function that has company-wide implications and affects both short- and long-term operations. An important management consideration is the fact that the same principles that apply to the administration of such business functions as finance, production, and marketing also apply to the training function. Even though there is general agreement among businessmen that the training of both old and new employees is among the many responsibilities of company management, there is no general agreement on the concept that such training should be an integral part of over-all company planning just as much as is any other vital phase of company operation. Haphazard training interspersed with an occasional formal program is not the way to accomplish fruitful results. In fact, many companies do not carry on any kind of formal training at all. In many instances, training is looked upon as something that takes care of itself because employees seem to know their jobs and the work gets done. The fact that most jobs are learned by trial and error with little or no system or attendant control and that the time taken to accomplish a reasonable skill level is much too long is one of the prime waste factors in American business. It is precisely this kind of situation that demonstrates the need for sound organization of the training function and a recognition of industrial training as an important activity that requires as much attention as any other major business activity.

RESPONSIBILITY FOR TRAINING

Attempting to fix the responsibility for training in any company is not a simple matter. Management literature is replete with statements and philosophies related to responsibility in the business organization. Many authors state principles of organization and management that have as their foundation the fixing of responsibility and the need for this. Unfortunately, in practice, something seems to happen to the good intentions about responsibility expressed in the management texts.

Is Training a Line Responsibility?

There is general agreement that training is a line responsibility. If we accept this premise—and it is a logical acceptance—then what happens to this approach to the fixing of training responsibility in practice? Some line supervisors and managers jealously guard their prerogatives and have no desire to relinquish responsibility unless it suits their convenience. In the case of training, however, it frequently suits their convenience. The most common excuse is that they do not have enough time to train any single employee. They claim that they must devote their energies to the whole job of supervision and cannot give special attention to any one individual. The unfortunate fact is that training is part of the whole job of supervision and that all employees need training on a continuous basis. The attitude of many supervisors is based on the notion that training is a one-shot proposition and that, once completed, the employee can be left on his own.

In many instances, no attempt is made to follow up on the amount of knowledge absorption or the skill level achieved.

Time for Training

The "lack-of-time" excuse is most commonly used by those who are on the first-line level of supervision. Their claim, which is often justifiable, is that their time is utilized by the work they have to perform and that consequently they have little left for the role of supervisor. Many of these supervisors have learned their jobs through the absorption trial-and-error method and have been promoted to a supervisory position because they have demonstrated an above-average ability for work performance. Since they can perform the work portion of the jobs they supervise quite effectively, they expect everyone under their jurisdiction to do likewise. Unfortunately, experience tells us that this is not often the case, and the failure on the part of the supervisor to recognize individual differences, human failings, various levels of motivation, and different goal perception results in a neglect to develop people effectively for job accomplishment. Another dominant characteristic of this type of supervisor is the simple fact that he does not know how to train people. There is an understandable reluctance on the part of an individual who learned his job the hard way to impart any information to a trainee that may enable him to reach a reasonable skill level in a shorter period of time than was taken by the supervisor to learn the same job.

Need for Specialists

Coincidental with this attitude is the lack of understanding of a logical approach to the teaching of a novice. Doing a job effectively and teaching a job effectively require quite different skills and aptitudes. It is becoming increasingly apparent in industry that successful training requires the efforts of specialists. If individuals are to be developed to their full potential and their skills utilized to an optimum degree, then something more than the usual observation-absorption method of training must take place. Regardless of the size of the company, training has to be accomplished. Even if no money is allocated for the training of new, transferred, or upgraded employees, money is being spent. In a company where little or no attention is paid to the formal training of employees, training must still take place. It is usually accomplished by the afore-mentioned trial-and-error absorption method. Typically, the mechanics of a job are shown to the novice by the experienced employee when he has some spare time to fill. A new employee may be broken in reluctantly because the training has to be finished as rapidly as possible so that the new employee can be left alone and the more experienced employee can get back to his job. When the new employee is trained in this manner, he learns the job in bits and pieces, and it may take him quite long to see the job as a whole and how the job fits into the organization structure. Worst of all, he is made to feel like a fifth wheel, and the atmosphere he lives in is one of fear and frustration. The fixing of responsibility for accomplishment is difficult, and the burden is usually on the novice. In some instances it results in an attitude of despair. Certainly, no loyalty to the company is built, and quite frequently the new employee leaves as soon as he feels he has enough marketable experience. In essence, the greater cost is borne by the company, with little or no return on the time investment in the new employee.

Responsibility Determination

The fixing of responsibility for training can be accomplished by management edict. The assumption of responsibility by the parties to whom the responsibility has been delegated is another matter. In general, training is considered a staff activity, usually under the jurisdiction of the personnel department. If the training division has no part in the choice of participants in any given program, then it is difficult to hold them responsible for the results. Over the years there has been a constant search for some sure-fire method to handle personal relationships in business organizations. Many techniques and ideas have been tried to bring about good relationships between people concerned with planning and people concerned with doing in the industrial concern. In the case of training we are still in the embryonic stages of development. This is partly due to the fact that formal training programs have been used on a wide basis only for a relatively short time. Most of the emphasis on training programs has developed since the end of World War II. Concurrent with this development of industrial training is the more incisive study of the role of a manager in the business organization. Many companies have found that if a man is to be a successful manager, he must be allowed to manage. This might sound like a paradox, but it is quite true that in many business organizations any given manager on any given level may be quite restricted in the scope of his authority. In some larger companies there are so many levels of supervision that the first-line level may be just a fiction on the organization chart and the person who holds the title of foreman or section head has little to do except to act as a policeman and keep records. If we accept the frequently expressed dictum that managers should be responsible for performance and results, then certainly we must include training and development as part of the responsibility for performance and results.

LINE-STAFF RELATIONSHIPS

Perhaps the traditional line-staff dilemma in the area of training can find a partial solution in an analysis of the line manager's role. While it is difficult to generalize about the role a person perceives in his job, there has been much written about line management and the performance of the line manager. On the lower levels of the organization structure, most line managers see themselves as individuals charged with the responsibility of getting the work out. To achieve this desired goal, they quite frequently pitch in and do some of the work themselves. This is frequently due to the fact that they were excellent workers before they were promoted and they derive a measure of security from work accomplishment. In addition to this, there is probably some desire on their part to set the pace for their subordinates and show them that they can still turn out a good day's work. This helps them exercise control over the group and also feeds their egos. This desire to have tangible accomplishments is even evident on the higher levels of line management. Even though many managers complain of excessive paper work, they are reluctant to delegate the work to subordinates who could handle many of the routine matters handled by higher executives. Perhaps this reluctance can be attributed to the desire of managers to see some tangible results of their efforts. This would be particularly true of those executives whose work is largely planning future actions of the company as well as formulating policy to accomplish such plans. Concurrent with the desire for tangibility of work performance traditional with line executives is the equally traditional suspicion and skepticism of the efforts of staff employees. The more established staff activities, such as engineering, production control, financial and economic planning, and legal counsel, quite frequently meet with opposition and resentment. So the fate of the more recent staff department concerned with industrial relations and personnel administration is usually less desirable than good management dictates. The line manager resents advice from the college-trained staff man who frequently does not have any line experience. The staff man who is anxious to see his ideas implemented often tries to usurp line authority either directly by ordering employees himself or indirectly by going over the line manager's head to higher authority in the company. This seems to be the heart of the problem in line-staff relationships. Underlying this problem is another closely related one that is equally important. Since staff people are greatly concerned with forward planning, particularly in personnel work and training, they are constantly recommending changes in the methodology being used. In fact, the recommendation of change is a fundamental characteristic of staff work. Most human beings are resistant to change, and, in the case of the typical line manager, this resistance is often directed against the changes that are proposed by the staff expert. This naturally causes the periodic difficulties that erupt between the line and the staff in many companies. Each is interested in maintaining his own personality, and each is loyal to his own judgment. The answer to this problem is not a simple one. But then there are no simple answers when dealing with the myriad of human problems that face every company in its day-to-day operations. The ideal to be achieved is the formulation of programs by the training department and the implementation of these programs by the line manager. This means that training has to be believed in by all management from the president of the company on down. If this feeling persists in the upper reaches of management, then it will permeate the entire organization structure because it is a widely accepted principle that any organization reflects the opinions and the quality of its leadership.

If we study the historical development of organization structure, we find that the original intention relative to staff departments was to have them aid the line managers in the managing of an enterprise. Business had become more and more complex, and a necessity for expertness arose concurrent with the realization that any individual line manager was limited as to knowledge and time to enable him to do the complete job. It is somewhat paradoxical that in many instances this staff advice which is intended to aid line management actually hinders it simply because of the conflict of interests and personalities involved. The fault does not lie entirely with the line manager, however. In his book, *Authority and the Individual*, Bertrand Russell presents a viewpoint which may give part of the reason for the cause of the poor relationships existing between line and staff in many companies. He states: "Since it is natural to energetic men to love power, it may be assumed that officials in the great majority of cases will wish to have more power than they ought to have."[1] There is no doubt that in many instances the staff man, in his desire to achieve success, may try to take over the functions of the line manager. This is why it is particularly important for the company to be well organized, with all activity clearly spelled out in an organization manual or some other similar document. If the line management can be made to appreciate the role of the staff man and if the staff man can, in turn, be shown that his effort is used and appreciated by the line manager, then the company has gone a long way toward solving the traditional dilemma.

TRAINING AND THE SIZE OF THE COMPANY

A fully staffed personnel and industrial relations department is usually found only in the larger business organizations. This carries the implication that the personnel function is not adequately administered in companies of all sizes. This implication is correct, and, if it is correct for the entire personnel function, then it certainly follows that formal training is neglected or not carried on properly in many companies. While size of company is not the only consideration, it is certainly an important one. The extent of specialization of any function is usually determined by the size and importance of that function. Related to size and importance of any function in a company is the amount of time and money available to carry out that function. The number of competent people to administer and staff the activities involved is also determined to a great extent by the size of the company. The one leveling factor is that the need for training is readily apparent in all companies regardless of their size. It is needless to point out that competent, well-trained people are needed in all kinds of business enterprises. Even though training takes place by the absorption method, whether it is formal or not, it is becoming increasingly necessary to recognize that organization of the training activity is vital to the optimum success of that activity.

Relationship of Training to Management

Further than this recognition of the need for organization of the training activity is the necessity for the most responsible people in the business enterprise to support this organization actively by direct and

---

[1] Bertrand Russell, *Authority and the Individual* (New York: Simon & Schuster, Inc., 1949).

indirect participation. Top executives should not just pay lip service to training plans and programs, but they should take an active part in those plans and programs themselves. This can be done by acting as instructors in some programs and by becoming participants in other programs. In addition, the training activity should be headed by someone that is respected in the company by all echelons, and he, in turn, should report to a member of the top management who is a key executive. In this way the employees will readily see that any training program or plan has the backing of the highest level of management in the company, and the program will have a much greater chance for success. The reporting relationship of the person responsible for the formulation of training plans and programs is particularly important, for if the job is to be done with optimum efficiency, he must be able to present his ideas and plans to people in the management who recognize the value of such plans and who are able to act on them with a minimum of discussion and other time-consuming maneuvers.

Even though the nature of the training organization will differ because of the size of the company, the basic methods are the same. This is simply because the function has to be implemented regardless of size of company. Any other business function such as sales, finance, staffing, and manufacturing is carried out in small, medium, and large companies, and the differences are largely of magnitude and detail. The same can be said for the training function. While this is true, practical necessities must be recognized. Needs relative to types of training and the personnel to be trained differ not only because of company size but because of the nature of the business enterprise itself. The nature of this book is such that specific types of businesses cannot be discussed. However, training activities and their relationships to the size of the company in which they are carried out do require examination. The ideas presented here can be adapted to any type of enterprise and used effectively, if the management of that enterprise accepts the basic premise that formal training organization is necessary to the success of the training function.

Training in the Small Company

When the term "small company" is used, the logical thought that comes to mind is the need for defining the word "small." For the purpose of clarification in this book, a small company is one that has at least two levels of management and employs more than fifty people and less than five hundred people. This would fit into the United States Department of Commerce definition of a small manufacturing company. There is no implication here that training is not necessary in smaller establishments or in companies with only one level of management. It is simply that training problems tend to manifest themselves more significantly in companies with more than one level of management and with the greater number of employees attendant with multiple levels of management.

Probably the greatest problem relative to training in the small company is to recognize the need for training. Most small businesses follow a practice of hiring experienced people whenever a job opening occurs. This lulls the management into a sense of false security and a high level of expectation in employee performance. What is usually not recognized is the fact that even the so-called experienced new employee needs training before he can fill his position to the satisfaction of his new employer. Along with this problem is the related one of nonrecognition of the fact that this training goes on for the new employee, whether or not it is formalized. The process known as "breaking in" occurs, no matter how experienced the employee was in previous jobs either in another company or in the present organization.

Recognition of the need for training and formalizing such training into some kind of program are the two major stumbling blocks to the successful organization and management of training in the smaller company. The executive must recognize that some of the problems he attributes to other causes can be traced to inadequate training. This recognition may come only after many bitter experiences, but it must come before any kind of formal program has a chance of success. Very closely related to this problem of need recognition is the value of realizing that even experienced employees need some training before they can do their jobs properly. Even though many executives in small businesses have achieved success and climbed to positions of financial security by learning the hard way, they must realize that such a learning process, even though commendable, is expensive, time-consuming, and weakening to the competitive position of the company. When the recognition of the need for training comes, then the most difficult hurdle is passed. The rest is relatively easy. The first step is to assign the responsibility for developing training goals and programs to a man in the company who has both the time and the desire to implement such a task. This is no idle suggestion, since executives in small companies are quite frequently concerned with many phases of business activity. Because of this, they tend to spend the most time on matters of immediate importance, and management takes on the characteristics of expediency, moving from one crisis to another. Consequently, it is difficult for many small-business executives to recognize the need for analysis and forward planning that must be accomplished before any training can successfully take place. Such a program may be organized by first completing an analysis of all the jobs involved in the company's activities. All the details of each job should be included. Next, the best way of doing each job should be determined, and then this information should be given to the people in the company who will do the training. These might include foremen and older, more experienced workers. From time to time, a follow-up should take place to ascertain that the proper teaching methods are being used and that the workers are absorbing the training. The same approach may be utilized for the supervisory jobs in the company. If there are not enough supervisors to support a program in the company, then these people could either be sent to the many management development programs available, or an instructor could be hired to carry out such a program. Many such programs are available on the local level through foremen clubs, YMCA's, and other local organizations. An important point for the small-company manager to remember is the fact that a training program does not have to be implemented all at once. Even a partial implementation with plans for a complete program over a period of years will improve the operations in such a company. If no individual in the company is available to accomplish the task described above, then an outside consultant can be obtained. He can develop the programs, and they can either be implemented by him or by someone from within the company. Quite a few small companies have found it useful to retain the services of an expert in the field from the faculty of a nearby college or university. Quite often, these people can work on a temporary basis, since many have flexible hours, and, once the job is finished, he can come back from time to time to help in its implementation. This is probably the least expensive method for the small company, since no permanent position is created until the company is large enough to support such a position and, in the meantime, the company has the services of a qualified expert with no permanent overhead cost. This procedure can be followed by any type of small business.

Naturally, most training in small companies will be skill training, since this area represents the largest number of employees in these companies and the results of such training are tangible and easiest to justify in the minds of the management. However, the important area of management development should not be neglected. A good many small companies have owner-managers, and they are frequently reluctant to delegate any authority or responsibility to subordinates. As a result, no one is capable of taking over either in an emergency or in the normal course of events. In fact, many small companies restrict their growth or go out of business because there are no trained managers to run the business when the owner dies or retires.

The minimum necessary in a small company would be an evaluation of the need for training, coupled with a job and skill analysis, to determine what should be taught. This could then be given to the various people responsible for performance. Skill training could be handled this way, and executive development could be handled on a day-to-day coaching basis, with the person or persons being developed placed under the guidance and observation of one of the senior executives in the company. There would be no need for a separate organization structure, and the company would benefit by reduced costs in such categories as less waste and spoilage, less labor turnover, less need for paying a premium for experienced employees, and less time required for an employee to learn his job, and training can improve morale and attitude because the employees will see that management has an active interest in their welfare. Above all, a reasonable approach toward training will help the business meet its competition with a higher level of effectiveness and also help assure the continuity of the business, which is, of course, one of the prime responsibilities of the management of any company.

Training in the Medium-Sized Company

Even though the medium-sized business usually has a separately organized personnel or industrial relations department, the problems it has relative to training are very similar to those of the small company. Very often this size of company has grown quite rapidly from a small business. The growth is frequently a sales growth, and, as a result, more and more employees have been added in a haphazard fashion. If the company has to deal with a union, then the need for a separate industrial relations division becomes apparent as soon as the problems become frequent and complex enough to utilize too much time on the part of the line managers. Another aspect of the personnel function also becomes prominent in the medium-sized company. This is the function of record keeping. Union dues check-off, social security data, insurance deductions, and other related payroll information soon create the need for a major record-keeping activity. As a result, the personnel division frequently grows around this record-keeping activity and the selection and screening activity carried on by most personnel departments. Other specializations, such as safety, medical, cafeteria, and recreation, are created, and the personnel department becomes known as the unit that takes care of employees and their problems, thus freeing the line supervisors and enabling them to get the work out. Of course, the line supervisors carry on with the usual kind of breaking-in of new employees, and any upgrading is usually accomplished by on-the-job training. When the lack of uniformity of instruction coupled with the perpetuation of incorrect techniques becomes apparent to the higher levels of management in the company, then talk of a training division begins. Recognizing that staff experts have helped in other fields of activity, the company hires a staff expert for training. Usually, his first job is to develop suitable training plans for the many skilled jobs and make these plans available to the supervisors, so that the training of new employees can be accomplished more rapidly and with greater uniformity than before. The training of employees is still carried out by the immediate supervisor or some experienced employee in the section to which the new operative is assigned. In fact, this is the most common relationship between a training division and the line management. Under this type of procedure, the training specialist is in the personnel department and is utilized only when the line management desires his services. He plays a passive role relative to forward planning, and his effort revolves largely around skill training, lesson plans, and perhaps an apprentice program. As the training function becomes more important in the sense that the results achieved by initial efforts are rewarding, then the training division will become more important. The next step is quite likely to be some kind of supervisory development program, since, in a growing concern, there is always a need for more competent supervision. Here the training specialist may play a larger role. He may plan the program and the subject matter it is to cover and even conduct the conferences himself. In addition to this, training specialists may be called on more frequently to aid in the training of employees. Perhaps a job instruction program is carried on to teach the supervisors the proper methodology for instructing employees. The training divi-

sion may now play an active part in the forward planning of the
personnel department relative to staffing problems throughout the company. Employee promotion policies may hinge on the value and success of the programs recommended and implemented by the training
division. It is entirely possible that a vestibule training program may
be established and that the training division begins to do skill and
supervisory training independently of the line departments. After this
stage of development, the company may begin thinking about management development for its middle management. The advice of the training specialist may be sought in this area, although many medium-
sized companies utilize outside agencies for this type of training.
Very often they send their middle managers to an executive development program that is established at a university or at some national
management association.

The foregoing description of the development of the training activity in a medium-sized company is typical. Very few companies of
this size start out with a training division in the personnel department.
While the description of the growth of the training activity is typical,
it is by no means an ideal situation. Actually, training organizations differ from company to company. This difference is based partly
on the needs of the individual company and the climate that exists in
that company for the development of the training activity. It is entirely
possible that, since the initial training programs in a medium-sized
company were skill programs, the training organization would come
under the jurisdiction of the line department where these skills are
used. The training specialist in a case of this kind would report to
the line head of that department rather than to the personnel or industrial relations director. It must be said, however, that the most
frequent approach to the organization problem is to place the training
director under the supervision of the head of the personnel and employment activity in the company concerned. The most important
aspect of training division organization that has to be considered is
its status in relation to other staff and service activities in the business.
In the growing medium-sized company it is very important to have the
top management wholly behind such an activity. Once this support is
made known throughout the organization, the training division has a
much better chance to function properly in its relations with the various line departments it serves. This is particularly important in the
growing company because the initial organization of the training
function and its ultimate acceptance by the line departments quite

frequently hinge on the early backing of the top management. Tradition is a powerful factor in the development of any business activity, and the pattern set when an activity starts in a company is very often the one that it follows for a good number of years.

The dominant characteristic of the entire organization structure in a medium-sized company is that there is not a high degree of specialization in each of the departments that function in the business. Managers frequently are responsible for many activities. If this is true of the entire company, then it is certainly true of the personnel–industrial relations department. The manager wears many hats, and this is reflected in the rest of the organization as well. All other supervisors and employees in the department are responsible for more than one activity. It is entirely possible that the training function may be carried on by a person who is also responsible for some other personnel activity, such as job analysis or wage and salary administration. This is normal in such a company and merely adheres to a widely accepted management practice in all companies. This practice relates to the size of functions and the degree of specialization required for the accomplishment of these functions. As the company grows and the function grows along with it, the degree of specialization increases. This is forced by the necessity to delegate on the part of the manager so that the work may be accomplished expeditiously.

While much of the description of the training activity in the medium-sized company given above applied to a growing company, the function would be carried on in much the same manner in a company that had stabilized at the medium-sized level. The differences would be largely ones of degree in relation to the training activity as well as other functions of the personnel department. In the growing company, recruiting of experienced personnel would be carried on with great intensity, and the training director might be largely concerned with orientation training. As the company stabilized its growth and its employment pattern, the training director would be concerned with many other types of training programs, as mentioned above. Certainly, supervisory training and management development would increase in importance as the employment pattern became stable. This would be especially true if the company wished to follow a policy of promotion from within. Naturally, the needs of the organization and the amount of money available for training would be important factors in determining the size and scope of the training unit. The scope of the training function will also determine the number of other specialists, assistants, instructors, and clerical employees necessary for the permanent staff. In addition, the number of outside personnel needed on a temporary basis is also predicated on need and budget considerations. The nature of the employment market in both the geographical area in which the company does business and the type of industry in which it is engaged also has a great deal to do with the importance and scope of the training function. An outstanding example of this problem is the tremendous growth of electronic and other space-age

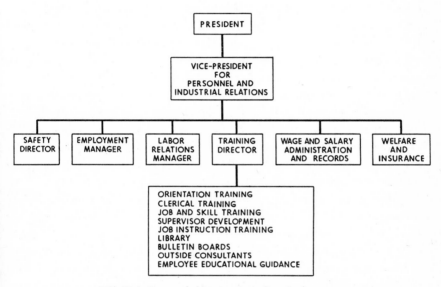

FIG. 10–1. Personnel department—medium-sized company.

medium-sized companies in the Route 128 area outside Boston, Massachusetts. In this locale there is a concentration of businesses that require highly trained scientists and technicians. Competition for their services is very keen, and the pattern followed is one of recruitment from larger companies and from universities in the area. In companies of this kind the training activity is usually directed to the clerical staff and the semiskilled personnel. The inference could be made that rapid growth and lack of stability of the employment pattern tend to mitigate training activity except in those areas where it is absolutely necessary, namely, orientation and skill training. It is therefore difficult to describe training in a typical medium-sized company, since this size of company can either be stabilized at this level or be small businesses which have just grown into the medium-sized category. At any rate, the usual place in the organization structure for the training

function is in the personnel department and there is no doubt that the
need for training of various kinds exists in all medium-sized companies. An organization chart of the personnel function in such a company may serve to illustrate the scope of training activities (Fig.
10–1, p. 243).

Training in the Large Company

The careful reader will find it simple to deduce that training cannot differ very much in the large company after reading the description of that function in the small and medium-sized company. His de-
duction will be partly correct. There is no doubt that the basic function of training is the same, no matter where it is carried out. The
difference is largely one of degree and scope in the large company.
The training problems that beset the smaller business organizations
are multiplied considerably in their bigger counterparts. One of the
characteristic problems of large companies is the maintenance of a
suitable organization structure so that the work of the company can be
carried on with reasonable dispatch.

Large companies fall into two broad categories. One of these is the
large company that is self-contained in one geographical location except for dispersed sales offices. The other is the multiplant, multi-
office, or multistore operation that is spread all over the United States
and, in some cases, in foreign countries also. Obviously, the single-
location large company has fewer organization structure problems
than the one that is geographically decentralized. The primary problem in most large-company organization structures has to do with
lines of communications. The gap between planning and implementation of these plans is naturally much wider in the large company.
This is doubly true of the large decentralized organization. This is
precisely why many large businesses have departments at the top level
of organization, headed by a vice-president, that are concerned with
organization planning and management services. Organization structure and line-staff relationships on all levels are under constant study,
and improvements in these vital areas are the concern of this department.

Since the end of World War II the educational and training activities of large companies have grown immensely. This growth was dictated by need and by the prosperous business conditions that have generally prevailed in the country. Rapid expansion has been the case in
many businesses, and this expansion has created the need for more

employees. Companies found that training could help them upgrade employees and lower costs of operation. They also found that promotion from within aided in the maintenance of higher employee morale. As a result, the training division became an important staff function with increasing scope and responsibility. All kinds of educational ventures were developed in the search for greater efficiency of operation.

As an organization grows in size, the personnel department is called upon more and more for training services. Even in the large company the scope of the training function varies with the individual company's concept of what education and training should be. This scope ranges from a fully integrated training division preparing programs for skill and supervisory and management development to simple on-the-job training. In order to meet the need for training, some large companies have set up training as a headquarters function, with a special school to serve as the training center for the entire corporation. One of the outstanding examples of such an operation is the General Motors Institute. It is a wholly owned subsidiary of the General Motors Corporation and has its own president and board of directors. A degree-granting institution, offering a variety of courses, it represents the ultimate in staff separation of the training function.

Companies which do not have such a headquarters school nevertheless offer a variety of programs to employees. The purpose is to allow for the almost universal implementation of promotion-from-within policies. The increase in fringe benefits, such as insurance and pension plans, has promoted a great deal of employee stability in industry. Rapid expansion in many industries has created a need for more highly skilled employees and for more management personnel. This has resulted in the increased activity of the training division in these companies. In addition to this, there is a growing recognition on the part of American business that the secondary schools, colleges, and universities can do only part of the training and education job. None of these institutions turns out people that are ready to step into positions in industry without additional training. Coupled with this is the desire of many individuals to grow in both status and stature. The large companies have capitalized on this desire by the development of training facilities and programs which will enable worthy employees to reach higher levels of achievement.

Both centralized and decentralized large companies seem to follow the same pattern when organizing the training function. Training is treated as a staff function within the personnel or industrial relations department. This department is usually headed by a vice-president, and the director or manager of training reports to him. In the company organization manual, great effort is made to spell out the relationships between the training division and the other departments and divisions in the company. Typical of such statements is the following in a booklet published by the E. I. Du Pont de Nemours & Company and called *Training within the Du Pont Company.* The Training Division of the Employee Relations Department is described in this

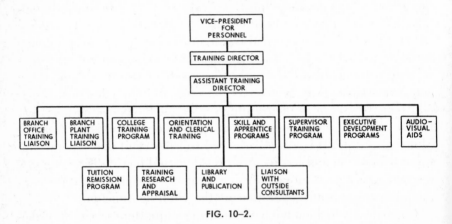

FIG. 10–2.

manner: "This division consults and assists employing units of all departments in training matters where needed. The Division has no authority within the plants and offices. As training problems arise, however, the solution of which require a broader perspective and a wide experience background in training, the plant or office can call for consultation and assistance from this Training Division."[2] Even though the foregoing statement is typical of the training function's scope in many large companies, it does not always play such a passive role. In a great many large companies the training director is cast in a more active role. He may help in over-all formulation of personnel policy relative to training and employee development and may develop and recommend various types of training programs. This is done without the line departments' first asking for training help and advice. In a relatively few large companies the training function is established as a separate department, often reporting to the

[2] *Training within the Du Pont Company* (Wilmington, Del.: Training Division, Employee Relations Department, E. I. Du Pont de Nemours & Co., Inc., 1955).

president of the company. In these companies the training activity has importance and prestige, and all training is done by the training department, with the line management assuming the passive role. Situations of this kind are in a distinct minority, and the prevalent role of the training division in the large company is that of a staff adviser on training policies, plans, programs, and problems. The organization chart of the training division in a large company demonstrates the nature of this activity and its reporting relationships (Fig. 10–2).

THE TRAINING DIVISION

After a description of the place of training in various sizes of business organizations, a more incisive study of the training division itself is in order. The extent of the training activity varies from company to company. From the small-company part-time function to the large-company fully staffed training division there is a variety of approaches to successful accomplishment of its purpose. This purpose is to help the company maintain and improve the performance of the work force. In order to achieve this goal, there is even further variety in approach relative to the type of program and individual company needs and resources. Perhaps a few illustrations will serve to show how various training problems are handled in individual companies.

Secretarial and Stenographic Training—Medium-Sized Commercial Bank

Faced with a constant shortage of competent stenographers and secretaries in a tight labor market, this bank decided to try a comprehensive training plan using girls with no previous experience. With an increasing salary scale for experienced employees dictated by the short supply of stenographers available, it was felt that the cost of the training program would be offset by the lower payroll costs incurred by hiring inexperienced girls. An autonomous unit under the jurisdiction of the personnel director for female employees was created. It was staffed with experienced trainers, and visual aids and representative equipment were installed in a separate soundproof room. The bank then hired a number of young girls who were attending high schools in the city and were taking a commercial course. Most of these girls had a year to go in high school, and, as a result, they worked at the bank on a part-time basis. They were given training in typing, shorthand, typing copy from various dictating machines, running duplicating machines, and various other related tasks. In addition to the technical training, these girls were taught proper grooming, correct English, telephone manners, customer-contact procedure, and other banking procedures. The girls developed through this program were assigned full-time jobs in the bank as soon as they finished high school. Loyalty was very high and labor turnover relatively low when compared with secretarial turnover previous to the program. In fact, the training program became known throughout the bank as the "charm school," and it is still furnishing well-trained secretaries to the executives in this organization.

In this bank a special need for a given type of employee determined the establishment of the program, which is actually a form of vestibule school. The line management turned to the personnel department for help with their problem, and the staff people took over the training function completely and turned out trainees that were capable of assuming responsible stenographic positions with little or no further training.

Headquarters Supervisory Training—Large Petroleum Company

This large company follows a very strict promotion-from-within policy. There are very few exceptions to this policy, and the company is very proud of its record in the fields of supervisor and management development. First-line supervisors and potential first-line supervisors of the headquarters work force are trained on a released-time basis by a professional training division. These people usually supervise clerical operations, and the company feels that training can take place effectively if they spend just part of each day in training conferences. The amount of released time is two hours per session, and the number of these sessions varies with the program being offered. These supervisors are given constant training over a period of years in various supervisory techniques, such as conference methods, performance rating, grievance procedure, and handling problem employees. The training is done in well-designed conference rooms in the training division and is carried out by experts in each area covered. These people are members of the parent-company training staff. The training division is under the jurisdiction of the company's employee relations department.

This might be called a classical example of supervisory training as practiced in large companies. The usual exception to this approach is the one where the supervisors are released from their daily jobs completely until the program is finished. In this case, the line management leaves the training of supervisors to experts in the training division. The feeling is that the work portion of the employee's job is learned on the job. The necessary supervisory practices and techniques to make him a competent supervisor are taught in the training program. In this way the company can get uniform exposure to its policies and procedures, and it feels that it can better determine the usefulness of the training programs, as well as the ability of the supervisors that are trained by the central training organization.

Clerical Training—Medium-Sized Office Services Company

This company has no separate training division. An assistant personnel director devotes part of his time to training activity. This activity centers largely around job definition and analysis. After suitable lesson plans are developed for each job description, the plans are turned over to the supervisors that are responsible for those jobs. The immediate supervisor is responsible for all training, and he carries it out when it is convenient for him and the employee concerned or when a pressing need for a particular clerical skill arises. There is no follow-up on training results by the personnel department. The only follow-up that does take place is a relatively constant revision of the lesson plans so that they meet changing job requirements.

In this organization all training is left to the line organization, and the preparation of training plans is only a part-time function of the personnel division. Most training is accomplished on a catch-as-catch-can basis, with little organization of the activity by the personnel department.

Human Relations Training—Large Commercial Bank

Banking is a relatively technical field of endeavor, and, as is common in many businesses, members of management attain their positions by virtue of expertness in a specialized area. With the growing interest in human relations apparent in business, this large bank decided to undertake a management development program for its executives. The emphasis was to be on the problems common to all types of management and supervision, and the conference technique was to be used. The personnel vice-president felt that no one in the organization was qualified to carry out such a program, even though the bank did have a training division and many formal programs. These formal training programs were all skill or technical programs, with the exception of their college trainee program, but, even here, the emphasis was on technical knowledge rather than supervisory knowledge. The vice-president decided to use an outside consultant for this program rather than hire a full-time employee because he felt that the program was experimental and that, if it did not work to the bank's satisfaction, the consultant could be released and it would not have the morale implications of releasing a full-time employee. The consultant hired for the program was a full-time faculty member of a large university who had had considerable experience with this type of program but who had never carried out such a program for a banking institution. Even though some members of the bank's executive committee were not convinced that an individual who had no banking experience could train bankers, there was sufficient support for the program and the approach outlined by the consultant to enable the bank to start. Briefly, the subject matter used in the individual conferences hinged about subjects which are generic to supervision, such as performance rating, employee grievances, self-development, promotion, employee problems, organizational relationships, interviewing, and selection and placement of employees. The conference covered each topic in a general way, but each participant was encouraged to bring his own problems to light at the meeting. After a number of conferences, the participants began to see that no one had exclusive problems and that the best results were achieved by the exchange of ideas among the various members of the group. The first group for the training program was carefully chosen from among the senior officers of the bank. They ranged from outright skeptics to people who had enthusiastically supported the program. At the end of the twenty-four-week series of conferences held two hours each week, a critique was held, and the program experiment was a success. A follow-up evaluation was carried out six months later to determine the usefulness of the program to the executives exposed to it, and it was found that some of the most adamant opposition had melted and that these individuals looked upon supervision in a much broader way than before. They recognized that skill alone did not indicate an employee's performance and that human relationships on the job were far more complex than they had thought they were before the program. As a result of this success, the bank decided to continue the program and make it available to all its supervisory personnel, as well as those individuals who had demonstrated potentialities for management positions. The same consultant was used because it was now felt that considerably more freedom among the discussants was possible in this manner and the point had been made that it was not necessary for the instructor or conference leader to have banking knowledge.

College Trainee Junior Executive Program—Large Rubber Manufacturing Company

This company attempts to integrate on-the-job training within the framework of a formal training program. The trainee is assigned to a given task, and he works with the experienced employee performing that task. Each assignment is for a specific period of time, the duration of which is determined by the complexity of the task being performed. At the completion of each assignment, the trainee is given a test, which is both oral and written, by the trainer, who then reports the results to the centralized training division in the company's home office. In addition, each trainee is asked to rate his trainer and the training received from him. In this manner the training division has a running record of performance at each stage of the trainee's development. After a period of six to eight months, the trainee has been exposed to a wide diversity of jobs in the company, and he has had the opportunity to develop a broad understanding of company operations. He is then sent to the home office, where he is given classroom training in company management policy, planning, procedures, philosophy, and other related topics. Major executives of the company, including the president, conduct these courses. The trainee is called upon frequently to offer suggestions and take part in the discussion, and at the end of five weeks he is given a battery of physchological tests, as well as a comprehensive four-hour examination covering all the material discussed during the classes in the home office. An assignment in keeping with the trainee's interests and desires and the company's needs is then given to the trainee, and his formal career in the company is launched. Up until this time, he has been on a training payroll, so that, while he is learning in the field, the branch plants and offices he is assigned to do not have to absorb any direct payroll expense for him. When he is given his permanent assignment, he naturally goes on the payroll of the unit to which he is assigned.

This company follows this procedure with its college trainees in order to give them a combination of practical and classroom experience on a co-ordinated basis. The testing program encourages the trainee to study on his own in the evening, as well as ask many questions of his trainer so that he will be well prepared for the examinations. The company has found that trainees can fill responsible management positions with a minimum of difficulty at the completion of the training period. In fact, a good number of the trainees have risen to higher management jobs in a few years after completion of the training. The close follow-up and testing during training allow the company to eliminate those trainees that are not developing properly, and they also enable the training division to keep a close watch on possible trouble spots in relation to trainers for the various task assignments.

Clerical Skill Training—Large Insurance Company

This company has a large, fully integrated personnel department. Within the personnel department is a training division with a manger that reports directly to the vice-president in charge of personnel. It is a well-staffed department with many kinds of training specialists, and it carries on a variety of formal programs for the company. Faced with a constant shortage of all clerical skills and mounting costs, the company decided to develop a vestibule school for clerical skills. One of the outstanding reasons for this was the fact that the usual on-the-job training was increasing in inefficiency because the clerical employees were overworked and could give little time to breaking in new employees. In addition, these clerical employees did not have any training ability, and they looked upon the job of training as an extra distasteful task which prevented them from completing their normal work assignment.

A vestibule school requires a considerable investment, since there is a need for space and duplicate equipment, as well as personnel to do the training. It was felt that the cost would be offset by the increased efficiency created by uniform training by the best accepted methods, as well as by the use of professional training people. The novice trainee did not have to learn her job under the pressure of actual working conditions, and there was no upsetting influence on the normal work force. When the trainee completed her training, she could fit into the work force as a skilled operator. The school trained employees for all the clerical operations necessary to staff the many departments of the company. Both male and female employees were trained here, although the dominant number were female employees. This vestibule school is also used as an experimental operation to test new techniques, procedures, methods, and machines. In addition, when a new machine is to be used in normal operations, the employees learn how to use it here on a released-time basis from their regular job assignments. The school is also used to train employees for clerical skills which will allow them to be promoted and receive more compensation.

Middle-Management Development Program—Large Electronics Manufacturer

The personnel department in this company has a training division, but middle-management development is under the jurisdiction of an administrative vice-president who heads the organizational planning department. The purpose of the middle-manager program is to develop executives for greater responsibility of a broader nature. In addition, the company has a need for more top-management personnel because of rapid expansion of the company as well as approaching retirement age for many of its top-level managers. The company's reason for having this program separated from the activity of the personnel department's training division is the highly personalized nature of the program and the fact that those chosen for the program are sent away to school. They feel that this is a program that calls for specialized attention on the part of a top-management executive and that the training division is fully occupied with lower-level supervisory programs, as well as a variety of skill and technical training activity.

The middle managers in this company are typical of their counterparts in other large companies, in that they have risen to their positions partly as a result of technical competence in a relatively narrow field of activity. The men chosen for further development are sent to Harvard University's Advanced Management Program. The company feels that the men will get a broader business knowledge as a result of this exposure. When the man returns to the company, he is given an opportunity to demonstrate his newly acquired knowledge by a carefully developed understudy-rotation plan. Each man is assigned to a major executive as an assistant to him. The assignment normally lasts six months but has been longer in special cases or where the man assigned has been definitely designated as the major executive's successor. An attempt is made to give the middle manager a diversity of administrative experience. Production and technical people are given marketing assignments and vice-versa. Thus far, the company feels that this program has been successful for them and is making no attempt to keep their executive development program a complete in-company operation. They feel that the time spent at Harvard exposes their executives not only to administrative practices but also to other executives in other industries and that this is a worthwhile fringe benefit.

Orientation Training—Medium-Sized Commercial Bank

The frequency with which new employees join this organization is relatively small. Even so, management believes that a centralized uniform orientation program is necessary. Many of the employees that are hired have no previous business experience, and those that do have business experience usually do not have any banking experience. The orientation program is not an extensive one, and it is under the jurisdiction of the personnel department.

Rather than give the new employee a quick walking tour through the bank, a set of color slides was prepared, depicting all the major operations in the various departments. These are shown and carefully explained, and the novice can ask questions without the embarrassment of holding up a physical tour. All the bank's fringe benefits are explained, and the employee is told about all the factors that will affect his employment status. Such things as tuition remission, promotion, transfer, probation, training, cafeteria, overtime work, and medical facilities are explained to the new employee. The employee reports to the personnel department for the first two days of employment, so that the orientation may be completed before he starts on his work assignment. At the completion of the program, he is turned over to his immediate supervisor, and his career begins. After thirty days, a follow-up is conducted by a representative of the personnel department, so that any additional questions the employee may have relative to his status can be answered. In addition, the employee is now taken to visit departments that have a direct bearing on the work he performs. It is felt that a physical visit to these departments at this time is far more beneficial than it would have been earlier, since the new employee now has an understanding of his work and will be better able to appreciate his position relative to other tasks in his own department as well as other departments.

While the foregoing examples are not all-inclusive, they will give a reasonably comprehensive picture of actual training practice in a variety of business organizations. They also demonstrate the lack of uniformity in handling various training problems. Actually, they follow what is normal for American business—that is, a pragmatic approach where the need as it arises dictates the methodology employed. Certainly a good number of companies copy the successful practices of other companies. Even though this is partially wrong, if the copying company adapts another company's program to its specific needs, then it is at least taking advantage of established practice and also being creative relative to its own educational task.

TRAINING ORGANIZATION RELATIVE TO TYPE OF TRAINING

From these actual examples of training programs, the reader can see that training of employees in business organizations is carried out in a variety of ways. This would indicate that there is no widely accepted methodology to cover all types of business and industrial training. This is true at least from an organizational viewpoint. A comprehensive study of training activity will demonstrate that it is placed under the supervision of a wide variety of executives and that its place in the organization structure is greatly determined by the type of training to be accomplished and the scope and importance of the activity.

One way of organizing training that is quite common is to place it under the executive who is responsible for performance in the particular field of activity. Even though the most widely accepted method of organization is partially to centralize training in a division under the personnel department's jurisdiction, as explained earlier in this chapter, there are many companies that organize training relative to the type of training. In these companies the training activity for an individual department becomes the responsibility of that department, and no attempt is made to co-ordinate this activity with training carried on by other departments in the same company.

The most frequent example of this is in the area of sales training, which includes training of company salesmen as well as dealers who sell the company products on a franchise. The dominant thinking seems to be that sales training has special problems and is a direct responsibility of the sales vice-president. In fact, this area of training could be called the classic example of line responsibility for performance as a result of training activity.

Another typical example of line management responsibility for training is in the area of skill training for both clerical and production skills. This would also include technical training of such people as laboratory technicians in a research laboratory. Here, also, it is felt that the people closest to the actual operation are more qualified to train operatives, and such training is frequently part of the first-line supervisor's job. The attendant disadvantages of such an approach have already been fully discussed. Needless to say, these approaches to the training problem do not recognize a simple management technique, that is, the use of staff experts and specialization.

Management and supervisory development also have adherents to the theory that no centralized training department can do the job as well as on-the-job training can. These companies follow an understudy approach, with the superior picking his heir apparent and developing him in his own way. The morale implications here are obvious. Not so obvious, however, are the other disadvantages. Perhaps the outstanding one is that the executive frequently chooses a person he can dominate and who gives him little trouble. Then, when the promotion does take place, a relatively weak supervisor is placed in a position of responsibility. In addition, any bad habits or incorrect techniques, as well as philosophy, are passed on to the new man. Even though there are disadvantages, there is no doubt that the "protégé" approach is very common in all phases of industrial training and for all types of jobs. It would be only fair to state that this method has advantages also. This is certainly true where the executive doing the training is a competent developer of men. He can build confidence by being an excellent teacher and can be a key factor in the company's future.

The Management of Training

As in the case of most staff activities, there is a definite tendency to create complexity and conflict where there should be none. If we accept the often expressed dictum that training is a very vital responsibility of an enlightened company management, then the problems relative to training are not so difficult to solve. It may be idealistic to think that a company's purpose is to attain optimum efficiency so that it can maintain its competitive position in serving customers and still make a reasonable profit, but if a business does not accomplish this, it ceases to exist. In today's increasingly complex economy with ever-changing technology, it becomes a necessity for a company to carry on an educational program for its employees. This is a simple fact of life for business. There are not enough trained people in the many skills required for successful operation to allow a business constantly to follow a program of pirating employees from other companies.

Role in Building the Organization

There is little doubt that a dominant personnel policy in large companies is based on promotion of present employees to positions of higher responsibility whenever this is possible. Companies that follow this policy find it both economically and psychologically sound. By this is meant that it is both less expensive for the company to train replacements as the need arises and it is good for employee morale to know that opportunity exists within the company.

It then seems logical that training should be an integral part of all management policy making and planning. Since countless businesses have found that they cannot find enough trained people through selection alone, they have been forced to assume the role of an educational institution. If the maximum benefit is to be derived from any such undertaking, then planning for training has to be a part of over-all planning. This is simply because the needs are so diverse in a large company that, if sound planning does not take place, training costs will mount out of proportion to the benefit derived from the training of employees.

Organization Planning

In a good number of large companies there is a relatively new department in the organization structure. It is usually called the "organization planning department." This staff activity is concerned with organization structure problems and with the staffing of the organization. It is here that the training of employees can be treated as part of the over-all plan for developing the organization for the future. Most large companies have short-range plans as well as long-range plans, and these have to be co-ordinated with staffing for the accomplishment of such plans. Typical of such planning is the example of a large electronic manufacturing company which estimates that there will be approximately fifteen hundred managerial promotions in the next ten-year period. Obviously, such an estimate requires some kind of development of employees so that they will be ready for promotion when the opportunity arises. This company has a well-organized training division and an excellent management development program, so that it is preparing to accomplish its long-range plans. On the other hand, there is a large chemical company that finds itself in the position of having about two hundred of its top and middle management positions open in the next five years because of retirement. This company has done little about forward planning and has always followed the approach of hiring from the outside when a position opened. Now that they are faced with this large recruiting problem and a shortage of available management personnel, they are going to undertake a development program as a stopgap operation. Which company do you believe has higher morale and greater efficiency?

From the foregoing examples it should be obvious that good management principles and practices have to be applied to the training function along with all the other functions of the business. If training is to be fully successful, it has to be integrated with the other phases of business activity. In fact, there are some writers in the management field who believe that staffing is a basic management function and that training is certainly closely related to staffing.

SUMMARY

If a company is to attain its goals, then it must have a loyal, well-trained work force. A training division can aid in this attainment. Widely accepted as a staff function, the training activity under the jurisdiction of a training director can help the line management get optimum performance from employees.

If training is accepted with the same confidence that other staff functions, such as engineering, legal counsel, and quality control, are, then the traditional line and staff relationships will be maintained. Only resentment based on supposed interference from staff people causes conflict between them and line operatives. A recognition that the training division is just as concerned with company success as any line manager is and only wants to aid in goal achievement will do much toward the achievement of a healthy relationship. There is considerable evidence to support the fact that training remains a line responsibility, even in companies with highly developed training divisions. It is only where line management is lax in assuming this responsibility that staff people fill the gap.

The function of training does not differ relative to the size of the company using it. The difference will be in scope and degree of specialization. Certainly it is as necessary in a small company as it is in a large one. The fact that many line managers are overburdened with their regular work creates the necessity for training specialists.

These specialists can prepare suitable training plans and teach the line managers to make maximum use of their training effort so that employees will benefit from their exposure to the training.

Formalized training programs of any kind are better than haphazard training. A company's training effort should be integrated with all the rest of its effort. Training should be given the same attention as the other major business functions if the company is to achieve optimum success. The increasing complexity of our economy and the growing need for many highly trained people in technical, as well as managerial, positions add daily importance to the function of training in American business organizations.

THINGS TO DISCUSS AND TO DO

1. Discuss why there may be line-and-staff frictions relative to the training of employees and what may be done to minimize these frictions.
2. Evaluate the training function in your own company or in some company you are familiar with and try to determine whether sound management principles and practices are being followed.
3. Outline a procedure that a company may follow to fix the responsibility for the training of its employees. In doing so, recommend suitable personnel policies that may be followed.
4. The smaller company quite frequently feels that training is a luxury that only the large business can afford. Discuss this problem and offer some practical solutions that may be followed by a small company at reasonable expense.
5. Discuss the reasons pro and con for the establishment of a separate training division in a company. Go to the library and do some research on the practices followed in this area by business organizations in this country.

II. ESTABLISHING TRAINING PROGRAMS—GETTING THE MOST FOR YOUR MONEY

Purpose of the Chapter

THE PREVIOUS CHAPTER emphasizes the need for sound management practices in organizing the training function. This chapter applies this concept to the establishment of training programs in a company. The natural result of good organization is the necessary implementation of policies that are developed. Training programs will aid a company to achieve the desired goals established for the training function. The chapter points out the many factors that have to be considered before starting any training program. Prior planning and evaluation can do much to insure the success of the program. Among the many things discussed are the determination of the need for training, selection of subject matter, selection of trainees and the nature of the training staff. The role of the training division is analyzed to demonstrate its role in the accomplishment of good training practices in a company.

Much of what occupies the time of managers centers around finding solutions to problems. The American businessman is a great pragmatist. In many instances the solution he finds is both practical and expedient, thus enabling him to move on to the next problem facing him. While problem-solving is a noteworthy effort, it does little to establish cures for the causes of the problems. Problems are merely symptoms that arise for reasons that are not always apparent. It may solve the immediate problem of a company that is in need of a major executive to hire him from the outside. The problem could also be solved by promoting an unseasoned subordinate in the hope that the new opportunity would force him to work harder and thus make up for his lack of experience. Neither of these solutions goes to the underlying cause of the problem, however. The next time the situation arises, the same approaches will be used if they have worked before. If they have not, then some equally expedient measures will be followed.

In a country unaccustomed to shortages of any kind, there are some very real shortages developing in the numbers of skilled employees and of supervisory and management personnel available for employment. A perusal of the employment opportunity pages of any large city newspaper will show the great number and variety of jobs available to people who have managerial experience or who have skills that require varied amounts of training. One of the reasons given for this shortage is the low birth rate of the 1930's. This reason is probably true, but it does not help the company that is looking for employees. Articles appearing in many business publications, as well as general-interest magazines, point up the skill and managerial shortages. Some of them offer sociological and psychological reasons for the shortage. While it is not the premise of this book to explore such possibilities, there is, no doubt, some cause for the belief that many individuals do not desire to spend the years necessary for obtaining certain skills, nor do they want to assume the responsibility necessary for management. However, one underlying cause that is discussed in many of these articles is within the premise of this book. This cause is related to training and the role of the business concern in this vital area. There seems to be no shortage of people, the shortage centers around skills. Perhaps one of the biggest reasons for the shortage is that industry in this country has not fully realized the impact of the tremendous postwar growth and expansion of our economy. This plus the increasing automation of factories and offices has created a demand for many new kinds of skills, as well as numerous supervisory positions. Many companies have found that the ratio of skilled workers to unskilled workers has increased as much as 100 per cent. In one large automobile manufacturing company there was a need for six skilled workers for every one hundred production workers in 1938. Now the ratio has increased to ten skilled workers to every one hundred unskilled workers. This phenomenon has also created a need for a new type of supervisor. No longer can the foreman be the strongest and toughest man in the group. He has to know how to handle people who have a great degree of technical skill and who also have a commensurate higher level of education. This fact has given birth to the many human relations–oriented supervisory training programs that have been instituted by a large number of companies since 1945.

The writers of articles about labor shortages all center around one cause and one apparent solution. The cause is either lack of training programs or not enough training programs. The solution—greater attention on the part of American industry to the huge educational task facing it and the need for an increasing effort in this direction if the shortages are not to hamper our industrial growth. Of course, training programs are not going to solve all the employee-shortage problems. Neither are they going to make business firms that are foundering into successful enterprises. The important thing to consider is that training in industry requires the same intelligent, purposeful effort that goes into technological improvement. Certainly, if a company is to achieve its maximum growth, it must recognize that it has a definite responsibility to train and develop its employees for new skills and for greater responsibilities.

WHY HAVE A PROGRAM FOR TRAINING?

One would be hard put to claim which of the functions of management is the most important. Certainly, planning ranks high on any list. It must precede any action that is to have an optimum chance for success. The dynamic nature of business makes planning an obvious necessity. Change is a constant characteristic of business enterprise in this country, and if a manager is to be successful, he must be concerned with the changing patterns affecting his organization. Any concern with change implies a concern with the future, and it is precisely this concern that requires planning. Planning involves choice from among various alternatives and the elimination of as much chance from the future as is humanly possible. To a great extent, planning is the function that is carried on to make things happen that would not ordinarily occur. It is also vitally involved in the elimination of haphazard choice and subsequent uninformed action.

Need for Sound Planning of Training

In earlier chapters of this book, much has been said about the haphazard characteristics of training in many business firms. The training of employees often involves a crisis-to-crisis stopgap operation. The thing that is amazing is that in many of these companies other functions are well planned and action does not take place without very careful analysis and consideration beforehand. A bank's officers will study the application for a loan at great length and analyze the prospective borrower's background and his business very carefully before granting the loan. Any successful bank has to do this, or it will not stay in business. It is presumed that a profit is made from this kind of effort. Whey, then, is so little attention paid to the type of training program used or to the trainees chosen for the program? A large consumer-goods manufacturer will spend a good deal of money on product design, market research, and product testing before a new product is introduced. This is done to remove as much of the risk element as possible from the successful acceptance of the new product by the consuming public. Yet, in this same company, twenty college graduates who are hired at a premium pay rate are put through an executive training program, and at its completion the company has nothing for five of the trainees to do and assigns them to innocuous positions merely to occupy their time. Faced with an unchallenging job, these trainees quit, and the investment in training these young men is lost to another company.

The foregoing examples among others are repeated in hundreds of companies in this country. Readers of this book will find no simple panaceas on its pages to answer the many problems facing them in the area of business training. They will find, however, a plea for the application of the same sound management practices to the function of training as are applied to the many other business functions.

It is reasonable to assume that the objective of a business is to offer such goods and services in sufficient quantity and quality to the public as to enable the realization of a profit. This takes a great deal of concentrated effort on the part of many employees with varied skills and abilities. To achieve such a goal consistently requires reasonably constant successful choice from among the available alternatives that always confront the management of a company. The future course of any enterprise is vitally affected by the policies, procedures, and programs that management chooses in the present. Nowhere is this more true in the operation of a business concern than in the area of employee development. Training, or the development of people, should be a major part of management's job. The improvement of the knowledge, skills, and attitudes of employees to enable them better to meet their present or prospective responsibilities is absolutely necessary if a business is to enjoy continued success.

The planning of the training function involves many considerations. The management of a company has to contend with some factors that are within their control and many outside factors that are beyond the control of any individual company's management. Among the factors that management has to consider and analyze when planning for training are the following:

1. *The Complexity of the Economy.* Increased difficulty is experienced by those companies that try to continue to operate today in the same manner as they have in the past. Idle reminiscing about the good old days will be of little use to a company faced with the task of competing for both customers and employees in the present and in the future. Increased foreign competition, a greater variety of products, an increasingly higher standard of living, changing government regulations, expanding markets, and wider choice of goods all spell trouble for the marginal producer. If a company is to take advantage of the predicted expansion of our economy in the next decade, then it has to plan carefully and prepare for this expansion. The luxury of going along with the tide is no longer feasible if the company is to maximize its profits in the coming era. Naturally, the nature of the economy of the country is an important consideration in the planning for employee training. Certainly, the more successful enterprises will be able to afford such training with greater ease and hence will usually continue to be successful. A well-co-ordinated training plan does much to aid a company in maintaining its competitive position relative to both the procurement of employees and the satisfaction of customers.

2. *The Changing Technology.* One only has to pick up a daily newspaper to find stories of the growing number of near-miracles produced by and for the use of American companies. A host of new machines and computers continually grab space on the pages of our newspapers. These news stories are the forerunners of more problems for the managements of the many businesses and industries in this country. If a company is to maintain its position in the industry or climb to a higher level, then it must keep abreast of the latest methods and techniques, and it must replace obsolete equipment with the most modern and efficient machines available. Doing this creates problems particularly in the area of employee training. When new methods or new equipment is introduced, employees must be trained in their use, or maximum benefits will not be obtained. In some cases employees with different training and background must be either hired or developed before the new machines can be used. As a result, changing technology and employee training are very closely related. The company that has well-formulated training plans, along with their plans for constant modernization, has certainly gone a long way toward achieving optimum benefits from our changing technology.

3. *The Nature of Individual Company Operations.*   Naturally, the complexity of a company's operations has a direct bearing on its training plans. A business that is in a rapidly changing industry, such as any of the space-age companies, has different training problems to contend with than a banking institution. Retail stores, manufacturing concerns, and service organizations all have varied training problems. The fact that a company may have unionized labor as a part of its work force also introduces another facet to the planning of training. Some unions have their own apprentice programs, some cooperate with company plans, and in some cases the company assumes all responsibility for training skilled employees. In a sense there is similarity in the planning of training in all companies, regardless of type and industry. Certainly, each company has to have as competent people as possible for each position, and training has to be planned with this fact in mind. In the important area of management development there is great similarity in the tasks of a manager in all types of businesses. So it is in the area of skill training that the major differences lie, and even here the techniques used to train employees are very similar, if not the same. The nature of a company's operations, then, is closely related to the number of programs and the amount of training necessary to maintain optimum effectiveness. There is no doubt that some companies with shortages of certain kinds of employees will have higher training costs than those companies that do not have such shortages or do not anticipate shortages.

The increasing stability of the labor force and its lack of mobility and the frequently stated policy of promotion from within also make it very necessary for a company's management to include training planning as a very vital part of any long-range planning program it undertakes.

4. *Educational Patterns.*   There has been much written recently about education in this country and its comparison with European and Russian methods and approaches. Be that as it may, many companies have found that they have to undertake an educational task that had not been necessary before. Executives in any number of concerns have found that clerical help does not know how to spell or write the English language properly. Many businesses have found the reading burden too much for its managers. To meet these needs, they have instituted reading improvement programs and business writing seminars. Perhaps this type of program does not get at the underlying failures of American education, but they do help a company to become more efficient at communicating information, and this is vital to its success. Certainly, planning for such programs that help upgrade employees in skills that are only partly job-related must be included in the training plans of the well-managed business organization.

Another interesting educational aspect is the changing composition of the working force of many American companies. The increased employment of college-trained manpower, such as engineers, scientists, and executive trainees, may force many companies to revise or discard previous approaches to training. Many of the people added to a company's payroll in recent years have strong desires for further education. They are used to it and have full knowledge of what it can do for them. As a result, these companies have started in-plant programs for Master's degrees and other related programs designed to make the employee more valuable to the company and to himself. This type of training, along with management development, has to be considered in the long-range planning of a business.

5. *Integration with Other Planning.* In an earlier chapter it was stated that training can be an integrating factor in the management of an enterprise. It certainly has a company-wide influence, and the quality and amount of training can affect the operations of a company for many years to come. It would then seem reasonable that top management would include training plans as a vital and necessary part of their over-all planning for the enterprise. This premise becomes obvious when one considers that most of the things that are involved in both short-range and long-range planning are firmly entwined with the employees of the company. When a company embarks on an expansion program, it will need not only more financing, additional space, and more customers; it will also need more trained employees to fill the jobs that will be created by the expansion program. It will be necessary either to hire these people from the outside or to promote from within or choose the middle course and do some of both. Other than hiring new employees from the outside, the course chosen would involve the training and upgrading of present employees to fill jobs with more responsibility or jobs that require different skills. There are, of course, many other examples of corporate planning that would support the contention that planning for training should be integrated with all other company plans, but the foregoing example will suffice to show the wisdom of such action.

6. *Relation to Staffing.* The often stated promotion-from-within policies of many companies make training plans a necessity. Whenever a promotion takes place, it usually triggers a number of job changes. All these changes imply that there are people who are ready to fill them. Any growing company experiences needs that result from such things as expansion, changes in methods, retirement of people, and normal attrition from death and labor turnover. The well-managed company tries to fill these needs by having trained subordinates who can fill the positions opened up by the above-stated events. Since our technology is becoming increasingly complex, another avenue of endeavor for the training division is to develop programs that will enable the company to have a pool of highly skilled technicians to handle the new machines and methods. Since none of these changes occur overnight, it becomes necessary to plan for them in advance, and the plans for training have to be considered at the same time that the plans for any change in operations are considered.

7. *The Personnel Program.* The last generation has seen the development of many highly detailed personnel programs in American business firms. This development has grown largely out of need, for the days have long since gone when the myriad of problems related to staffing an industrial concern could be handled on a part-time basis. Over the years, the personnel department has been the one responsible for the development of training policies, plans, and programs that would enable the company to operate effectively under various sets of circumstances. Quite frequently the effectiveness of training in a company is in direct proportion to the position of importance given to the personnel department and its programs in the corporate hierarchy. If training is to be successfully utilized on all levels of the business, it must have the backing of top management. Obtaining this backing and seeing that training is included in other corporate planning are the direct responsibility of the individual who heads up the company's personnel function. It is he who can and should continually try to convince the president and other top-ranking executives that the development of the work force is as important to the welfare of the company as any other major activity. Part of this responsibility is obviously the planning of such training programs and procedures as are necessary and recommending them to the line management for implementation.

8. *Effective Utilization of Training Staff and Facilities.*
Machine downtime always is a cause for concern in a manufacturing
company. Any time that equipment is not being utilized spells monetary loss for the company. The same result is true of staff functions
which are not utilized for optimum benefit. Planning takes the haphazard characteristics out of doing, and in the area of employee training it allows for the maximum use of the programs devised by the staff
and such physical facilities as the company may have set aside for the
carrying-out of training programs. Nothing is so frustrating to staff
employees as to see their efforts wasted by lack of proper implementation. This usually gives rise to the bitter feelings that are so often
written about when line-staff relations are the topic. Planning is certainly not a panacea, but it can do much to mitigate unwise actions if
these actions are fully contemplated before they take place. It is always easy to theorize about what should have been done after the act
takes place. Planning at least helps to test some of the theory before
a crisis arises. Any efficient corporate management wants to utilize
its staff and facilities as efficiently as possible. Wise and sound planning merely helps this desirable eventuality come about.

9. *Choice of Programs.*   There are many factors that affect
the type and number of training programs that any individual company may choose to carry out. This will be discussed in greater detail
later in this chapter. Planning plays its part in this choice if it is integrated with other company planning. As was explained earlier, other
company plans, such as those for expansion, have a direct bearing on
the amount and the type of training that a business will find it necessary to undertake. This obvious statement needs to be said because
many companies choose and develop training programs simply because some of their competitors have done so. In fact, in some cases
it has become a fashionable necessity to have a management development program, even though the number of possible opportunities for
trainees is considerably less than the supply that the program turns
out. Equally useless programs are started in some companies by the
whim of an executive who has a fetish about some phase of company
operations and sufficient power to start such a training venture. Even
though this is a book on training, there is no desire to push training
merely for the sake of justifying the training division and for giving
it an importance when there is no need for it. It is precisely for this
reason that training programs should be carefully planned and
closely related to company needs before they are started.

10. *Selection of Trainees and Trainee Utilization.* After proper deliberation takes place in the choice of training programs, it would follow that similar careful deliberation should take place in the selection of the people who are to benefit from these programs. As many training directors well know, this is not always the case. Quite often people are chosen for training who are either not ready for it or have no ability to assimilate the subject matter. In other instances, the prospective trainees have neither the desire nor the motivation necessary to gain anything from their attendance. Admittedly, it is difficult to predict beforehand who will and who will not benefit from any particular training program. The suggestion is that more careful attention be paid to trainee selection, to minimize the number of training failures that come about and often jeopardize a program that would be of value to the company. Some years ago one of the authors was conducting a supervisory training program for a large electronics laboratory. Among the trainees chosen by the management to participate in the program was a supervisor who had five months to go until retirement. The program had nothing to do with retirement planning, and this supervisor obviously could not gain anything that would benefit him or the company. In addition, many technicians were chosen for this training program who had absolutely no desire to be supervisors and had expressed this lack of desire freely throughout the program, to the detriment of interest on the part of other participants. It is this kind of selection that should be avoided. The numbers of people given a particular type of training mean little to a company. It is the type of person chosen for training and his ultimate chance for successful learning that benefit a company undertaking a training program. This requires careful planning on the part of the individuals responsible for selecting trainees. The best training program is only as good as the trainees in it, and nothing is so frustrating to the training director as a failure in a carefully developed program caused by poor selection of trainees for that program.

Closely allied to the selection of trainees is the ultimate utilization of these trainees after the training program is completed. Since most programs are designed to develop new skills and methods or develop attitudes and ideas, the trainee should be able to utilize his new knowledge as soon as possible after the completion of his exposure to the new knowledge. First of all, it will be fresh in his mind, and, second, he will be most anxious to use it to see whether it works. If he returns to a job climate that largely frustrates such desires, then any benefit resulting from the program will be lost. To enable the trainee to utilize his training requires planning on the part of management. Again the difficulty in accomplishing such a goal with infallibility is recognized. In a large company it is not always possible to place a trainee in a job requiring his new skills immediately upon completion of the training program. However, this is a goal that a company would find worthwhile. At least, the trainee should be told about the circumstances surrounding his job assignment, and, if the company is developing a pool of individuals with a particular kind of training, he should be told this also. This approach may deter many trainees from quitting after they have received their training and going to another company that will immediately utilize their newly acquired skills. It is certainly worth a try, and management should make every effort to keep those trainees that have successfully completed a given training program.

Training Should Be an Organized Activity

It should be obvious from the above description of the planning that should take place prior to implementation of training that the function of training has to be a highly organized activity if success is to be maximized. Management theory tells us that planning is of little use if, after careful analysis of alternatives, there is no attempt to organize and control the chosen plan of action. Any activity that a business organization undertakes has to be of benefit to the company, or else it should not be attempted. Since business is a highly complex operation, certain precautions have to accompany the efforts of managers to make their enterprises more effective. While employee training is widely recognized as being necessary to the welfare of a business, this does not mean that it should be carried on without making provision for the measurement of its usefulness to the company.

Given proper attention, employee training can definitely help a business to realize greater profits in the long run. Not given this careful approach, it can be more trouble than it is worth, and a company would be better off hiring employees with the needed skills from outside rather than attempt to develop them in a haphazard manner. As in many other areas of endeavor, the need for highly trained specialists is necessary in the development of training programs. In most instances, line supervisors have neither the interest nor the desire to prepare themselves properly for the job of instructing employees who work under them. In more and more companies, management is turn-

ng over the function of training to staff specialists, and, by doing so,
hey obtain better results at lower costs and in less time.

Efficient Operation of the Training Program

When a company has a training division in its personnel department, it has accomplished the most important step toward more efficient training of its employees. In a well-managed company, the
staff training division does not discourage training on the part of
line supervisors. In fact, in many instances it enhances the training
activity that the line managers have been carrying on. Some of the
programs that a company may want to carry out, particularly those
that require a high degree of specialized technical knowledge, may
be taught by one or more line people. In this manner, co-operation
between line and staff is developed, and a better program results.

If the programs are organized and developed by the training division and then recommended to the line management who have co-
operated in their development, then such programs will have a much
better chance for success. Since one of the prime objectives of any
training program is to maintain and improve performance standards, it is wise to have both the training specialists and the line people concerned work on the development of suitable programs. There
are many benefits that accrue to the company that properly organizes
the training activity. They may differ in the case of highly specialized
programs in individual companies, but the following advantages are
generic to all training programs.

1. *More Prestige throughout the Company.* A well-organized and publicized program enjoys greater prestige among the employees of the company. If it is felt that management is interested and
participating actively in the training function, then the employees
tend to feel that their efforts during the training period will be more
readily recognized. This gives the program greater acceptance, hence
making the program have more impact not only on the people exposed
to it but also on other employees and supervisors. Acceptance is of
particular importance in the case of supervisory personnel, since they
will have the trainees assigned to them either during or after the training period and the usefulness of the training will be in direct proportion to its acceptance by the line supervision. If they discredit the
program as being unrealistic or impractical, then the employee will
soon learn that if he is to get along with his supervisor, he will have
to adapt to the supervisor's methods. Certainly one of the ways to

have the supervisor's methods and the methods taught in the program coincide is to consult with the supervisor when developing the program.

2. *Uniformity of Knowledge Presented.*   One of the main problems confronting a company that does not organize its training is the lack of uniformity in the methods, techniques, and procedures taught to new, transferred, and promoted employees. Perhaps the best service that a training division can render is to collect all the knowledge available about a particular job by careful analysis and, after consultation with the line supervisors concerned with that job, develop lesson plans incorporating the best methods and techniques. In this manner all employees taught that particular job will be exposed to the same knowledge.

3. *Training Time Lessened.*   By accurately appraising the job situation and thereby determining training needs, the amount of time required for training will be materially shortened. The only reason for embarking on any program of training is to make the work force more effective. Obviously, time is an important factor in the achievement of such a goal. The preparation of uniform lesson plans for the various jobs that have to be taught lessens the amount of time necessary to train an individual. There will be no need for learning various methods and unlearning others. Once the proper way to do a job is determined by the training division in consultation with the line supervisor, that is the way the job will be taught until a better way is found to do it.

Since employees often become impatient during a training period, it behooves the management of a company to minimize the time spent on training but still teach the job thoroughly. There is a natural desire on the part of novices in any field of endeavor to try out their newly acquired knowledge and skills. The quicker they are given this opportunity, the better it is for both the company and the trainee. Placing a well-trained enthusiastic employee on the job is the worthwhile goal of any training director. He realizes that the increased productivity that will result from this kind of achievement will enhance his reputation throughout the company and will enable him to secure the co-operation of the line management in future training program proposals.

4. *Proper Scheduling of Training.*   When attention is paid to the organization of the training activity in a company, it is not introduced in haphazard fashion. It is not some secret venture that is in the province only of staff specialists. By consulting with the line supervisors about their training needs, the timing of any program becomes apparent. Their co-operation is secured more readily for the necessary released time of their employees because they have had a part in the development of the program and can see the benefits that they will get from the training of employees under their supervision. In addition, since they have had a very active part in the planning of the program, they will be more prone to want to see it succeed. As a result, they will implement the program when the employee is assigned to them and will follow up the formal program with such supplementary training as may be necessary.

DETERMINING THE NEED FOR FORMAL TRAINING PROGRAMS

At various places in this book it has been demonstrated that some companies start training programs without properly determining their usefulness to the company. The reasons for this are varied. Some managers have great respect for all kinds of education and feel that it will benefit those who are exposed to it. Other companies are forced into establishing certain kinds of programs because their close competitors have done so. In still other companies an overzealous training director may believe his success in the company depends on how many programs he has going at any given time. Whatever the reason, there is sufficient evidence to support the contention that many training programs undertaken in business and industry are superfluous.

How Training Needs Are Determined

In order to gain maximum benefit from every dollar spent on training, very careful attention has to be paid to exactly what training can do for the company. Training needs usually manifest themselves in specific employment problems. Certain skills are required, and employees with these skills are not readily obtainable, so a program to train employees in these special skills is undertaken. On the other hand, there are many needs that cannot be filled by training. An employee will not be satisfied with a training program if the need is really better wages. Improved selection procedures may eliminate the need for training new employees in certain jobs. An improved organizational structure, with better analysis of executive and supervisory positions, may postpone the need for an executive training program. In other words, the training of employees has to be considered in relation to the entire personnel program and then integrated in such a way that it supplements and enhances the other personnel practices that are carried on by the company. Training should never take place in a vacuum. All the employees concerned with the problem to be solved should be consulted before training as a solution is decided upon. Training programs should be used only when they are the appropriate measure to fill the need.

The Approach to Be Used

Since employee training is not something carried on without a point of reference, it has to be related to both the present and the anticipated needs of the business organization. The training director is responsible for surveying these needs and for recommending programs that will help fill them. He should use a methodology as scientific as possible, leaving a minimum to chance, personal likes, and company politics. Naturally, he has to sell his superiors on the programs that he feels are necessary, and he has to recognize budget limitations. This implies a training timetable for most companies, since many organizations are not equipped to carry out all the varieties of programs that may be desired.

As has been pointed out earlier, co-operation between line and staff is a hallmark of a successful training program in a company. When undertaking a survey to determine training needs, the training director has a unique opportunity to build sound relations between his department and the other departments in the company. The training director has to ascertain what the line management considers to be the major shortcomings in the company. He should also try to determine which problems are thought of as pressing and of immediate importance. Training in the abstract may be helpful, but if it can be related to some of the problems that management considers critical, then it has a much greater chance for acceptance and ultimate success. There is an adjunct benefit to this personal approach by the training director. By talking to many managers and employees and by observing the work of each department visited, he can more readily see for himself what goes on and where training may be needed. Naturally, there are disadvantages to this approach also. Many line managers will have personal axes to grind, and the training director may be caught in the middle. Unless there is an unlimited training budget—and this is highly unlikely—he will have to choose which programs should be done and set up those which he believes have precedence. In doing so he will probably alienate those managers who do not get their desires fulfilled. Since his efforts are advisory, he should recommend to his superiors those training efforts that he believes are imperative to the welfare of the company. If his advice is accepted by higher-line management and they act upon it in a positive way by active approval of his efforts, then his choices have a greater chance of acceptance down the line. Explanations should be given to those line managers whose ideas about training were not immediately acted upon. In this way, long-run understanding is built. If the company is very large and the time is limited, the training director may want to use a questionnaire to supplement his personal visits. He may also ask supervisors to prepare an inventory of their work force both qualitatively and quantitatively. Most companies also have records which the training director should consult. Among these records, the following may prove useful in assessing training need.

1. *Job Analysis and Specifications.* These show what skills are required for the various jobs. They will also indicate the kind of experience and training necessary to fill these jobs. By comparing what is expected on the job and what the supervisor believes is occurring, the training needs for particular jobs can be ascertained. In addition, the job specifications can be reconciled with what actually exists in the labor market, and in this manner the company's jobs can be brought up to date. While this is not the responsibility of the training division, it is within the realm of the personnel department, and the training director can aid by bringing discrepancies to the attention of the persons responsible for job analysis. Another possibility is the development of new methods to do some of the jobs, and then the training division will have to prepare a program for this and for work simplification.

2. *Merit or Performance Ratings.* A large number of companies carry on an annual or semiannual program by which employees' performance on the job is rated by their superiors. These forms can be a fruitful source of training data. The areas of performance and attitude that show up negatively should be analyzed for frequency and for type. The traits in which employees have been rated below average can then be determined, and it can be ascertained as to whether or not training may help upgrade employees. Caution should be taken, however, since many of the rating forms used in industry have highly subjective categories and the supervisor may not be entirely accurate in his analysis of employee performance. This may point to a need for supervisory training in the area of merit rating and a further analysis of the rating program by the personnel department.

3. *Analysis of Personnel Records.* It is well known that the personnel department in a good many companies is the repository for many kinds of employee records. These records can aid the training division in the job of arriving at what kind of training programs should be developed. If records are kept of the number and kinds of grievances that occur, they can be analyzed to determine the need for further skill training, or they may point out certain lacks in supervisors which may be rectified by inclusion of grievance-handling techniques in a supervisory training program. An analysis of transfer requests and demotions may indicate poor supervision or poor working conditions, or it may indicate popularity for a certain type of work or a certain department. Training may help rectify the problems encountered. Promotions of employees may help to point up the nature of the qualities and skills necessary for promotion, and these may be included in future training programs. Many companies have tuition-remission programs under which employees may attend schools on their own time for self-improvement and the company pays the tuition. By analyzing the type of course that is taken and the number of employees taking such courses, the training director may get an indication as to what education the employees desire. This will help in the design of executive development programs, as well as skill programs. For example, if a number of employees are taking public speaking courses, the training director might decide that it would be economical to carry on such a course on the company premises for the employees. By the same token, subject matter that is desired by employees can be included in company programs.

4. *Other Company Records.* Among the company records where the training director may find useful information are accident records, cost and production records, attendance records, and labor turnover records. Accident records may indicate the need for further skill training, as well as a need for a safety-training program for supervisors and employees. Production and cost records will show the spoilage rate, and an analysis of the type of spoilage and rejects may indicate that skills are lacking and that training may help reduce the spoilage rate. Methods may be outmoded, or new machinery may be indicated, and this would call for retraining also. Costs may indicate a lack of cost consciousness on the part of both supervisors and workers, and a training session in profit improvement may be the answer to this. Absenteeism, lateness, and labor turnover may all show possibilities of poor working conditions or low-quality supervision. Here, too, the training division can aid in rectifying the problem.

Specific Needs versus General Needs

Training policy, over which the training director may or may not have control, is closely related to the number and types of programs that the company carries on. If a company desires to use training as a remedial mechanism to improve immediately apparent problem situations, then the training director will be largely concerned with skill programs and supervisory training at the first-line level. If the long-range goals of the company are co-ordinated with its training policies, then training will take on a preventive characteristic, and programs will be developmental in such areas as executive training and technical training for jobs which may not exist at the time the training takes place.

Specific Needs

Training programs that can help to solve specific employment problems can be established to achieve the following possible results:

Reduce the time required to perform a particular job
Minimize learning time for many skills
Reduce the breaking-in period of new employees
Help lower the amount of overtime paid by the company
Increase safety and reduce accidents
Increase efficiency by reducing rejects, reworks, and spoilage
Reduce absenteeism, lateness, and labor turnover
Increase the usefulness of methods, systems, and procedures and
  introduce new ones
Minimize the number of grievances
Raise employee morale and job satisfaction
Improve worker flexibility and versatility
Reduce the amount of close supervision necessary
Prepare some employees for more responsibility and for promotion
Enhance employer-employee communications
Develop a pool of trained workers and supervisors for company
  expansion

Of course no one training program can accomplish all of the things listed above. However, problems arise quite frequently, and when they become outstandingly apparent and the same problem occurs with great frequency, then management feels that something has to be done to prevent or minimize future occurrences. In this manner, training becomes a remedial process and, if given a chance to do its job, will quite often remedy the problem. The remedial type of training program is usually in the area of skill training. New machinery, a change in operations, introduction of different methods and procedures for doing a job, and the introduction of new products often form the basis for a company training program. This is the kind of training program that the training director will find easiest to sell to line management. Because the need is so apparent and line managers are usually anxious to have their problems solved with a minimum of difficulty, they will more readily implement the skill remedial type of program than any other kind. Another reason for this ready acceptance is the fact that results are easily seen after the program is completed. In fact, increased skills become apparent during the program, and this reinforces the faith in the program. As a result, the skill program is the most common type of training in industry and forms the backbone of the training efforts of many training divisions.

Preventive Training

A comprehensive training policy is often built on the success of efforts by the training director to establish and develop useful skill programs. At least, it becomes easier for him to convince his superiors of the usefulness of training after he has had a number of successful experiences with training programs in the company. There is no doubt that many corporate managements are concerned with dealing with immediate problems and seeking solutions to these problems. It is, however, the responsibility of the training director to point out and advise top management that a comprehensive, well-integrated, long-range program should be included in the planning of the company's future. If the training man can obtain from management a clear-cut expression of policy and an appreciation by management of the wisdom of extended planning for employee development, he has a suitable foundation upon which to base his programs. Since costs are an important consideration in any business undertaking, the wisdom of a long-range program can be demonstrated in the language most management people understand—dollars and cents. If the intention of a particular training program is to solve an immediate need, it will probably help, but, like other expedient measures, it may prove to be of only temporary benefit. In some instances the training program may come about because a particular group in the line management desires the particular program and has sufficient power to put it through. It may or may not have any definite relation to immediate need. In other cases a program may be hastily planned and prepared to meet some immediate desire, and the results do not come up to expectations. Consequently, training in general is downgraded, and the training division faces great difficulty in its role as an adviser to management on training policy and procedure. The often too familiar distrust of staff functions comes to the fore on the part of the line management, and the training director is relegated to the extreme background.

In order to be fully effective, training has to be a definite part of the over-all staffing program. Any well-managed company has to be concerned with long-range planning. Quite often this type of planning revolves around as many tangible aspects as possible. Such things as finances, space, equipment, and supplies occupy the time of the planners. While staffing is considered, since people to implement plans are an obvious necessity, these considerations are not given as much attention as the afore-mentioned material things. As a result, many companies find themselves with all kinds of employee skill shortages when the plans start to bear fruit. The rush is then on to find individuals to fill the positions that have been created by implementing the plans made years before. Hastily developed training ventures are started, and extreme pressure is placed on the personnel department to find sufficient skilled individuals as rapidly as possible. Very often a premium price is paid to these new employees, upsetting the established wage and salary structure of the company and causing much employee discontent among the employees who have been on the payroll.

It can be readily seen that an over-all survey of company training needs is much better than attempts to set up a piecemeal program. The training director would be doing his company an injustice if he did not point out to the top management the advantages of the over-all approach. Even though some management people place too much emphasis on experience and give lip service to training effort, the cost of hiring experienced personnel, coupled with the fact that even this kind of employee has to be trained, should help the training man convince them of the benefits of a comprehensive program. Each company has certain goals, and it is recognized that people play an important part in any corporate goal achievement. Therefore, training goals should coincide with the goals of the company. Naturally, this approach will necessitate some short-run expense for long-run purposes. If training is to be preventive, then, obviously, employees will have to be trained before the need is imminent. It is precisely for this reason that the training man has a difficult time convincing management that preventive training is useful. They are reluctant to risk the time and money for a training program if they feel that the knowledge will not be put to immediate use. On the other hand, management accepts the risk of machinery purchased and not fully utilized and of building space rented or bought and not used immediately. With the increasing complexity of business and the need for staying abreast of technological improvements so apparent, it would seem logical that a company be prepared with the necessary technicians and supervisors as well as equipment.

The Determination of General Training Needs

Specific training needs are relatively easy to determine, since the areas of ineffective operation in a company are readily isolated. However, a successful training division cannot always be concerned with therapeutic measures. In the long run, it is not only cheaper but more rewarding in a broader sense if employees are taught to perform their individual jobs without causing problems rather than solving these problems after they develop. The training director should not be placed in the position of being at the mercy of operating emergencies as they develop. To accomplish his best work for the company, he has to present and develop programs that anticipate staffing problems and offer fundamental cures. A lack of understanding of the nature of general company needs on the part of line management often forces the training director to acquiesce in their desires for the expedient type of training.

The nature of the training program that results from a comprehensive survey of general needs may not be different from the program that comes about in a haphazard manner. It is simply a matter of emphasis. Something that may be of use to one section in a company may be brought to the attention of the training division. If a program is designed for this one section, it may help solve the immediate problem. Other parts of the company may have need for the same type of training some months in the future, and the program is then duplicated. A survey of general needs will usually unearth this more widespread need, and the program can then be developed for a greater impact on the operations of the company. An example of this would be a job-instructor training program. In such a program the trainees are taught how to teach their skills to others. In a good many concerns there is a need for this kind of training throughout the company. Rather than restrict it to one department, a general survey would indicate this over-all need, and the program could then be integrated with other training plans, so that it could be given with maximum benefit to those employees who are in a position to train others in a variety of skills. This approach could conceivably minimize skill training costs and still give the company a sound reservoir of multiskilled employees.

As was demonstrated above, general training needs are frequently the outgrowth of a determination of specific needs. When the specific need is found to be evident in many of the departments of the company, then it becomes a general need. There are, in addition, some skills that have a wide application. Such skills as public speaking, reading, business letter writing, and conference leadership all may become part of a general training program. The training director should also survey sources other than those within the company. A study of other companies' activities, as well as the programs that are being carried on by colleges, universities, and other organizations, may indicate some usefulness for an individual company contemplating a broad training program for its employees. In some instances the retention of an outside consultant may benefit the company, for he can give the unbiased, fresh viewpoint so often necessary to a really scientific survey of training need. It is very important that the training director gather his information from as many sources as possible so that, when he presents his survey results to management, he has a variety of useful alternatives available for their ultimate decision.

Considerations Other than Training Program Subject Matter

There is no doubt that the nature of the training program and what material should be included in it are probably the most difficult aspects of an evaluation of company needs, but there are other factors that have to be considered comprehensively before any anticipated program can be started. Among these factors are the following:

1. *Instructional Personnel.* When a company institutes a comprehensive training plan, one of the first obvious needs that arises is that for sufficient and adequate instructors. For certain types of training, such as human relations and supervisory development, the training division may furnish the instructors, since it may be staffed with enough competent teachers to implement such a program. In many areas of skill training, however, instructors are often recruited from among the line employees that are fully qualified in these skills. In this case they may have to be taught how to teach, so that the skills will be properly presented to the trainees. It becomes evident that job descriptions for instructors have to be prepared and some provision made for the evaluation of instructional effort. The ratio of trainees to an individual instructor also has to be determined. This may vary, depending on the nature of the training effort. Another aspect of the instructional effort on behalf of the training division may be the preparation of daily lesson plans and course material, so that the instructor has guideposts to make his teaching most effective in the time allotted for the program.

2. *The Physical Environment for the Training Program.* Here again the nature of the program has a definite bearing. The space for a large orientation lecture on company history would be quite different from that required for a conference or seminar type program in human relations. Ventilation, lighting, decoration, type of classroom equipment, maintenance, and accessibility all have to be considered before the program can begin. As a result, many companies design their training space for a variety of programs. The use of sliding walls will allow the creation of a number of small conference rooms as well as one large hall for bigger groups. Where space is limited and expensive, the company cafeteria or recreation rooms may be used. In fact, some companies have rented space in outside buildings for training purposes. In the larger, centrally organized company there is a definite trend to set aside space for the training division and have it designed for maximum utilization with the latest equipment conducive to efficient instruction.

3. *The Preparation of Teaching Aids and Materials.* One of the main functions of the training division is the preparation of suitable materials to supplement the instructional effort. Even if the instructors are not furnished by the training division, they do prepare the lesson plans, visual aids, mock-ups, charts, and reading lists so that the instructor can be as effective as possible. Here another opportunity for co-operation between the staff of the training division and various line personnel presents itself. This is especially true in the preparation of charts and mock-ups. The training specialist may know how to present the material visually, but the line employee will know what to present, and in this way the best results will be effected. If the training budget allows, filmstrips, sound slide films, and motion pictures may be prepared under the jurisdiction of the training division. Careful thought should be given to this phase of training, since material that appeals to as many of the learner's senses as possible will make the learning process easier and more efficient.

4. *Record Keeping and Evaluation.* If a company is to maximize its benefits from the training of its employees, then a constant search for better materials and methods has to be carried on. Records should be kept of the performance of trainees during the program, and their performance after the training is completed should be observed. In this manner the rate of knowledge absorption can be determined, as well as the trainee's utilization on the job of the knowledge gained. Instructors and the material they have used in the program should be evaluated by the trainees, so that any improvements indicated can be included in future programs. The scheduling of the training and the amount of time given to particular subject matter should also be a consideration. This type of research may indicate the need for refresher courses in certain aspects of the program, so that the employees will be able fully to absorb the information necessary to his successful performance on the job. Constant vigilance should be maintained on job characteristics, so that any training has a direct relationship to job requirements. Using internal experience along with as much information as can be gathered from the experience of other companies with similar training activities, tests for the selection of trainees, and the evaluation of the training should be prepared. In fact, all the resources of the training division should be used constantly to revise and improve the training effort. Any failures of either program or personnel should be incisively analyzed, so that such failures can be minimized in the future. In this way training can offer the company a continuing effort that will upgrade employees and maintain peak efficiency in both operations and managerial tasks.

THE ROLE OF THE TRAINING DIVISION

There is no doubt that the entire organization has to participate if a comprehensive training plan is to be effected. Much has been made of the fact that training can and should act as an integrating mechanism for the company. Top management, middle, and first-level managers, as well as individual employees, all have a part in making any program a successful venture. People in authority in any company recognize the usefulness of having efficient workers on the payroll. Trouble arises when they pay only lip service to this goal. Management has not only the responsibility to develop people for the future, it has to see that training is given proper funds in the present. It also has to be prepared to take active part in training either by participating in a program as a trainee or by acting as a trainer where needed. This premise holds true for all levels of management.

Obviously, the training division has an important role in bringing about company-wide acceptance of a comprehensive training plan. It should be the focal point from which training ideas and programs emanate. By co-ordinating the requests of the many divisions in a company for various kinds of training, the training director can aid considerably in keeping costs at a minimum and still give the company suitable training programs for both general and specific needs. By assuming the responsibility for expertness in the field of training, this division has to be on the alert for all new developments in the field and measure their possible effect on the company. The training director has to gain the respect of management and employees by developing an understanding of the line manager's problems and field of operations. After accomplishing this, he will be better able to recommend the kind of training that will help the company achieve its objectives.

The Training Staff

The size of the company and the nature of its operations would have considerable bearing on the characteristics of the training staff. Another important factor would be the scope of the training plans that the company desires to implement. In a good many small and medium-sized organizations the training staff is kept to a minimum, and outside consultants are used whenever necessary. These consultants often teach specialized skill programs and supervisory and executive development courses. In such companies the training staff consists of a director and perhaps one or two subordinates in addition to the necessary clerical help. The programs in these companies are largely of the expedient type, designed for a specific present need. Little attention is paid to future developmental needs, since the staff is too small to prepare the comprehensive type of program that is necessary to support general needs. Many companies carry on a job training program where the supervisor does the training with training aids of various kinds furnished by the training division.

In the large company the training division may have a staff of specialists who are able to handle all contingencies. They prepare and recommend programs as well as teach them. In addition, they may make training aids of all kinds. In this kind of operation the training function is closely related to the over-all personnel program and plays a vital role in all staffing problems that the company may encounter. This is the type of corporate climate in which the training function can offer its best. By being integrated with the other operations of the company rather than acting as an adjunct expedient, the training division can aid its company to maintain and develop an effective, well-trained supervisory and work force.

SUMMARY

It is increasingly apparent to American businessmen that managerial and technical personnel are becoming more difficult to obtain. As a result, greater attention is being given to the training function. To maximize the benefits of training, there has to be sound planning for it in much the same manner that any other major business function is planned for. The planning for the training function involves many considerations. Among these are the complexity of the economy, changing technology, the nature of company operations, educational patterns, integration with other company planning, relationship to staffing, the personnel program, utilization of training staff, choice of programs, and the selection of trainees and their ultimate utilization. In order to be fully effective, training has to be a well-organized activity. If proper planning takes place prior to the implementation of the training program, certain benefits result. Training enjoys more prestige throughout the company, uniform knowledge is presented, the length of time required for training is lessened, and scheduling is more efficient.

Part of the planning process involving training is the determination of the need for training in the company. Any training program should have a direct relationship to both the short-range and the long-range staffing problems of the company. The training director should use as many sources of information as possible in his search for the types of programs that will be most useful to his company. His research will most likely indicate certain specific, as well as general, needs. In some instances the specific need of one department will grow to a general need after the whole company is surveyed. One of the prime responsibilities of the training director is to point out to management that training has to be preventive as well as remedial. If it is to be of long-range benefit, then training has to develop people for the long haul and not serve as an expedient to solve immediate problems.

Once the subject matter is determined, the training director has to be concerned with other aspects of training program administration. Instructors, facilities, teaching aids, visual materials, and provision for record keeping and evaluation of performance all have to be considered and planned for if the over-all program is to be successful. The training division and its staff can play a very vital role in the efficiency and growth of the company. A company that has a well-staffed training division can maximize a promotion-from-within policy and maintain an efficient work force.

THINGS TO DISCUSS AND TO DO

1. Discuss the reasons why a formalized training program has a better chance to develop a well-trained work force than haphazard trial-and-error methods may have.
2. Choose a particular area of interest such as clerical work or supervisory training and develop a series of arguments to present to top management for the establishment of a formal training program in the area of work you have chosen.
3. A company may have many critical training needs and at the same time have limited funds to expend on formal programs. Outline a suitable procedure that such a company may follow so that critical needs may be filled within budgetary limitations.
4. Discuss the steps management may take to try to insure the efficient operation of training programs once they have been established in the company.
5. Research and discuss the concept that formal training programs should be an integral part of the staffing procedure rather than a stopgap measure used to meet critical needs.

12. JOB, SKILL, AND SPECIAL TRAINING PROGRAMS—GETTING OFF ON THE RIGHT FOOT

Purpose of the Chapter

THIS CHAPTER is designed to demonstrate the need for a variety of skill-oriented training programs to aid an individual company in the maintenance of an efficient work force. It is based on the assumption that technological changes will continue in American industry, thus creating the need for an increasing number of highly skilled individuals in many occupational specialties. The skill training needs of both manufacturing and white-collar organizations are considered since the problems in each are somewhat different. A number of methods for the accomplishment of effective skill training are described at length so that the management of a company and students of personnel practices may understand the scope of the training function in this area. The growing complexity of American business has given rise to the need for increased skills in areas where training has not been considered necessary in the past. These areas are discussed in the chapter to suggest that such training may help a company make optimum use of the services of their employees.

It has often been said that the company management that believes training programs cost too much is already spending too much money on training. This self-delusion seems to be a characteristic of planning in relation to training in a great many American business organizations. In the race for world domination in which we and the Russians are engaged, we can ill afford not to pay attention to anything which may aid in increasing the individual's productivity. We can no longer be satisfied with the so-called normal 3 per cent annual increase in our productivity that has been the status quo in our economy for a number of years. The next decade will bring American industry a work force that will be the best-educated group in the history of our country, since more young people are going to and completing high school and college than ever before. Of course, most of these people will have a general education, and they will be lacking in the specific skills necessary for many of the jobs in business and industry. This changing work force and the need for properly utilizing it will be one of the major challenges for the United States in the near future.

The Role of Management

Since it is already very difficult for a company to obtain employees with necessary skills for the effective operation of the business, it becomes apparent that this problem will continue to grow in intensity and scope. While we certainly do not advocate turning to training as a last resort, there seems to be no alternative left to the company that wants to continue to grow and secure its share of the market for the goods and services that it sells. There is no doubt that training of employees will occupy the efforts of managers to a very great extent in the forseeable future. The role of management centers around the planning and co-ordination aspects of training. Certainly, the financial resources of the company also have to be considered. The money argument is just as common as the time argument when training programs are discussed. It would seem that there must be some considerable change in the thinking relative to employee education if business is to maximize its opportunities in the next decade.

Conversations with supervisors and managers on every level in a business organization quite frequently center around the performance of the people they supervise. In many instances this conversation involves a stream of complaints about the quality of the help that is being hired. The old cliché, "They don't make them the way they used to," is often mentioned. Rarely, if ever, does the manager consider that the employee has not been trained properly for the job he is doing. Very often a new employee is expected to work efficiently almost immediately after employment. Sometimes this is not a conscious expectation on the part of the supervisor. Rather, it is the result of pressure placed upon him to get the work out. In a good many companies a position opens as the result of some type of emergency situation, such as an unforeseen accident, a separation without notice, or a very rapid expansion of business. Couple this with the fact that most job applicants oversell their past experience and that references are either superficially checked or not checked at all, and the problem of poor performance begins to come into focus. Regardless of the reasons why employee performance is not up to par, the manager still has the responsibility for getting the work out as efficiently as possible. If the problems involved in effective employee performance are widespread today, then we can only look forward to the time when these problems will magnify and become universal. A visit to any trade or industry show or a cursory reading of the literature of a particular industry will demonstrate conclusively that there are a myriad of new processes and procedures being developed for use in factories and offices. Any seasoned personnel executive knows that he cannot fill all his job requests from outside the company. So the pathway becomes clear for the company that wants to maintain optimum effectiveness.

Need for Forward Planning

In order to remove or minimize the "crisis-to-crisis" characteristic so evident in many businesses, it becomes necessary for management to take some long, hard looks at the future. It is one thing to complain about the quality of applicants available to the company and quite another thing to be ready for the growth possibilities that the company may encounter. It may mean a complete change in company philosophy relative to the training of employees. Probably the greatest change that many companies will have to make is a departure from the haphazard on-the-job training methods to a more formalized approach to the training of its new and present work force. The implications here are more significant than they appear. A departure of this kind will involve a greater immediate expenditure of time and money than the company is used to, and herein lies most of the difficulty.

1. *A Typical Example.*   Consider this reasonably typical example. A small manufacturing company in a suburban community was in need of a variety of trained technicians. Among the jobs to be filled were wiremen, solderers, and electronic technicians. The need had come about because the company had been successful in selling its products and business had expanded rapidly. The shop was on constant overtime, and each foreman was continually haranguing the personnel man for additional help. Advertisements had been placed in the local newspapers, and employment agencies had been contacted. In addition, the existing work force had been asked to recommend friends that might be interested in the job openings. In other words, the usual effort was being expended to handle the problem.

The personnel man was under great pressure not only from the foremen but from the sales manager and from the president to find the people necessary so that existing orders could be filled and customers satisfied. Any applicant that came in or telephoned was given the royal treatment. When the applicant outlined his past experience, he quite naturally built it up. If it sounded even partly applicable, then the man was hired and put to work immediately. The personnel man took the new employee into the shop with a triumphant grin on his face and told the foreman that he had found an experienced workman. After a quick introduction to the foreman and the other men he was to work with, he was assigned a spot on the bench, given a set of tools, the necessary blueprints and wiring diagrams, told where he could obtain additional supplies, and was then expected to turn out work on a productive basis. While he was not given any performance test before he was hired, the foreman did observe him more carefully than he did an employee who had been on the payroll for a period of time. Naturally, the new man was nervous, and, with close observation, he was bound to make mistakes. The fact that the foreman was under pressure to get work out added to the tense atmosphere, and the inevitable result was poor performance on the part of the new employee. If he withstood this baptism of fire, the chances are reasonably good that he would learn his job by trial and error after a period of time. Unfortunately, not too many new employees of this company lasted very long. Some of them stayed long enough to develop skills which they did not possess when employed, and others left the same week they were hired. Needless to say, this represented a considerable expense to this company, but it was one not readily recognized by management. As a result, they continued the wasteful practices mentioned above and have a very high labor turnover.

2. *An Atypical Example.* In a large steel manufacturing company which had followed a rather strict promotion-from-within policy over the years, a recent analysis of their managerial force revealed some startling things. Because of a recently adopted compulsory retirement plan and a decentralized organization structure plus the acquisition of two other companies, a rapidly growing shortage of management personnel was developing. The company found that they would have to replace about a 5,000-man management team in a five-year period. A single top-level retirement caused considerable job shifting and upheaval. In addition to the existing need for managers, another need became apparent. The company had been growing quite rapidly and anticipated that this growth would continue. This meant that additional managers would be needed over and above replacement requirements. If the promotion-from-within policy was to be adhered to, then there was only one solution: rapid training of lower-level managers as well as training of nonmanagement personnel in the theory and practice of management. This company was very aware of the responsibility for training and development that goes with a promotion-from-within policy. They felt that a good portion of the company's success had come about as a result of this policy, and they had every desire to continue it—hence an incisive look at their training of management personnel. Their planning included a survey of existing executive development programs in other companies, as well as what was being done by universities and various management associations. In addition to training, the company maintained elaborate personnel records and carried on a well-developed performance appraisal program. This was done so that all possibilities were considered when a management opening occurred. The usual centralized training program, in which the program is carried on at the home office and candidates are brought in for the training, was discovered to be inadequate to fill the growing needs. Since the company was undergoing decentralization, it was decided to carry on training of managers on a decentralized basis also. The need for rapidity of training with maximum coverage of the potential trainees in a minimum of time also became apparent. Even decentralized training of the usual kind would not answer the need or insure the uniformity of presentation of the company's management philosophy. The company then hit upon an unusual method of presentation for so abstract a subject as management theory. An outside organization prepared black-and-white films in 16-mm. size. Coupling these with supplementary visual aids and case studies helped make the subject matter alive and interesting. This was a complete set of lectures on the subject of management on film. They were presented as a frame of reference for small group conferences which were led by the managers who supervised the trainees. The conference leaders were given a manual as a guide and could also adapt the material to local problems and conditions. In addition, the trainees were shown a film which gave the history and organization of the company. The course was given in two-hour sessions over a period of several months and, in most cases, on the trainee's own time. While the results of such a program are difficult to measure, the company felt that it would expose a maximum number of potential managers to the company's philosophy and its management principles and practices and that the program would help all participants to gain a uniform exposure to training. While the content of the program was not different, its method of presentation was, and the preparation of such a program required considerable forward planning. It is precisely this kind of forward planning that may aid the company in overcoming future shortages of managerial personnel.

3. *Technological Advances and Training.* The greatest need for skilled people will most likely come about as a result of the increasing improvement in machines and equipment and the resultant changes in methodology. Many companies are extremely anxious to introduce the latest equipment, in order to increase efficiency and lower their overhead costs. The ever-narrowing cost-price squeeze on American businesses makes the job of selling new equipment a relatively easy one. Many companies have been dazzled by the glamour of so-called automation and have hurriedly placed orders for the rental or purchase of the necessary equipment. This is frequently done without the necessary planning in relation to ultimate cost and the preparation of employees and physical facilities. One bank decided to lease a computer, the monthly rental for which was $16,000. Further analysis showed that they would have to send ten employees to school for the training necessary to use the new machine at a cost of $6,500. In order to maximize their use of the computer, they had to spend $60,000 for additional equipment and raise the floor in the room where the installation was made, at a cost of $10,000.

While this book is not particularly concerned with capital spending, it is necessary to consider capital spending in relation to training, since any new piece of equipment that a company purchases involves change and employees have to be trained to work with the new equipment. If training new employees for the use of this equipment was a one-time cost, it would not be too significant. The fact is, however, that the training must be continuous for a number of reasons. One reason is that most of the electronic data-processing equipment rented or purchased is not utilized effectively. Each day brings new uses for this type of equipment, and employees have to be instructed in these new techniques. Another very important factor is the scarcity of people who have the proper skills to run this equipment. The pay scales are considerably higher than that of clerks who may be replaced by the machines. Quite frequently, these clerks are the ones who are sent for the training. After acquiring the necessary skills, their pay must be raised. Very often a company is reluctant to raise this pay too rapidly because it will affect the entire white-collar salary structure. As soon as these newly trained clerks gain some practical experience with the equipment, they begin to recognize how valuable they are, and any gratitude they may have toward the company for the training which has increased their value disappears in a welter of job offers from other employers at considerable salary increases. If the company does not choose to raise their pay, then they must have other persons ready to fill the spot, and this means continuous training. If the company chooses to meet the market as far as salary is concerned, this means a re-evaluation of the salary structure in the company, which will also raise costs considerably. This is in addition not only to the training necessary for the people who are going to run the equipment but to the indoctrination and orientation of the other people in the company as to the uses and impact of the equipment on company operations.

The foregoing description may have many negative connotations and seems like an appeal for turning back the clock and forgetting about progress. Such is not the intention. The appeal is for proper and total forward planning and the recognition of more than the surface implications involved in technological advances. Naturally, the training aspects of such advances loom large in this consideration, and any management would be deluding itself if they thought that any new equipment was going to solve all their problems without creating other problems which may be greater.

4. _The Impact on the Trainee._ Not the least of the problems connected with the introduction of new equipment and methods is the effect on the people chosen for training. It is well known that people are resistant to change and that they tend to become comfortable in a given position. This is probably one of the great deterrents to ambition. Of course, there are some ambitious people, but even these are resistant to rapid changes in the set patterns. When an employee is chosen for training and removed from his job, the set pattern is changed. This is a very critical period in the life of the trainee, and it is imperative that management plan adequately for the proper orientation of the trainee so that the money spent on the subsequent training program will be well spent and the maximum number of trainees retained by the company. Along with the trainee, his supervisor should be well informed as to the status of the trainee and the results that are expected of the training program. If the trainee is to be transferred because of newly acquired skills, then provision must be made for restaffing in the department he has left, if the need arises.

5. *Management Considerations before Undertaking Skill Training.* There are a number of factors that management should consider carefully before undertaking any kind of skill training program. These considerations will aid the company in carrying out any subsequent program and give the training the maximum chance for success. This list is not all-inclusive and can be enlarged or contracted, depending on the conditions which exist in the individual company. It is intended as a guide to anyone concerned with the development of training programs to increase or change the skills of a work force.

a) *Consider the Nature of the Problem.* Is there a complete change in the methodology anticipated? If this is the case, then the undertaking will require considerable planning. An incisive analysis of the work force will have to be carried out to determine the number of job changes necessary and how many people will be affected. If the change is a minor one involving changes in only a few jobs, then the training may take place as a regular part of the job, and the persons performing the job may be the only ones trained in the changing job. Actually, many jobs change over a period of time, and this goes on as an evolutionary process with little disruption to the work force performing the job.

b) *Co-ordination of Equipment Acquisition and Training Plans.* There is usually a considerable time lag between the management decision to acquire new machinery for either the office or the factory and the time that the equipment is delivered. This can act as a built-in safety factor for the training director. If he is kept fully informed on the plans evolving around the new equipment, he can render excellent service to the company. The estimation of needs can be carried out under ideal conditions and the trainees and trainers carefully chosen. The changes can be introduced gradually, and the chances are that the new equipment has a maximum chance to be utilized effectively when it is delivered.

c) *Enlisting the Existing Work Force.* Ignoring the people who will have to play a key role in any contemplated change in jobs and work methods only makes the change introduction more difficult when it does have to take place. On the other hand, when the existing work force is brought in on the planning, they frequently contribute excellent ideas, and the ultimate change is much smoother because they have had a part to play in its introduction. In fact, they quite often look upon it as their contribution, and their complete co-operation is an asset. The human's natural desire to be included in planning which affects his future is satisfied, and the work is performed more efficiently because abnormal uncertainties about the future are eliminated. Any rumors which are likely to start because of lack of information are quickly thwarted because the employees know what is going on almost from the start of the project.

d) *Choice of Trainee and Trainer.*   Much has been said in this book of the need for careful selection of both instructors and the people they are to train. Needless to say, a careful choice in this area gives any program a much better chance for success. Any company is limited by its available work force and the talent it possesses. But this limitation does not mean haphazard selection. There are varying degrees of suitability on any work force, and it is management's responsibility to spend the time necessary to obtain the best people available.

e) *Use of Outside Organizations and Consultants.*   Many of the companies that sell and service office and factory machines also maintain schools for the training of operators for these machines. In some instances they will even send instructors to the plant or office of the buying company to train the employees. In the case of an outside school, the employees can be sent a few at a time so that the normal work flow will be subject to minimum disruption. In some instances these few employees that are sent to school can become the trainers for the rest of the staff when the machines are delivered. In this way the training expense is minimized. The smaller company may find it useful to hire an outside training specialist who can help in setting up the program and prepare subject outlines and even train instructors. The large company may have such a specialist in the training department.

f) *Continuous or Intermittent Training.*   There are many factors that have to be considered before deciding on the length and type of training. If a complete change in a work process that is a major part of the effort of the company is contemplated, then it would be logical to establish a program that could be a continuous one. This would be particularly necessary where the skills required are in short supply and a higher labor turnover is likely to result. It may also be necessary where the nature of the changes in methodology are such that the work flow will increase in size and more people will be needed over a prolonged period of time. A minor job change affecting a few people would be the kind of program that may require only intermittent training. The program could be set up and then implemented only as the need arose. Continuous training may be indicated for instructors, so that a suitable group of trainers is available to teach new and transferred employees.

g) *The Manufacturing Company.* Since the vast majority of manufacturing concerns in this country are unionized, the labor unions involved must be taken into consideration before any change in work methods or jobs is instituted. The nature of the industry and its traditional approach to change will play a big role in any undertaking of this kind. Faced with increasing competition from abroad, many companies must make their plants more efficient or close them down. Labor unions in these industries are beginning to recognize some of the realities connected with this problem. Some of the unions are cooperating with management in the training of people to run new equipment and increase productivity by job changes and changes in work methods. Others are setting up their own schools to help workers increase their skills, or they are working with existing trade and vocational schools in the community to develop programs which will help their members obtain better-paying positions by increasing their value to the employer. One such example occurred recently in a medium-sized manufacturing city with approximately one hundred thousand population. Located in this city is a vocational and technical high school. Students are trained in a variety of skills for the local labor market. This community contains a number of research laboratories and electronics companies, as well as a variety of companies using draftsmen, wiremen, engineering assistants, machinists, tool and die makers, and other precision skills. Under the provisions of the National Defense Education Act of 1958 and in conjunction with the state board of education a program has been designed to meet the needs of the area labor market. Courses are designed to furnish engineering aid and to increase the knowledge of persons currently filling technical positions. It is also designed to prepare persons for eventual employment as engineering technicians. To be eligible for the program, a candidate must have a high-school diploma and show proficiency in algebra, plane geometry, and physics. A successful candidate is awarded a diploma after completing this evening technical institute. Aptitude tests are given periodically to applicants, and the successful graduates find ready positions in local industry.

Some labor unions are even underwriting the tuition of members that desire to attend evening school so they may learn new skills and be ready for the new equipment and machinery when the company they are employed by installs it.

h) *The White-Collar and Service Organization.* Rapidly changing job methodology has become characteristic of the white-collar job in the past decade. Every indicator points to even more rapid change in the future. Pressed by ever-spiraling overhead costs, the company employing large numbers of white-collar workers is always seeking ways to lower these costs and make their operations more effective at the same time. The techniques of motion study and work simplification applied to the factory for many years have now been applied to office procedures, and a resulting change in many jobs and work procedures has resulted. In many companies the teaching of work-simplification techniques to various employees is a skill training program in itself. Since so-called paper work has grown so rapidly in the last twenty years, a logical place for improved job efficiency is in white-collar work. Each year the manufacturers of business machines develop equipment designed to help the managements of organizations employing clerical staffs cut down on the cost of processing paper work. Some of the developments in this area border on the miraculous. From electric typewriters to huge computers, the machines are all designed to simplify the tasks and increase the efficiency. If the company is to take advantage of these new developments, it must have trained employees to operate these new machines. Since service organizations are rapidly increasing in size and clerical needs are constantly growing, it is in this area that the training function can play an increasingly effective role by preparing training programs for employees to enable them to increase their skills so that they are able to operate the equipment when it is purchased by the company.

i) *The Nature of the Jobs Performed.* Any company that maintains a continuous job analysis and evaluation program finds that some jobs change more rapidly than others and that still other jobs are entirely eliminated or are replaced by newly created jobs. Certain jobs have grown more complex over the years and, because of this complexity, require more skills or increased educational requirements. A change in company policies or an expansion in its markets or product line has an effect on a variety of the jobs performed and the training necessary for these jobs. In a dynamic economy such as ours, job changes occur with great frequency, and it is necessary for the training division to be alert to these changes so that proper programs are developed to insure a properly trained work force. In some industries as many as 50 per cent of the jobs being performed at present were not in existence twenty years ago. Such industries as electronics, plastics, chemicals, and data processing were either not in existence or in their infancy. Their rapid development has created many new positions directly in the particular industry and indirectly in those industries using the products developed. In some instances the job changes are subtle. A person performing the job will not notice these changes because they occur over a relatively long period of time. It is not until a new person has to be trained for the position and some thought is given to the material to be taught that the changes become apparent. Quite frequently, because of lack of organization of material and priority of importance of presentation, certain items are taught to the new employee which are no longer necessary in the performance of the job. Another possibility is that jobs are continued in existence merely because they are traditional rather than presently necessary. Supervisors are frequently reluctant to admit that a job under their jurisdiction is no longer necessary, since they may feel that this will narrow their area of responsibility and diminish the status of their position.

6. *The Accomplishment of Skill Training.* When any business organization decides to undertake a program of self-analysis, it finds that there are a variety of problems confronting it. As in the case of an individual, the company is understandably reluctant to admit its faults. This is additionally true if the organization is competing successfully in its industry. Any self-analysis, however, will point up weak spots in the organizational structure and will indicate immediate and future needs that have to be filled. Not the least of these needs will be those that indicate somewhat less than optimum performance in the various skilled positions that are necessary to the particular business. Certain skills are needed for the particular business, and others are generic to all companies. The frequency of error and the importance of the particular skill often determine the priority of training program development. Obviously, no company can solve all its training problems in one fell swoop. In fact, success in one type of skill training will very frequently convince a company management of the usefulness of a broader approach to skill training programs.

The important fact to be considered is that such training is necessary if the company is to continue to grow and operate efficiently. The next important fact to consider is where to start. In other words, what type of training need is most apparent, and what type of program will have the most significant impact on the company's operations? Any fully integrated company will have a variety of needs to be filled, and the approach to be followed in determining these needs is carefully outlined in the chapters on research methods for training. After arriving at an order of priority, the company must decide how to implement the training. One of the outstanding roadblocks to the successful accomplishment of any training is the lack of co-operation of the people who are supposed to benefit from the training. These are the trainees and the line supervisors who employ these trainees. This is precisely why it is important to use the existing organization to accomplish the training whenever and wherever it is possible. Eliciting their opinions as well as their direct aid frequently enables the program to be accomplished successfully in a shorter period of time. The simple key here is that it becomes their program rather than one designed by a staff man, who, they feel, does not understand their needs. Once the decision is made to start some type of formal training program, the logical question that arises is where to begin. This is difficult to answer in a general sense because individual companies differ in the degree and scope of their problems. Perhaps the best way to develop an answer to this question is to present a reasonably comprehensive list of the many varieties of skill training that are in existence in American industry. These may be adapted for individual company use, and combinations of them may apply to specific situations.

On-the-Job Training

The most common and widely accepted method of training employees in the skills necessary for job performance is on-the-job training. It is carried out in a variety of ways ranging from informal trial and error to a formal program with a training specialist doing the training. In most instances the supervisor or another employee undertakes the training. Naturally, there are advantages and disadvantages attendant on this type of training. The underlying disadvantage is tied to the fact that in most instances it is carried on with little or no planning and is looked upon by the trainer as an interruption to the normal work pattern. If emphasis is placed on production rather than learning, the new employee will probably learn his job only partially, and his efficiency will be impaired. Frequently, safety is disregarded in the haste to build the employee to the speed of older employees. When the job is not taught in an organized manner and the new worker learns haphazardly, he is apt to retain these sloppy work habits as long as he is performing the job.

When done properly, on-the-job training has many advantages for both the trainee and the company. The employee gains experience on the job and in the environment in which he will be working. He actually learns by doing the job as he will be required to do it when the training period is over. In order to accomplish on-the-job training satisfactorily, the following practices should be observed:

1. The person selected to do the training should be a good teacher.
2. He should know the job he is to teach thoroughly.
3. He should prepare an organized training plan or have it prepared for him by the training division.
4. He should be given sufficient time to carry out the training effort and, if possible, be removed from his responsibility for work production.
5. He should have access to information about the person he is to train, so that he is able to gauge the trainee's needs as accurately as possible.
6. He must be able to perform the job at a normal pace in the proper manner. He does not have to be an outstanding performer. In fact, outstanding performers frequently lose patience if the trainee does not learn the job rapidly.
7. A timetable should be developed so that the trainer can assess the trainee's progress and report on it to both the trainee and the supervisor.
8. If the supervisor does the training, then he must be able to devote the time necessary without neglecting his other supervisory and work duties.
9. Try to assign the trainee to the work station he will ultimately be employed in, in order to maximize the advantage of working in the job environment.
10. After the trainee has developed sufficient skill to be left on his own, let him know that he can call on the trainer for further guidance.
11. The trainer should follow up on the trainee as often as is necessary to ascertain the results of the training and the amount of job knowledge retained by the trainee.

On-the-job training is usually carried on where the job is not conducive to group training or the number of similar jobs to be taught is not large enough to warrant the setting-up of a classroom-type program. Companies of all sizes use this type of program, and it is found almost without exception in the small company. This type of training is often less expensive than other types, since there is no need to duplicate the workplace or prepare mock-ups or models and even the slow performance of the new worker may result in usable finished products. When the new or transferred employee is trained on the production line, in the office, or behind the counter, he is exposed to the many problems that he will continue to face when he is finally left alone on the job. He does not have to go through any transitionary period, and this fact makes on-the-job training a time saver when carried out effectively. If he has good supervision and instruction, he can be rewarded for his progress, and his errors can be corrected before they become bad habits.

It must be remembered that organization of the training and the choice of good instructors is the keynote to success in on-the-job training. Even though these two factors are important in all types of training, they are even more important here because on-the-job training is so open to haphazard methodolgy and pressures of production not present in a classroom situation.

Apprentice Training

Apprentice training is one of the oldest formalized approaches to the training of individuals in a variety of skills. The basic methods have changed very little from the Middle Ages, when young boys attached themselves to a master craftsman in order to learn the skills of the particular trade. Servitude is no longer present in apprenticeship today, but there is usually some type of contractual arrangement which exists until the apprentice finishes his training. Apprentice training differs from other types of job training because it is usually of longer duration and is more formalized. Many of the trades and crafts taught in this manner take from two to six years to learn under the guidance of journeymen and master craftsmen. Frequently, the program includes classroom instruction as well as individual on-the-job training. In some companies the apprentice program is highly developed and has even furnished some of the company's executives, who have moved up in the company after starting as apprentices. Brown and Sharpe Manufacturing Company even has dormitories and recreational facilities and has developed an enthusiasm for its program that is similar to that developed at college. The automobile companies and major electrical manufacturers also have well-developed apprentice training programs. Apprentice training received impetus in this country in 1936 when the Congress passed a law establishing a permanent Federal Committee on Apprenticeship Training in the United States Department of Labor. This committee has promoted apprentice training, along with state committees and similar committees in many local communities. The advantages of apprentice training can best be summarized by a publication of the United States Department of Labor which pointed out ten ways in which apprentice programs are beneficial:

1. Maintenance of skilled worker force
2. Immediate returns
3. Quality workmanship
4. Satisfied customers
5. Higher production
6. Lower production costs
7. Lower hiring costs
8. Increased loyalty
9. Opportunity for America's youth
10. National security[1]

This program seeks to provide a skilled force of manpower for the country's needs. It furnishes written agreements specifying the type of training to be given, the length of time of the apprenticeship, the hours to be devoted to training on the job and in the classroom, and the wages of the apprentices. The bureau will help establish programs in apprentice training as well as training for the variety of jobs which do not require the length of time that apprenticeship does. Bureau employees do not take an active role in the program. This is the responsibility of the training personnel in the company and in the union if the union plays a part in the program. There are approximately three hundred skilled occupations under 110 trade classifications for which apprentice training is given. The specific trades and occupations can be obtained from the bureau.

Managerial, clerical, selling, professional, semiprofessional, and agricultural occupations are not included in this program. There are usually quite specific state regulations governing apprentice training in addition to the federal regulations.

Vocational and Technical Education Programs

In 1917, Congress passed the Smith-Hughes Act, in order to stimulate and promote vocational education. Public trade schools and vocational industrial high schools were developed over the years.

---

[1] *Apprenticeship Pays Dividends* (Washington, D.C.: United States Department of Labor, Bureau of Apprenticeship).

During World War II the Engineering, Science, and Management War Training Program dealt with many phases of technical and vocational training problems. A large part of the program was on what is called the "technical institute level," which provided extension as well as classroom courses in many technical fields. After the war the large number of veterans desiring technical training caused the development of a number of vocational schools. Technical institutes and two-year community colleges now offer a wide variety of technical and vocational courses in day and evening programs. Quite frequently these courses are tied very closely to the needs of the area in which they are located, and the staffs of these schools work in close conjunction with the training personnel of area industries, so that the labor needs of the community are more readily met. Among the types of vocational and technical education offered in these schools are the following:

1. _Day Programs._ These programs are designed to train students who are preparing for a variety of technical positions in industry. The nature of these courses is described below.

1. Posthigh-school courses with broad technical content in specific industrial fields to prepare people for engineering technician positions.
2. Curriculums designed to prepare people for technical specialist positions in one area of an industry and usually on the posthigh-school level.
3. Vocational and technical courses in technical high schools which are similar to the above but designed to prepare the participant for jobs on a lower level.
4. Programs which combine technical courses with sales and cost content and also given on the posthigh-school level.
5. Technical and vocational courses outside the engineering area to prepare people for such occupations as biological laboratory assistant and medical assistant. These also are on the posthigh-school level.
6. A variety of short intensive courses for specific technical occupations to prepare people for jobs on a relatively low level.

2. _Evening Programs._ These programs are designed for the presently employed individual who desires to learn additional skills or increase his competence in a present skill. The nature of these courses is as follows:

1. Courses for technicians to enable them to keep up to date in

their fields and to make up any deficiencies they may have.

2. Courses which will enable workers to upgrade their skills to obtain better jobs.

3. A series of courses given over an extended period of time to prepare employed workers for higher-level positions.

4. Technical supervision courses to aid people who are in, or who aspire to, supervisory positions in technical employment.

5. Short and intensive courses to prepare people for low-level technician jobs.

The following organizations are interested in technical education for a variety of reasons. Some are concerned with manpower problems and others with educational programs. Trade associations are concerned with the problems of their particular industry. Regardless of the reason, most of these organizations have furthered the cause of education in the technical vocational area. The following list of such organizations is not complete but will demonstrate the scope of interest in technical and vocational training:

American Association of Junior Colleges
American Society for Engineering Education
American Society of Training Directors
American Technical Education Association
American Vocational Association
Atomic Energy Commission
Electronic Industries Association
Foundation for Instrumentation Education and Research
National Association of Manufacturers—Educational Department
National Education Association
National Home Study Council
National Manpower Council
National Science Foundation
President's Committee on Education beyond the High School
President's Committee on Scientists and Engineers
United States Department of Labor
United States Office of Education[2]

Vestibule Training

When a company has to train large numbers of employees in similar skills for positions in either clerical or production work, they may consider the advisability of setting up a vestibule school. During World War II many companies used this method of training

[2] *Vocational-Technical Education for American Industry* (Circular No. 530) (Washington, D.C.: U.S. Department of Health, Education, and Welfare, 1958).

and found it quite successful. It is particularly advantageous when time is a factor and the work to be taught is relatively simple in nature. Many semiskilled production and clerical jobs can be taught in this manner with great success. In vestibule training we are concerned with job training which is not complex enough for an apprentice program. The length of training may be a few days, or it may be several months. Most frequently a simple job is taught, and it usually represents just a portion of the work of a given department. The advantages of this type of training are obvious. The interruptions that accompany the learner-teacher situation in on-the-job training are eliminated. The learner is under no pressure to turn out actual production. He can build his confidence at a pace more natural for him than the pace he may have to work at if trained on the production line or in the actual office. The company is assured of uniform training done under ideal conditions with the best instructors available to the company. The only pressure placed on the trainee and trainer is to complete the program in the prescribed time allotted to it. Exceptions can be made even here for a slow learner who has otherwise demonstrated that he can do the job he is being trained for. Whatever weaknesses the learner may possess soon become evident to the trainer, since he is under no pressure to turn out work. He can then spend such time as he feels is necessary to strengthen the trainee's weak spots, and, as a result, a new or transferred employee who might not have worked out if trained by conventional on-the-job methods is developed as a productive employee for the company. Generally speaking, people who are employed in semiskilled occupations represent the highest labor turnover potential in a company. It becomes necessary to train these people as rapidly as possible so that they can be utilized on the job as soon as possible in a productive capacity. This more rapid utilization of an employee is possible through the use of a vestibule school because the training is systematic and is carried out by training specialists. The fact that the worker is brought up to normal production standards more rapidly tends to increase his self-confidence as well as his earning power. Inevitably, the well-trained worker is more productive, and he usually stays on the job longer, thus reducing labor turnover. In the long run, the increased productivity of individual workers and the lower labor turnover pay for the investment in a vestibule school.

The vestibule school is usually established away from the actual workplace. This is done to remove it physically from the place where actual production is taking place, so that the training can be carried on without the interruptions that occur in the actual working environment. The same equipment, machines, tools, and materials are used in the training that are used in actual production. Actually, an attempt is made to duplicate the workplace in every way except for the pressures. The disadvantages most frequently mentioned in relation to vestibule training come about from this very method of establishment. Critics say that the training in a vestibule school lags behind the actual work processes because of the systems established in the school. It is claimed that the methodology becomes stagnant and that the training specialists are reluctant to change the methods. In addition, the "actual-experience" adherents say that a certain amount of retraining is necessary before the worker can make the transition from training to actual production. The fact that vestibule training is done at a much more leisurely pace than that required on the job itself is also a source of criticism. Since the worker is not used to doing the job under actual pressures, he does not think in terms of the necessary time limitations placed on him when he starts on a production basis.

1. Overcoming Disadvantages. While the disadvantages mentioned above are not always easy to overcome, they can be minimized by more effective management of the vestibule effort. Where the nature of the work is such that large numbers of workers are needed frequently for unskilled and semiskilled jobs, the vestibule school is the logical answer. If the training specialists work in close co-ordination with the line supervisors, they can keep the training up to date in relation to the actual jobs for which the training is being done. Frequent meetings as well as observation of the workplace by the trainer can increase the co-operation between line and staff. In fact, in some companies line supervisors are assigned to the vestibule school as trainers on a rotation basis. To help the employee make the transition from school to actual work performance, the trainer can aid in the follow-up after the trainee is placed. The trainee can also be introduced to the actual job on a gradual basis by going to school part time and working part time as his skill grows. When it reaches a desired level, he can be assigned to the job as a full-time employee. This will also help minimize the transition training which some supervisors feel is necessary for the vestibule trained employee.

2. Examples of Vestibule Training. The following examples of vestibule training indicate the various ways of working out the plan.

a) *Large Insurance Company.* All stenographers and typists, regardless of experience, are sent through a vestibule school in this company. The amount of training they receive is determined by the amount of job experience they have when employed by the company. At the least, they are given an orientation to the company's policies and procedures, and an inexperienced girl just out of high school is given instruction in the use of various typewriters and other office machines, such as adding machines, duplicating machines, and copying machines. Filing techniques are also included. All this work is done in a classroom atmosphere with no pressure placed upon the learner. Much of the training is done by role-playing, so that the new employee gets used to some of the varied situations she may face in the actual job. In addition, each new employee is given sufficient practice in typing and stenography that the desired speed and accuracy levels may be reached before assignment to a permanent position in the company. This school also serves to upgrade the skills of employees. If a typist wishes to become a stenographer, she may learn shorthand in evening classes.

This vestibule school furnishes clerical and secretarial help to the many departments in the company only after they have become familiar with company practices and procedures, and, as a result, there are many fewer complaints after job assignments from supervisors, and the girls have greater confidence in their ability to do the job well. New-employee jitters are removed, and the girl has gained the poise of experience when she is finally assigned to a job. The length of training varies according to the degree of skill and experience the employee has when the training starts. The shortest period is one week for the experienced employee and as long as six weeks for the novice who has just finished high school.

b) *Restaurant and Retail Food-Store Chain.* In this vestibule school the classroom atmosphere also prevails. Each new employee starting in this company reports to the school in the chain's central headquarters. A film depicting the history of the company is shown, and then varied training courses are pursued, depending on the new employee's ultimate job assignment. All the actual jobs are covered, such as waitress, coffee service, retail sales, supervision, and fountain work, together with lecture courses on company methods and procedures. The groups are small, and great attention is paid to individual instruction. The employee is trained in the particular skill until he is ready for job assignment. Each time a new technique or method is established, supervisors are sent to the school, so that they may train their employees in the latest techniques that are developed by the company's training department.

Here again, this company has met with success in the vestibule approach. Probably the outstanding factor in the training is the uniformity and the individual training. The management feels that this enables them to maintain each branch operation at an optimum level of efficiency and remove the burden of employee training from the manager so that he can devote maximum time to the operation of the branch store or restaurant.

c) *Large Commercial Bank.* This vestibule duplicates the actual banking operation of a branch. Employees are trained in a variety of jobs, such as teller, machine operators of varied kinds, clerical workers, and other necessary skills. This school is operated just as if it were an actual branch except that the situations are not real. Role-playing is used, and the work performed is not part of the bank's regular business transactions but examples developed by the bank's training department. These examples attempt to cover as many actual possibilities as can be obtained from daily experiences. The training department collects these and inserts them in the training program at the appropriate place. The desire is to develop an employee that can be assigned to a branch banking operation who can fit into its operations with a minimum of adjustment.

3. Training by Simulation. Very closely related to vestibule training is training by simulation. This type of training was used by the various military services during World War II to train men as rapidly as they could assimilate the knowledge and skills necessary for the particular function they were being trained for. Among the types of simulation used were gunnery for the training of aircraft gunners and bombardier training. The trainees were instructed in the use of their respective equipment on the ground under simulated conditions. In this manner they became familiar with the operation of the equipment and attained a suitable skill level before using the equipment in flight. This kept down accidents and expenses. Similar training is done in industry today for precisely the same reasons.

One of the prime users of simulation are the airlines, who train pilots in the use of new airplanes by using a mock-up of the plane on the ground. When new jet aircraft were purchased and the airlines were waiting for delivery, the pilots became familiar with the cockpit and instruments before they flew the aircraft. Thus they were able to become proficient and familiar with the new jet planes before they were delivered. Mock-ups of many kinds are used in manufacturing and service industries in a similar manner. They are particularly useful when new equipment is to be introduced and relatively large numbers of employees have to become familiar with the equipment. Costly mistakes are not made in actual production, and the company can train employees under ideal conditions. Then the conditions can be changed to represent any situation that may be encountered in actual job performance. Stress situations can be created, and the employee can be observed to see how he will react to such situations. In this way, misfits can be eliminated before production is upset or costly mistakes ruin valuable production equipment. In the next chapter we shall discuss a relatively recent innovation in simulation. It is decision-making simulation for the training of managers.

Special Training Programs

As a company grows and its problems become more complex, it begins to recognize the need for many types of training programs to meet the requirements of the work force. These programs are all conducted by means of one of the general methods described earlier in the chapter. Some of them are given on the job, while others are given in classrooms, and many are carried out by a combination of methods. Some are designed to fill a specific need and then abandoned, and others are carried on a continuing basis as long as they are necessary. Probably no one company has need for all the programs that are conducted throughout industry, but the numbers of special programs is growing each year, and the educational efforts in some companies rival that of an educational institution.

1. *Orientation Training.* One of the most common and widely used special training programs is involved with the orientation and indoctrination of new employees. The need arises from the desire of a company's management to have a new employee learn as much as possible about the company in a short period of time so that he will be more able to adjust to the environment and become more productive. Its need also stems from a recognition by management that a new employee will receive all kinds of information about the company from his fellow employees and the orientation program will give him a frame of reference from which to judge the varied impressions that he will receive in his early days with the company. Whether there is a formal program or not, the new employee has to be introduced to his fellow employees and the work environment. The terms of employment, such as the hours to be worked and the length of a probationary period, if any, have to be presented to the employee. Very often the new employee is nervous and ill at ease, and the orientation program is designed to help him adjust to his new surroundings as rapidly as possible.

The nature of the orientation program will differ somewhat, depending on the type of employee and also the size and type of company. In many large companies, executive trainees undergo an extensive program, during which major company executives speak to them. In addition, they are given plant and office tours and a complete history of the company. This history is often a color motion picture or a sound slide film and is usually quite comprehensive. Lower-level employees may be inducted by a member of the personnel department and then turned over to the immediate supervisor, who shows the employee his workplace and introduces him to his fellow workers. One successful method used in many companies of all sizes is the "buddy system." The new man is assigned to an older employee who is responsible for the newcomer until he becomes adjusted to his new position. This individual sees to it that the new employee is shown the washrooms, the eating facilities, and other necessary aspects of the physical environment. He also answers the many questions that a new employee may ask, or he anticipates these questions and explains the policies and procedures of the company that the new employee will be most concerned with. In any event, an orientation program allows the new employee the opportunity to get to know his new company more rapidly, and frequently he becomes more productive because he feels welcome and is not treated as an interloper. To supplement the verbal orientation, many companies give the new employee a booklet which usually contains a letter of welcome from the chairman and the president and an explanation of all the policies and procedures that are important to the new employee. Such things as vacations, holidays, leaves, insurance, pensions, rules of conduct, grievance procedure, and other pertinent company policies are included in this induction manual. In some instances, a follow-up program is conducted by the personnel department after the new employee has been on the payroll for a period of time, to ascertain how well he has adjusted to his new job and to determine whether any doubts or fears have developed in the employee's mind. Frequently, the man's supervisor is also contacted, so that his impression of the new employee can be correlated with the impressions of the employee.

2. *Safety Training.* While safety instruction is an integral part of any job being taught, the importance of maintaining safe procedures and a safety-conscious work force makes it necessary to supplement the job instruction with constant safety training. The large and medium-sized company will have a safety director as a member of the personnel department. It is his responsibility to develop a safety program that can be implemented by the line supervisors. He may also act as the instructor for group safety instruction. The insurance carrier will also help by furnishing literature on general safety problems, as well as providing guidance for safety programs through its staff of safety engineers. Even the small company can have a professional safety program in this manner if they utilize the efforts of the insurance company which carries its policies.

3. *Reading Skill Improvement.* One of the major complaints of many supervisory and management people, as well as research employees and others required to do a large amount of reading to keep up with the changing situations in the business world, is the extra time necessary to accomplish this task. Many companies have found that their employees had difficulty simply because they could not read rapidly enough and that, when they had finished reading, they did not understand what they had read. To alleviate this situation, some companies have sent their people to reading improvement clinics or have had an expert in this field hold classes in reading skill improvement on the company premises.

Programs of this kind are usually of short duration and are given to people who have heavy reading loads and who do not have the reading and comprehension rate to match their intelligence level. The results obtained from such programs has been very tangible. Many employees have more than doubled their reading speed, and their rate of comprehension has gone up as well. The expenditure for such a program is easily justified by the increased reading productivity. The results are easy to measure because the employee can be tested before being exposed to the training and then tested again at the end of the program. In addition, the employee's morale is usually affected in a very positive manner, and this shows him that training is worthwhile. In fact, such a program often creates a favorable climate for many other self-improvement programs which will enable the company to upgrade its work force and make it more effective.

4. *Letter-Writing and Public Speaking Programs.* Since communication is such a vital part of our lives, the necessary skills to communicate verbally and in writing are extremely important in business. A great many companies have found that letters that were being sent out by employees to customers, suppliers, and others that the company was doing business with were stilted, poorly written, and difficult to understand. Since even the best product or service cannot sell itself, these companies realized the importance of sound letter writing to their businesses. A typical program to improve written communications is one that was started about seven years ago by a medium-sized New York bank. The management hired a college professor who taught business writing at a local university. His course started with various members of the top management group, and he is still in the process of covering the organization. It is planned to reach everyone in the bank who has any responsibility for writing internal as well as external material. The classes number approximately twenty people, and they are conducted for two hours once each week for twelve weeks. Using examples of material written at the bank, the instructor helps each individual to improve his writing ability. Much individual attention is given, and over the years this bank has found its written communications considerably improved. In addition, the instructor prepares a monthly bulletin which is distributed to all employees in the program with helpful hints about bettering their writing techniques.

Public speaking programs are conducted on much the same basis as the letter-writing program described above. It is well known that businessmen are called upon frequently to be speakers at various functions in the business community as well as in civic activities. The impression that the public has of an organization is frequnetly formed at such a function. Public speaking classes have contributed to better verbal communications and clearer expression of daily conversation conducted in the normal course of business.

5. *Co-operative Training*. In many communities high schools, colleges, and vocational schools have co-operative training programs with local business firms. In this manner, practical training on the job is given to students attending these schools. They attend school part of the day and work for a company in the skill area they are learning about in school. The employee is compensated for the time he spends on the job, and in many instances he is offered permanent employment with the company when he graduates. This type of training has been successful in various clerical occupations, manual trades, retailing, sales, engineering, technical and laboratory jobs, and even lower-level management positions.

6. *Technical Training for College Graduates.*   The growing complexity of business enterprises has created the necessity for a wide variety of technical training programs for college graduates. They serve a dual purpose for the company using this type of program. First of all, they aid in the recruitment of college graduates who are desirous of expanding their knowledge about a particular field, and, second, the company develops young people in needed specializations to strengthen the existing work force. These programs run the gamut from short courses in a particular skill area, such as production control or time study, to Master's degree programs in such areas as electrical and mechanical engineering.

A number of these programs are conducted in co-operation with colleges and universities located near the plants and offices of the sponsoring company. One large company has arrangements with several universities throughout the country located near branch plants so that qualified employees may do their graduate work conveniently. A large aircraft company has established an in-plant program for advanced engineering degrees by having the faculty of an engineering school give classes in company classrooms. A number of federal government installations have similar programs for both civilian engineers and technicians and qualified military personnel.

Short skill programs are usually conducted on company premises, some of them by experts within the company and others by outside instructors who are frequently university faculty members located in close proximity to the plant. These courses include such subjects as production control, electronic data processing, time study and motion economy, system and procedure analysis, work simplification, and such specialized areas as metallurgy and plastics.

7. *Sales and Dealer Training.*   Even though many companies conduct sales and dealer training under the supervision of the marketing or sales department, it falls in the category of special training programs. In some companies the training division is called upon to render technical assistance in the development of suitable programs, which are then implemented by the sales department. In still other companies this type of training is carried on by the training division of the personnel department. Of course, there are those organizations that conduct such training in the same haphazard manner that other training is carried out. Nevertheless, sales training of all kinds is receiving increased attention from business managers in this country. Probably the prime reason for this is the fact that we are in an economy of abundance in a number of business areas and that, if products and services are to be marketed successfully, the sales force has to be properly trained. Couple this with the fact that many products are becoming increasingly complex, requiring of the salesman much more than a gregarious personality, and the problem of sales training begins to come into focus.

Many books have been written and more will be in the future that cover this particular area of training. It will serve the purpose of this book to describe briefly the dual problem of training company salesmen and dealers. In a good many large industrial organizations, college graduates are hired for the sales force. One such program is conducted by a large business machine company. The college graduate is initially sent to the home office for a period of four weeks, during which he is trained in company policies relative to over-all operation as well as sales. Formal classes and seminars are held by company executives in various subject areas, such as pricing, distribution, advertising, and sales promotion. Then the trainee spends another four weeks in the manufacturing plant producing the products he is going to sell. He is given formal instruction in the manufacture of the products, and he observes the manufacturing processes. The thought here is to familiarize the trainee with the equipment so that he is able to answer technical questions that customers may ask. At the completion of this phase, he is sent to the district to which he will be assigned and turned over to a senior salesman, whom he understudies. In addition, he is given continuous formal training at the branch office in sales techniques peculiar to the sale of the comapny product line. At the end of one year of this training, he is given a territory, and he is on his own.

8. Dealer Training. This type of training may range from a one-day yearly meeting of dealers, where new products are displayed and explained along with new pricing policies, to comprehensive programs of varying duration held both in the field, at regional training centers, and at the home plant and offices. Frequently, the dealer is an independent businessman selling the company products under a franchise agreement. It becomes necessary to convince these dealers that training is necessary and that it will help them maximize returns from their investment. Dealer programs include both sales and mechanical training programs. A number of manufacturing companies conduct training programs for technicians from dealer organizations, so that company products may be properly installed and serviced. Appliance and automobile companies are prime examples of those businesses conducting such programs. In addition, dealer salesmen are trained in sales and sales promotion techniques which will enhance their sales efforts. Quite frequently they receive training similar to that given to the company's own sales force. The primary reason that a company would undertake such a broad program of dealer training is to protect its investment in the products and services it sells and to maintain as high a level of goodwill with the consuming public as possible.

Summary

This chapter has endeavored to show the various considerations and problems that a company must recognize before undertaking the development of skill and special training programs. Management's responsibility for comprehensive forward planning to minimize the resistance to change and to maximize the benefits to be gained from the introduction of new equipment, techniques, and procedures is discussed at length. A variety of training approaches is explained. Among these are on-the-job training, apprentice training, vocational and technical training, vestibule training, simulation training, and both day and evening outside training programs in local schools.

Special training programs to fill specific company needs have grown in importance over the years. The recognition on the part of management that many skills are required to operate a business successfully supplies the impetus for many of these programs. Better-written and verbal communication is simply good business practice, and, since many employees are lacking in this vital area, company programs to rectify this lack become important. Proper orientation of new and transferred employees helps raise morale and makes the transition from inexperience to experience much easier for the employee. This means that the employee becomes productive more rapidly, and this makes him more valuable to the company.

Safety training to minimize the number of lost-time accidents is also to the self-interest of the company. Employees who practice safe procedures are more productive, and insurance costs are lowered. In addition, employee morale is enhanced by such training, since the employees feel that the company has a definite interest in their welfare.

The ever-increasing amount of literature that has to be read, if a responsible employee is to keep up to date in his area of activity in the company, has given rise to reading improvement programs in a number of companies. Both reading speed and comprehension are improved as a result of such programs. Co-operative training of young people who are going to school pays many dividends for the company utilizing such a program, since many good permanent employees are obtained from the school source when the employee completes his education. Along with co-operative programs, a number of companies have found it both useful and profitable to conduct a variety of technical programs for college graduates, to enable these people to upgrade their skills and in some cases work toward and complete graduate degrees. Rounding out the area of special training programs is the training of salesmen and dealers. This is being carried out on a wide scale by many companies so that they can gain an optimum return from their production and advertising investment.

It is apparent that the American business organization is becoming quite an educational institution. It is beginning to recognize that schools and colleges cannot turn out finished skilled technicians and that it has a responsibility for the maintenance of a continuing high level of productivity in the economy.

THINGS TO DISCUSS AND TO DO

1. Go to the library and research the idea that well-trained employees may have higher morale and be more productive and efficient.
2. Evaluate the training needs of your company or one with which you are familiar and choose a skill area where needs are critical. Outline in detail a skill training program which will help to alleviate this critical need.
3. Choose a skill in which you are lacking, such as public speaking, reading comprehension, or typing, and develop a self-improvement program which both you and other interested individuals may use to increase their skill.
4. Discuss the reasons why a first line supervisor charged with the responsibility for the skill training of subordinates may not accomplish such training effectively.
5. Discuss the many problems that may arise when a company purchases new equipment that may require skills which the present work force does not possess. In your discussion, consider the relationship of training to these problems and the contributions that effective training policies may make.

13. SUPERVISORY AND MANAGEMENT DEVELOPMENT PROGRAMS— CAPITALIZING ON LEADERSHIP ABILITIES

Purpose of the Chapter

THIS CHAPTER will offer no simple solutions to the sound development of management personnel for all levels of the organization. Rather it will discuss some practical approaches to this goal and offer some opinion on how such a goal can be achieved. It will point up the need for more careful evaluation of the manager's job and also what is expected of training programs for management. The training program examples and experiences are offered to stimulate thinking on the part of training directors, students, and management personnel responsible for the selection and placement of individuals in management positions. This chapter is also designed to demonstrate the usefulness of a formalized program for the development of business executives. It also emphasizes that sound development is a long-range process and that no single program can guarantee a supply of adequately trained individuals to fill supervisory and management job openings as they occur.

LEADERSHIP AND BUSINESS SURVIVAL

There is little argument among businessmen, educators, politicians, and other interested members of our society about the continuing and growing need for wise leadership in the business and industrial community. In recent years many studies have been undertaken by a variety of organizations in order to define more clearly the role of the manager in the business organization. In attempting to define this role, the next logical problem has been to define clearly and simply what a manager is. This has led to the numerous studies which have tried to determine how a manager can be trained.

The universality of the need for supervisory and management development has been well documented in a large number of business books and periodicals. Countless numbers of companies, whether they realize it or not, have found, or will find, that such development is a critical necessity. The top managements of these organizations have a growing recognition of the fact that the development of executives on all levels of the organization cannot be left to a hit-or-miss absorption of the necessary knowledge for competent performance.

Importance of Development Programs

Shortages that exist in the area of business leadership are even more critical than shortages of materials, capital, and machinery. Staffing executive positions in business organizations has grown in importance and significance because of the many changes in business itself. We have seen increased competition, growth in the size of companies, trends toward big labor unions and big government, and, because of this growth, an increased need for better communications and more astute decision making. There are very few enterprises left in this country that can afford the luxury of chance availability of necessary managerial skill. In addition, technological developments have been rapid in the years following World War II, and these changes have created human problems that were not previous considerations. Administrative knowledge and capacity quite frequently cannot cope with the rapidity of technological change that has occurred. There is growing acceptance of the fact that human understanding and greater administrative skill are needed to cope with the complexities involved in managing a modern business. The idea that, as the occasion demands, someone will rise to such an occasion is being rapidly diminished, and this attitude is being changed toward the more positive and fruitful one of methodical development of an adequate supply of managerial personnel.

Each year vast amounts of money are spent to protect the physical assets of business organizations. Naturally, neglect of these physical assets can endanger the future growth of any enterprise. Similarly, the neglect of the managerial assets of a business can place the company in comparable straits. Continuing success is possible only when the organization is aware of the need for maintenance of executive effectiveness. As was stated earlier, much attention has been focused on this problem in recent years. This attention has shed light on many aspects of management development and education. It has also done much to establish more clearly the goals desired by business for its management personnel. The approach followed in much of the research has been two-pronged. The function of management has been studied in order to define more clearly the role of the manager, and the nature of education for management has been studied in order to understand more readily what type of knowledge is necessary to attain effectiveness in this role.

While over the years much has been done to establish basic concepts with reference to supervisory and management development, perhaps the greatest effort in this direction has taken place in the last ten years. Because the role of business in our society is being recognized as a vital and important one, more attention is being focused on the nature of the people who run our industrial and business complex. In 1952 a study of some significance was undertaken jointly by the American Management Association and the Fund for Adult Education, an independent establishment created by the Ford Foundation. Since this chapter is concerned with education for management, it might serve a useful purpose to include a summary of the press release which announced this study before it was started. A careful consideration of the points mentioned in this press release will give a broader understanding of the need for a continuing program of executive development in American business organizations.

The summary of the above-mentioned press release follows:

Basic Propositions Underlying the Joint Decision of the American Management Association and the Fund for Adult Education Established by the Ford Foundation to Undertake a Study of Management Education for Itself and Its Employees

This Study rests upon certain basic propositions:

1. That management is playing an increasingly important part in modern society and is becoming, though to a degree about which we have no exact knowledge, aware of this and anxious to equip itself to meet its enlarged responsibilities.

2. That the first of these responsibilities is to play its part in the maintenance of a free society. By "free" in this context is meant a form of society in which each individual has opportunity and encouragement to develop to his or her fullest potential in character, capacity and personality.

3. That management is engaged in leading groups within the community

toward definite objectives in a way which, by satisfying those it serves, gives a sense of achievement to those who render service.

4. That management does this by getting results through people and that people can give of their best only if they are given opportunity and encouragement to develop the best that they have to give.

5. That the basic purpose of management is therefore identical with that of a free society—to provide a climate in which individuals can grow, so that in each cell of which American society is built up the individual may feel in his or her own experience that for which the nation stands.

6. That it is the responsibility of the individual manager to work to achieve this end.

7. That the influence of management extends beyond the individuals actually supervised to the lives of all others with whom those individuals are in contact.

8. That, among all the leadership groups which must play their part if any semblance of a free society is to be preserved, management has a unique position and task, since it has more frequent and more continuous contact with more elements in the broad working population than does any other group.

9. That management is an activity which calls for particular qualifications, attitudes, skills and preparation.

10. That for all these reasons it is of great national and social importance to know what is management's own attitude toward its task, the extent of its influence upon the American economy and society, how far it accepts its responsibilities, and what it is itself doing to insure a continuous supply of individuals progressively more competent to discharge them.

The American Management Association has undertaken this inquiry because it is dedicated to the study, improvement, and dissemination of management knowledge. Through its constant contact with more than 14,000 members actively engaged in management, it is in a unique position to find out what they are thinking and doing. The need for such a study has been widely felt. Its obligation to undertake the task is therefore clear, and it has had the encouragement and the help of the Fund for Adult Education established by the Ford Foundation in doing so.[1]

It can readily be seen that the foregoing summary makes a rather strong plea for competence on the part of business executives in the performance of their duties. The entire study certainly indicated the need for training and development on all levels of management within a company. An unusual and interesting discovery was made in the segment of the study that surveyed management development

---

[1] Lyndall F. Urwick, *Management Education in American Business* (New York: American Management Association, 1954), Appendix 1, p. 117.

practices in American industry. A quotation from the study will epitomize this discovery. It follows:

There are few if any absolutes in connection with management development activities. A company can be said to have a plan of management development when the management people of that company, despite the absence of formal procedures and system, feel or believe that there is a plan of management development. Similarly, regardless of formal procedures and system, there is no effective plan or program when the management thinks there is none. Moreover, a company can be said to be achieving satisfactory results in whatever it is doing to develop management personnel whenever that company feels that it is receiving its desired benefits. Hence management development is primarily a state of mind, a philosophy of management, a way of business life—*not* a system of forms and procedures.[2]

Perhaps the keynote of the paragraph above is the statement that management development is a way of business life. It is particularly important that business organizations recognize this, for in this recognition lies the key to business survival.

THE NATURE OF SUPERVISORY AND MANAGEMENT POSITIONS

The implication that management development is a philosophy may lead one to the conclusion that all a company has to do is think about developing managers and they will appear, ready to take on responsibility. There is no doubt that the training of managers is a controversial subject, since relatively little factual information is known about it. To be sure, much has been written over the years, and there are many principles pertaining to leadership that have come down to us from military and political spheres. The fact is, however, that all too few business organizations apply these principles and a good many people still believe that leaders are born and not made. Probably every business executive has his own pet theory as to the development of subordinates for greater responsibility. This theory is usually based on the way the particular individual concerned reached his position. Then training in this area has been plagued with a variety of fads and quick courses. Many companies have been disappointed with the results because in many instances they expected too much from their investment and in other instances

---

[2] Joseph M. Trickett, *A Survey of Management Development* (New York: American Management Association, 1954), p. 23.

they did not know what they were looking for. As is pointed out in Chapter 14, too little research is done to determine the usefulness of training or to assess its results accurately. In most cases training results are judged emotionally rather than scientifically. The indefinite attitude about management development is aptly summed up in a statement made by O. A. Ohmann, manager of employee relations for the Standard Oil Company (Ohio), at a recent round-table discussion held by the National Industrial Conference Board. He states:

> I have some misgivings about being here today. Just five years and two days ago I had a similar part on an NICB panel discussing management development. At that time many companies had no formally organized program of management development, so the panel could speak with confidence—and it did. The other day I reread my paper for that occasion and was consoled only by the dependability of human forgetfulness. A fair percentage of what we thought and did then we no longer think and do. Extrapolating, I should be able to give you a "discount factor" to apply to my remarks today; the only difficulty is that I cannot tell you exactly *which* of the things I will say today are untrue.[3]

What Is a Manager?

Perhaps the outstanding factor in trying to determine the effectiveness of supervisory and management development programs is to define more clearly what we are trying to accomplish with such programs. The obvious answer should be the development of suitable managerial personnel. But the obvious answer does not come close to being an accurate answer. In the first place, there is constant controversy as to whether or not individuals can be systematically trained for leadership positions in business organizations. Part of this controversy hinges on the concept of leadership that a given individual possesses. The time-worn arguments that surround the ancient cliché which states that leaders are born and not made still seems to pervade many discussions on the training of supervisors and managers. Even as far back as the time of Plato, there seems to have been discussion about the qualities of leadership. In Plato's *Republic* he mentions that no two persons are born exactly alike and that they differ from each other in natural endowments. We certainly recognize this today, but we also recognize that different individuals can be given the same training and that all can benefit from it. The main difficulty arises from the belief that we cannot train leaders. This

---

[3] "Management Development Today," *Management Record*, Vol. XXII, No. 4 (April, 1960), p. 29.

belief centers around the lack of understanding of what is necessary for competent performance of the managerial job. Even though many companies firmly agree that some kind of program is necessary, they do not know what to include in such a program. Closely related to this problem is the concurrent one of too high a level of expectation on the part of the program to develop people rapidly. The mass-production orientation of the assembly line of feeding in raw material and turning out a finished product has spilled over to the training function. This may be based on the assumption that you can assemble a program based on a variety of techniques and skills which can be readily learned and that, by exposing individuals to this training, they will automatically become leaders. The engineering approach of developing a list of desirable attributes and skills that an executive should possess and then trying to teach people this ideal list is probably one of the main causes of controversy in the field of management development. This attitude is aptly summed up in an article by a well-known writer on management subjects, Perrin Stryker, who states:

> The assumption that there is an executive type is widely accepted, either openly or implicitly. Yet any executive presumably knows that a company needs all kinds of managers for different levels of jobs. The qualities most needed by a shop superintendent are likely to be quite opposed to those needed by a coordinating vice president of manufacturing. The literature of executive development is loaded with efforts to define the qualities needed by executives, and by themselves these sound quite rational. Few, for instance, would dispute the fact that a top manager needs good judgment, the ability to make decisions, the ability to win respect of others, and all the other well-worn phrases any management man could mention. But one has only to look at the successful managers in any company to see how enormously their particular qualities vary from any ideal list of executives' virtues.[4]

The Generalist versus the Specialist

The first step in any attempt to define more clearly training needs in the area of supervision and management is to ascertain what we want the manager to do. As the foregoing quotation points out, there are varying needs which are dependent on the level at which the manager functions in the organizational structure. Yet the usual concept of leadership focuses around the ideal image of the valiant knight on a white charger leading his forces into battle. Paradoxically, the

---

[4] Perrin Stryker, "The Growing Pains of Executive Development," *Advanced Management*, Vol. XIX, No. 8 (August, 1954), p. 15.

same individual that will demand the need for strong leadership on the national scene will resent this type of leadership if his superior exercises it over him. People who say that they work their best when not prodded are often the ones who let the work slide and complain that they are not given clear instructions. The fact that the business environment requires a variety of approaches to get the job done escapes the individuals who are subjected to these approaches. One situation may require autocratic leadership, and another situation that arises just a few moments later may require a more democratic method of leadership if it is to be successfully administered. It is precisely this need to be a human relations virtuoso that causes much of the difficulty in the design of effective executive development programs.

As was mentioned earlier in this book, technical skill and competence are frequently the first characteristics that management notices about an individual. The fact that a person can perform with a high degree of efficiency in a narrow skill area may be the outstanding factor that recommends him for promotion to the first-line level of management. While outstanding technical skill may be a necessary requisite for job success, it may not be absolutely necessary for success as a supervisor. In fact, many highly skilled individuals find it impossible to supervise the work of others because they have too high a level of performance expectation on the part of their subordinates.

Closely related to this problem in industry is the problem involved in the proper development of young people for responsibility in business. The constant argument of generalist versus specialist has been with us for a long time. It is not unusual for the president of a large corporation to give a speech at a college commencement extolling the virtues of a broad liberal education and to have the personnel manager of that same company recruiting technically trained specialists on the same campus. Much has been written about the usefulness of a broad educational background for administrative positions in industry, yet hiring practices seem to indicate a preference for the rather narrower educational disciplines of engineering, accounting, law, and business administration.

Education for business has come under rather close scrutiny in recent years. Many people who have paid little attention to this important aspect of our educational complex are now at least becoming aware of it, if nothing else. A recent article in *Business Week* magazine points up this attitude. The article was reporting on the 1960 McKinsey Lectures given at the Graduate Business School of Columbia University. The topic was business vitality, and of particular interest was the reporting of discussion among executives that took place after the conclusion of the lecture program. Among the discussants were the heads of a wide variety of major American businesses. These executives turned their attention to education for business as follows:

After some discussion of stockholders' meetings, the executives turned a critical eye on management textbooks and graduate business schools. This touched on a point made by Kappel in his lecture that afternoon. "I have found very little in the literature of management that has helped me to be a better manager." He went on to say that to help build vitality "business organizations, including my own, might well do a lot more to study their own important experience and write about it so that all might profit by it."

With more than a little relish, the executives attacked most management books as having little value because people without business experience usually wrote them, and the subject defied rational analysis anyway. As one company president said: "We just don't know the qualities one must have to become an executive or how one becomes an executive." Said one chairman of the board of a billion-dollar company: "It's the seat of your pants that tells you how." One executive summed up the feeling about a well-known textbook: "It's not worth the powder to blow it up."

When one of the three business students present asked if the executives really thought graduate business schools were worthless, Dean Courtney C. Brown of Columbia B-School entered a spirited defense. The schools can do three important jobs, he argued:

Acquaint students with the vocabulary and processes of management.

Develop intellectual qualities that will be helpful later.

Help the student to think about some of the characteristics of his society that affect business and so help him to develop ethical standards.[5]

Can Supervisors and Managers Be Trained?

Needless to say, this quotation displays the attitude of some executives toward education for business. The effect on business organizations would not be too great if this attitude were not relatively widespread. Even in companies that have been spending large sums of money on a variety of supervisory and executive development programs, one hears voices of doubt as to their usefulness. Many individuals who are sent to university programs in distant cities or to courses sponsored by various associations look on these

[5] "A Vital Topic—Business Vitality," *Business Week*, May 14, 1960, pp. 86 and 91.

trips as pleasant junkets away from the pressures of the job. Many go merely because they are told to go, and still others look upon the course as a reward for hard work rather than an opportunity to learn more about the managerial task.

The essence of the problem is not training as such. Rather, it is the formalized training program, that has become prominent since the end of World War II. Few business executives will deny the fact that experience on the job over a period of years is really training. Most companies readily recognize that a period of indoctrination is necessary even for experienced managers. Certainly, the individual employee that is promoted from within the organization must learn his new job. The question is whether he can learn more effectively by actually performing the job over a period of time or whether some type of formalized supervisory development program will accelerate his competence level. There are, of course, some people who believe that little or nothing can be done to train a manager or supervisor. These individuals believe that a man is the product of his heredity and environment and that, by the time he reaches a position of responsibility in business, there is very little that can be done to change his basic personality. A long nurturing process over a period of years results in the end product that the company has to work with, and either he fits into the proper place in the hierarchy or he does not.

Another aspect of the problem centers around what is expected of training and development. In many instances a company will expect some kind of uniform ideal man to emerge from the training program. They will expect this man to possess all the necessary skills and knowledge for successful job performance and, in addition, to be aggressive, dynamic, honest, tactful, decisive, flexible, co-operative, and individualistic. Not only are many of these qualities paradoxical, but there are very few human beings who possess even a portion of them. It may be of some interest to note that the authors have conducted a series of executive development programs for a variety of companies over the years, and one of the questions we ask of conference participants is to define the qualities they would like to see in their superiors. In most cases this list is pursued with vigor, and invariably the group comes up with a compilation of godlike characteristics. Upon further analysis and questioning, they begin to see the impossibility of such a human existing in the company, and they sheepishly admit that it does no harm to indulge in wishful thinking. If management training is to be at all successful, such wishful thinking must be eliminated from the minds of those individuals who design training programs, as well as of the people who participate in them.

Knowledge, Skills, and Attitudes Necessary

With the great amount of interest and emphasis on mental health in recent years, the general public has become more aware of the complexity of the human being. It is increasingly apparent that we know very little about the mind and its actions and reactions. If one reads the many articles in business publications related to management development, further confusion results. These articles range all the way from unqualified praise for formalized programs to outright discounting of the need for any type of formalized training for managers. Many of these articles are based on experience in a particular company or a particular program. A careful reading will tend to demonstrate that original objectives were often hazy when a program failed to measure up to the expectation, and where success was achieved the article will indicate that the expectation was realistic. In other words, there seems to be a high degree of correlation between what a company expects an executive development program to accomplish and its degree of success in that company.

Any attempt to generalize from individual experience is fraught with the dangers of illogical reasoning. Yet this is very often done when evaluating the results of management development programs and in trying to develop a suitable program for use in a particular company. In relation to management development it is probably unfortunate that we seem to adhere to a hero approach to leadership. Many individuals envision a leader as an individual leading the troops into battle. This concept, along with the rags-to-riches Horatio Alger concept, has firm undercurrents in our business life. In trying to assess what is necessary for successful business leadership on all levels, our thinking is frequently clouded by the above-mentioned concepts of leadership. Autobiographical and biographical articles and books appear frequently in this country and tend to perpetuate the notion that leadership requires hard work and a firm hand on the tiller and that any young person can achieve success if he follows this advice. Unfortunately, the development of supervisors and managers in business requires somewhat more sophisticated thinking if it is to have a chance for success.

Even though much of the advice about success in business seems to center around simple black-and-white reasoning, there is considerable evidence to support the need for more incisive analysis of the ingredients of successful achievement in supervisory work. We tend to put human beings into types and categories that are quite arbitrary, not recognizing that each individual is complex and that each leadership situation has nuances and shadings which require unusual handling and to which no simple formula can be applied. It has become increasingly popular to characterize people in business by placing them in such convenient categories as "organization man," "typical steel company executive," "conformist," "Madison Avenue," "Wall Street," "banker," "white collar," and a host of others too numerous to mention. Perhaps this comes from the predilection to place people in racial, religious, and nationality categories; but, whatever the reason, it is increasingly prevalent in business. In addition, many employees place their supervisors in the "good" or "bad" category based on their reaction to a particular event or order. This tendency to oversimplify has led us to the many lists of executive characteristics which now prevail in business literature.

Nevertheless, there is some usefulness in trying to develop a set of knowledge, skill, and attitude criteria by which executive development can be measured. The caution focuses around the desire to oversimplify such lists and apply them to all leadership situations in business. It is difficult to separate into categories the many things that successful business executives possess that go into their personalities. The many articles, self-help books, and biographical interviews seem to point in particular directions, however. Even though widely divergent individuals can be successful in a variety of business situations there is a common ground on which they all seem to meet. Among the common factors found in many studies are the following:

1. Knowledge. The successful supervisor on any level must possess technical knowledge related to the jobs he is supervising. The amount of this knowledge varies with the level of supervision. The first-line supervisor must have a great deal of such knowledge because he is frequently called upon to train operators as well as fill in if the need arises. As the supervisory responsibility broadens, the supervisor requires less specific technical knowledge of the jobs performed, but he must have a general understanding of the nature of the work for evaluation purposes. He must be familiar with a variety of administrative practices, such as planning, organizing, control, delegation, and decision making. The higher the level of management, the greater the need for this kind of knowledge. Insight into human nature is also a necessary requisite to successful supervision. Part of this knowledge can be obtained from training and part from on-the-job experience.

2. Skills.   Naturally, knowledge is relatively useless unless one possesses the necessary skill to apply it. The supervisor must exercise skill in the area of administration and must particularly learn how to assume responsibility and delegate tasks to other individuals. This implies the development of sound judgment not only of situations but of human beings as well. Probably one of the greatest reasons for executive failure is the lack of skill and ability in the area of judgment. Conceptual skill is perhaps the most necessary skill that the supervisor must have to be successful. Effective co-ordination of business functions and the people who must perform these functions requires an ability to see the entire area of responsibility as a whole, rather than in segments. The supervisor can be lacking in technical skill and still succeed in getting the necessary work done if he can recognize the relationships that exist among the various jobs on any level of the organizational structure. It is the ability to judge human beings soundly, their relationship with the equipment, and the judicious use of available funds that makes for executive success.

3. Attitude.   This criterion is probably the most difficult to define. It can be best described by the oft-repeated statement "He failed because he did not have a management viewpoint." The development of this management attitude or viewpoint is of vital necessity, but it is usually the most difficult thing to attain in an executive development program. To be effective, a manager must be able to encourage other people to do their best on a continuing basis. Obviously, in order to do this, he must set the example. His attitudes are reflected throughout the group he supervises. It is generally agreed that attitudes are built up over a long period of time and that they are very difficult to change. Quite frequently the way a given supervisor perceives his job and the attendant goals determines not only his level of performance but the level of performance of the entire group. If he happens to be a top-level executive, then the attitudes displayed will have a good deal to do with shaping the so-called corporate image.

SUPERVISORY TRAINING PROGRAMS

Generally speaking, there are three levels of management in most business organizations. These levels are given many names by different writers in the field, but the most readily understandable widespread ones are top management, middle management, and first-line management. Recognizing the fact that the exercising of supervision on any level is quite similar, the training of people on different levels of supervision requires a variety of approaches. Even though the basic principles are the same for all managers, it is the application of these principles to the daily situations that arise that differs in magnitude. Closely related is the fact that the trainees differ in education, experience, and background, and, as a result, their rate of knowledge absorption may differ also. It has been the authors' experience that first-line supervisors require much more explanation of management theories, concepts, and principles than do their more experienced superiors on higher levels in the organization. It is a reasonably safe assumption that content differs in degree rather than in subject matter when comparing supervisory training on different levels in the same organization. The first-line supervisor has to be given many concrete and practical examples rather than abstract theory and philosophy. He must be shown how the subject matter of the program may help him on his job, so that it is a good idea to draw as many examples as possible from the work experience of the group being trained.

Choosing Participants

In a large number of companies, first-line supervisors are chosen from among the existing group of employees. It is on this level that any promotion-from-within policy is most strictly adhered to. As was mentioned earlier, promotion to this level is frequently given as a reward for outstanding job performance, long company service, or both. As unfortunate as this may be in some instances, it is still a widespread practice and should be realistically recognized as such by the training director. He should, however, make every effort to convince management in his company that other criteria should also play a part in the selection of individuals for training as supervisors. Even first-line supervision is a complex job and requires abilities other than outstanding work performance and longevity. As nebulous as it may sound, it does require the ability to handle people and inspire them to greater work performance. Anyone who has supervised the work of others knows that this is no small accomplishment. Under the conditions that exist in many business enterprises, the first-line supervisor is frequently chosen on short notice and in a haphazard manner. Very often the man or woman is a worker one day and a supervisor the next day. With little or no orientation to the responsibilities of supervision, it is no small wonder that the chances for success as a supervisor are considerably diminished. In companies that follow this approach to selection of supervisors, one usually finds a similar approach applied to the selection of training programs and trainees to participate in these programs. The chapters in this book devoted to research methods point up the need for much work in this area, and no company, whatever its size, should neglect the "ounce of prevention" that research will accomplish in making a program more successful. When one considers the amount of money spent on training and the costs involved in time off the job, it seems prudent to devote some effort, time, and money to the choice of participants and programs, in order to realize a greater return on the training dollar investment.

What to Look For in Prospective Trainees

Certainly, the outstanding reason for any supervisory training program is the more rapid development of suitable supervisors for the various lower-level management needs of the company. In addition, this initial selection may prove to be the starting point for greater responsibility for the individual chosen. What, then, should management look for in the prospective supervisor that will indicate that he is promotable and suited for such training? As was indicated earlier in this chapter, this is no easy task. There are, however, some indicators that have proved successful in many companies. Among these are the following:

1. *Ability to Understand and Carry Out Oral and Written Instructions.* This is an important factor because a good part of

the supervisor's job is to give instructions and see that they are carried out properly. A person who can accomplish this when a worker has a good chance for success in the supervisor's role.

2. Emotional Stability. If an individual can accept extraordinary situations when they arise and use good judgment in the handling of such situations, he indicates that he may be able to stand the stresses involved in supervision. This does not imply that he has to be a placid individual with no temper, but it does mean that he should not be prone to emotional outbursts under stress and that he should be able to work successfully under pressure. Even though the job he does before promotion to supervision may not be a pressure job, the responsibility of supervision presents many situations in which the individual will have to act wisely so as to develop stability among the group he supervises.

3. Ability to Organize His Work in an Orderly Manner. If the individual being considered has evidenced an ability to plan his work and then execute it with a definite purpose in mind, this would indicate a talent for organization which would help him considerably in supervisory work.

4. Ability to Deal with Fellow Workers Successfully. Fellow workers and their estimation of an individual can be an excellent indicator of future success as a supervisor. If a person is respected and has the confidence of his peer group on the job, he is on the way toward being a successful supervisor. In a poorly supervised group this type of individual may even be the informal or de facto leader to whom the employees turn with their problems, grievances, and ideas.

5. Ability for Oral and Written Expression. Communications ability is of paramount importance to the successful supervisor. The need for giving clear instruction and for reporting on the performance of the group is inherent in the supervisor's job. If the potential supervisor shows by his daily efforts that he can communicate effectively both in writing and by speech, he certainly demonstrates that he can be trained to supervise others.

6. Loyalty. Quite often an individual will not be promoted because he is not management-oriented. What is implied here is that the individual is a complainer and constantly criticizes management actions. Constructive criticism is useful, but the carping and petty gripes indicate poor morale and a lack of understanding of the over-all implications of the many courses of action that management must take in carrying out its responsibilities. Successful supervision implies a dedication to the company that transcends pettiness and bickering. The supervisor must set the example for his men, and if he reacts negatively as a worker, the chances are that he will not change appreciably if he is made a supervisor.

7. Seniority. While this factor was partially discounted earlier in the chapter, it should be considered when choosing a person for supervisory training. Certainly, an individual who has given long service to the company deserves consideration for promotion. However, he should not be chosen for this alone. If he has shown that he possesses other qualifying characteristics, then seniority should be in his favor, but promotion to supervision should not be thought of simply as a reward for service to the company.

8. Accuracy and Competent Work Performance. Here, too, we have one of the frequent pitfalls that govern the selection of participants for training programs. An outstanding performer on the job is naturally readily noticed by his superiors. They must be careful not to let this performance be the prime factor in selection. Very often the outstanding performer is something of a perfectionist, and he may not recognize individual differences, and, as a result, he will get into frequent arguments with employees when they do not perform up to his high standards.

9. Ability to Learn and Grow. In many companies attempts are made to force training on unwilling individuals. If a person has shown by attending evening school or by taking correspondence courses on his own that he wants to learn, this is a good indicator that he will absorb training satisfactorily. Job performance and its improvement plus a willingness to learn new jobs are also good indicators for further growth on the part of the individual.

10. Desire to Assume Responsibility. Opportunities frequently arise when extra work must be done in an emergency situation or extraordinary overtime becomes necessary. Some individuals are the so-called "nine to five" types, and they refuse to co-operate in such emergencies. This type usually does not have the proper attitude for supervisory responsibility. Many companies take part in a variety of charitable drives, such as blood donations, community chest, and the like. If an individual has demonstrated leadership ability in this area, he may be a worthwhile risk for supervisory training. In companies that have a recreational program, the employees who attain positions of leadership in such groups as bowling leagues, picnic committees, and camera clubs can apply this experience to job supervision and become successful supervisors.

The Nature of the Supervisory Training Group

The preceding list of attributes is by no means intended to be all-inclusive. Individual company experience will dictate changes and additions to any list of desirable characteristics. If it stimulates thinking in the positive direction of making the choice of participants less of an emotional one, then it will serve its intended purpose. Each manager that is confronted with the need for choosing people for a developmental program has usually acquired a personal list of criteria to measure people for training and possible promotion. All will agree, however, that there is considerable need to minimize failure in any attempt to train supervisors and that personal likes and dislikes should be secondary in the selection procedure.

Any company that has been in business for a period of years will be able to evaluate the performance of its supervisors based on actual experience. Even if the evaluation is not as scientific as it should be, management will have some fixed ideas as to what type of individual is successful and what type has proved to be unsuccessful. It is a well-known fact that much of the knowledge gained by business organizations is pragmatic. To a great extent, American businessmen measure performance by results, and if a particular supervisor has a suitable record of achievement over a period of time, he is looked upon as a successful supervisor, and other individuals chosen for the supervisory role are frequently measured against this type of standard.

Closely related to the measurement of individuals by some preconceived standard is the composition of the group that will be exposed to the training venture. Company thinking and desires relative to promotion, training needs, and what they expect from a supervisor all have a vital role in the selection of candidates. Naturally, emotional factors also loom large in the selection procedure. Such things as company politics, salary levels, and the desire of a particular executive to sponsor a protégé may hamper a completely rational selection. The authors have had considerable experience in the development of lower-level supervisory training programs for a variety of business and governmental enterprises, and numerous problem areas have become apparent over the years as a result of this experience. This experience may prove useful to the training director and other members of management in addition to the student. At least, it may furnish something of a guide when considering supervisory training.

1. *Company Climate and the Training Program.* Probably the most frequent criticism of any supervisory training expressed by participants is related to the usefulness of the subject matter. Very often the material learned in the course cannot be applied on the job because it differs from the ideas and practices of the man's superiors. Many first-line supervisors feel that any training is wasted on them if their bosses do not receive similar training. The attitude of middle and top management toward first-line supervision has a great deal to do with the success or failure of the program. This is particularly true in the case of any human relations training, as is pointed out in Chapter 1. The climate existing in the company is probably the outstanding determinant as to whether or not human relations training can effect any significant change in supervisor-employee relationships.

a) A Negative Example. One of the authors had an interesting experience in this regard. He was called into a company employing approximately 1,200 people to help the personnel department design a suitable supervisory training program for first-line supervisors and some employees who were not as yet supervisors but who were identified as promotables. The program was developed with much care and many conferences. Finally, it was approved by the personnel vice-president, and a date was chosen for the first session. The participants were chosen, but, unfortunately, no one had told them of the choice. Three days before the program began, some of the people were told that they were going to be trained, and the rest of the group were told on the morning of the same day that the program was to begin. Needless to say, the conference leader had some small difficulty with the group at the first session in trying to convince them of the usefulness of such a training program. Most of the participants looked on the program as an interruption of their more important daily work. They felt that if management did not think enough of them to give them suitable advance notice, then the program could not be very important. None of them were told the purpose or nature of the program or what was expected of them as participants. The first session and two subsequent sessions had to be devoted to attempts to soothe battered egos and to point up the usefulness of the training. In a climate of this kind it is certainly difficult to justify the cost of supervisory training because the trainees will have little opportunity to use any of the knowledge. It became apparent that such training was undertaken simply because the personnel vice-president had heard about a similar program being done for a competitor and thought that it would be a good idea if his company kept up with the competition.

b) A Positive Example. In another business organization about twice the size of the one in the foregoing example, supervisory training was undertaken also, but the circumstances were quite different. In the first place, before any program was developed, company records were carefully checked to determine the need for supervision over the ensuing 5-year period. Needs were directly related to company expansion plans. Performance ratings of all supervisors were checked, in addition to the performance ratings of individuals who were being recommended for promotion by their superiors. The personnel department tried to determine what characteristics made for successful supervision in the company. Various key members of management were consulted for their opinions and ideas. These included the president, line vice-presidents, key members of middle management, and many first-line supervisors. After extended study on the part of the company, one of the authors was called in to help in the design of the program, and he was given complete access to all the information that had been previously gathered. He was also allowed to discuss the program with any one in the company that he chose. The selection procedure was undertaken by the personnel department with the complete knowledge and co-operation of the line departments and such staff departments as were concerned. Each selected trainee was called in for a conference with his supervisor and a senior member of the personnel staff. He was told about the program, what his part in it was, and what was expected of him. In addition, he was told of the importance of the program relative to his future development with the company. Prior to the first meeting, the conference leader, who was one of the authors of this book, interviewed each trainee individually. The purpose was to get to know the trainee and to exchange information, so that the opening session could concentrate on the subject matter of the program.

This program has been continued for a number of years and is still going on in this manner. Each trainee is closely watched by his superiors after the conclusion of the training, and, even though everyone exposed to the training has not improved, the results have been excellent, and many middle- and top-management supervisors have gone through the program prior to their promotion. The program is looked on with great pride by each participant, and it has become something of an honor to be chosen to participate. In fact, many of the early participants have been sent through again for a refresher course. With the exception of a few die-hards in the company management, the program is considered a success and has the complete backing of management on all levels. The trainee is given every opportunity to apply what he has learned. In fact, the chances are very good that his superior has gone through the program in a previous year and will discuss the various conferences with him. This, in turn, becomes a constant learning tool for the trainee's superior, and it gives him the opportunity to learn more about his subordinate under ideal circumstances—discussing something which each has in common.

2. *Are the Trainees Promotable?* This is not the simplest question to answer and is the cause of much controversy in the area of supervisory and executive development. The intention here is not to enter into that controversy but rather to point out that the training director or whoever has the responsibility for the training function should know the purpose that the training program is to serve. In some companies training groups are made up of individuals that have been identified as promotables by their superiors. Here the purpose is to give these employees a certain amount of training, so that they will be able to assume further responsibility and perhaps even go beyond the first level of supervision. In some cases the employees chosen for supervisory training have been supervisors for some time, having been promoted from among the work force. They are given training to help them understand more fully the role of the supervisor. In still other companies a human relations training program can be looked at as a means for the reorientation of troublesome employees—in other words, employees who have a poor record of dealing with others on the job, troublemaking, lack of a positive company attitude, or some other related factor. If this is the case, then the person designing the training program should be fully aware of it. Under no circumstances should a group be made up of people who are definitely thought of as having promotion potential and other people who are thought to need rehabilitation to make them better employees.

A few examples of trainee groups may help point up the need for careful selection of the participants.

a) *The Negative Individual.* He is doing the company a favor by submitting to training, since he knows everything there is to know about his job and no one can teach him a thing.

b) *The Silent One.* He never wants to get involved, and he goes along with the premise that silence is the safest way. He acts this way on the job, and he was assigned to the training program in the hope that he would change.

c) *The Troublemaker.* He has been on the brink of being fired on several occasions, but management is giving him another chance, and they feel that human relations training will show him the error of his ways. It won't.

d) *The Dominator.* He is a long-time employee of the company and knows all the folklore of company politics. He grasps every opportunity to make speeches about his connections in the company and the fact that he started thirty years ago with this or that vice-president.

e) *The Skeptic.* He knows that the subject matter covered in the program is all theory and cannot be applied on the job. Book learning is for children, and, besides, his department is different and requires special handling which no one but he can give.

f) *The Comedian.* Life is one big joke to this individual. He has a new joke for every meeting (at least he thinks it's new). He has no problems with his group, since he knows how to keep everyone happy.

g) *The Keyman.* He is the highest-ranking supervisor in the group, and everyone looks to him for an opinion before they speak. They are afraid they might not follow the party line, and, as a result, he exercises a negative dominance over the group.

h) *The Dictator.* All employees are lazy, and they will not give a good day's work unless they are browbeaten. The only thing that employees understand is force, and that is the only way to get the work out. Training is a waste of time, but he comes to the meetings just to prove how wrong the instructor is and how right he is.

i) *The Ingratiator.* He is the conference leader's friend and agrees with everything that is said. In this manner he bolsters his lagging security; actually, he does disagree but is reluctant to express himself.

j) The Hedger. He never takes sides in any discussion and has an opinion to offer which expresses no viewpoint. He rarely makes a firm decision on the job, and this carries over to the training program.

k) The Do-Gooder. This is the group errand boy. He will get sharp pencils, fresh pads, and ashtrays. Opening windows and arranging chairs are also fortes of this individual. After all this physical work he is worn out and has little or nothing to say in the discussion.

h) The Social Butterfly. He is not much good during the discussion period, but when it is over, he comes to the instructor with all kinds of comments and invitations to coffee or stronger beverages.

Every training director and conference leader will recognize some of the above detractors and will even be able to add some of his own. The fact is that supervisory training is made a much more difficult task when a group is populated with any of the personality types mentioned above. Careful selection will not eliminate them, but it will certainly help to minimize the disrupting influence. Where a group has a healthy attitude about training and the complete backing of management, the training program has a much greater chance to accomplish its goals.

3. Placement after Training. The sooner any learning can be implemented, the better the chance for its use. This watchword is particularly important when the trainees are not supervisors but have been defined as promotables. This is perhaps one of the prime areas of difficulty in all supervisory and management development programs. When a person is chosen for training and is not yet in a supervisory position, he obviously feels that he is designated for rapid promotion soon after the program is completed. If this event does not take place with reasonable speed and he is given no reason for it by his superiors, he will think less and less of the training as time goes on, and it will even have a negative effect on him in many instances.

Another aspect of the placement problem is related to the first factor discussed above—company climate. If he is placed at the head of a section where his superior gives him no opportunity to exercise sound supervisory judgment, then his subordinates will lose respect for him, and he will become frustrated in any attempt to grow. If the company climate is such that his opinions and judgment are sought and acted upon by higher management, then his supervisory job will be easier, and he will be able to develop into a manager who can continue to assume responsibility and go on to higher positions in the company. In his daily tasks, the typical first-line supervisor deals with many people outside his own section. Many of these individuals are on the same level of supervision in the company, and others are members of staff departments. It becomes obvious that, to maximize the benefit of any supervisory training program, a large number of people in the company should be exposed to it. If the supervisor finds that what he has learned is not practiced by either his peer group or his superiors, he will quickly stop trying to implement what he has learned and will try to please his bosses.

A common practice in many companies is to give a man a provisional promotion. He is frequently called an "acting" department head or some similar designation. Whether it is reluctance on the part of management to make a decision, poor planning, or some other reason, it adds up to a vote of no confidence and is so interpreted by the supervisor. He may be hesitant to act with firmness because he does not want to incur the displeasure of his superiors when actually he may never get the permanent designation because they will feel that he is afraid to make decisions. Closely related to this is the promotion that is tendered with no raise in pay, even though the new position calls for a higher rate. The supervisor is told that he will receive a raise after he proves himself or that he will be taken care of in the next performance-rating period. Even a token increase in salary at the time of promotion will do much to build the supervisor's self-confidence and motivate him to superior performance. It is not the amount of money as much as it is the confidence the supervisor feels his superiors have in his ability to do the job.

Types of Supervisory Training Programs

A study of supervisory training manuals used in many company training programs as well as those used by university extension courses and other off-premises programs will indicate the impact that the Training Within Industry (TWI) programs of World War II have had on supervisory training. At the risk of boring the seasoned training director, a brief description of this program must be included. The success of these programs during that critical period gave great impetus to the training of supervisors immediately after the war. This trend has continued, and the present-day modifications of these programs have been and continue to be successful.

The TWI Program had three parts: Job Methods Training, Job Relations Training, and Job Instructor Training. Each of the programs consisted of five 2-hour sessions usually given by company employees who were previously prepared and coached by the TWI Service. If the company found it impossible or impractical to furnish its own trainers, the trainers were also furnished by the TWI Service from other companies. The rapid growth of industry during the war pointed up the need for a great number of supervisors, and the large majority of them came from the work force of the company needing them. As it is today in most cases, these people had little or no supervisory experience, and certain of the highly practical skills of supervision had to be taught to them in a hurry. The entire program was based on the assumption that every supervisor has five needs. These needs are as follows:

1. *Knowledge of the Work.*   Materials, machines, tools processes, operations, products, technical skill, and information.

2. *Knowledge of Responsibilities.*   Policies, agreements, rules, regulations, safety, schedules, and interdepartmental relationships.

3. *Skill in Leading.*   Increasing production by helping supervisors to improve their understanding of individuals, their ability to size up situations, and their ways of working with people.

4. *Skill in Planning.*   Improving job methods by having supervisors understand and study each operation, in order to combine, rearrange, and simplify details affecting the use of materials, machines, tools, and manpower.

5. *Skill in Instructing.*   Shortening training time by breaking down jobs into simple operations, making the learner receptive, presenting the instruction, trying out his performance, and following up for results.

With this over-all frame of reference, supervisors were trained in three areas. No attempt was made to give standardized solutions or rules. The purpose was to build confidence and resourcefulness among potential supervisors so that better teamwork and more production were the result.

Job Methods Training

The main idea in this program was to build an attitude among the participants which would enhance their efficiency. Emphasis was

placed on such small improvements that any supervisor could personally implement in the pursuit of his daily work. The improvements did not have to be spectacular but of a continuing nature. New
ideas and better ways of doing things were encouraged. The supervisors were given four steps to follow. They are broadly presented as
follows (in the actual program they were given in much greater
detail) :

Step 1—Break down the job.
Step 2—Question every detail.
Step 3—Develop the new method.
Step 4—Apply the new method.

Job Instructor Training

The need for additional skilled workers in large numbers became
readily apparent early in World War II. The problem was to teach
as many novices a variety of critical skills in as short a time as
possible. Trained workers and supervisors were given this training
in teaching methodology so that they could teach their skills to
others with a minimum of difficulty. Increased skill production was
the goal, and it was achieved through the implementation of this
program. Here is a brief description of the steps involved in this
program:

How to get ready to instruct:
  1. Have a time table.
  2. Break down the job.
  3. Have everything ready.
  4. Have the work place properly arranged.
How to instruct:
  1. Prepare the worker to receive instruction.
  2. Present the operation.
  3. Try out his performance.
  4. Follow up on his performance. If the worker hasn't learned, the instructor hasn't taught.

Job Relations Training

A reasonably practical way was developed to enable supervisors
to get better results from the people whom they were supervising,
not only as individuals but as a team. Emphasis was placed on the
simple fact that results are achieved through people. The supervisors
were firmly reminded that good relationships and problem-solving
skill were necessary for better supervision. They were encouraged

to treat people as individuals and were given basic psychological principles that would help them build an understanding of their subordinates. Some of these are:

1. Let each worker know how he is getting along.
2. Give credit when it is due.
3. Tell people in advance about changes that will affect them.
4. Make best use of each person's ability.

Also included in this program were some simple steps related to the handling of problems:

1. Get the facts.
2. Weigh these facts and decide on a course of action.
3. Take action.
4. Check results.

The student who reviews the above brief descriptions carefully and then does some individual research into today's supervisory training programs and practices will make a simple discovery. Very little has changed in the years since the TWI programs were developed. Many present-day company programs and even university programs are either exact duplicates or enlargements on the above themes. There are various reasons for this. The experience that companies had with this program proved to be a very positive one. It was found that individuals who had little or no supervisory experience reacted very favorably to the three 10-hour programs. They became better supervisors, and productivity increased in the groups that they supervised. As a result of this experience and the concurrent needs of expanding postwar industry, many of the companies simply continued the programs on their own. The basic soundness of approach to the training of first-line supervisors inherent in the TWI program encouraged some businesses to expand on the originals. This was particularly true of the Job Relations Training program. This formed the nucleus of many so-called human relations programs that sprang up in companies, institutes, campus, and off-campus programs. The authors' experience indicated that these programs are still meeting with success in many companies today.

An Example of a Present-Day JIT Program

One of the authors has been carrying on a Job Instructor Training program in a large metropolitan bank for a number of years. Perhaps a brief description of this effort will serve to illustrate the continuing usefulness of this type of training for other business organizations. One of the problems this bank faced was very similar to what was faced by a wide variety of business organizations during World War II. Expansion and increased costs coupled with a tightening labor market made this bank aware of the need for developing a well-trained staff with available employees and such others as they were able to hire. Growing mechanization of many of the operations also added to the problem. It was decided to embark on a JIT program with a group of 15 employees who possessed the needed skills but who had no supervisory or teaching experience. This group met once a week for 5 weeks. Each session was 2 hours in length. The only change from the original JIT program was the introduction of bank clerical examples for instructional purposes. The initial experience was followed up by the same program the next year. These employees were observed by their supervisors, to determine whether or not they were applying the methods taught in their instruction of novice employees. It was noticed that much of what was covered in the program was retained and used and that the employees were grateful for the techniques and knowledge they had gained. In addition, a number of these employees went on to become supervisors and were also trained in the bank's human relations training program. There have been some modifications in the JIT program as a result of experience. There are still five weekly sessions, but they are only $1\frac{1}{2}$ hours each. The last session is now devoted to a discussion of training problems which the employees encounter on the job. The post-training experience continues to be successful, with higher productivity and better morale among the employees. In addition, each job is more carefully analyzed and written up in the preparation of the lesson plans for skill training. This example demonstrates the continuing usefulness of Job Instruction Training for more effective performance in the training of new and unskilled employees in those skills necessary both for current jobs and for possible upgrading.

In-Company Supervisory Training Programs

Supervisory training that has been formalized and developed into a continuing program is most prevalent in large business organizations. Smaller companies usually do not have the need for continuing programs, nor do they have the financial resources to support such an effort. The smaller company that believes in formalized training will frequently make use of training institutes in local colleges or bring in an outside expert to do their training for them. Of course, large companies follow this approach also, but it is frequently in addition to the training carried on by the training division of the personnel department.

There are many types of supervisory training programs in use throughout American industry. Even though it was mentioned earlier that the work of the manager is basically the same regardless of the level in the organization he functions on, the training programs have to differ in approach and scope, depending on the level of management being trained. Supervisory training on the first-line level is usually steeped in techniques and methodology. Much time is spent giving concrete examples drawn from work experience in the particular company. Any attempt to introduce theoretical concepts and abstract principles usually meets with boredom and subsequent failure. The pattern seems to be one of a high degree of practicality coupled with information that the trainee can take back to the job and use immediately. Lower-level supervisors are rarely theorists or philosophers, and they will look with disdain on information they do not understand. In general, these programs are concerned with the following kinds of information:

1. Responsibilities of a supervisor
2. Quality control
3. Waste control
4. Cost control
5. Work planning and scheduling
6. Delegation
7. Dealing with subordinates
8. Interviewing
9. Training of employees
10. Performance rating
11. Simple essentials of organization and types of organizational structure
12. Interpretation and implementation of company policies
13. Safety
14. Disciplining employees and handling grievances
15. Relations with labor unions and organized labor
16. Communications
17. Effective discussion
18. Conference methods
19. Leadership
20. Simple psychology, such as individual differences, motivation, and morale

This list will give a general idea of the scope of typical supervisory training programs. Individual companies will have favorite subject areas that they want to cover, and the amount of time spent on each subject area depends on the nature of the group, the length of the program, and the importance attached to the particular subject by management.

In addition to the above subject areas, many companies give their supervisors a variety of special training programs in material and information in which the management of the company may be interested and which they may feel the supervisors will find useful. Typical of these programs are courses in basic economics and the functions of the free-enterprise system, the functions of government and the democratic process, and others that fall in the category of broadening general education.

Some actual examples of lower-level supervisory training carried on by large-company training divisions will demonstrate what is being done to develop first-line supervision.

1. *A Basic Management Training Program—Large Bearing Manufacturer.* This course has been developed in the central training division, and it is given by trainers in all branch plants of the company. It is a weekly 2-hour session given over a period of 12 weeks. No more than twenty people take the course at one time, and frequently the number is less. A combination lecture, discussion, and conference method is used, and at the completion of the program a certificate is presented to each graduate by the local plant management. The course is human relations–oriented and covers such subjects as organization, need for managers, control procedures, human relations skills, training, line and staff relationships, and personnel procedures.

2. *A Basic Supervision Course—Large Petroleum Company.* This course is given to individuals who are either current supervisors or who have been chosen for promotion to supervisory jobs in the near future. It is given in a central training division conference room by qualified instructors from the training division. The program runs for 10 days and occupies 7 hours daily. This company feels that a concentrated effort rather than one that is spread out over a period of weeks is more effective. The employee is taken off his job for the 10-day period, and he returns after the program is over. This program is also human relations–oriented and is conducted on what the company calls a "conference method," but actually much of the instruction is lecture-discussion. A wide variety of subjects is covered by instructors who are expert in the area to be covered by the particular conference. In some instances the instructors are drawn from operating departments, in addition to those used from the central training unit. The company looks on this instructional process as a form of management development for the instructors, and they are frequently rotated, so that many individuals from the same operating department are given the opportunity to instruct. Among the subjects covered in this program are company history, management teamwork, qualities of a supervisor, induction of new employees, tools of management, cost control, human relations problems, order-giving, attitude development, union-management relations, personnel administration policies and procedures, salary administration, employee rating, and communications.

3. *Conference Leadership—Large Manufacturing Company.* This is a 30-hour course which is given to supervisory personnel who may have the responsibility for leading conferences. It is given on a weekly basis in 2-hour sessions over a period of 15 weeks. The course is quite comprehensive and covers the conference method thoroughly. In the beginning it is descriptive in nature and covers such topics as the job of a conference leader, description of conferences, physical preparation for a conference, and the actual conducting of conferences. This course is given primarily in the company's centralized training division by trained instructors, but a very complete instructor's workbook has been prepared, and, as a result, the course has been given in company branches by local personnel officers. Human relations subject matter is woven into the discussion throughout the training sessions, so that the course serves a dual purpose. It acts as a refresher in human relations for the supervisors who are exposed to the conference program.

4. *Training New Supervisors—Large Insurance Company.* This company obtains its supervisors from many sources. Many are promoted from within from the work force, others from outside the company with supervisory experience, and still others from outside the company with little or no work experience. The latter are mainly college graduates hired for supervisory jobs. These people are all given an intensive 2-week orientation and training program revolving mainly about company policies, procedures, and traditions. Some are then given a rotating assignment which gives them experience in a number of departments, particularly those that they will be working closely with on their permanent assignment. In addition, they are given special assignments, such as the development of a new procedure manual or a more effective method of doing a certain job.

5. *Correspondence Course in Supervision.* This technique is in use in a number of large companies that have widely scattered branches with relatively few employees at each branch. Rather than use a course prepared by a commercial correspondence school, these companies have developed their programs to meet their specific problems. The subjects covered are very similar to those described above and are usually heavily interspersed with human relations topics. The employee reads his particular lesson for the week and then may answer a short quiz and also do a case problem, both of which are supplied to him in the course. His corrected answers are then sent back to him for further study. In addition, he may be given such assignments as the preparation of a case problem and its solution for his own job experience. The length of these courses differs, depending on the amount of information covered. Some cover as few as ten lessons and others as many as thirty.

6. *Supervisory Development—Medium-Sized Manufacturing Company.* This company has a less frequent need for trained supervisors. Nevertheless, they have a well-formulated developmental program which has the complete co-operation and backing of top management. The heart of the program is a conference-methods program given to ten carefully selected people at a time. Pertinent subject matter is covered in the conferences, and each man is given the opportunity to lead one or more conferences. At the completion of the conference course he is given either a supervisory assignment or a complete explanation of why he has not been made a supervisor and a prognosis of his future development. Each candidate is carefully observed by his superiors and is frequently told of his progress. In addition, any weak points that he may have are openly discussed, and he is told how to improve. In fact, freedom of communications between the supervisor and his superiors is stressed emphatically, and the supervisor is definitely encouraged to seek advice any time he feels he may need it. He is formally reviewed every 6 months in addition to the many intermittent conferences he has with his superiors. He is also given the opportunity to lead frequent conferences on such subjects as safety, company policy, insurance programs, and union relations. Over a period of time the man builds his self-confidence, and this company has developed many excellent supervisors through this method. Some of these individuals have gone on to more responsible middle- and top-management positions, and the company has had to hire from the outside only a few supervisors in the 15-year period that this program has been used.

The above examples of lower-level supervisory training have all been used successfully. Naturally, there have been failures in other companies. In fact, all the people who have been trained in the successful programs have not gone on to be good supervisors. The foregoing descriptions serve to illustrate the point that there is no one successful method or approach. The predominant climate is one of experimentation, and this is as it should be. Since business is dynamic, it is necessary for a well-managed company constantly to evaluate the results of their supervisory training efforts. Many companies have done and are continuing to do outstanding work in this area. The need for competent supervisors will be with us for a long time. So will the need for sound developmental programs.

7. *Off-Premises Supervisory Training.* A large number of business concerns use facilities other than their own for the training of potential and present supervisory personnel. The personnel director of any company receives hundreds of mailings each year describing a wide variety of courses to which he can send candidates. These courses cover much the same subject matter as those programs described here. The major difference is that they are usually more general in nature and do not cover the problems of a specific company. This is particularly true of those programs which attract individuals from many different companies. There are situations when a company will send ten to twenty candidates to an off-the-premises program, and it will be tailor-made to the company's specifications. New York University has an Office of Special Services to Business and Industry and a Management Institute, both of which carry on general supervisory training programs for individuals from many companies, as well as programs designed specifically for one company; these are given at the university in both the day and the evening. This approach is duplicated by colleges and universities all over the country, and no companies located near such a facility need do without supervisory training because of their size. The cost is moderate for these programs, and their success is implied in their continuing growth. In addition to university programs, a number of other organizations administer off-premise supervisory training. Among these are the American Management Association, the American Institute of Banking, local chapters of the Society for Advancement of Management, various management clubs, chambers of commerce, management consultants, and individual college faculty members. Perhaps an example of one of these programs will serve to illustrate what is being done in many places throughout the country.

8. *University-Sponsored Program.* A number of small banks and brokerage firms felt the need for formal supervisory training for their employees. None of the firms was large enough to support its own program. They approached a local university and discussed the problem. A course was developed which met the general needs of all the companies concerned. It was a 12-week program with 2-hour conferences weekly on mutually agreed-upon topics. Each of the companies sent one individual to the group. There was a total of twenty participants. The subject matter was similar to the list of topics mentioned above on page 345. Each of the members of the group was encouraged to participate in the discussion and to lead conferences. The exchange of information and problems was perhaps the most valuable aspect of the program. The participants learned that their problems had duplicates in other companies, and they also learned about successful solutions to problems in other companies. As a result of this initial success, the program has been carried on annually, and a larger number of firms are now participating.

Management Development Programs

The lower-level supervisory training programs described above are quite common in many companies. Not too much doubt exists as to the value of presenting potential supervisors as well as supervisors with little experience a program which gives them knowledge and instruction about the widely accepted techniques of their task. When the training of managers on higher organizational levels is considered, there is considerably more controversy involved. There is a plethora of opinion about the education of business executives. Concurrent with this opinion is the abundance of programs and approaches to accomplish this goal. Some of the attendant difficulties have already been pointed out earlier in this chapter. Certainly, the profile of a manager that a particular company considers its ideal will have a lot to do with the type of training it decides on. When the topic of management development comes up for discussion in any company, one will find adherents to many schools of thought as to its successful accomplishment. Recent opinion centers on the need for making such training as practical as possible. The "learning-by-doing" group is certainly becoming more vociferous. On the other hand, many experts feel that the understudy method and exposure of the potential manager to the supervision of other managers will not either give him sufficient background or indicate success or failure when he is given the chance to perform. There are hundreds of thousands of individuals enrolled in formalized programs all over the country, and this would give some indication that the formal training approach is thought of highly by a wide segment of the business community.

Management Development Practices

A careful study of management development practices that are now being used in contrast with programs of 5 and 10 years ago will certainly show how far we have come in a relatively short period of time. Middle- and upper-management training years ago was frequently a capsulized version of the program given to first-line supervisors. Many companies felt that a shorter version of the same program was all that was necessary. Higher-level executives had experience in administration, and a 20-week supervisory program was arbitrarily cut to 10 weeks for middle managers. Frequently the same subject matter was covered in condensed versions, and little attention was given to the needs of the particular group being trained.

Many companies have sent candidates to a particular executive development program outside the company simply because it had a good reputation or had considerable prestige. This is particularly true of programs given at well-known universities in various parts of the country. While there is considerable merit in some of these programs, little attempt was made to relate the particular program to the developmental problems in the company. In many instances the people chosen were favorites of some top manager, and they were sent because the manager wanted to do something for his protégé. Competitive reasons often dictated the decision relative to embarking on executive training of some kind. It was found that a company had to offer such opportunity if it was to attract better-quality candidates for openings. The attitude that if the ABC company could send its men to X University for executive training, so could our company, was all too frequently the prime motivating factor dictating the decision. In addition, the choice of individuals for higher-management training is often made on factors other than potential competence as a manager. Educational, social, racial, religious, and environmental backgrounds loom large in the minds of many people who are charged with the responsibility for choosing promotables. This does not mean that these factors should be discounted or that they are not important, but it does mean that graduating from a particular college or worshiping in a particular church should not be the sole criterion for original consideration for advancement. Unfortunately, in many instances this approach is the one used, and if an individual is not a member of the "in" group prevalent in that company, he does not have a chance even to demonstrate his potential.

Another interesting aspect of this problem is related to the common human weakness of a lack of desire to admit a wrong decision. Once a choice is made and a given individual is developed for greater responsibility, it seems as if the die is cast. In many instances a protective cloak covers his efforts, and this cloak is put there by the higher executive who made the choice. Even though the person is not developing to the expected level of accomplishment, his sponsor will make excuses for him and attempt to prolong his training. He will be rotated in a variety of jobs so that he can "find" himself. Failure may be admitted only after much expense and anguish. The reluctance to admit a wrong decision is understandable because this reflects on the judgment ability of the sponsor, as well as the accompanying deflation of his ego. While there is no simple solution to this problem, awareness of its existence may help to minimize its impact in company planning for executive staffing.

The fact that a company has a program of sorts should not delude them into thinking that this will guarantee them a supply of future executives. As is pointed out in the last section of this book, much research is necessary to arrive at sound solutions to this problem. Many programs train young men for jobs as they are presently constituted. Not enough attention is paid to the changing nature of business in general and the individual company in particular. The "seat-of-the-pants" approach quoted earlier in this chapter has to be put in limbo if sounder practices are to be achieved.

Improving Executive Training

One of the outstanding fallacies of many executive training programs is the belief that exposure to training guarantees some kind of success. In the postwar rush to develop managerial personnel on all levels in a company, all that was thought necessary was the selection of individuals for training and the subsequent in-company or off-the-premises program. Not too much attention was paid to subject matter, follow-up after training, and even initial selection of trainees. After many bitter experiences and costly errors of judgment, business organizations are now assessing their management development efforts more carefully.

While it may be hard for some people to believe, there are many individuals who do not want to grow and assume responsibility. They may complain about lack of advancement, but when they are confronted with situations which will give them the opportunity to demonstrate management potential, they either turn away or try and fail. They may be lacking in initiative, enthusiasm, knowledge, or capacity; but, whatever the lack, there is little usefulness in training such people. As difficult as it may be to admit, many people reach their career peaks relatively early in their business lives. They prefer to remain at a given level of responsibility for a variety of reasons, and little or nothing can be done to shake them from their lethargy. Obviously, there are very few, if any, business organizations that have as many self-starters as they need. The people who are responsible for executive staffing and forward planning have to recognize that supervisors are needed on every level and that some people are just not promotable.

The major effort should be expended on those individuals who have shown that they can develop into more capable supervisors. This emphasis on self-development rather than spoon feeding is becoming one of the more outstanding criteria for the definition of promotables in a company. The assumption is that if a man is willing to put forth the extra effort to assume greater responsibility, to learn more about his job, to expand his knowledge of other operations in the company, and continually to give that extra measure of enthusiasm and willingness, then he should be given every opportunity to grow. There is a variety of methods by which this potential can be assessed. Most of these methods are based on the ability of senior management personnel to judge the performance of subordinates with wisdom and without bias. Some of these methods are relatively long range, and others are incorporated into management training programs. They all seem to hinge on the ability of the individual to work effectively under the many stress situations that arise in the daily functioning of any business. A brief description of the more common varieties of such programs will help illustrate what is meant by self-development and individual growth.

1. *Job Rotation.*   This is perhaps the most common method of developing an executive in broad job experience. It is particularly useful when the program is formalized and the individual is carefully observed in each position by a seasoned executive. Each job assignment should be for a specified period of time, sufficiently long to allow the person to gain knowledge and insight into the position and to demonstrate his ability to perform. He should be given a series of assignments that not only are instructional but will give him ample opportunity to exercise judgment and to make decisions. If sufficient stress situations do not occur, then they should be fabricated by the manager so that he may be able to judge the trainee's performance in a variety of circumstances.

2. *Understudy or Assistant To.*   This method is very similar to job rotation in its basic philosophy. The difference lies in the fact that the trainee gets experience in only one position. A number of companies use this method to train a person to fill a specific job. It may also be used to expose a trainee to a particularly good senior executive who has a past record of accomplishment in the development of young people for further responsibility in the company. These two methods are frequently used in conjunction with junior executive training programs for college graduates.

3. *Simulation.*   There are two methods used in an attempt to simulate actual job conditions. In addition, the case method and the incident method of instruction also attempt to set up practical situations where the trainee can demonstrate his ability to gather information and make decisions based on this information. Both methods have come into prominence in recent years. One is the business game. It can be played either with the use of a computer to process data more rapidly, or it can be done less expensively with prepared material available from business-book publishers who have prepared this material for use in college classrooms as well as in executive training programs. Briefly, these games attempt to demonstrate the close relationships that exist among the many functions and departments of a business. The trainees are given a certain amount of information relative to a company's operations and the related problems that exist. The problems that are faced are as realistic as those that actually occur in the operation of the business. The trainee must plan, direct, and control in much the same way that he would if he were making the decisions in a real situation. If a computer is used to process data, then the effects of decisions can be assessed more rapidly and the future impact of the trainee's decisions can be measured more effectively.

A number of other companies have developed another type of simulated situation. The outstanding characteristic of this method is that the trainee does not know that he is not faced with a real situation. The circumstances are all carefully planned in advance, and stress circumstances are created. The trainee is placed in the job and is given the situation to handle. He gets actual problems relating to people and conditions which have occurred in the past. Of course, he does not know that these things have already occurred. To him it is an actual, live, present-day condition. He is carefully observed by his superiors, and his ability to work under stress conditions and to exercise sound judgment and make useful decisions is carefully evaluated. This method is perhaps the closest that management training can come to learning by doing without putting the trainee in the actual job.

4. *Other Programs.*   Most executive training through the use of formalized methods is done in much the same way that lower-level supervisors are trained. A conference technique is used, and the subject matter is usually human relations–oriented. The length of the program varies from company to company, depending on which level is being trained and on the size of the training budget. These programs are conducted either by the individual company or by sending the trainees to an established program at a college or university or to such organizations as the American Management Association. The principal difference between these programs and those offered for lower-level supervisors is the sophistication of presentation and the scope of the subject matter. It is assumed that the people in these programs have greater business knowledge and more administrative experience. Less detail is covered, and more abstract theory is presented. Concepts and philosophy are discussed, and the functions of a manager are introduced with far less emphasis on techniques and procedures and far greater emphasis on human problems and impact on the company as a whole.

There are a number of special management training programs which have come into some prominence in recent years. The hallmark of these programs is their emphasis on broad educational goals. Many business organizations have found that the primary barrier to effective functioning on the higher levels of management seems to be the narrowness of the executive's viewpoint. The complexity of business organization requires the use of highly trained specialists in a variety of activities. These individuals normally develop in their narrow areas of specialization. They are given greater responsibility, but they generally manage the function they have been trained in. When the time comes in their development to promote them to a position of broader scope, the promotion is made, but the man has considerable difficulty in adjusting to his new position. He continues to see his problems and his activities in the narrow frame of reference that he has been used to over the years.

In recent years, management development for middle and higher management has emphasized broad education. Of some interest is a postwar development in England. Sir Noel Frederick Hall established the Administrative Staff College. This institution was founded on a number of sound premises. First, it was assumed that the best thinking develops from practice. The college was founded with the objective of discussing not theory but improved practice. Second, it was felt that men and women who have evidenced capability for higher management would find it useful to leave their jobs for a period to gain greater perspective and insight into the functions of their organizations. Third, it was believed that exposure to other individuals of similar capacity but from a variety of business, public, governmental, and military organizations would also have a broadening influence on each other. The program lasts 3 months, and a conscious effort is made to have the group members come from different activity areas, such as production, finance, sales, engineering, and purchasing. These individuals are then forced to lead groups in areas other than their own specialty. A short description of the course will serve to demonstrate its scope.

At the present time the course of studies divides into five major parts, three of which are further sub-divided. There are also some supplementary subjects which are not closely knit into the general structure of the course. This structure is set out on page 12 of the current number of the College Handbook as follows:

Part I   Comparative Administrative Structures
Part II   Internal Organization and Administration
     (a) Management of the Individual
     (b) The Structure of Organization and Inter-relation of Departments

(c) Delegation, Control, and Accountability
(d) Organization for Production
 1. Production
 2. Research and Development
 3. Office Services

Part III External Relations
 (a) Commercial Relationships
  1. Consumers and Customers
  2. Purchasing
  3. Sources of Finance
  4. Trade Associations
 (b) Organized Labor
 (c) Central Government
 (d) Local Government
 (e) Industrial and Commercial Financing

Part IV Constructive Administration
 (a) Adaptation to Economic Change
 (b) Adaptation to Technological Change
 (c) Imparting and Maintaining Vitality

Part V The Administrator.[6]

There have been some adaptations of this approach in this country, and there are many similar executive development programs in major universities throughout the country.

Another interesting method of development for higher executives has occurred in recent years. This approach is based on the assumption that candidates for higher management already have sufficient knowledge and background in business and management subject matter. These programs attempt to broaden executives by exposing them to the great books of our civilization. It is felt that everything that man does has its parallel in what man has done before. Since a good portion of the accumulated wisdom of the ages has been published, a penetrating analysis and study of the past through the medium of the great books, along with conference discussions on these studies and their relationship to the present-day business climate, will aid in creating deeper meaning and broader understanding for the participants in such a program.

Regardless of the method used, it is becoming increasingly apparent that executive training for higher management must break away from technique and procedure and emphasize the need for sound evaluation and subsequent effective decision making.

---

[6] Sir Noel Frederick Hall, *The Making of Higher Executives: The Modern Challenges* (New York: School of Commerce, Accounts, and Finance, New York University, 1958), pp. 50–52.

Higher Management's Responsibility

The management personnel of any company has the prime responsibility for the development of people for individual growth as well as company growth. They must remember that the training of executives is a continuing process. No one method or program is the answer. Most well-managed companies use a combination of the methods described in this chapter. The development of a sound executive is like the aging of a fine wine. It takes many years and a variety of careful evaluations before it can be accurately ascertained whether or not a particular person has become a good manager. No 2-week institute or 13-week program is going to turn out a seasoned business executive. The exposure to knowledge will help a young man with potential to understand his responsibilities, but it will not give him the long years of experience that are necessary for sound judgment and effective decision making. Careful appraisal and performance evaluation, with the full participation of the subordinate being rated and the superiors who are doing the rating, are necessary if a company is to gain optimum benefit from its management development efforts. It takes a considerable period of time for an individual to learn the many facets of the managerial job, and the fact that it changes over the years makes the task all the more difficult. The growing executive should be given every opportunity to demonstrate his capabilities. Formal training and on-the-job experience should be combined to accelerate his growth if possible, but it is wise to consider that sound management development is a long-range proposition and that the challenges of the future are such that business will require men who are unusual in their ability to handle the growing complexities of American business.

SUMMARY

There is a high correlation between the development of effective managers and the growth and survival of a business enterprise. A universal need exists for good management on all levels of an organization. As a result, more attention is being devoted to the determination of a manager's duties and responsibilities and the knowledge, skills, and attitudes he must possess for successful achievement. Companies are faced with the problem of selecting competent people for training as managers, since promotion-from-within policies have become more prevalent. This is because there is a definite shortage of managerial personnel and the only apparent solution is for a company to train people who have demonstrated that they can assume further responsibility.

It is imperative that a company recognize what it expects from its training efforts and relate this to a realistic evaluation of the manager's job in that company. They must develop a corporate climate which allows an individual to reach his optimum potential, and they must allow him to use the training he is exposed to. It follows that any management training must have the complete backing of top executives in the company, and they must continue to insist that the individuals exposed to the training programs be chosen carefully and evaluated as scientifically as possible, once they are assigned to positions of responsibility.

THINGS TO DISCUSS AND TO DO

1. Survey executive development programs to determine the weaknesses that you think exist in them and make suggestions for improvement.
2. Develop a practical profile of an effective manager in a particular company.
3. Try to determine the differences that exist in the manager's job on different levels in the organization structure.
4. Outline a sound executive development program for your company or for a hypothetical company in an industry you are interested in.
5. Discuss the merit or lack of merit in the argument that leaders are born and not made.
6. Meet with a group of your peers and discuss a practical approach to developing yourself for managerial responsibility.

Unit IV

TRAINING EVALUATION
AND RESEARCH

14. RESEARCH AND TRAINING—
SUBSTITUTING EVIDENCE
FOR OPINION

Purpose of the Chapter

THE PURPOSE of this chapter is to present an introduction to the field of research. Specifically, emphasis will be placed on the part that research plays in the successful operations of a training program, the need to relate and to integrate research into the training program, the meaning and the importance of research and the role of systematic and logical thinking involved in conducting research. Furthermore, the purposes and the barriers to research will be reviewed, and the survey and experimental methods of research will be introduced.

Training conducted without research is like an automobile without a driver. Driverless, the automobile moves without a destination, heedless of direction and control, building momentum and zigging and zagging this way and that, its course dependent on the happenstance contours and ruts that appear in the road. Such aimless movement not only is dangerous but is most inefficient.

To drive the automobile effectively, the driver must be equipped with the essential knowledge, be adept at the proper skills required, be inculcated with the necessary attitudes, and be experienced. But knowing how to drive the car is not enough, since it is equally important to understand where one wishes to direct the automobile.

Beyond a doubt, most of us would run for cover if someone sat behind the wheel of a car without the necessary knowledge, skill, and experience in driving. Yet no one runs for protection when training programs are conducted in business without the necessary knowledge, skills, and attitudes. Whether one operates a car or controls a training program, it is necessary to do a certain amount of reflective thinking,

363

in a systematic manner, in order to arrive at the facts, data, principles, and generalizations that are fundamental to all activity.

"Research" is the name given to the general procedure for investigating and studying a problem. The word "research" implies the need to search for "something," and the purpose is to find facts and principles. Research is a critical inquiry into any matter that is characterized by doubt and uncertainty. It embraces the application of logical, reflective, and systematic thinking for the purpose of arriving at facts and principles that can be related to the solution of problems.

Training Research

Training research is concerned with the facts, data, and principles that are necessary to carry out training programs. With regard to the problems related to training which require systematic research, the following command attention:

1. *Should a Company Start a Training Program?* In many cases training is considered the cure-all for any of the problems faced by management. It is obvious that this is not always the case, for many other causes may exist for the dilemma that the company must solve. For example, the company organizational structure may be unsound, the policies may need clarification, the lines of communication may be faulty, and many other barriers may exist that are responsible for the company's inefficiency.

Accordingly, it should be self-evident that the first step in instituting a training program is to determine through systematic research whether training is needed at all. Thus research is a valuable tool to use in discovering the sources of a company's failures, and at the same time it is helpful in determining whether an investment in training is required.

2. *What Should Be the Policies and Objectives of the Training Program?* Policies and objectives lend guidance and direction to all management practices, including training. A company that is manufacturing fine precision instruments must be guided by training policies that will insure the highest-skilled employees.

3. *What Should Be the Content of the Training Program?* Content refers to the knowledge, skill, and attitudes that must be imparted to an individual in order to change behavior in the direction of systematically predetermined ends. The content of a training program should be determined by a careful, systematic analysis of the job or jobs for which employees must be trained. Basically, this can be accomplished only by carrying out some preliminary research, which means that logical, reflective, and systematic thinking must be applied to a study of the nature and breakdown of each job. If the content is faulty, so will be the training results.

4. What Methods Should Be Used in Order to Insure the Success on the Training Program? In general, method refers to the means that will be utilized to impart the essential content to the learner in a training program. Should the method be one that emphasizes the lecture approach, the conference, case-study, problem-solving approach, or trial and error. Again the success of training depends upon finding the best method for transferring the content to the learner.

Guesswork or hunch will not secure the best method and can never replace sound research. Methods must be analyzed by conducting careful experimentation and evaluation, for in this manner comparisons of different methods can be made and decisions arrived at which justify the use of a method on the basis of verified facts and data.

5. Who Is to Do the Training? Along with sound content and efficient methods it is necessary to have teachers or trainers that are properly selected and adequately trained. Problems that require research with regard to trainers include such areas as the personality of the trainer and the knowledge and the attitude he possesses. There is only one way to arrive at a determination of who will be the better teacher, and that is through a carefully conducted research program.

6. How Is Training to Be Evaluated? Perhaps the most important area for research and in many cases the most neglected is in determining how effective a training program really is. Is the training actually producing the changes in the behavior of the learners in the predetermined and desired direction?

The foregoing does not reflect in any way the complete variety of areas in which research is necessary in training. The questions posed serve only to point out some of the more important questions that must be answered, and at the same time they emphasize the inseparable and integrated nature of training and research.

The Relationship of Training and Research

To believe that training and research can be separate functions is a fallacy. In a sense it is impossible to conduct training without using the tools of research. Research is the built-in weather vane that is necessary to determine the direction, the means, the needs, and the results of training. In another sense research comes before, during, and after training is conducted, and then it repeats itself over and over again. As a consequence, research is inseparable from training and is continuing in nature. The measurement of results is one of the most effective controls that management has, and research is the best way to measure training results.

To illustrate how some business concerns ignore the inseparable nature of research and training, consider the training program of a large company, employing some two thousand people. A personnel director is in charge of the training program and is assisted by three members of his department. Training programs are in operation for several levels of the company, and in their order from top to bottom they are as follows:

1. *Executive Development Program.*   All the vice-presidents of the company are participants in the program. The main purpose of this training is to develop ability to solve problems and to think creatively and independently. The conference method is used, with emphasis on the case-study technique. The assumption is that the participants will develop themselves by the process of solving top-management problems.

2. *Supervisory Development Program.*   All supervision below vice-presidents are included in this phase of training. The main purpose is to provide knowledge and improve skills in handling employees and at the same time to solve problems effectively. A combination of conferences and lectures is the basic method used.

3. *Trainee Program.*   Each year approximately ten college graduates are selected and are subjected to a series of conferences, lectures, rotation in different departments of the company, and in dealing with the solving of management problems.

4. *Job Training Program.*   This is the largest segment of the program in terms of personnel. It is concerned mainly with teaching the necessary job skills in order to acquaint new employees with their duties and responsibilities. This training is done by line supervisors mainly, who provide an instructor, and the training is essentially on-the-job experience.

On the surface, a glance at the brief description of the training program of this company would seem to indicate that the program is comprehensive and efficient. Yet, when a careful analysis is made of the training program, many weaknesses are revealed, the most important being that little or no research has been conducted. When management is asked why the training program has been inaugurated, the answer is that problems have appeared from time to time which indicate that training is necessary. However, when one inquires whether any research has been conducted to determine what the nature and causes are for such problems, where they are located, and what the circumstances are surrounding the difficulties, few answers are available. In general, management feels that a training program will change the behavior of its management and employees and, as a result, produce better co-operation, harmony, teamwork, and efficiency. Hasty and generalized assumptions and conclusions of this kind are the result of failure to carefully analyze problems without adequate research. If a serious study had been undertaken to discover the actual causes for the company's difficulties, it is possible that the solution might have been entirely different. This was proved to be the case when the training program failed to produce the results that management "guessed" would occur. Later, a more careful research project was started, and this clearly demonstrated that the company employees were loyal, co-operative, and capable but that the real source of the trouble resided in weak and ineffective management practices. Improper separation of functions, poorly defined responsibilities and duties, overlapping of authority, inadequate personnel practices, and inept communications were found to be the real causes of the difficulties. What this company really needed was an overhauling of its organization and not a training program. With intelligent direction of research, much money, time, and effort might have been saved.

But assume that the company in our illustration did have sound management practices, does this indicate that the training program was therefore effective? Not necessarily so, since a closer study of the training program reveals that no research was conducted in order to isolate the problems, to define and clarify them, to determine where and when and to whom training should be given in order to remove the difficulties. As a result of inadequate research, the objectives of the training program were hazy, the content of the conferences were inconsistent with the actual needs, the methods used proved to be faulty, the instructors were picked and trained haphazardly, and little was done to study the effectiveness of the program.

The illustration described serves to emphasize the importance of relating research with training. Before embarking on any training program it is of primary importance to analyze and study the causes responsible for management problems. Once it is determined that training of employees is definitely related to the problems, then research must be continued to discover objectives, content, methods, instruction, and means of evaluating the program. In consequence, research cannot be separated from training, it must be a part of the built-in strategy for planning and co-ordinating training with the entire company operations. Furthermore, research must be a continuing process, for it must be ever alert to evaluate all facets of the training program, including content, methods, instruction, and improvement in job performance.

It is an oddity that, even where research is conducted, companies fail to evaluate their programs. In a survey of approximately 150 companies the *Conference Board Business Record* states:

Determining the ultimate value to the company of individual research results is a difficult, and at times, impossible task for many cooperating companies. In fact, more than half the participants have no method for assessing the value of their research after its conclusion.[1]

The study points out that some companies are trying to develop more orderly and systematic methods to evaluate their research programs and that "many more companies, however, apply no measurement whatsoever to their final research results or rely on the 'exercise of judgment' and 'informal' appraisals."[2]

It appears obvious that any improvement in training contemplated or in operation in business can be eventualized only when managers begin properly to relate research with such programs.

However, recognition of the fact that research and training are inseparable and interrelated merely prepares the way for careful investigations to take place. To carry out effective research, it is necessary to understand the basic principles and knowledge of research, to acquire the skills and tools, and to develop the proper attitude toward systematic problem-solving. In this regard McGehee points out:

The failure to make adequate evaluation of training techniques and methods arises from two sources. First, training personnel, by and in large are not acquainted with the exact methods of controlled research and statistical technique. Second, and perhaps even more important, industrial executives have

---

[1] "Allocation and Control of Research Expenditures," Conference Board Business Record, Vol. XV, No. 9 (September, 1958), p. 390.
[2] *Ibid.*

not been indoctrinated into the necessity of careful evaluation of training as well as other personnel activities.[3]

Evidence of this kind suggests that one of the basic requirements for anyone who seeks to conduct training is to acquire the knowledge and the skill of research methodology. Logically, the acquisition of research knowledge must proceed from an understanding of the meaning and nature of research.

The Meaning and Nature of Research

To the uninitiated, the idea of entering into a discussion of the technical aspects of research may produce feelings of awe and foreboding. Lest this be the case, it might be wise to point out what C. F. Kettering, one of General Motors most successful practical researchers, said on the subject:

> Research is a high-hat word that scares a lot of people. It needn't. It is rather simple. Essentially, it is nothing but a state of mind—a friendly, welcoming attitude toward change. Going out to look for change instead of waiting for it to come. Research, for practical men, is an effort to do things better and not to be caught asleep at the switch. The research state of mind can apply to anything. Personal affairs or any kind of business big or little. It is the problem-solving mind as contrasted with the let-well-enough-alone mind. It is the composer mind instead of the fiddler mind; it is the "tomorrow" mind instead of the "yesterday" mind.[4]

Even a casual analysis of this statement reveals some of the important aspects of the meaning of research. First is the fact that research is largely influenced by a state of mind or an attitude which simply means a predisposition or a mental set characterized mainly by an intellectual curiosity. Those with such curiosity seek to know the reasons and the causes behind events and behavior. They are not content to accept things as they are or on the basis of authority or tradition alone. It is the critical mind. Training research requires an attitude of inquisitiveness, of questioning, of seeking to understand the reasons for actions, of searching for facts and data, and a strong will to avoid acceptance of the status quo.

In its attempt to improve safety, a nation-wide railroad system makes use of a safety book that includes several hundred rules which

---

[3] William McGehee, "Persistent Problems in Training," in *Current Trends in Industrial Psychology* (Pittsburgh: University of Pittsburgh Press, 1949), pp. 97–114.

[4] C. F. Kettering, "More Music Please, Composer," *Saturday Evening Post*, Vol. CCXI (1938), p. 32.

each employee must carry with him at all times. The employee must also make every effort to memorize and apply all the rules in the safety book. This method of safety training has been used for many years and has become imbedded in the tradition and the way of life of railroad employees. Actions that result from the force of authority and tradition alone tend to create an atmosphere of slavish acceptance and, at the same time, to destroy the wholesome research attitudes that are essential for improving the safe practices of the railroad. In this case the let-well-enough attitude seems to persist, and there seems to be little or no desire to analyze critically and inquisitively the relationships between the rulebook and safe practices. No one appears interested enough to avoid being caught at the switch. Little research is conducted because there seems to be weak resistance to tradition and authority.

On the other hand, in a large trucking corporation that operates on a national scale the atmosphere and the research state of mind are entirely different. The management is driven by a desire to avoid the traditional and, as a result, has conducted research of every conceivable kind, ranging from careful investigations in selecting and training truck drivers to mechanical safety design of trucks, engineering studies of motors, truck equipment, and even studies and research on the relationship of personal habits, such as sleep, diet, and drinking, to safety. In this case it is obvious that this company is not standing still and that it welcomes change by seeking facts and data that will result in improvement and greater efficiency.

But a state of mind is not enough to describe the full nature of research. It is equally important to recognize that research is fundamentally a systematic inquiry and that, as such, it requires mental skills like logical reasoning and problem-solving. Associated with these mental skills are such mental habits as orderly attention to detail, persistence, concentration, and ability to organize projects.

Logical reasoning and problem-solving can be better understood if one studies the elements and steps that are involved in the thinking process. John Dewey, noted philosopher and educator, provided the following analysis of a thought process;

1. The occurrence of a felt difficulty
2. Definition of the difficulty in terms of a problem statement
3. Occurrence of a suggested explanation or solution—a guess, hypothesis, inference or theory
4. The rational elaboration of an idea through the development of its implications, by means of the collection of data [evidence]

5. Corroboration of an idea and formation of a concluding belief through experimental verification of the hypothesis.[5]

T. L. Kelley adds to the process of problem-solving by suggesting that the thought mechanism should be carried one step farther. Specifically, it is suggested that, once the solution is reached, it is essential to evaluate the new findings in the light of future needs and applications.[6]

In summary it can be said that the thought process first begins with a feeling of inadequacy or deficiency, then an attempt to define and delimit the problem follows; this leads to the search for assumptions and tentative conclusions, which are critically evaluated in the light of present evidence; and then a process of experimentation follows, in order to corroborate or reject the assumed conclusions.

For purposes of amplification of the thought process involved in problem-solving, consider the situation of a small company in the food-distribution business.

The F-A Company distributes and sells a variety of food products, such as potato chips, pretzels, and assorted kinds of crackers and peanuts and candy to small groceries, independent supermarkets, and chain stores. The company employs some 75 route salesmen, who drive trucks, keep records of sales, and do merchandising and promotion work in order to sell the products.

For the past year the company has been experiencing trouble in keeping its employees on the job for more than three months. It is during this period that the new man undergoes induction and orientation training. In an informal manner the personnel manager followed the process of logical reasoning that has been previously mentioned. This procedure of thinking may be detailed as follows:

1. *Felt Need.* The company faces the problem of excessive labor turnover, which is costly and inefficient. Sales are falling off, and customers are dissatisfied. The difficulty felt is obvious to the personnel manager, and the general question arises as to what can be done to reduce the labor turnover.

2. *Definition of the Problem and Delimitation.* The problem was carefully analyzed and delimited. A statement of the problem was attempted—What is the nature and causes of labor turnover and what can be done about it? Further analysis of the problem revealed that the problem could be delimited to the training program.

[5] John Dewey, *How We Think* (New York: D. C. Heath & Co., 1933), p. 12.
[6] T. L. Kelley, *Scientific Method: Its Functions in Research and Education* (New York: Macmillan Co., 1932), p. 5.

3. *The Hypothesis Is Formulated.* The hypothesis is an intelligent guess as to the explanation or causes of the difficulty, and it suggests a possible solution. The hypothesis is not arrived at by hunch. Instead, a careful study of the possible causes is undertaken. Wages are compared with other similar businesses, along with hours of work, advancement opportunities, and fringe benefits, such as hospitalization, life and retirement insurance. Vacation plans, supervision, and other conditions were examined. As a result, the tentative hypothesis was made that the difficulty probably could be found in the training program.

4. *The Collection of Evidence to Corroborate the Hypothesis.* The next step in the process of logical thinking is to analyze and break down the possible sources of difficulty in the induction and orientation training program. This was accomplished by surveying the reasons for employees leaving the job, by interviews with trainees, trainers, supervisors, and customers. Along with this analysis, the training program was carefully scrutinized with regard to objectives, content, methods, teaching personnel, and the like. As a consequence of this research, the entire training program was reshaped, and a training assistant was given the responsibility for conducting the program.

5. *Experimentation Is Conducted.* Along with the new procedure of training, careful observations were made, and evidence and data were collected for a period of six months. It is important to remember that the only conditions that were changed resided in the training program. All other conditions remained about the same. At the end of the experimental period, labor turnover had been reduced by 60 per cent.

6. *Applying the Results to Future Needs.* If the principles of research, especially with regard to the application of logical thinking, can be successful in the case of training, then perhaps they may be applied to other problems facing the company.

In this example it is clear that the nature of research is characterized by intellectual curiosity, in the sense that one is not content with the status quo but seeks to find the reasons and causes behind existing problems; while at the same time the application of reflective thinking and the use of a logical approach is manifested.

Furthermore, research is characterized by systematic organization and the collection of data that are intelligently interpreted. This is evidenced in the food-distribution company in connection with the experimental stage, as well as in the phase of formulation of the hypotheses. In each of these instances it was necessary to gather a great deal of evidence and to organize, classify, and interpret the facts in an objective and detached manner.

Two other characteristics of the nature of research should be mentioned, they are courage and innovation. Courage implies the willingness and the fortitude to accept the consequences regardless of the results. It is not unusual for facts and conclusions that result from serious research to be shaped and molded to fit the desires and ambitions of personal needs. It is obvious that conclusions that are maligned and twisted, in such cases, can be regarded only as biased and false. Consequently, the courage to face the facts and to seek the truth regardless of the cost to individuals is an inherent necessity to the nature of research.

Innovation refers to the ability to devise and concoct new and different approaches to a problem. Most people follow a habit pattern in thinking that is so narrow and fixed that they cannot innovate new alternatives. The successful researcher has the facility to formulate new hypotheses and to devise different techniques. In a sense, research requires imagination and creativity.

Another way to approach the nature of research is to study the personal traits and qualities of outstanding men of research. T. L. Kelley, in a series of lectures given at Ohio State University in 1928, suggested that, although people and cultures might be different, certain characteristics of the researcher might be listed. These were listed as follows:

1. The great man of science is industrious, shows great mental energy, and is persistent on the trail of discovery.

2. He questions authority, at least in the one line of his greatest achievement.

3. He is apt at drawing inferences and is therefore ingenious in making hypotheses.

4. His sense of logic is sound, so that he is perspicacious in making deductions.

5. He is a keen observer of natural phenomena.

6. He is dependent on observed facts.

7. He is inventive in matters of technique.

8. He is rich in his variety and number of hypotheses.

9. He is not "inspirational," in his chosen field; that is, his feet are always on the ground—his hypotheses are always amenable to some test of a factual or observational sort. But he is inspirational in the sense that a vision not the common property of fellow-men urges him on.

To summarize the meaning and nature of research, it is important to remember the following key points:

Research is a critical inquiry that involves the application of reflective, logical thinking conducted in an orderly and systematic manner for the purpose of arriving at facts and principles that can be related to the solution of problems.

By its very nature, research is characterized by such mental activities as the following:

> Intellectual curiosity
> Reflective and logical thinking
> Systematic organization
> Attention to detail, persistence, and concentration
> Courage and innovation

Research and training are inseparable and interrelated. Research is a built-in and interwoven part of a training program. It is utilized to start a training program, to modify the training, and finally to evaluate the effectiveness of the program. Finally, research must be a never-ending and continuous feature of training.

The Purpose of Research in Training

Although the discussion thus far has presented several of the purposes served by research in a training program, a more orderly and comprehensive presentation is needed.

The most general purpose of research in training programs is obviously the improvement of the efficiency of the training. The problem is to investigate critically every facet of the training mechanism, in order to determine whether the objectives of the program are attained. It must be understood that the objective of any training program is to change human behavior in a predetermined direction aimed at the improvement of the efficiency of the company. Since the research conducted is an inseparable part of training, it therefore follows that the main purpose of a training program must also be directed toward the improvement of human efficiency. Consequently, the main target upon which research is focused is the human being or the employee whose behavior is to be altered.

But changing human behavior means that alterations must be reflected in the knowledge, skills, and attitudes of the learner. Accordingly, research must be aimed at a critical inquiry into the kinds of knowledge that must be transferred to the trainee—for example, is it company organization, policies, personnel rules and regulations, products, machines, materials, safety rules, and any other pertinent knowledge that are essential to the daily life of an employee?

Along with knowledge, research must analyze the skills required to accomplish a task efficiently—skill in the operation of a machine, a typewriter, an adding machine, a drill press, a lathe, or skills in using tools, such as a screwdriver, wrench, micrometer, and the skills required to do bookkeeping, accounting, and other clerical tasks.

Finally, research must study the complex task of changing the attitudes of the learner. Attitudes have an indirect relationship to the manner in which an employee will adjust to his job, to the company, to fellow workers, to superiors, to his home life, and to the community. It is contended that if an employee is happy and satisfied with his work, he will therefore be a more productive worker. Consequently, research is seriously interested in studying the nature of attitudes, as well as the means to alter unfavorable attitudes so as to produce a more satisfied and better-adjusted employee.

Thus it is evident that the most fundamental purpose of research in training is to assist, in a critical and analytical manner, by finding the facts and principles that will facilitate the processes of changing human behavior.

More specifically, research aids in developing an efficient training program by providing the evidence that makes it possible for management to come to sound decisions. Such decisions include the problem of deciding whether training is necessary, where it is required, to whom it should be given, when it should be done, how long the training period should be, what the content should cover, how training should be done, by whom it should be conducted, and whether the training is efficient.

With regard to the problem of evaluating the efficiency of a training program, research is imperative, in order to determine whether human behavior changes are truly meeting predetermined objectives.

Barriers to Research in Training

The obstacles that interfere with the conduct of research in a training program are numerous. They run the gamut from financial limitations to personality traits that are unfavorable to research programs.

From a financial standpoint, many businessmen view research as a waste of money, especially where expenditures for investigations are related to human values. In a sense it could be generally said that managers spend millions of dollars each year on research that is concerned with technological advances but, in contrast, spend "pennies" with regard to human behavior research. Perhaps one of the reasons for such a lopsided state of affairs is the fact that most businessmen regard efficiency in a rather narrow light. They think of efficiency as a matter of achieving the greatest amount of production with the least possible cost. This is an exemplary and necessary objective of any business concern, but when the means to attain these objectives fail to include and give value to the role that human beings play in its fruition, then the logic of the argument collapses.

The narrow viewpoint of efficiency is all too often reflected in the objectives of many training programs, for most research that is conducted is concerned mainly with immediate changes in skill and knowledge that will be reflected in terms of immediate increases in productivity. The emphasis in such training is usually placed on effecting changes in human behavior without regard for the feelings, attitudes, and opinions of employees. The fact is that human beings cannot be cut into parts, since humans operate and function as totalities. In a word, skill and knowledge cannot be separated from human values and attitudes. Research in training, regardless of whether it is job training, supervisory, or developmental, must be aware of the human equation and must seek ways to instruct and develop men in order to make them more satisfied and better adjusted to their environment.

It is equally important to understand that many businessmen fail to realize that a business enterprise, no matter how small or large it may be, has a social responsibility to fulfill. To achieve this, management must utilize training to educate for safety, health, human relations, and economic concepts commensurate with the ideals of our democratic way of life. To do less is to train for immediate profits and self-aggrandizement and to deny the fact that our economic system can succeed only when workers are adequately trained and adjusted to all jobs and working environments.

Therefore, one of the most important obstacles standing in the path of research in training is the attitude of top managers, among whom a narrow interpretation of profits and efficiency prevails.

Training research requires the co-operation and co-ordination of many levels of the management team, including the employees. Yet, when participation is required, it is not always forthcoming. Top managers, middle managers, and supervisors often feel that it is an imposition on their time and an interference with work schedules. Unaware of the importance of training research, they unwittingly place many obstacles in the path of training directors and researchers.

Likewise, the training researcher is also at fault, especially in his ability to understand management problems and terminology and in his failure to be "practical." He is sometimes considered too academic and theoretical, since he is not usually concerned with surface symptoms but with basic principles and causes. Such viewpoints tend to clash with the desire by managers to get quick answers to difficulties.

Finally, as previously indicated, many training directors are not properly equipped in the methods and tools of research.

To offset the obstacles that confront training research it is necessary to achieve the following:

1. Change the attitudes of management toward research.
2. Give research in training the high status it requires.
3. Provide the financial backing it deserves.
4. Generate the co-operation and co-ordination of all levels of the management team.
5. Educate for an appreciation of the importance of research.
6. Train the training directors in the tools and methods of research, as well as train researchers to understand the limitations and problems of management.

The Methods of Training Research

Although all the obstacles listed are of importance, the main emphasis for this discussion is focused upon the need for a better understanding of the tools and methods of research. Research has been characterized as a critical investigation into areas of doubt and uncertainty—applying logical, systematic, and organized thinking, in order to find facts and principles that will solve difficulties. However, to achieve this end, the research technician must be equipped and expert in the knowledge and skill to do his job effectively. Like the financial expert who must understand budgeting, investments, and credit; the marketing specialist who knows advertising, distribution, and selling techniques; the production manager who is versed in production planning, routing, scheduling, layout, and the like; and the worker who must be skilled in the use of tools and equipment, so, too, the researcher must be adept and skillful.

Accordingly, the following chapters will attempt to describe the tools and the methods that are of importance to the research technician. First will appear a discussion of the survey method of research, then an exposition of the experimental method will follow, and, finally, the future of training will be viewed.

An attempt to present the practical and realistic side of training research will be emphasized with ample examples.

Summary

In summary, this chapter has presented the viewpoint that the safe road to successful training is to substitute facts for opinion. And that this is best accomplished by an understanding of the meaning, nature, and interrelatedness of research to training.

Research involves the application of logical and reflective thinking to the solution of problems. In the training area such problems include the following: the need for training, the policies and objectives, the content, the methods, the trainers, and the evaluation of training. To solve these problems the training director should be capable of understanding the nature and the meaning of research and the mechanics of its applications. In this connection one should be alert to the fact that logical thinking proceeds from a felt need to the definition of the problem, to the formulation of hypotheses and the collection of supporting evidence, thence to experimentation, and finally to the application of the findings to future uses.

Finally, it has been pointed out that certain barriers exist which interfere with training efficiency, and these include the attitudes of top management and the failure of those responsible for training to attain the skills required to conduct research.

THINGS TO DISCUSS AND TO DO

1. Who should be responsible for research in training?
2. Discuss the qualities or characteristics required in a training researcher.
3. Why is systematic and logical thinking important in conducting research?
4. Explain how you would use research if you were planning a long summer trip in your automobile.
5. Assume that you had three positions available and that you had to select the best one for your future career objectives. Explain how you would apply the steps of thinking postulated by John Dewey.
6. Make a visit to a large and a small company that are using training programs. Critically analyze the training programs in each company from the

following viewpoints: (a) Are the objectives of the program clearly defined? (b) Is the content of the training courses in line with the stated objectives? (c) Are the trainers selected and trained to instruct? (d) Is the training evaluated from opinion or from carefully conducted research? (e) Is research done to determine the effectiveness of the methods of instruction?

7. Make a visit to the library. Look through such publications as the following: (a) *Journal of Applied Psychology;* (b) *Personnel Journal;* (c) *Journal of the Academy of Management;* (d) *American Society of Training Directors Journal.* Find as many articles concerned with evaluation of training and the application of research to training as time will permit. Critically evaluate each article from the viewpoint of the meaning and nature of research.

15. THE SURVEY METHOD—LOOK
BEFORE YOU LEAP

Purpose of the Chapter

EFFECTIVE TRAINING requires a systematic, studied, and cautious investigation before it can be launched. It is advisable to look before one leaps; therefore, this chapter will stress the importance of systematic research before one commits mistakes that are irksome to mend. Fewer mistakes will be made if the researcher understands the meaning of survey research and learns how to employ the job activity analysis, the normative survey, the case-study method and the documentary method. Furthermore, the accuracy of the several forms of research will be increased by a careful use of such information-gathering tools as observation, interview, questionnaire, and the attitude scale.

A student who had graduated from the university some five years ago suddenly found himself in the predicament of instituting a training program for a small company. It seems that he was working as a "Jack-of-all-trades" as a systems man, personnel, and accounting assistant, when his boss called him and said that he believed that a training program was needed in the company. The boss explained that the company was about to consummate contracts that would require the addition of a large number of new employees.

Imagine the confusion and bewilderment of facing a new experience without adequate preparation for the task. Where does one start a program? What kind of training is needed? Who is to be trained? How will the training program be organized? Who will do the training? What should the new employees be taught? How long will it be necessary to train the employees?

Experiences of this kind are not uncommon among college graduates, whether they happen to be employed in large or small companies.

380

Yet, among all the questions that are aroused, in a situation of such complexity the one question that is paramount and most pressing is the most obvious, namely, Where does one start?

Devoid of the emotionality that is a consequence of being confronted with a complex and sudden problem, the simple place to start is by learning something about training and to realize that the experiences of others in similar situations might be investigated. This can be accomplished and should be done before one dashes headlong into a training program and seeks to learn by a trial-and-error method. It is obvious that a hit-or-miss approach to problem-solving is costly and wasteful in terms of money, time, and energy expended. The best way to safeguard against such wastefulness is to approach the difficulty with a logical, systematic, and problem-solving attitude.

Start with a Research Survey

It is necessary to recall that research is a process of applying logical reasoning in a systematic and orderly manner, in order to solve some felt difficulty. Furthermore, it is well to recognize that there are available certain methods of research that can help one to study a problem in an orderly and systematic manner. One of these methods is called "survey research."

A simple rule to follow, when in doubt, is to "Stop, Look, and Listen," and if this simple admonition is applied, then survey research might mean "Reflect, Investigate, and Learn." The young man about to embark on a new training program would do well, therefore, to begin a systematic and organized attack upon his problem by conducting a survey, bearing in mind that a research survey is a carefully organized procedure for investigating current practices in training. In another sense, it is a serious investigation that deals with a cross-section of training practices that are currently being used. The main purpose of such research is to determine what current training practices are and then to classify, generalize, and interpret them, in order to find a scientific guide to action.

Consequently, when one is confronted with a problem that is difficult to answer, the best place to begin is with a survey. It is only by conducting such a survey that one can answer the eternal questions, "Where do I start?" and "What is the best thing to do?"

But a word of caution is necessary before one jumps to the conclusion that a survey research is merely the application of "common sense." Rather, as has been pointed out, such research is scientific in the sense that it is a carefully organized procedure that utilizes certain tools that have been developed systematically.

The Meaning of Survey Research

Survey research is the scientific method of collecting and examining pertinent data, as objectively as possible, concerning a specific problem, in a systematic manner and then to analyze and interpret such data in order to improve existing conditions. The beginner should remember that survey research is concerned largely with descriptive reporting of data objectively and as it actually appears. This requires that the researcher must record data as they truly exist, devoid of bias and inaccuracies. Furthermore, it is important that the investigation be concerned mainly with current practices in a given and specified area. For example, the novice in starting a training program would do well to study the experiences of similar business concerns that have faced the same kind of training problems. The survey would be directed toward the gathering of data in a systematic manner so that it can be logically and intelligently interpreted. The objective of such a study would be to find a technique that might be applicable to the training problem that must be resolved. Specifically, the survey is aimed and directed toward finding a norm from the available similar experiences that are studied. It is advisable also to bear in mind that the phrase "current practices" refers to data that are presently in use or that are of fairly recent origin. In a negative sense the investigation should not be concerned with a historical study of training problems from early Greek times; rather, it should deal with "recent" current practices, for example, in terms of the past five or ten years. Accordingly, current practices should relate to recency in terms of time.

It is obvious, therefore, that the reason for any survey is to determine a norm that acts as a guide to action. Consequently, a carefully conducted survey could provide the beginner with a definite training program that could be modeled and suited to the specific requirements of any given situation. As a word of caution, it should be understood that the training procedure that emerges from the survey is, in essence, a "starting point" only and not a "finished product." In a scientific sense the study provides a place to start and thus answers the question of "Where does one start?" It should, however, be kept in mind that the true effectiveness of the program can be determined only by a careful follow-up and evaluation of the training program. In other words, the survey supplies the hypothesis necessary to inaugurate the training program, but it is equally important to test the assumptions that have been derived. The hypothesis thus formulated provides an "intelligent guess," not a hunch or some idea that flows from thin air. The intelligent guess is the result of a systematic collection of data that are carefully interpreted and developed into a plan of action. In summary, the survey assists in accomplishing the following:

1. Aids in defining the problem
2. Helps in arriving at hypotheses or guides
3. Establishes the basis for a definite plan of action
4. Assists in evaluating the effectiveness of the program

Survey Research in a Large Company

Faced with an impending shortage of supervisory and executive manpower, the president of a large bank called his department heads for a conference. He explained to the dozen executives present that the company was faced with a serious problem concerning the bank's future. He explained that the policy of the company had always been to promote employees from within the organization and that a careful survey had been conducted by the personnel director, aimed at studying manpower needs. The survey revealed the startling fact that the most pressing area for manpower replacements existed in the supervisory and executive positions. It was also explained that this was due to the fact that the company had done little to develop new talent and now found itself in the awkward position of realizing that almost half its executive staff would have to be retired in the next few years. He pointed out that the company had been too busy and too successful to be aware of the problem sooner and that the years had gone by with a very capable staff of executives but that the time had arrived when action should be taken. What should be done? The consensus of the group was that a manpower development training program should be started at once, but the inevitable questions arose:

What kind of training was required?
What kind of a training procedure was best?
Who should be trained?
How should they be trained? By whom? When? Where?

Finally, one of the conferees suggested that the company conduct a survey immediately to determine how other banks were developing executive and supervisory manpower. The personnel director was given the responsibility for conducting the survey and was told to have a complete report in the hands of the president in approximately two months. The report was also to include specific statements concerning policies of the program, aims and objectives, and a definite plan of action which could get the training program started.

The personnel director began his assignment by first attempting to define and clarify the problem. He was certain that he could not conduct the survey properly until he was able to prepare a detailed and specific statement of the problem. In order to accomplish this, it was necessary to understand clearly and to define the meaning of "executive." Accordingly, answers had to be found for the following questions:

> Who is an executive?
> What positions do executives hold in the company?
> What duties and responsibilities do the executives perform?
> What are the present techniques being used to train executives?

The reason for answering such questions was to make certain that the survey that had to be conducted would be specifically oriented and directed, compactly and tersely stated, and delimited to the specific needs of the company's problem.

Consequently, before the personnel director could actually begin his survey of other companies it was imperative that study of the executive problem be undertaken first. The main purpose of a preliminary survey, obviously, is to make certain that the study of other companies will pertain to the central problem at hand. For example, the term "executive" may have a different meaning from one company to another; likewise the duties and responsibilities may be different, and the place in the organization structure may not be the same. Therefore, it is necessary to be clearly certain of exactly what should be surveyed and which companies offer similarities in practices that may be helpful to the solution of the present problem.

The preliminary survey does more than help in the definition of the problem. If it is sensibly handled, it can also provide criteria, standards, or yardsticks that may later be especially important in evaluating and comparing the experiences of other companies in the light of present needs. These generalities can be better clarified and understood if the procedures of the personnel director in the bank are more specifically explained.

Job Activity Analysis Survey

One of the techniques for conducting a survey is to carry out a systematic investigation of the jobs presently being performed in the company. In management terminology this procedure is called a "job analysis." It is actually a survey of current jobs, with the objective of classifying, naming, and describing the jobs in question. Thus a job analysis will aid in establishing job classifications and job descriptions. With respect to the executive development survey that the bank must conduct, the job analysis will therefore help to define the nature of the executive position by giving a clearer definition, establish the place in the organization, identify the problem better, and render a statement of the duties and responsibilities.

To carry out a survey of any kind, including a job analysis, the personnel director has a choice of several tools that can be used to collect and gather the facts and information needed. Tools may be considered as aids necessary to the accomplishment of any task. Just as a carpenter needs tools, such as a hammer, plane, and screwdriver, so a researcher requires tools to conduct a survey. Furthermore, the tools that are used for one technique or method of survey research can be used for carrying out all types of surveys. Since one of the methods for conducting a survey research is the job activity or job analysis technique, the following tools will be applied thereto.

The tools that are most frequently used are as follows:

> Observation
> Interviews
> Questionnaires
> Attitude and opinion scales

The purpose of a job analysis survey is to study the nature of a job as well as the human requirements that are essential to performing the task. With reference to the executive position that must be analyzed, the personnel director seeks to investigate the functions that must be performed, the duties, and the responsibilities, as well as the human requirements, such as the skills, knowledge, and attitudes. This can be done by conducting a systematic analysis of the job with the aid of a carefully organized procedure of observation.

Observation as a Tool for Job Analysis Research

Observation means more than viewing a picturesque landscape for sheer emotional enjoyment or watching a worker perform a job from the standpoint of admiring his skill. In a general sense, to observe means to watch, to view, to perceive, to notice, or to attend to something. Usually, in the layman's observations, the approach is informal, casual, and unsystematic, while, in the scientific sense, observation is purposeful, directed, controlled, systematic, and formal. When the survey is used to study a job, the approach is scientific. The scientific approach is mandatory because all human observations are open to suspicion. This fact can be readily appreciated if one realizes that human observations are the result of the observer's ability to observe accurately. Furthermore, accurate observations are more directly the result of human perceptions, which involve the sense organs and the interpretations occurring from what is observed. Since it is generally accepted that human perceptions can be inaccurate and faulty, techniques must be devised to reduce the possible margin of error. In scientific observation this is accomplished by preparing and following a detailed plan of action.

One way to investigate the executive position in the problem under consideration might be to observe in an organized manner the knowledge required to do the job, then to study the skills necessary, and, finally, to view the attitudes or human qualities needed. This can be facilitated by developing a job description from the observations of the actual performance of the position. The job description thus prepared should render a clear picture of the duties and responsibilities involved in the task. If possible, the use of more than one observer might be employed so as to insure greater accuracy in reporting the detailed description of the job.

However, the survey research which employs a job activity analysis that is accomplished by using the tool of observation does not end with a job description. At this point the researcher is equipped only with the facts concerning the nature of the job. Now the procedure requires some careful analysis and interpretation in terms of the knowledge, skills, and attitudes involved in the job.

In summary, one should remember the following key points:

1. That, before one embarks on a survey, it is necessary to define and clarify the problem to be investigated.
2. That one of the techniques used to define a problem is the job activity analysis.
3. That one of the tools that may be employed to conduct the analysis is controlled observation.
4. That a job analysis results in a job description.

5. That the job description must then be analyzed and interpreted so as to classify in an organized way the complex facets of the job.
6. Finally, that the job analysis aids in delimiting the forthcoming survey and directs it more efficiently to the problem at hand.

The Interview as a Tool for Job Activity Analysis

Another tool that is often used to study and survey a job is the interview. Like the use of observation, the interview must also be carefully organized and systematically employed. The major differences in the two tools is that, in the one, observation is emphasized, while in the other conversation and face-to-face contact is predominant. It should be understood that both tools are overlapping and complementary. Which is to say that, in the analysis of any job, both tools can be used to supplement each other when a job analysis survey is conducted.

Therefore, it is wise to remember that observation is a noncommunicative tool, while the interview is communicative. The interview has often been defined as a "conversation with a purpose." Conversation in this case is the means of communication. However, the conversation is not aimless; rather, it has a direction and a purpose. Where a job analysis survey is conducted, the purpose is to collect accurate information concerning the skills, knowledge, and attitudes required to perform the job being analyzed.

The main purpose of the job analysis interview, therefore, is to collect as much pertinent information as is possible from those who are actually performing a job or from those who possess authoritative information concerning its essential details. Usually such persons to be interviewed are the workers themselves or their immediate supervisors. As previously mentioned, it is necessary to have a carefully prepared list of questions available, in order to secure the accurate information needed to survey a job adequately. Specifically, questions should be directed to the sequence or the steps involved in performing the task, to the special skills required, to the abilities and the knowledge involved, and to the attitudes essential to the job.

It is not always possible or expedient to attempt to interview all the workers doing the same job; therefore, it is sometimes advisable to sample the group. This can be done by taking a percentage of the workers, such as 10 per cent, and making certain that they represent the characteristics of the larger group. The interview is of value because it permits of two-way communications and, as a result, allows the interviewer to probe in greater detail into the job requirements. Furthermore, it also gives the worker a better opportunity to enlarge and render information that the interviewer may not have realized as being important.

The interviewing tool also provides some difficulties that should be taken into consideration. First, interviews take time to prepare properly; time is also a factor in conducting the interview, and perhaps the cost and the time consumed are not efficient for the purpose. Also the interview requires that individuals be trained adequately to secure the interest and the information required.

A practical approach to the survey is to use both the observation and the interview tools, for in this way a more accurate recording of the facts can be accomplished. This is best done by a sampling procedure, wherein the jobs are limited to a small percentage of the total number.

The Questionnaire as a Tool for Survey Research

One of the most practical and least costly tools for the collecting of information is the questionnaire. The questionnaire is a one-way stream of communication and is characterized by the fact that it is a "paper-and-pencil" form of gathering information. Questions are carefully prepared and suited to the purpose of the investigation, then they are written out or printed in various ways and are sent to the respondents.

Generally, such questionnaires are prepared so as to incorporate the following:

An introductory statement which seeks to enlist the aid of the respondent to render accurate information and to secure his co-operation. Sometimes it is beneficial to orient the respondent by giving him some idea of the purpose of the questionnaire and why it may be important for him to answer the questions accurately.

Next usually come the directions for answering the questions, for example, whether the questions are true or false statements, or fill-in, or multiple choice.

Then the actual questions should be properly arranged and set forth clearly.

As a rule, the respondents are not asked to sign their names. The advantages of the questionnaire approach to information gathering are related to practicability and ease of collecting and scoring the data. Many respondents may be contacted in a short time, and the information can be classified and scored with a great deal of ease. Another advantage of this tool is that the results can be listed and treated numerically and therefore can be made more intelligible. Thus, if one desired to determine how many companies are presently conducting training programs for supervisors, one of the questions might be "Do you conduct a supervisory training program in your company?" From the responses to such a question it would be possible to determine the quantity or number of companies involved. Now suppose that the intention of the questionnaire was to also acquire knowledge concerning the nature of such training and the content, among a number of other things that might be sought. Then the questions would be directed and stated along the lines of the desired information.

Accordingly, the answers can be tabulated, and the totals for each question can be determined. Thus it can be seen that the questionnaire makes it possible to express numerically the results with relative ease. At the same time, many companies can be requested to submit answers to the questionnaire, and in this manner a large sample is also possible.

But, lest one assume that the questionnaire tool to survey research is infallible, it should be noted that it also has some weaknesses. Above all, the validity or worthwhileness of the tool is questionable because many respondents will not reply, and, when they do, there is little evidence to support the fact that the data reported are accurate or even in existence. Therefore, caution must be the rule in interpreting and drawing conclusions from the results. Even when the evidence is trustworthy, the questions may be interpreted by the respondents in different ways. Consequently, where questionnaires are used, they must be carefully prepared, and the results should be interpreted with caution.

The Attitude and Opinion Scale as a Tool in Survey Research

While the questionnaire is concerned mainly with quantitative results, the attitude scale is more interested in qualitative data. It should be recognized that the attitude scale is primarily used as an evaluative tool and is generally employed to measure morale. At the same time, it can also measure the opinions and the feelings on respondents toward any situation. For example, the Gallup and the Roper polls are attempts to ascertain the opinions of segments of the population regarding current issues confronting the people. Therefore, they are actually forms of survey research aimed at studying the feelings and opinions of the population. In many companies, attitude surveys are conducted in the same way, in order to determine the feelings and opinions of segments of the working force toward the companies' policies, their supervision, conditions of work, and similar factors that affect the workers' behavior.

The attitude scale is more often used as a means of measuring the opinions of trainees in supervision programs than as a technique for gathering information from other companies, and it will be more adequately dealt with in the following chapter, concerned with evaluation of training programs.

The personnel director referred to at the beginning of the discussion can now take stock of the discussion and of the available tools he has at his command. As previously mentioned, his first task is carefully to define the jobs of supervisor and executives in his company. This he can do by using any of the tools, namely, observation, questionnaire, interview, or attitude scales. It should be understood that all these methods are complementary and supplementary to each other and that any combination or single tool will aid in clarifying the problem.

Since the first task confronting the personnel director is one of describing the executive and supervisor jobs, how would you advise him to proceed? Should he use the interviewing tool? If so, then how should he prepare the interview, and how should it be conducted? Or would you recommend any of the other tools to perform the job analysis?

With regard to the conduct of a job activity analysis, it is necessary to remember that such an analysis is actually a method of survey research. Furthermore, the inception of any training program regardless of its nature—for example, job training, supervisor or executive training—must depend upon the gathering of information that accurately describes the jobs in which training is required. Remember that a training program's content depends upon accurate job knowledge.

Job knowledge is acquired by research that is called "job activity analysis," and the tools that can be used to perform such an analysis are observation, interview, questionnaire, and attitude scale. The following key points should be carefully noted with regard to job analysis research:

1. Job analyses are conducted within the company and for tasks that require training.
2. Job analysis research helps to define the job.
3. Job analysis provides the content for the training.
4. Job analysis establishes the criteria or standards for evaluation and measurement.
5. Job analysis aids in the preparation of the content of the tools of observation, interviewing, questionnaire, and attitude scale. It is impossible to prepare a tool of scientific inquiry without knowing what it is that must be inquired into.

Equipped with such information and having prepared and chosen the tool that should be used, the personnel director can now utilize several other methods of research to determine what current practices are in other companies. Thus the young college graduate or the personnel director now is in a position to explore the experiences of others, in the current scene, in order to answer the question "Where do I start?" and then in logical order the question "What should be the composition of the training program?" can next be pursued.

Normative Survey Research

Late in the year of 1942, when we were engaged in the darkest hours of World War II, it became necessary to train large numbers of people in a relatively short time. Production in armaments and especially in aircraft became the primary objective of most of American industries. The main obstacle in the path of meeting the enormous goods needed was not material as much as it was manpower. Most of the youth and the trained people had been or were being called into the armed services, and therefore any new personnel had to be recruited from the remaining part of the population, most of whom had never worked in a factory, or even at all—women of all ages, men who were not fit for service, old and young, teachers, lawyers, merchants, and the like.

One of the areas that required special attention was the need for civilian inspectors, whose main job was concerned with the problem of inspecting all materials manufactured for the Air Force. A civilian director was placed in charge of the entire operation for the Eastern District, and he was charged with the responsibility for establishing a school in as short a time as was possible. The objective was to train civilian inspectors who would be equipped with the knowledge, skills, and attitudes that would facilitate the production of aircraft.

As with the young graduate and the personnel director of a bank, the eternal questions arose: Where do I start? What should be the content of the training program? How can people learn most rapidly? On and on went the questions, but action was required.

The first thing to do was to determine the nature of an inspector's job. This was accomplished by conducting a job activity analysis. Since most large manufacturers had many inspectors and had much experience in training them, teams were sent out, with carefully prepared tools, to determine exactly what was involved in an inspector's job. Utilizing the tools for surveying jobs previously discussed, such as observation, interviews, and questionnaires, the teams, who sampled many aircraft plants, classified and interpreted the data gathered by them in a very short time. The data reported by the observers and interviewers, along with the information returned on the questionnaires, resulted in a job activity analysis. The analysis helped to describe the inspector's job, and this included detailed statement of duties and responsibilities.

The first phase of the new training program was thus completed because a clear-cut definition of the job was now available. This phase clearly indicated that the training of inspectors involved the following kinds of knowledge and skills that were required to perform the job of inspecting effectively:

> *Knowledge required*
> Shop mathematics
> Metallurgy
> Aircraft motors and parts
> Human relations
> *Skills required*
> Slide rule
> Tools and gauges
> Blueprints
> *Attitudes required*
> Respect for human behavior
> Motivation of people

Now the question of how to best train novices to become inspectors had to be answered. To conserve time, the original team that had done the job activity analysis was also instructed to survey and report in detail the methods that were currently being used by many of the aircraft manufacturers to train their inspectors. This was accomplished while the job analysis was being done.

This was the second phase of the program and involved the use of another method of research called the "normative survey research." The purpose of a normative survey is to investigate current practices in training so as to arrive at a standard or guide for future action.

Normative survey research is an investigation of present practices employed by others, so as to arrive at a workable procedure that, upon analysis, would appear to be the best solution to an existing problem. Basically, the objective of normative research is to determine what is best to do, in order to resolve some problem, which in this case is to find the best way to train inspectors in a short time.

Often practical businessmen are inclined to scoff at what they would call the waste of time that results from such investigations. Such individuals are apt to rely on opinions, prejudice, and guesswork as the means of deciding on a course of action. The fallacy of such an argument should be obvious, since the methods of guesswork and opinions are wasteful in terms of time, effort, and money expended. Methods of this kind are trial-and-error approaches to problem-solving and as such, are "hit-or-miss" solutions. In another sense the "practical" approach leaves the chances for error wide open, while, in contrast, the scientific survey method considerably reduces the probability of risk. The scientific approach substitutes blind action for reasoned and logical planning based upon verifiable evidence.

Therefore, it is important to recognize that, before action can take place, it is imperative to investigate scientifically the nature of a problem and then to establish a procedure that may be tested. To be assured that the scientific approach is properly conducted, it is wise to remember that two main principles are involved in normative survey research, and they are:

1. The data and the principles derived from the investigation should be pertinent and directly related to the problem at hand. For example, the need to determine the best way to train inspectors can be fulfilled only if the problem is clearly defined and the methods of securing data are carefully developed and carried out.

2. There exists a probability that the facts and the principles derived have a fairly good chance of being applied to the solution of the problem. For example, the aircraft plants that were investigated in order to set up a school for inspectors did not in all cases offer data and principles that were relevant to a training school. Only those that had similarities to the defined need offered such pertinent information.

Guided by the main principles for conducting survey research, it is equally important to understand that certain criteria must also be adhered to for such research to be efficient. The criteria or requirements that are needed are discussed below.

1. *Normative Research Must Be Accurate, Objective, and Quantitative.* Opinions and loose judgments cannot be tolerated, for they serve only to reduce the probability that the evidence and principles being investigated will work in the problem situation. Accuracy requires great diligence, concentration on facts, descriptions of what actually exists, proper attention to all facets of the investigation, and clarity in written rendition of the data. Imagine yourself as a witness to an automobile accident, and suppose that you were asked to report your account of the mishap. Could you be accurate in your report as to the exact time of the accident, the speed of the cars involved, the direction of each car, and all other relevant data that should be observed? The same criteria for accurate reporting on the training program in an aircraft company would be required for it to be effective and helpful.

Objectivity refers to the ability to report data as they actually appear, not tainted by feelings, bias, prejudice, or emotion. Preconceived concepts and "notions" can be deterrents to objective reporting; for example, if one has rigid and strong viewpoints as to what constitutes a good training program, then it becomes possible to observe only what fits into preconceived ideas. In effect, observation becomes a process for observing only what one wants to observe and not what actually exists.

Although survey research is characterized by observation, this should not be construed to mean that quantitative expression of the investigation is not possible or desirable. On the contrary, wherever it is possible to effect quantitative values for that which is observed, so much the better. For example, when a normative survey is conducted in many companies in an endeavor to determine the best training program for a definite purpose, it would be wise to express numerically as much of the data as possible. Numerical expression could include the number of people being trained, the number in each training section, the time needed for training, the progress of the trainees, the number who succeed after training, and the effects upon production, on labor turnover, and any other pertinent data.

2. *Normative Survey Research Must Be Valid and Reliable.* It can be said that if the survey does not measure or investigate what it has predetermined to study, then it is not valid. Consequently, validity refers to that necessary requirement of scientific investigation that assures that the survey is actually observing and investigating what it is intended to study. The most important quality of validity is relevance. This simply means that the survey must conform to certain predetermined and clearly defined criteria or standards. In the instance of setting up a training school of inspectors, it will be recalled that the first essential requirement was to carry out a job activity analysis. The purpose of this phase of the survey was to establish certain criteria for the job of inspecting. Once this was accomplished, analysis then followed, which culminated into a clear-cut and carefully defined statement of the duties, the responsibilities, and the human qualities needed to perform the job successfully. Accordingly, any further research, such as a normative survey of several companies who have been training inspectors, would, of necessity, be so conducted that all the investigation would be oriented toward the predetermined criteria or standard. In this case the standard is the specific job requirements. Normative research, like all kinds of research, must therefore be relevant to some definite criteria or standard, for it to be properly directed and for it actually to investigate what it really is supposed to study.

Reliability is another necessary requirement of effective normative survey research, since it refers to the consistency of the survey. Consistency means the control of those conditions that make a survey uniform and standardized, so that the same factors will be observed and investigated in similar ways under different situations. Maintenance of reliability, therefore, requires that the objectives, methods, tools, and personnel doing the investigation must be so controlled that the entire study, ranging from one company to another, will be conducted in a similar manner. If this condition is not met, then the survey could result in confusion, as the result of different observers studying different factors in various ways that might not be properly related to the defined and stated criteria.

3. Normative Research Requires Accurate and Adequate Description.   To report whatever is observed requires effective communications, and one of the barriers to scientific survey methods is the failure to transmit information in a manner that reveals exactly what has been observed. In a sense it is possible for an observer to observe accurately and at the same time fail to convey to others the nature of the actual data collected.

Communications refers to the means of conveying or transmitting information from one place to another. In general, the means usually consist of oral or face-to-face transmission and written forms of communication. In a normative research survey both forms of communication are used, with major emphasis usually placed upon the written media. Failure to transmit observed data in a clear, intelligible, and understandable manner to others can seriously distort the facts and lead to false conclusions. Accordingly, it is imperative in survey research that all reports be written in simple language and in a compact, detailed, logical manner. Generalities and vagueness should be avoided. Words can mean different things to different interpreters, and great care must be used to be certain that a description of any situation will convey the same meaning to all interpreters.

4. Normative Research Must Result in Valid Conclusions. The culmination of survey research that is valid, reliable, accurate, and adequately described is the formulation of sound conclusions. Any conclusions that are drawn from the data collected must be consistent with the facts as reported.

Conclusions can be formulated in a consistent manner only when all the data collected are organized, classified, and arranged in an orderly manner. For example, if ten aircraft companies were surveyed, in order to determine a norm or average of the training methods used, then the data collected might be arranged under separate classifications, as follows:

Why is training done?
Who is being trained?
When? How long?
What is the content? The methods?
Who does the training? How selected? How trained?
What is the nature of the job? How is it evaluated?
What criteria are used?

Furthermore, classifying data requires subclassifications under each of the major headings. This process of organizing data and evidence may be analogous to a master sheet that is laid out with a complete and detailed classification scheme, where one takes all the data and carefully separates and enters them in the proper column on the master form. Conclusions can be formulated intelligently only when the evidence makes sense, and this occurs only when all evidence is properly organized.

Finally, it is important that the conclusion be relevant to the facts.

Thus all conclusions reached must be evaluated against the stated objectives, definition, and needs for training that were initially formulated.

Whether one is a young college graduate, a personnel director of a large bank, or an individual interested in setting up a training school for inspectors, the normative survey method of research can be of vital importance in the solution of training problems, especially when adherence to these general rules are followed:

1. Where a felt need or a problem exists in training, carefully state and clarify the nature of said difficulty.

2. Define the nature of the job or jobs that require training. Through the use of the job activity method of survey research, determine the exact responsibilities, duties, and human qualities required to perform the job successfully.

3. Determine the methods and the tools to be used. When the job activity and the normative methods are employed, select the tools, such as observation, interview, questionnaire, or attitude scale or possibly a combination of these.

4. Prepare the tools carefully. From the job analysis select the items that must be surveyed and incorporate these into the body of the content of the tool, such as the question to be asked in an interview or written into the questionnaire.

5. Give the tool a trial run. Try it out on some of your own employees or in a small sample of respondents outside the company. Look for the weaknesses and iron out the kinks.

6. Now select and train the observers. The success of the survey will depend upon the care with which observers are selected and trained. In selection it is important that the observers be interested in the project, mentally fitted, acute in powers of observation, adept at reporting detail, unbiased, efficient in systematic procedures, and equipped in social skill and language communication.

Furthermore, the observers should be trained in the techniques of gathering data, in the nature of the survey and its purposes, and in the skills required to carry out the survey.

7. Select the sample to be surveyed, and secure permission. What companies and how many should be surveyed. Remember that normative research seeks to establish a norm of several companies. Accordingly, the companies selected should possess common elements that are similar to the predetermined needs of the survey.

Permission should be secured to survey the companies chosen. It is best to acquire such permission from top management where possible.

8. Conduct the survey and gather the evidence and the data desired. The members of the team or a single individual now carry out the purposes of the survey by collecting the evidence according to the predetermined plans and with the tools that have been developed.

9. Classify, analyze, and interpret the data and evidence. This stage requires that all data be assembled and organized in a systematic manner so that they may be analyzed and interpreted. The goal of intelligent and logical analysis and interpretations is the development of a plan of action.

10. The plan of action is put into operation. It is at this point that the answer to the question What is the best training program to use for the stated purpose? has been tentatively found. Thus the normative survey research has assisted in the formulation of a norm for a training program.

Supplementary Methods of Survey Research

Two other methods of research, beyond the job activity and the normative survey techniques, that are of importance to the student of training research are the case study and the documentary methods. Both these methods require the same consideration and conditions and utilize the same tools as all the methods of survey research.

The case-study method may be distinguished from the normative survey in that it is concerned with a single case at a time rather than several cases. For example, the normative approach may gather evidence from several companies, while the case-study method would concentrate on a single company. The single company involved might be the same one that the investigator is employed in at the present time or another company.

The case-study method is also characterized by the fact that it is causal and evolutionary. It is causal in the sense that it stresses the search for causes for an existing difficulty, and it is evolutionary because it investigates the development and historical background of a single case. Perhaps the most prevalent use of the case method is found in the work of clinical psychologists, psychiatrists, and doctors. Such practitioners seek to use a diagnostic approach, with emphasis upon studying the background and history of the patient, so as to arrive at a true definition of the causes of a problem. However, it is important to recognize that the search for causes is preliminary and necessary to the application of remedial action.

In the business world the case-study method has many applications. To illustrate, assume that a company has found its production falling and that labor turnover has increased and that it wishes to correct the difficulty. A case study might be instituted to find the causes, and this in turn might reveal that the cause may be faulty training. Furthermore, such an investigation may pinpoint the difficulty to a specific aspect of the training program. Then some form of remedial action would be recommended. Perhaps the training time is too long, the method faulty, the instruction poor. The same procedure would be applied to the case-study method as those applied to the normative survey.

Documentary research is another form of survey that is usually employed as an adjunct to the other methods. It is an informational analysis of recorded and printed material that represents the current state of conditions. The doctor may have a recorded written report of a patient's past medical examinations that is accurate and complete. Using this information, he may be able to analyze the ailment more successfully. The businessman may not have records of blood pressure and the like, but he does have production and personnel and financial records that can reveal the pulse rate of his company's activities.

Production, personnel, and financial records are of inestimable value to the businessman in determining possible symptoms before difficulties arise, and they are equally important in helping to discover problem areas after they have occurred. It should also be recognized that accurate record keeping is also important in helping to determine criteria for evaluation purposes. To determine whether or not a training program is effective, it may be necessary to study and evaluate the effect of the training upon production. This aspect of documentary research will be more fully described and discussed in the next chapter.

Summary

This chapter has dealt with the methods of survey research that may be of benefit to business in answering the problems related to the organization and origination of training programs. It has stressed the viewpoint that an investigation along scientific lines can be of value in setting up a training program and that this can best be accomplished by studying current practices in a single company or in many. These methods include the job activity analysis, the normative survey, the case method, and the documentary approach.

Of noteworthy importance is the fact that the results of survey research is the development of a plan of action. But it must be emphasized that such action is not the cure-all for problems; rather, it is merely the start of a program which must then be followed up with further research to determine its effectiveness. This problem of the relationship of research to evaluation will be discussed in the next chapter dealing with the experimental method of research.

THINGS TO DISCUSS AND TO DO

1. If you were requested to start a training program in a small company, explain how you would use the survey form of research to get the program started.

2. Select any job which may be familiar to you and conduct a job activity analysis.

3. From the analysis of the job you selected set forth the content that would be necessary to train someone to do that job.

4. Do a survey of several companies in order to determine the procedure that might be used to start an executive training program.

5. What is the value of documentary research?

6. How can the case method be used to start a training program?

7. Discuss the criteria necessary for normative research to be effective?

8. Outline in detail the factors that you would observe if you were to do a job activity analysis of a teacher's job.

9. Prepare in detail the interview that might be employed for the same job.

10. Devise a questionnaire that would be used to determine the need for new courses or for modifications of present ones in the school you attend.

11. After gathering your information, classify, organize, and interpret the findings along with your recommendations.

16. THE EXPERIMENTAL METHOD— THE PROOF OF THE PUDDING

Purpose of the Chapter

THIS CHAPTER attempts to demonstrate that the way to justify the existence of training is by the intelligent application of the experimental method of research. The purposes and the meaning of experimental research will be explained with appropriate examples to illustrate its applications. Three ways of conducting experimental research will be reviewed, namely, the single-group, the equivalent-group, and the rotation methods. Finally, the problem of determining the criteria for the evaluation will be mentioned with emphasis upon the evaluating of job performance from the detailed aspects of the job to the evaluation of job performance from summary criteria.

"We have an excellent training program in our company," said the training director of a large company to a group of visiting students. "If you will notice," he continued, "three floors of this main building, located in the lower part of New York City, are devoted to training. Training of all kinds is conducted here, ranging from job training to supervisor and executive development. On the first floor all new employees are put through an orientation and induction phase of training, then the trainees are moved down the floor to another division, where they are trained in job skills and observe all the machinery and equipment available. We advance the trainees from the very simple to the very complex aspects of the jobs they will eventually perform, and I think that you might be interested in the training rooms also; notice how the seats and the tables and equipment are arranged. At the same time, look at the blackboards, the projectors, and the other visual aids we employ to teach our trainees. And let me also tell you that our instructors are all carefully selected and trained and that they use the best methods of training available."

One of the visiting students observed that it probably required a

great deal of time and money to establish and keep a training program of such size and complexity in operation. To this the training
director replied, "The budget for this program runs into many thousands of dollars, to be sure, but we feel it is worth it. But of more
importance is the fact that the training program was not put together by guesses or opinions, we went out and investigated many
companies and determined how they were trying to train for similar
jobs, and only after a careful survey did we decide on what to do in
our company."

"Does the training program ever change?" asked another student.
"Yes, from time to time we have changes in methods, machinery,
and procedures that cause us to change the training in one way or
another."

From another student, "How can you be certain that the cost of
such a training program is really worth it?"

"We are fairly certain that the program works because we are
constantly surveying the trainees, and they seem to indicate that the
program is effective. But we don't stop there, for we also ask the instructors and supervisors to let us know if the program is working
properly. Furthermore, our production records indicate that we are
producing more and that we have less labor turnover. I think that
proves the effectiveness of the training."

Does the conclusion of the personnel director actually prove that
the elaborate and expensive training program briefly described is truly
effective? Whether or not proof is available to substantiate such
claims, it is not uncommon in the area of business training for those
responsible for the evaluation of training to conclude hastily that
training is effective on the basis of evidence that has rarely been
subjected to controlled experimental research. Conclusions that are
hastily drawn from empirical evidence do not necessarily prove that
causes of behavioral changes, which, in this case, are assumed to be
training, are related to the effect, which is stated as opinions of
trainees, supervisors, and production records. It is possible that
many other causes might be responsible for the changes that are
claimed—for example, the employment and selection procedures may
have been improved, with the result that better employees are presently
being trained; perhaps the wage and salary program has been altered,
or union contracts may effect the motivation of the trainees; likewise,
supervisors may be better equipped to train employees on the job;
conditions of work may have been improved, such as better methods,

incentive plans, changes in illumination, use of music, rest periods, and music. One could add a host of other possible causes that might have been responsible for the alleged changes of the personnel director.

Acceptance of generalized conclusions also ignores the possibility that the training program might be improved and actually places a "blindfold" over the eyes of those responsible for evaluating training. Since top management usually wishes to insist upon immediate, practical, and monetary results, they force many training directors to become "penny wise and pound foolish." Thus long-range viewpoints and improvements in training are often ignored in place of immediate results. This is probably due to the attitudes of managers who view training as a supplement to business activity, not as a necessary part of the total management function.

Another reason for such narrow concepts of evaluation of training is the fact that many training directors believe that, once a survey has been made, the training program must be assured of success. As already mentioned, a survey merely serves to establish a program of action where none previously existed. It does not guarantee that the training program will be successful. It is much like a calculated risk that must be followed up and tested experimentally. This means that the validation of training must be concerned with experimentation that not only will render empirical evidence of proof but must also give logical support to the effectiveness of the training program. Logical validation is concerned with the "innards" or parts of a training program that make up the total training process. These parts include such factors as the selection and the training of instructors, the content of the courses, the methods of teaching, the recall and retention of material learned, the requirements of motivation, the application of teaching aids, the time for effective learning, and the determination of standards or criteria. To the automotive engineer the fact that an automobile engine is functioning as a totality is not enough, for it is equally important to know the logical question of validation, which is concerned with the manner in which the hundreds of parts that comprise the motor are functioning. Thus pistons, spark plugs, distributor, compression, generator, fuel pumps, and the like must also be experimentally tested.

It is a paradox that management will invest large sums of money in training programs and at the same time will fail to determine experimentally whether such investments are worthwhile. It may be said that the future of training, its status, prestige, acceptance, and stability as a basic part of business practices, will depend upon how well experimental methods of research are applied to all training factors.

THE PURPOSES OF EXPERIMENTAL RESEARCH IN TRAINING

Experimental research aims to answer two basic questions:

1. Does the training program change the behavior of the learners in the predetermined direction that has been desired?

2. What laws can be formulated that can be applied to all training conditions?

With regard to the problem of changing human behavior, it can be generally stated that the purpose of all training is to attempt to equip the learner with new knowledge, skills, and attitudes that will be carried over to the actual working situation. Psychologically, this is known as the "law of transfer of training," which simply means the transference of knowledge, skills, and attitudes from one situation to another. College students seek to attain degrees in one specialization or another, and thus they acquire many changes in their behavior, which, it is believed, will be transferred to the attainment of careers, of citizenship, and successful living. Likewise the purpose of business training is to equip the learner to transfer his behavioral changes to the job so that he may become a proficient worker.

A necessary prerequisite to the problem of answering the question of whether or not human behavior is changed is that one related to the determination of criteria. It is impossible to measure anything accurately unless some definite yardsticks, standards, or criteria are first established. In the business world the usual criterion is production—namely, quantity and quality of work performed by an employee. Although this criterion is necessary and valuable, it fails to view the whole worker in relation to the total demands of the job. For example, the worker's adjustment to the company, his fellow workers, his supervision, his community; and his attitudes, motivations, aspirations, and potentials must also be considered since they may influence productivity.

The determination and evaluation of training, therefore, must take into account more than production. Where training criteria are narrowed to the material aspects of job performance, the total requirements of job success are ignored. Consequently, the purpose of experimental research should be viewed as twofold: first, it should seek to determine the total meaning of successful job performance, and, second, it should then be used to evaluate whether or not the training program is meeting the requirements of the determined concepts of job performance. In essence, experimental research, therefore, first seeks to establish criteria and then tries to ascertain whether the changes in human behavior that have occurred in the training program are, in fact, transferred to the requirements of successful job performance.

The second basic question that experimental research seeks to answer is concerned with the formulation of laws and principles related to training. Experimental research is basically a process of mental activity that stresses a controlled search for facts and evidence that will accurately explain the cause-and-effect relationships of a phenomenon. For example, the law of transfer of training was formulated after much research in the field of the psychology of learning had been conducted. Thus the law today is used as a guide for all training programs. Laws or principles of learning are important to training directors because they help to direct and guide actions along proved lines. Consequently, when training programs are used in business, it is possible to establish through experimental research certain laws and principles that can then be employed to aid all other training needs.

In summary, it may be pointed out that experimental research aids in the following ways:

1. It serves as a tool to evaluate the effectiveness of training.

2. It helps to determine criteria that are essential to evaluation and measurement of training.

3. It helps to discover laws and principles that may facilitate the training and learning process for future requirements.

THE MEANING AND NATURE OF EXPERIMENTAL RESEARCH

Experimental research is that type of controlled research in which the variables affecting human behavior are isolated and in which one variable at a time is permitted to affect an individual or a group of individuals. Variables are those factors or conditions that may cause individuals to behave in certain ways. For example, one may well ask why it is that some workers learn to do a job faster and more accurately than do other workers. Even a moment of reflection will indicate some of the probable variables that may account for the difference. Perhaps one has more intelligence, is more mechanically inclined, has better motivation, can see better, has more experience, is less affected by noise—and a host of other reasons may be added. Therefore, if one wanted to ascertain in a more definitive manner what specific variables accounted for the differences, it would be necessary first to isolate all the variables that could affect the workers, then it would be necessary to take one variable at a time and subject each to controlled conditions, where only the one factor being tested could affect the learner. If all the variables were then treated in the same manner, it would be possible to determine which one of all the factors was responsible for the differences.

Accordingly, the main features of experimental research are control, isolation of variables, and permitting only one variable to operate at a time. Experimentation can best be conducted if the following considerations are kept in mind:

1. The problem should be carefully defined and isolated, so as to avoid confusion.

2. The variables that may enter into the experiment must be isolated and labeled.

3. One variable that is to be evaluated should be chosen and defined.

4. The technique to be used for the experiment should be selected.

5. The criteria needed for adequate evaluation should be determined.

6. A detailed and careful reporting of the results must be made.

7. There should be provision for a repetition of the experiment.

As a means of accomplishing these considerations, experimental research employs specific techniques. The first important technique may be likened to the familiar "before and after picture" that many have seen used in advertising and selling. In the selling of a hair cream, the picture of a young man with unkempt and unruly hair is first shown, then the hair cream is applied, and the smooth shiny hair is then displayed. The untidy hair is first shown, in order for the potential buyer to establish a criterion or standard in his mind, so that he may be able to evaluate and compare the difference when the experimental factor is introduced, which in this case is the hair cream.

In experimental research in the training area the same technique is utilized in a more formal and scientific sense. The "before and after picture" is attained by making provisions for a controlled phase and an experimental phase. In the controlled phase all variables that may affect the learner are left as they usually would be, while in the experimental phase only one variable is permitted to influence the learner. The control phase provides the means to determine criteria or standards that can be compared later with the changes that may have occurred as the result of introducing a new factor. In a large factory the question arose "Do supervisors become better decision makers and problem solvers as the result of conferences that permit of free discussion, or are better results achieved by controlled methods?"

One of the authors was given the responsibility for conducting an experiment that would help to find evidence to solve the problem. It should be noted that the problem arose because the company involved had been conducting supervisory training conferences which utilized the free discussion method. After several years, many complaints were registered by management, and the participating supervisors indicated that the method was not effective. The following experiment was devised and conducted and attempted to incorporate all the considerations previously mentioned, as well as the technique of a controlled and experimental phase.

The Forced-Response Conference Method

1. *Purpose.* To control and force the participants in a conference to respond and enter into active discussion by forceful means. Specifically, the method seeks to force the participants to alter and change their mental habits slowly and gradually.

2. *General Theory.* Psychological and sociological evidence suggests that changes in human behavior can be effected when habits are altered. And this is especially true in the case of mental habits, which are related to such mental activities as reasoning, including abstraction, comparison, judgment, and decisions. These are the basic components underlying the ability to solve problems, to reflect critically, and finally to become decisive. Changes in mental habits may occur from self-control and from the control of forces outside the individual or from a combination of both. The forced-response conference method is premised on the theory that control and cautious pressure applied intelligently can produce advantageous changes in the mental habits of participants in a conference. Finally, the suggested method maintains that all the conditions of present conference procedures should prevail except for the introduction and addition of the forced technique to be described.

3. The Limitations. Individual differences and the variability of human behavior make it possible that some individuals cannot be influenced in a favorable direction. The forced-response method does not and cannot claim to be a complete theory for conducting conferences; rather, it is a modification and addition to present methods.

4. The Method. It is suggested that three pieces of apparatus be used: a stop watch, a rotary card rack, and a response list. The stop watch remains in the possession of the conference leader and is used simply as a timing device to control the amount of time allotted to each participant for discussion.

The rotary card rack is designed like a pin wheel and contains the names of the participating members in the conference. The card rack should be large enough that the conferees can plainly see their names. The names of the participants are to be printed on the face of the circular card and in the same position on the back. The back of the card is left open to the conference leader, while the front of the card is entirely covered except for a rectangular opening at the top of the card. When using the card, the conference leader can thus view the names of all the conferees along the rim of the circular card while the members of the conference can see only the one name that appears in the opening at the top. The card is set up on a stand, in reach of the leader, who can rotate or spin the card easily to the desired name.

The response list is simply a listing of the names of each of the people attending the conference; however, the list should be prepared in advance so that the names appear in a random order. If the participants are to be called upon more than once in the same conference, then different lists should be prepared in advance, with another random order appearing for each separate list. The response list is kept confidential so as to prevent the conferees from knowing when their names will appear. Since the purpose of the forced-response conference method is actually to force the members in the conference to speak at specified times, the leader is now equipped with the necessary apparatus to carry out this function with ease and facility. This is done by merely reading the first name on the response list and then spinning the card-rack wheel to that name. At the same time, the stop watch is started and later is stopped when the speaker is told by the conference leader that his time limit has expired. The same procedure is continued until the response list is exhausted.

It should be noted that other variations of the same procedure are possible; for example, the card rack can be dispensed with, and the leader may simply call the names as they appear on the response list. Experience convinces that the pin-wheel card rack is desirable because it is an exceptional attention getter.

The time allotted for each speaker to talk in the conference deserves a few words of consideration. It is recommended that, at the first use of the forced-response conference method, no more than one minute be permitted for each discussant. Longer intervals of time may cause confusion and embarrassment. However, as time and familiarity with the method increase, the time limit should be gradually extended. The maximum time is best left to the discretion of the conference leader. The obvious limitation of the time interval is, of course, the size of the group and the amount of time for the duration of the conference.

Application of the Forced-Response Conference Method

First, assuming that a series of conferences are to be held over a period of time, the conference leader should conduct several of these conferences in the normal manner. This grouping of several conferences should be viewed as the control phase of the total series of conferences. During this time, the conference leader should direct his attention to a careful appraisal of each of the participants, for it is here that he can learn a great deal about their behavior. Mental impressions should be carefully recorded during or after the conference. Once this has been done to the satisfaction of the conference leader, he is now ready to apply the forced method. This is best done by carefully informing the group of the nature, purpose, and method to be used. Motivation can be strengthened by pointing out the benefits to be gained by the use of the method and by willing and active participation.

Second, as the group acquires experience with the method, start to increase the time interval slowly and progressively. It should be noted that experience with the method has demonstrated that some quiet men do not respond even with a small time interval. The leader should carefully and tactfully avoid any long lapses of silence by cutting the time quietly and moving to the next name on the response list. Remember the quiet man is not changed easily.

Third, when, in the opinion of the leader, some definite changes in the behavior of the quiet man in the conference are observed, then the forced method should be dropped, and the conference should proceed under normal conditions. Again, experience suggests that this should be done wthout notice to the participants. At this point, the leader can study and analyze the changes in behavior that may have taken place, and, at his discretion, the method can be reactivated where it is necessary to do so.

Fourth, the leader should be constantly on the alert, in order to evaluate the behavioral changes that may take place. This is best accomplished by dividing the series of conferences into three parts— the precontrol, the experimental, and the postcontrol. For example, assume that a series of fifteen conferences is to be conducted for a group of supervisors and that the purpose is to develop their ability to solve problems and become more decisive. Then the series of conferences might be divided as follows: precontrol for four conferences, experimental for seven, and postcontrol for the last four. In the first part, the leader observes the characteristics of the conferees in the group, while in the second part the forced-response method is applied and observations are recorded, and in the final part he determines what behavioral changes have taken place and appear to be stabilized.

Changes in the participants should be evaluated in terms of the number of times they respond and the content or quality of responses.

The experiment described is still being evaluated, and results at the moment are meager and insufficient to draw any definite conclusions. However, it may be said that the participants have been interviewed, and all express interest and feel that the experiment will be successful. However, the opinions and the viewpoints are not enough to justify the conclusion that controlled techniques are better than noncontrolled conference methods. Since the experiment was started, two weaknesses emerged, which are presently being corrected. One of the corrections pertained to the fact that the conference leader was the sole judge of the changes occurring in the problem-solving ability of the participants. The criteria used by the conference leader were changes in the number of responses made by the conferees as a result of the forced-response technique and the quality of those responses. At the present time two observers have been unobtrusively placed in the group and will also rate the participants; furthermore, a better and more definitive rating scale is now in the hands of the leader and the observers. Another yardstick for evaluation has been the introduction of case problems that are chosen and identified by the supervisors, and they are asked to answer in written reports throughout the series of conferences. Thus each participant will now solve one problem for each of the three phases of the experiment, namely, the precontrol, the experimental, and the postcontrol. These reports are to be examined to determine whether any changes in problem-solving skills have been effected by the controlled response method.

Does this experiment carry out the seven considerations previously mentioned in the chapter? It is suggested that the reader carefully review these considerations and determine for himself whether or not they have been adequately employed in the experiment.

THE SINGLE-GROUP TECHNIQUE IN EXPERIMENTAL RESEARCH

The experiment described employed the single-group technique. This technique requires that the same individuals be used in the experiment throughout all the phases of the investigation. Suppose that one wished to train a group of twenty truck drivers to learn the skills necessary for changing a tire. The group of twenty drivers could be treated as a single group for purposes of experimentation. Furthermore, assume that you wish to determine whether the use of visual aids would aid in the learning process, to the extent that fewer mistakes would be made, the time involved could be shortened, and safety would be improved. Since the single-group technique requires that the same individuals be a part of the total experiment, then the control phase would consist of permitting the drivers to learn under the present conditions for a specified time. This would be the control phase of the experiment, and during this phase records would be accurately made of the mistakes occurring, the time involved to change tires, and the number of accidents that took place. It is the control phase that permits the researcher to establish the standards needed for evaluation. The experimental phase then starts, and the visual aids selected are introduced into the training program. Notice that all conditions remain the same as in the control phase, except for the use of visual aids. Again records are made of the mistakes, time, and accidents, so that a comparison of the achievements of the two phases can be made.

Although the single group of experimentation is practiced and probably the easiest and most frequently used, it has certain disadvantages that should be understood. The main weakness occurs as a result of the fact that the drivers are a part of both phases, and, as a result, another variable is introduced and is not controlled. This variable may be recognized as a prelearning factor, and it operates as an influence on the experimental phase of the study. This might be stated as a question: "To what extent has learning, during the control phase of the experiment, affected the learning in the experimental phase?" Since the drivers have already been subjected to the learning of skills in the first part of the experiment, how is it possible to conclude that any changes occurring in the experimental phase can be truly attributed to the introduction of the visual aids?

To lessen the effect of prelearning, it is usually good practice to conduct the experiment over as short a period of time as is possible. However, this precaution does not eliminate the danger. One of the better techniques that can be employed to achieve more scientific results is usually called the "equivalent-groups technique."

THE EQUIVALENT-GROUPS TECHNIQUE IN EXPERIMENTAL RESEARCH

The equivalent-groups method of experimentation is used when the purpose is to determine the superiority of one experimental factor over another. Again, the two main considerations of the single-group method are adhered to: specifically, the law of the single variable and the rule of using controlled and experimental phases. The major difference in the two methods is the fact that in the equivalent-groups method, two groups of trainees are used, while in the single group only one group of trainees is used. Consequently, in the single-group method the same subjects are used for both phases of the experiment.

Suppose that the equivalent-groups method had been applied to the situation of training truck drivers, mentioned before, then the twenty drivers would have been divided into two groups composed of ten drivers in each group. One group would be identified as the control and the other as the experimental. The control group would be trained under the normal, existing conditions with all the variables held constant, or exactly as they would have been in the usual training program, that is, without the experimental factor, which in the situation was the use of visual aids. Then the other group would be trained under exactly the same conditions, except that visual aids would be introduced. Since, in this case of training, the purpose was to determine the effects of the use of visual aids upon learning, it can be seen that the law of the single variable is obeyed.

Both groups are now trained during the same time interval, one with the visual aids and the other without them. Observations of the time to learn, the number of mistakes, and the number of accidents are carefully recorded, and then comparisons are made. Conclusions are then formulated, and recommendations are offered. The following diagrams will help to understand the experimental research technique employed in both the single and equivalent methods of investigation.

THE SINGLE-GROUP METHOD APPLIED TO
TWENTY TRUCK DRIVERS

Diagram A

Control Phase	Experimental Phase
Usual conditions. Records are kept and standards are determined.	Visual aids are introduced. Records are kept and comparison made with control phase standards.

THE EQUIVALENT-GROUPS METHOD APPLIED TO
TWO GROUPS OF TRUCK DRIVERS WITH TEN
IN EACH GROUP

Diagram B

Control Group	Experimental Phase
Ten men subjected to usual conditions of training. Records are kept and standards set.	Ten men subjected to visual aids in training. Records are kept and comparisons made with control phase standards.

An analysis of the two diagrams will reveal that in Diagram A the same group of twenty workers are used throughout the entire experiment, first for the control phase, then in the experimental phase. Diagram B reveals that the twenty men are divided into two groups of ten each, one group operates in the training experiment as the control and the other as the experimental group.

The experimental research technique of equivalency groups can also be used to include the use of other variables by introducing into the experiment more than two groups. Three or four groups are often used and sometimes more; however, the more groups added, the more difficult the experiment becomes to manage effectively. For purposes of illustrating the use of more than two groups, assume that the experiment's objectives included the study of other variables, such as "trial-and-error learning" and "individual instruction." The objective of the experiment might now be viewed as a study of the relative values of each of the following experimental factors: visual aids, trial-and-error learning, and individual instruction. The following diagram will serve to illustrate the technique:

THE EQUIVALENT-GROUPS TECHNIQUE APPLIED TO TWENTY
TRUCK DRIVERS WITH FIVE IN EACH OF FOUR GROUPS

Diagram C

Control	Experimental Groups		
Normal Conditions	(1) Visual Aids	(2) Trial and Error	(3) Individual Instruction

Analysis of Diagram C will reveal that the group of twenty trainees was divided into four groups of five in each. Furthermore, that each of the groups were instructed for exactly the same specified time period, but under the influence of each of the different experimental factors. The control group is instructed with the normal methods, and records are kept of accidents, mistakes, and speed of learning. With group two, all conditions are held constant with the control group, with the exception of the introduction of visual aids, while in group two the same conditions prevail, except that the trainees are permitted to learn by themselves or by trial and error; finally, in group three, individual instruction is employed, while all other conditions remain the same. Results for each of the four groups are collected and analyzed, and comparisons are made so as to determine the effectiveness of the various experimental factors that were studied.

Probably the difficulties and the time required for conducting experimental research with the equivalent-groups technique account for the fact that most experiments conducted in industry and business are accomplished with the single-group approach. Most of these difficulties are related to the time and care necessary in preparing to conduct research with the equivalent method. Such preparation involves the problem of assuring that the different groups used in the experiment must be equalized, so that they may be compared properly. To equalize or equate the groups requires that the individuals composing the groups be approximately the same in their potentials and abilities. The chief difficulty in achieving this end is the fact that it is necessary to control all the factors and conditions involved, so as to isolate those which are to be studied and, thereby, insure that the law of the single variable is adhered to properly. When groups of human beings are used in experimental research, it is possible for many variables to affect the results; among these variables are such human abilities and capacities as intelligence, mechanical aptitudes, sex, experience, physical strength, motor co-ordinations, attitudes, and motivations. Applying this to the truck drivers, it would be necessary to equalize the groups to be used so that they would be comparable. For example, suppose that only the experienced truck drivers, those of whom many have previously been taught to change tires, were all placed in one of the groups and that in another group only those who had never had experience happened to be located; then it would not be fair to compare the speed, accuracy, and number of accidents of the two groups and to conclude that the differences found were due to the introduction of visual aids. Actually, the variable of experience might have been a causative factor to influence the results, and the possibility of concluding that visual aids affected the results would be false. Unless all the possible variables that might affect the results are controlled, so that the single variable can truly be said to be effecting the results, the experiment is faulty.

It is obvious that one of the most important conditions necessary for conducting research with the equivalent method is, at the same time, the major difficulty. This requirement not only is so with the training of truck drivers but holds true with all kinds of training, from typists to file clerks, to machinists to supervisors and salesmen. To insure that the groups are properly equated requires that testing and appraisal of the characteristics of the individuals in the experiment must first be done before the groups are arranged. Since this requirement is time-consuming and costly, most practical researchers prefer to use the single-group method rather than the equivalent-groups method. However, it can be said that, regardless of the cost and time, statistically the equivalent-groups method is superior and productive of more refined results.

THE ROTATION-GROUP TECHNIQUE IN EXPERIMENTAL RESEARCH

Many researchers view the rotation technique as one of the best ways of securing accurate results in training research. As a matter of fact, in many of the studies done in the field of learning and educational psychology, the rotation technique is used. At the risk of incurring the disfavor of research directors in the business training area, it is suggested that the literature in the research field of educational psychology be read and used. The problems of training in business and in education are basically the same, and, since the field of educational psychology has many more years of experimental research behind it, many ideas are to be found that can be of value to the training researcher.

The rotation technique is similar to the equivalent-groups approach, except for the fact that the groups are rotated so that each group has a chance to be influenced by the several variables to be investigated. In this method, either the groups or the experimental factors to be studied are rotated or changed. Actually, it is a technique that uses the two previous techniques already discussed, since it can use two or more of the single groups or it can make use of a combination of the single and the equivalent groups. The procedure is useful especially when the groups are small, as in the case of the truck drivers, where five men would be in each group. One of the good features of this method is that the individuals in each group do not necessarily have to be equated, as in the equivalent-groups technique.

A study of the following diagram will help to understand how the rotation technique operates.

THE ROTATION TECHNIQUE APPLIED TO TWENTY
TRUCK DRIVERS WITH FIVE IN EACH OF
FOUR GROUPS

Control	Experimental		
A	B	C	D
Usual and normal conditions	Visual Aids as the variable	Trial and Error as the variable	Individual Instruction as the factor
B	C	D	A
C	D	A	B
D	A	B	C

Assuming that the four groups of truck drivers were subjected to one week of training for each of the four factors—namely, control, visual aids, trial and error, and individual instruction—at the end of four weeks all the groups would have been influenced by each of the factors to be studied. This is accomplished by rotating the groups through each of the experimental factors at the end of each week. Thus, for the first week, the order of the groups would be: (A) for Control, (B) for Visual Aids, (C) for Trial and Error, and (D) for Individual Instruction. The second week would then have group (B) for Control, (C) for Visual Aids, (D) for Trial and Error, and (B) Individual Instruction. The fourth week, (D) for Control, (A) for Visual Aids, (B) for Trial and Error, and (C) for Individual Instruction.

It is readily observed that the rotation technique tends to overcome the weaknesses of the single-group approach, since the subjects in each group are influenced by all the experimental factors. Accordingly, it is obvious that the experimental method of research may be conducted with any one, or a combination of, the single groups, the equivalent groups, or the rotation techniques.

EXPERIMENTAL RESEARCH: THE METHOD OF TRAINING EVALUATION

A training program is only as good as its proved worth. The most lavish and extravagant training program is worthless unless it can provide evidence to substantiate its existence. As is often remarked, "The proof of the pudding is in the eating," so too, it is with training in business. One of the surest ways to test a training program is by scientific and controlled experimentation. Experimental research has one fundamental purpose, and that is to find the evidence to prove the value of a training program. This is usually referred to as the "process of evaluation of training." To evaluate means to measure the worth of training, to determine verification for the usefulness of training. Evaluation is impossible without some standard or yardstick against which to judge the worthwhileness of training. In a practical sense, the evaluation of training is related to the primary objective of all business training, that is, to prove that a training program makes it possible for a trainee's behavior to be so altered and changed that he will perform successfully on the job. This is tantamount to saying that the evaluation of training depends upon how effectively the trainee can transfer the knowledge, skills, and attitudes that he has learned in a training program to the actual performance of the job.

The criteria standard or yardstick must therefore be related to the requirements of successful job performance. The problem of evaluation consequently depends upon the establishment of accurate criteria, which in turn depend upon the definition of exactly what constitutes successful job performance. Evaluation, like any statistic, is never perfect. Rather, it seeks to eliminate and reduce the possible wide range of errors that can result from opinion, tradition, and subjective judgment. Subsidiary to evaluation, as measured against scientifically determined criteria, is the problem of discovering the causes for training failures. Suppose that a training program had been evaluated against sound criteria, and it was found that the job performance of the people who were trained did not improve, then it would be logical to pursue the investigation with the objective of discovering why the training had failed. Continued research along such lines might reveal that the training program was faulty in content, methods, time, objectives, and the like. Discoveries of this nature should lead to further experimental research aimed at removing the faulty factors in the training program. This is the process of utilization of experimental research as a preventive tool. In this way, experimental research serves two purposes, namely, to establish criteria which are basic to evaluation of training and to uncover causes that may be removed.

With regard to criteria, it is important to recall that the job activity form of survey research can be helpful in determining the requirements of successful job performance. For purposes of establishing the criteria for a job it is necessary to understand that there are two broad types of criterion measures. One type uses procedures for evaluating performance in specific and detailed aspects of the task to be performed, while the other type is referred to as a summary type in which evaluation is made on the basis of a large segment or a total picture of the job.

EVALUATING PERFORMANCE FROM DETAILED ASPECTS OF THE JOB

There are four types of criterion measures that may be used in order to evaluate job performance. These types are as follows:

1. Tests of knowledge and information
2. Objective performance scores
3. Observed scored job samples
4. Rated job samples

Perhaps the most easily established criterion for estimating job performance is to measure the changes in knowledge and information through the use of tests. Since one of the objectives of training is to provide the learner with the knowledge required to perform the job adequately, it is essential first to determine the kinds and amount of knowledge and information needed to do a job, then to incorporate this into the training program, and, finally, to test the learners to ascertain how much has been retained and used in the actual work situation. In the case of training typists, it would first be necessary to decide what knowledge and information were needed for the typist to perform the job; this could be determined by the use of the job activity analysis and with the help of experts in the area of typing. Once this had been answered, then such knowledge and information would be made a part of the training program. To evaluate whether the training program was truly providing the learner with the necessary information and knowledge, tests could be constructed and given. The scores on these tests would then be compared with the criteria of knowledge, and judgments could be made to determine whether the training program was effective. The procedure used is to prepare at least two tests that are equivalent in difficulty and then to use one at the start of the training course—this is usually called the "pretest." After the training period ends, another test is given, which is called the "final test," and comparisons are then made between the two tests, to determine the changes in knowledge and information that have taken place.

The second type of criterion measure uses the evidence that can be collected objectively from actual job performance. Again in the case of the typist, certain criteria or standards may have been set for successful achievement in the job; in turn, the training program would seek to teach the learner to achieve these standards, and, finally, evaluation of the training program would occur when an objective record was kept of the typist while performing the job. Such objective records might include speed and accuracy, and, if objective records were kept, then they could be compared with the criteria and the training effectives. The same procedure is used for many kinds of jobs, including assemblers, file clerks, bank tellers, machine operators, accountants, and telephone operators.

Observer-scored job samples provide another criterion for evaluating the effectiveness of training. Some jobs do not provide the possibility of making objective records of job performance, such as a truck driver, a supervisor, and foreman. The procedure used in this instance follows the logical and scientific pattern already detailed, with the other measure of criteria mentioned, except that an observer is introduced. The observer becomes the measuring "instrument," insofar as he observes and scores the performance of the worker in the task. Evaluation of training then proceeds as a result of the scores obtained by the observer, and these scores in turn help to determine how well the training program is meeting its objectives. To aid the observer to judge the job performance, it is necessary to prepare detailed rating and scoring forms and to train him in the technique of observation. In this way the weaknesses of the observer-scored method is minimized to some extent, since the danger in the method is the possible introduction of opinion and bias in the judgments made. Another means of insuring a greater degree of objectivity is to break the job into units and to permit the observer to score each of the units separately. Then a total score is accumulated from the results of each of the unit scores. Obviously, the better methods are the objectively rated approaches.

In certain jobs it is not possible to break the job into units, and often the job can be evaluated only in terms of the total performance of several large segments of the task. This is the case in the evaluation of the supervisory position, the teacher, and all jobs that cannot be broken down into small units. Again an observer is used to measure the job performance, with the attending dangers of subjective judgments involved. For example, a supervisor may be rated on such samples of his job as counseling employees, disciplining men, selecting new workers, rating, promoting, transferring, and motivating his employees. Although there are dangers to such ratings, the same precautions as those used with the other rated methods can diminish their effects.

EVALUATING PERFORMANCES FROM SUMMARY CRITERIA

Training can also be evaluated from scores that are obtained from the performance of a worker over a long period of time. Suppose that one wished to evaluate the achievement of a trainee in a training program that extended over a year. As previously pointed out, tests of knowledge could be given; objective scores of attendance, grades, accuracy, and speed could be determined; raters might judge the performance of the trainee in some of the units of the training program.

However, a total score for the observations and the records and a picture of the trainee's entire performance could also be used. This last procedure is called the "summary approach to evaluation." In a sense an evaluation of a unit of the task might serve only to indicate how training has changed the behavior of the learner in only a phase of his total responsibilities, while the summary report would give a total evaluation.

Two types of summary criteria are generally used in the evaluation of training; one is the summary of performance records over a period of time, and the other is a summary of ratings that have been recorded over a time period.

The most practical and widely used criterion is the summary of performance, and this includes the production and personnel records of a trainee that have been compiled over a long period. Production records of those who have finished a training program can be compiled from the accumulated evidence of performance and can then be compared with the objectives of the training program. Production records refer to the quantity and quality of work done by a worker. If one of the objectives of training is to improve the quantity and quality of work, then the effects of training should be reflected therein. The success of the summary performance method depends to a considerable extent on records that are accurate, understandable, and available at all times. The "before and after" picture mentioned earlier is commonly used with this method of evaluation.

In many companies ratings systems are used to evaluate employees, and it is possible to use summaries of many ratings over a period of time as another type of criteria. Some personnel people require ratings by supervisors of their employees and others on a quarterly, semiannual, or annual basis. The rating, therefore, of a man for only a period of six months may not be criterion enough to justify the fact that a training program is successful; it may require a longer view of the worker's performance to render a more reliable conclusion.

While the criteria developed from detailed aspects of the job are important and necessary, the fact is that they are weak, insofar as they measure only a segment of the task. Most studies reveal that learning is usually effective, as far as retention, recognition, and recall of material taught, when it is evaluated immediately following, or in a short time after, training and learning. Often the question arises as to how long the material learned will hold. In this respect the summary reports are of vital importance, since they render a total record of training over a longer period of time. Finally, it is important to understand that the problem of establishing criteria is the most vital and the most difficult to achieve. Therefore, no single method is sufficient, and, without question, as many as possible of the methods that are practical and expedient to employ should be used.

Summary

In summary, this chapter has stressed the experimental method of research as the major tool to be used in the evaluation of training. It has pointed out the purposes of experimental research, the meaning and nature, the methods to be used, and some of the techniques for establishing criteria so as properly to evaluate training.

THINGS TO DISCUSS AND TO DO

1. Why is experimental research important in evaluating a training program?
2. Discuss the major considerations that should be kept in mind when conducting experimental research.
3. What is the most important characteristic of the nature of experimental research?
4. Assume that you are presently subjected to the lecture method and the conference method of instruction in two of your classes. How would you use the experimental method of research to determine the better method?
5. If a company asked you to evaluate its program for training clerks, and wanted results in a short time, which of the three methods of experimental research would you use? Why?
6. How would you proceed to evaluate the performance of a worker from a study of the detailed aspects of the job with the aid of each of the following: (a) tests of knowledge and information; (b) objective performance scores; (c) rated job samples.
7. Review several articles from the journals mentioned at the end of the last chapter and determine the following: (a) Are there many research articles employing the experimental form of research? If not, why not? (b) If experimental research is used, then what form is used (single-group, etc.)? (c) Criticize the study. Are there any changes you would recommend in the procedure?
8. Like the students in the chapter who visited a company, do the same and ask some of the questions they asked of the training director.

17. THE FUTURE OF TRAINING—
PROFESSION OR TECHNIQUE

Purpose of the Chapter

TRAINING CAN RENDER contributions to investors, managers, employees, and the community. However, such contributions will remain ineffective and unfulfilled until training attains the aura of a profession. Therefore, the purpose of this chapter is to suggest guides for training leaders that may be helpful in elevating training to a professional status. To assure the future of training, the following considerations will be reviewed: First, the meaning and basic requirements of a profession will be clarified; then the reasons for sound policies and objectives will be stated; following will be the importance of establishing an organized body of training knowledge; finally, the need and application of philosophical research will be demonstrated. It will be contended that the future success and status of training will depend upon how effectively these considerations are resolved.

The status of training today may be viewed as that of a second-class citizen. Although training has progressed in business over the last twenty-five years, it has failed to gain the professional status that it deserves. One attempt to professionalize training has been the co-ordinated effort of training directors to organize themselves into an association called the American Society of Training Directors. One of the main purposes of this Society is to improve the status of training by a mutual exchange of the knowledge and experience of the membership through periodic meetings and the establishment of the *Journal of the American Society of Training Directors*. Through this medium of communication, the Society publishes articles that encourage an enlightened interest in the improvement of training. The Society has also established certain qualifications necessary for acceptance into the organization.

Notwithstanding the serious intentions of the Society, the fact remains that training still has a difficult task in convincing management that it must be recognized as a first-class citizen. The problem of convincing management rests to a large extent on the practitioners of training, such as personnel and training directors, aided by professional educators in the colleges and universities.

Some Problems That Make the "Profession" of Training Unprofessional

Since it is here contended that training is viewed as a second-class citizen and that it lacks prestige and status, then the problem concerns the need to give training the professional character that will cause management to accept it in the same manner that other important functions, such as finance, engineering, and marketing, are regarded. The basic problem, therefore, is to professionalize training.

The more important problems that must be answered in order to professionalize training are:

1. To understand the meaning of a "profession"
2. To formulate sound objectives and policies for the conduct of training and to organize a body of knowledge
3. To perform effective and prestige-producing research

A profession is regarded as the business or vocation which one professes to understand and to practice; such an occupation is distinguished from a trade or handicraft. A profession is usually characterized by the fact that a collective group of people is engaged in, or practicing, a special occupation or vocation. One who is a member of such a group and is practicing the special vocation is recognized as a professional, as in the field of medicine, engineering, or teaching. A profession is more than a technique which is solely concerned with the mechanical performance, the skill, or the details and methods of performing a vocation; rather, it is more concerned with the integration of knowledge and skills that are organized into a totality which is guided by clearly defined objectives and policies. At the present time, objectives and aims differ from company to company, and there are as many objectives as there are training programs.

In most cases training is conducted by opportunism or as the need arises and is, in general, a crisis-to-crisis method of dealing with training needs. The treatment of training in this manner will hardly produce a profession, since a profession requires that certain aims and purposes must be fundamental to all training. Furthermore, crisis-to-crisis training serves only to make training subservient to present needs and places a heavy reliance upon techniques and, as a consequence, can result only in training that is viewed by management as a tool. In reality, it should be recognized as an integrated part of the total functioning of a business. The longer training remains a technique, the less chance it has to become a profession.

A profession also requires an organized body of knowledge that is capable of providing the broadness of scope that makes it possible to deal with training problems on all levels and in a diversity of training needs from company to company. This body of knowledge should include management principles of organization and administration that are related to the instituting and conducting of training programs. Psychological knowledge is also important, especially with relation to the principles of learning and habit formation. Much of this knowledge has already been organized by other disciplines, especially in the field of educational psychology. Another most important area of knowledge concerns the methods of research which is so important in giving training greater prestige and acceptance. Within the framework of these broad areas of knowledge should be incorporated the numerous techniques and skills required to carry on effective training.

The body of knowledge of a given profession also requires deductive analysis that will result in guiding principles and laws that will serve to provide the general direction of training. As an outgrowth of the policies and aims of a profession, there must be developed a code of ethics that will serve as a guide to the behavior and conduct of the members of a profession. Most authorities would also agree that a profession is characterized by an association of members, whose functions include the enforcement of the profession's standards, the advancement and dissemination of knowledge, and, to some extent, control over membership requirements for the profession.

An examination of the training field, as it operates today, reveals that few of the criteria mentioned are in use. Training cannot be identified as a profession as long as it is possible for anyone to practice as a trainer without the necessary knowledge, skills, and values required to do the job in the manner of a professionally respected vocation. Admittedly, it is extremely difficult to enforce a code of ethics for the profession of training and equally difficult to set up standards for entry into such a profession; however, the time is "ripe" for the development of a more systematic and orderly presentation of the body of knowledge and skills that have been developed. If a profession of training cannot be established to include all the criteria necessary, then at least a start in the right direction would be to establish those standards that are presently obtainable, and this can be done in the area of knowledge and skills. Therefore, the unprofessional regard for training can be somewhat removed if those who practice as training experts attempt to define aims and objectives and the body of knowledge which they must employ to "ply their trade."

In a practical sense anything that can be done to prove to management that training is based upon an integrated body of knowledge that is guided by sound policies and objectives, laws and principles, should be done, whether it is on a scale that encompasses all training done for all kinds of business or in a single business enterprise. The ultimate goal of any attempt to professionalize training would be to incorporate all the criteria for all training, no matter where it is done in business; but the attainment of this end may not be realistic. Therefore, it would seem expedient to employ these criteria in single companies where a training director may be capable of integrating the training program into a respected totality merging into the entire management function. It is where training is not done in this manner that the aura of a profession is lacking and, in turn, results in loss of respect and a regard for training as a second-class citizen. When training is conducted without clear-cut objectives, without delineation of the role of the training director, without definition of the real needs to be served, without adequate research to evaluate the effectiveness of training, and is guided by opportunistic or crisis-to-crisis services resulting in a hodgepodge of training programs, then it will never make its voice heard, and little respect can be expected. Operating in this manner, training can be and will always be viewed only as a supplement and not an integral part of the management team.

The viewpoint expressed suggests that the road to training acceptance must be paved with the results of effective research that is aimed at proving conclusively to management that training not only is necessary but is likewise profitable to employees as well as management. When the results of such research are organized into a body of knowledge from which principles, concepts, and guiding policies and aims can be formulated, then training will be on the way to greater acceptance.

Since it is suggested that the road to the professionalization of management training depends on the establishment of objectives and on a systematic and organized body of knowledge, then the logical question that follows concerns the manner in which this goal can be attained. Five avenues of approach to the problem of training improvement are suggested:

1. Effective research
2. Integration of research evidence
3. Understanding the meaning of philosophical research
4. Applying the methods of philosophical research
5. Strong leadership

Effective Research—the Basis of a Training Profession

The importance of research with respect to the evaluation of training has been discussed in previous chapters; however, it is also necessary to understand that the results of research can provide the foundation for the body of knowledge required for training to become a profession. No matter how effective research may be in evaluating various areas of the training program, it still remains, for the most part, a segmented and piecemeal accumulation of facts and evidence, and, so long as it remains in such a condition, it will fail to impress management with the importance of training. The most important problem to resolve in the ultimate sense is that of unifying all the proven evidence acquired from research into an integrated and organized body of knowledge. Research in training seeks to validate the results of training in both the immediate and the ultimate sense. The immediate goals of research are to determine the present effects of training, that is, to justify, whether or not it can be proved, that training is actually changing human behavior so that the effects of training can be reflected in the improvement of production and the satisfaction of employees. Overemphasis on empirical results that insist upon seeing only the immediate can distort the ultimate goal. The ultimate goal of training is concerned with classification, analysis, and interpretation of all the facts and data assembled by empirical research, in order to develop a body of knowledge that will provide a set of objectives, principles, and laws that will make it possible for training ultimately to be recognized as a profession.

Integration of Research—the Method for Integration Is Philosophical Research

Overwhelmed by an emphasis upon materialistic values, the business world has all but lost sight of the important uses of philosophical research. Businessmen and training directors feel that they cannot afford the time and money to consider the probable theories which attempt to explain the ultimate goals of training, nor are they much interested in the synthesis of training knowledge, when they can find in their laboratories the evidence to prove the validity of the immediate problems that must be solved. Businessmen are more interested in answering the daily problems that are necessary for survival, and this is understandable. A man must make a living, and, therefore, he is concerned with those things which will assist him in the attainment of that purpose in the shortest possible time and with the least cost. To speculate about the origin or the possible outcome of things makes little or no appeal to the businessman. What he desires are facts and data that can without much difficulty be translated into immediate action.

These opinions, so widespread today, arise from a false or narrow view of philosophical research. This view holds that science and philosophy are separate and unrelated; moreover, it is too often forgotten that philosophy is not a particular kind of science, nor can the methods of any special science be compared to the methods of philosophy. Philosophy is a "general science." The field of philosophy embraces the final facts which have come from scientific investigation. These facts are of such a character that they defy further analysis by the methods available to empirical science. Philosophy attempts to take these facts beyond their immediate usefulness and seeks to use the method of synthesis to answer such questions as "Where do these facts come from?" "What do they mean?" "How can they be related to the philosophy of business management?"

To illustrate the role of philosophical research, consider the report of Secretary of Labor James P. Mitchell, which appeared in the *New York Times* on February 7, 1960. The facts to be presented can also be found in a Labor Department study titled, *Manpower Challenge of the 1960's.*

The *Manpower* report points to the following facts:

The number of workers will increase by 20 per cent in the next ten years.
The number of older workers will rise to the extent that two out of every five workers will be over forty-five years of age.

There will be a small increase among workers between twenty-five and thirty-four years of age.

There will be fewer workers between the ages of thirty-five and forty-four.

These facts are derived from an analysis of the birth-rate statistics for some previous years, and the *Manpower* report attempts to project them into the future population trends.

One of the most basic purposes of philosophical research is to analyze the facts presented and then to apply reflective thinking so as to determine their future applications. Viewing the facts from their potential applications for long-range planning it might be possible to answer the following questions:

Where do the facts come from?

Are the facts valid and reliable?

What do the facts mean with regard to the kinds of training required for future employees?

Do training policies and objectives need revision to satisfy future requirements?

Do the facts suggest that more trainers will be needed?

Will future trainers have to be selected and trained differently?

What changes in the methods of training may be required?

Are adequate facilities available to meet the projected changes in training needs as suggested by the facts?

In what ways do the facts relate to the total needs of operating a successful business?

Even a casual analysis of the questions asked will reveal that one of the major purposes of philosophical research is to "go beyond the facts." Philosophy takes the facts and conclusions accumulated by scientific and empirical investigations and uses them as raw materials for further reflection. This simply means that the facts have gone about as far as they can go and that reflective thinking is needed to put them to further use. As a result, philosophical research aids in formulating more inclusive and broader points of view that can be projected into long-range plans and to the integration and synthesis of all the facts accumulated by science. John Dewey comments that

. . . the work of philosophy is confined to the things of actual experience. Its business is criticism of experience as it exists at a given time and constructive projection of values, which, when acted upon, will render experience more unified, stable and progressive. Defects and conflicts of experience as it exists demand thorough criticism of its contents and procedures. This phase of inquiry is not, however, final; criticism does not end with mere intellectual discrimination. It provides the basis for protection of values as yet unrealized, values that are to be translated into ends that move men into action. Philosophy thus conceived does not involve flight and escape to that which is beyond experience. It is concerned with making the best possible out of experience, personal and social.[1]

In consequence, the objective of philosophical research is to make possible those value judgments that will aid in decision making for the determination of long-range business planning with respect to the future needs of a business enterprise. Philosophical research can help by going beyond the facts in ascertaining and projecting sales forecasts and product development, as well as alterations in training programs. It is important to recognize that, when businessmen restrict their decisions to the immediate facts of scientific investigations, they fail to move on to the realm of prophecy, which is so essential to the synthesis of all business functions, as well as to long-range planning. It is equally important to respect the interrelatedness of science and philosophy, for one provides the facts, while the other studies them so as to make future plans. The importance and purpose of philosophical research is ably attested to by Frederick L. Whitney:

> Philosophers, frontier thinkers have always been sadly needed. We believe that this need is now more crucial, because we do not know the past and are nearer to the present. The status of modern education and modern economics and politics is fundamentally not much, if at all, above Greek culture. The outstanding philosopher is lacking in every field of human endeavor. However, present leaders should be nourished and commended for any level of farsighted thinking that they do engage in, but they should be condemned for refusing to learn philosophically from the past experience of the race. It is the function of philosophical research to point out the supreme value of reflective thinking on the level of the largest generalizations of widest import, to give information about the methods and techniques of philosophical reasoning, and to stimulate to whatever ordered research is possible on this level of reflection.[2]

The Meaning of Philosophical Research

Philosophical research may be defined as reflective thinking on levels of broad generalization, beyond the realm of the fact-finding sciences. Accordingly, any discussion related to the methods of philosophical research must necessarily be concerned with the processes involved in reflective thinking. At the same time, reflective thinking must be systematic and orderly, to be conducted effectively. Some

---

[1] John Dewey, in F. L. Whitney, *The Elements of Research* (New York: Prentice-Hall, Inc., 1942), chap. x, p. 243.

[2] Whitney, *op. cit.*, pp. 243–44.

popular concepts of "philosophical thinking" suggest that it is flight from reality into the realms of fantasy. It is thought that philosophy should be relegated to dreamers and to speculators whose conclusions are arrived at by hunch and intuition. Such notions ignore the true nature of reflective thinking as a process of logical thinking that is founded upon verifiable evidence and which reflects upon such evidence, in order to arrive at more inclusive points of view. The purposes of such reflective thinking may be listed as follows:

1. To evaluate the validity and reliability of the facts provided by scientific research
2. To determine whether such facts can be improved
3. To suggest better methods for the improvement of the search for facts
4. To deduce the basic principles and laws that can be derived from the facts
5. To better the integration and synthesis of facts
6. To utilize the facts for future planning

The meaning and the purposes of philosophical research can be better understood when the methods used by companies for long-range planning are considered.

Future planning is conducted in many organizations for both short- and long-term periods, since it would probably be financially disastrous to wait for a crisis or a need to appear. The manufacturers of automobiles do not wait until the end of a current year to decide upon the design, number of autos to produce, tools and machinery, capital budget, manpower requirements, and other needs. Planning in advance requires that the manufacturers have many facts from which to project their needs. In general, it may be pointed out that all forward planning involves some element of risk, although short-term planning—for example, one year ahead—may be less of a risk than long-range planning for five or ten years. Regardless of the time involved, forward planning is not done by "intuition"; it is accomplished by gathering valid facts and data, by organizing, classifying, verifying, integrating, and analyzing such evidence. In other words, the facts alone "have gone about as far as they can go," and what is needed is the application of reflective thinking to develop the generalizations and principles needed for future action. The student would be aided in understanding the meaning and purposes of philosophical research if the six purposes previously mentioned were put to the test of forward planning, for a one-year period and then to a five-year period in the automobile field.

Another example, in the electrical appliance field, reveals that a systematic procedure for forward planning is used. Facts are determined for the following broad areas:

1. Product Development and Invention. Engineering changes and new products are a continuing part of the research program.

2. Manufacturing Techniques. The possible applications of automation, tools, dies, layout, and other items are carefully studied.

3. Market and Economic Research. The potentials of the future market are analyzed, along with sales, advertising, and distribution. At the same time, the economic trends are suggested from past and present facts.

4. Financial Needs. What will it cost? How much will be needed to meet future plans?

5. Administrative and Organizational Plans. Will future plans demand changes in the corporate echelons of the organization? Will different leadership skills and knowledge be the same? To what extent will future plans affect the organizational structure? What changes for the operational levels of the company may be needed?

6. Personnel and Training. Wage and salary projections, promotional plans, manpower audits for future needs are required. Training needs must also be reviewed in the light of the future. Availability of manpower, fringe benefits, welfare, and community needs must be appraised.

7. Labor-Management Relations. Future desires of labor organizations, contractual obligations, effects of legislation, and the like must be estimated.

Specialists in forward planning are given the responsibility for gathering the facts from all valid sources. These facts are then synthesized and integrated, since all the areas studied are obviously interrelated. Then, by the application of reflective thinking or the method of philosophical research, plans are projected for the future.

For the most part, large companies adequately attend to all the requirements for future planning with the exception of training. Training seems to be the last item considered and again appears to be treated as a supplement and not a vital part that should be given as much attention as the others. With regard to training, evidence is sorely needed with respect to future training needs.

For training to be adequately integrated with all the problems of future planning, the following questions should be answered: "Will changes in products, manufacturing processes, sales, distribution, and the like require future changes in training needs?" "Will the training personnel have to be enlarged?" "Selected differently, trained in some other way?" "Are present methods, facilities, etc., adequate to satisfy future needs?" The reader can easily add to this list.

To repeat, unless training is given its proper status, the principles, laws, and facts from training research will always be given second rating, and training will never gain the position of a profession.

The Methods of Philosophical Research

Reflective thinking is systematized by the application of the methods of philosophical research. The three methods which have been most generally used have been the following:

1. Analytic method (inductive)
2. Synthetic method (deductive)
3. Analytico-synthetic

The Analytic or Inductive Method

The analytic or inductive method of philosophical research is an adaptation of experimental research and relates philosophy to the natural sciences. It consists in the observation, accumulation, and verification of facts. In the strict sense, the analytic method insists that all speculation or theorizing outside or above observable fact is unscientific and therefore incapable of producing truthful results. The method is inductive because it proceeds to an investigation of parts and then arrives at generalizations. The values to be derived from the applications of the inductive method have been previously discussed in connection with the experimental method of research.

From the standpoint of philosophical reasoning, the main objections are leveled against the *exclusive* use of the inductive method in philosophical research. By confining investigations to observable phenomena, there is the danger of ignoring the causes as they affect the facts and, as a result, give only a "partial understanding" to the problem under consideration. For example, when evaluating a job training program, it is possible to fall into the trap of merely employing production changes (facts) as the criterion for the effectiveness of training. Slavish adherence to the facts in this instance may cloud the investigator's search for the true causes responsible for the changes. Any method which ignores causality is one-sided. It is as though the facts alone are of value; but facts in themselves have no cognitive value, nor are they bound together by any principles or laws. Facts should be viewed as the catalysts of thought; they certainly have practical value, especially in resolving immediate problems, but they are, in no sense, in themselves related to underlying truths.

In many training programs, reams of experimentally verified facts can be found, but little is done to use the powers of reflective thinking to unravel the problems of causation or to deduce underlying principles and laws that will provide the "glue" for an organized body of training knowledge. When training programs apply reflective thinking to the facts, then the chance for professionalization may be realized.

The Synthetic or Deductive Method

The synthetic method is the opposite of the analytic because it establishes a generalization as the result of intuitive processes and then proceeds to provide the evidence to support the premise. In the training area this may be illustrated by the application of both methods to the problem of determining training needs. The analytic or inductive method would begin with the small parts, such as facts related to production records, personnel records, labor turnover, and the like, and, as a consequence, would determine training needs. On the other hand, the synthetic or deductive method would begin with the intuitive idea that training needs are generally understood, then would proceed from the generalization to supply the reasons to support the premises. The main criticism of the synthetic method is that it makes little, if any, use of vast funds of facts and information that have been accumulated as the result of experimental and inductive methods of research. It makes the error of having theories precede facts rather than recognizing that facts should precede, not follow, the theories. At the same time, it is an error to assign causes without examining the facts. Training programs that are based solely on the theories of specialists without the support of facts can lead to an unfavorable attitude toward professionalized training. When facts are properly related to theories, they serve as excellent checks and audits of a priori generalization.

The Analytico-synthetic Method

This is the true method of philosophical research, since it is a combination of the analytic and synthetic methods and is not open to the objections when either of them is used separately. Furthermore, it is considered by practically all authorities as the accepted process of mental activity where reflective thinking is employed. Most advocates of the experimental methods of research agree that the analytico-synthetic method is necessary in their empirical approach to problem-solving. It can be said that reflective thinking "ebbs and flows" between the extremes of inductive and deductive reasoning. The mental processes involved in problem-solving may therefore begin at one moment by reflecting upon the parts, such as isolated facts, and then follow toward the unifying of knowledge, the search for causes, and the derivation of principles and laws. At other times, reflective thinking may start with the general presuppositions and then lead to facts that will prove the generalizations made.

Much has been said concerning creative thought, which emphasizes the interrelatedness of the analytico-synthetic methods of reflective thinking. In general, creativeness employs the mental processes in order to seek new or novel approaches to present problems. In a sense, it works from the unknown to the known to a greater extent than does the inductive, which operates from the known to the unknown. Creative thinking requires freedom from conformity, whether it be toward tradition, authority, or existing factual procedures. It also demands that the habits of mental activity, that are conditioned in all human thought, be changed. Conformity to habits of thinking may be likened to a train running along on tracks with little freedom of choice as to direction. Creativity breaks from the binding chains of routine and searches for new routes and different methods.

Leaders in management stress the importance of creative thinking as a means of bettering and improving the efficiency of the enterprise. Notwithstanding, the area of training still adheres almost totally to the conforming techniques of tradition. Professionalizing the training area requires creative thinking in order to innovate new and better approaches. This is possible when the analytico-synthetic method of philosophical research is used more frequently.

Although creative thinking stresses deductive reasoning, it should be understood that the analytico-synthetic or inductive-deductive form of reflective thinking must, first of all, be analytical. By reflecting on the facts and assumptions of training programs within a company or among all training programs in all companies, it is possible to arrive at a body of presuppositions that are common to all training programs. For example, training presupposes the existence of a trainer, of a mind for learning, and of the law of causality. The problem of philosophical research is to sift, criticize, accept, or reject these common assumptions. It is then ready to proceed to a synthesis, to a construction of a system of thought which will both justify and explain, in the widest possible generalizations, the implications imbedded in all training programs. Fortified with certain basic generalizations related to all training, it is then possible to construct an organized body of knowledge that is far more than a mere statement of techniques. Until training acquires such a respectable posture, it will remain only a second-class citizen.

The Need for Strong Leadership

The road to wisdom is difficult, hazardous, complex, and never final. Yet the challenge demands that a beginning must be made, and this suggests that a motivational force is necessary to begin the movement. Intelligent, knowledgeable, and purposeful leadership can be recruited from the following broad sources:

1. Management personnel
2. Employees
3. Labor organizations
4. Community

The ideal condition would be for leadership to emerge from top-management levels, because their backing and stimulation are most necessary and important. However, in many instances top management must be educated and motivated to respond to the need for recognition of training. This is perhaps best accomplished by such members of the management team as personnel directors, training directors, department heads, and staff specialists. Through their efforts in applying all the methods of research discussed, it is hoped that top-management acceptance will result.

Employees on all levels have a stake in the benefits that can come from training, insofar as their own growth, development, and self-fulfillment are concerned. Job training, supervisory, foremanship, and executive development programs provide excellent possibilities for growth both to the company and to the individual. If employees on all levels give the co-operation needed for training to transcend the technique phase, then by their interest it may be possible to alert the strong leadership needed.

The impact of labor leaders upon management practices is attested on all sides, yet their influence on training is still not properly utilized. Labor leaders might consider the benefits that can be given to their memberships by implementing and supporting a movement toward broader concepts of the values of training to all concerned— management, labor, and the community.

The community has an opportunity to work with business in the improvement of the members of the locality. Chambers of commerce, educational institutions, religious groups, and the like could co-operate in various ways with business; likewise, business might co-operate with the community in serving the training needs of all concerned.

Philosophical Research—the Road to the Professionalization of Training

Reflective thinking applied to training can help to make the facts accumulated by research meaningful in relation to the broad problems required to make training more of a profession. Those requirements, previously stated, that must be resolved are the following:

1. Training must attempt to meet the conditions necessary to professional status.
2. Training must broaden its objectives and policies to embrace all training needs in business.
3. Training must perform more effective research.
4. Training must integrate its facts into a soundly organized body of knowledge.
5. Training must formulate basic principles and laws.
6. Training must raise its sights to future needs.

Some of the questions that may be within the future province of business training are as follows:

1. Should training enter into the realm of the health improvement of its employees?

This means more than the physical health, for the need to deal with mental health is becoming more of a problem. One may wonder whether it is the social responsibility of management to be concerned with the mental aberrations of its employees, including alcoholism, and gerontology, which is concerned with adjustment of aging employees.

2. Should training be directed toward the teaching of knowledge and skills to be utilized during the leisure time of the employee?

With the impact of automation, it is probable that employees will have more leisure time. Again, to what extent should management and its training programs play a role in serving such future needs?

3. Should training prepare employees for retirement?

Some companies, notably Esso Standard Oil Company of New Jersey, are already embarked on programs that are designed to aid employees to make successful adjustments to retirement. Is this area one that management should tackle?

4. Should training go beyond the immediate practical needs of employees? Is it possible that training should lift its objectives to include many educational areas of instruction, such as economics, human relations, politics, and the like, in order to educate employees to accept and assume the roles and responsibilities of efficient citizens?

Without any question of doubt these are controversial issues; yet the application of philosophical research to such societal problems may be another way through which the future professional status of training may be assured.

Summary

This chapter has presented the viewpoint that the future success of training will be assured when a profession that is guided by clear-cut policies, augmented by an association of members, selected with high standards, and with leadership that can enforce a code of ethics and organize a body of training knowledge is a reality.

Furthermore, it has been demonstrated that the formulation of policies and a body of knowledge will depend primarily upon an intelligent awareness of the value and application of research methodology. Although all forms of research are assets in elevating training, it is the responsibility of philosophical research to integrate the facts into an organization of knowledge that will then lead to the development of principles and laws. Philosophical research employs reflective thinking in order to transcend the facts and this is done by the use of both inductive and deductive reasoning or by analytical and synthesized thinking. Consequently, the reader has been introduced in a superficial manner to the methods of philosophical research, with emphasis placed upon the true method, concerned with the analytico-synthetic approach to reasoning.

Finally, it has been suggested that another way to professionalize training is for training experts and management to project their vision into the future needs of the community. Training may have a social responsibility that goes beyond the immediate needs of training a worker in a job skill. Training can "lift its sights" just as education must.

THINGS TO DISCUSS AND TO DO

1. Explain the conditions necessary to the establishment of a profession.
2. Select a club or a society of which you are a member and analyze its status as a profession.
3. What is meant by analytic reasoning?
4. What is meant by synthetic reasoning?
5. Why is the analytico-synthetic method the true method of philosophical research?
6. Secure the Labor Department report, *Manpower Challenge of the 1960's*, and suggest the more important implications for future training needs.
7. Do you believe that training should go beyond the immediate needs of a company?
8. What should be the moral and ethical obligations of a company where training is concerned?
9. Visit a company that has a well-defined training program and determine how philosophical research has been used.
10. Read a textbook dealing with philosophical research and suggest how the knowledge you gained may be applied to training.

THINGS TO DISCUSS AND TO DO

BIBLIOGRAPHY

BIBLIOGRAPHY

AHERN, EILEEN. *Handbook of Personnel Forms and Records.* American Management Association, Research Report No. 16. New York, 1949.

ALLGOOD, M. B. *Demonstration Techniques.* Englewood Cliffs, N.J.: Prentice-Hall, Inc., 1947.

ALMACK, JOHN C. *Research and Thesis Writing.* New York: Houghton Mifflin Co., 1930.

ALTICK, RICHARD D. *Preface to Critical Reading.* New York: Henry Holt Co., 1951.

ANDREWS, KENNETH R. "Is Management Training Effective?" Part I, *Harvard Business Review,* Vol. XXXV, No. 1 (January–February, 1957). Part II, *ibid.* (March–April, 1957).

ARGYRIS, CHRIS. *Personality and Organization.* New York: Harper & Bros., 1957.

———. *Understanding Organizational Behavior.* Homewood, Ill.: Dorsey Press, Inc., 1960.

AUDIO VISUAL AIDS COMPANY. *How, What and Why of Audio-Visual Education.* 50 frames, b & w filmstrip.

BARNARD, CHESTER I. *The Functions of the Executive.* Cambridge: Harvard University Press, 1946.

———. *Organization and Management.* Cambridge: Harvard University Press, 1949.

BARRY, F. GORDON, and COLEMAN, C. G., JR. "Tougher Program for Management Training," *Harvard Business Review,* Vol. XXVI, No. 6 (November–December, 1958).

BELLOWS, ROGER M. *Creative Leadership.* Englewood Cliffs, N.J.: Prentice-Hall, Inc., 1959.

———. "Management's Use of Personnel Research in Training," *Handbook of Applied Psychology* (ed. DOUGLAS H. FRYER and EDWIN R. HENRY), Vol. I. New York: Rinehart & Co., 1950.

———. *Psychology of Personnel in Business and Industry.* Englewood Cliffs, N.J.: Prentice-Hall, Inc., 1954.

BELLOWS, R. M.; ESTEP, M. F.; and SCHOLL, C. E., JR. "A Tool for Analyzing Training Needs: The Training Evaluation Check List," *Personnel,* Vol. XXIX (1953).

BELMAN, HARRY S., and HULL, THOMAS F. "Preparation and Follow-Up of Participants in Training Programs," *Journal of the American Society of Training Directors,* Vol. XXI, No. 8 (August, 1958).

BIGGONE, ROBERT J. "How We Determined Training Needs," *Personnel Journal,* Vol. XXIX, No. 1 (May, 1950).

BLACK, JAMES M., and PICCOLI, J. GEORGE. *Successful Labor Relations for Small Business.* New York: McGraw-Hill Book Co., Inc., 1953.

BLOCKER, CLYDE. "Evaluation of a Human Relations Training Program," *Journal of the American Society of Training Directors,* May–June, 1955.

BLUM, MILTON L. *Readings in Experimental Industrial Psychology.* Englewood Cliffs, N.J.: Prentice-Hall, Inc., 1952.

BURSK, EDWARD C. (ed.). *Human Relations for Management.* New York: Harper & Bros., 1956.

BYRNES, A. F. "Your Money's Worth from Your Tape Recorder," *Instructor,* Vol. LXIII (January, 1954).

CENTI, PAUL, and DOYLE, PAUL. *Basic College Skills,* Vols. I and II. New York: Rinehart & Co., 1959.

CHRISTENSEN, C. ROLAND. *Management Succession in Small and Growing Enterprises.* Boston: Division of Research, Graduate School of Business Administration, Harvard University, 1953.

COMMINS, W. D., and FAGIN, BARRY. *Principles of Educational Psychology.* 2d ed. New York: Ronald Press Co., Inc., 1954.

COPELAND, MELVIN T. *The Executive at Work.* Cambridge: Harvard University Press, 1952.

CROW, RICHARD R. "An Organized Approach to Training," *Personnel,* Vol. XXIII, No. 6 (May, 1947).

DAHL, ROBERT A.; HAIRE, MASON; and LAZARFELD, PAUL F. *Social Science Research on Business: Product and Potential.* New York: Columbia University Press, 1959.

DALE, EDGAR. *Audio-Visual Methods in Teaching.* Rev. ed. New York: Dryden Press, 1954.

DALE, ERNEST. *Planning and Developing the Company Organization Structure.* American Management Association, Research Report No. 20. New York, 1952.

DALLMANN, MARTHA, and SHERIDAN, ALMA. *Better Reading in College.* New York: Ronald Press Co., Inc., 1954.

DANIELSON, LEE E. "Your Manpower Needs of the Future," *Michigan Business Review,* Vol. I, No. 1 (January, 1958).

DAVIS, KEITH. *Human Relations in Business.* New York: McGraw-Hill Book Co., Inc., 1957.

DAVIS, RALPH C. *The Fundamentals of Top Management.* New York: Harper & Bros., Inc., 1951.

Defining the Manager's Job. New York: American Management Association, 1958.

DE KIEFFER, ROBERT, and COCHRAN, LEE W. *Manual of Audio-Visual Techniques.* Englewood Cliffs, N.J.: Prentice-Hall, Inc., 1955.

DEPHILLIPS, FRANK A. "How to Activate the Quiet Man in the Conference," *Journal of the American Society of Training Directors,* Vol. XIV, No. 4 (1960).

Developments in Supervisory Training. Studies in Personnel Policy No. 124. New York: National Industrial Conference Board, Inc., 1952.

DEWEY, JOHN. *How We Think.* New York: D. C. Heath & Co., 1933.

DOANE, R. C. "Demonstration: Before, During, and After," *Industrial Arts and Vocational Educational Education,* Vol. XLIII (January, 1954).

DOOHER, JOSEPH M., and MARQUIS, VIVIENNE (eds.). *The Development of Executive Talent.* New York: American Management Association, 1952.

DOOHER, JOSEPH M., and MARTING, ELIZABETH (eds.). *Selection of Management Personnel,* Vols. I and II. New York: American Management Association, 1957.

DRIVER, R. S. "Methods for Spotting Training Needs," *Personnel,* Vol. XXI (1944).

DRUCKER, PETER F. *The Practice of Management.* New York: Harper & Bros., 1954.

DUBIN, ROBERT. *Human Relations in Administration.* Englewood Cliffs, N.J.: Prentice-Hall, Inc., 1951.

DUNBAR, JAMES C. "Surveying Training Needs," *Personnel,* Vol. XXV (1948).

E. I. DuPONT DE NEMOURS & CO., INC., TRAINING DIVISION, EMPLOYEE RELATIONS DEPARTMENT. *Training within the DuPont Company.* Wilmington, Del., 1955.

ECKER, P.; MacRAE, J.; QUELLETTE, V.; and TELFORD, C. *Handbook for Supervisors.* Englewood Cliffs, N. J.: Prentice-Hall, Inc., 1959.

EDGERTON, HAROLD A. "Some Needs in Training Research," *Personnel Psychology,* Vol. VIII, No. 1 (Spring, 1955).

ELY, D. P. "Check Your Resources for Audio-Visual Aids," *New York State Education,* Vol. XLI (April, 1954).

ESSO STANDARD OIL CO. *How to Set Up a Job Training Program,* New York, 1948.

Executive Development Courses in Universities. Studies in Personnel Policy No. 142. New York: National Industrial Conference Board, Inc., 1954.

FILE, Q. W., and REMMERS, H. H. "Studies in Supervisory Evaluation," *Journal of Applied Psychology,* Vol. XXX (1946).

FLYNT, R. C. M. *Use of Training Aids in the Armed Service.* Washington, D.C.: U.S. Office of Education, 1945.

Forms and Records in Personnel Administration. Studies in Personnel Policy No. 175. New York: National Industrial Conference Board, Inc., 1960.

FRYER, DOUGLAS H.; FEINBERG, MORTIMER R.; and ZALKIND, SHELDON S. *Developing People in Industry: Principles and Methods of Training.* New York: Harper & Bros., 1956.

GARDNER, BURLEIGH B., and MOORE, DAVID G. *Human Relations in Industry.* Homewood, Ill.: Richard D. Irwin, Inc., 1955.

GILBERT, DORIS G. *Power and Speed in Reading.* Englewood Cliffs, N.J.: Prentice-Hall, Inc., 1956.

GLOVER, JOHN D., and HOWER, RALPH M. *The Administrator: Cases on Human Relations in Business.* 3d ed. Homewood, Ill.: Richard D. Irwin, Inc., 1957.

GOODACRE, DANIEL. "The Experimental Evaluation of Managerial Training," *Personnel,* May, 1957.

GORDON, ROBERT A., and JOWELL, JAMES E. *Higher Education for Business.* New York: Columbia University Press, 1959.

HAIRE, MASON. *Psychology in Management.* New York: McGraw-Hill Book Co., Inc., 1956.

HALL, SIR NOEL FREDERICK. *The Making of Higher Executives: The Modern Challenges.* New York: School of Commerce, Accounts, and Finance, New York University, 1958.

HALSEY, G. D. *Supervising People.* New York: Harper & Bros., 1953.

————. *Training Employees.* New York: Harper & Bros., 1949.

HARVEY, O. L. "Measuring the Value of Training," *Personnel,* Vol. XXIII, No. 1 (July, 1946).

HILGARD, ERNEST R. *Introduction to Psychology.* 2d ed. New York: Harcourt, Brace & Co., 1957.

————. *Theories of Learning.* 2d ed. New York: Appleton-Century-Crofts, Inc., 1956.

HOLDEN, PAUL E.; FISH, LOUNSBURY S.; and SMITH, HUBERT E. *Top Management Organization and Control.* New York: McGraw-Hill Book Co., Inc., 1951.

How to Establish and Maintain a Personnel Department. American Management Association, Research Report No. 4. New York, 1953.

HULL, THOMAS F. "What Should We Evaluate?" *Journal of the American Society of Training Directors,* Vol. XIII, No. 1 (January, 1959).

HULL, THOMAS F., and POWELL, ROBERT F. "Evaluating a Supervisory Training Program," *Journal of the American Society of Training Directors,* Vol. XIII, No. 11 (November, 1959).

JACKSON, B. B., and MACKINNEY, A. C. "Methods for Determining Training Needs," *Personnel,* Vol. XXXVI, No. 5 (September–October, 1959).

JENNINGS, EUGENE E. "Two Schools of Thought about Executive Development," *Personnel Journal,* Vol. XXVII, No. 10 (March, 1959).

JUCIUS, MICHAEL J. *Personnel Management.* 4th ed. Homewood, Ill.: Richard D. Irwin, Inc., 1959.

JUDSON, HORACE, and BALDRIDGE, KENNETH. *Techniques of Reading.* New York: Harcourt, Brace & Co., 1954.

KELLEY, T. L. *Scientific Method: Its Function in Research and in Education.* New York: Macmillan Co., 1932.

KELLY, WILLIAM A. *Educational Psychology.* 4th rev. ed. Milwaukee: Bruce Publishing Co., 1955.

KIRKPATRICK, DONALD L. "Techniques for Evaluating Training Programs," Part I, *Journal of the American Society of Training Directors,* Vol. XIII, No. 11 (November, 1959).

————. "Techniques for Evaluating Training Programs," Part II, *ibid.,* No. 12 (December, 1959).

————. "Techniques for Evaluating Training Programs," Part III, *ibid.,* Vol. XIV, No. 1 (January, 1960).

————. "Techniques for Evaluating Training Programs," Part IV, *ibid.,* No. 2 (February, 1960).

KOONTZ, HAROLD, and O'DONNELL, CYRIL. *Principles of Management*. 2d ed. New York: McGraw-Hill Book Co., Inc., 1959.

KORNHAUSER, ARTHUR; DUBIN, ROBERT; and ROSS, ARTHUR M. *Industrial Conflict*. New York: McGraw-Hill Book Co., Inc., 1954.

KRUGMAN, H. E. "Management Development Training: Who Profits Most?" *Personnel*, Vol. XXXVI, No. 3 (May–June, 1959).

LAWSHE, C. H., JR. "Eight Ways to Check the Value of a Training Program," *Factory Management and Maintenance*, Vol. CIII (1945).

Leadership on the Job. New York: American Management Association, 1957.

LEARNED, EDMUND P.; ULRICH, DAVID N.; and BOOZ, DONALD R. *Executive Action*. Boston: Graduate School of Business Administration, Harvard University, 1951.

Learning Theory, Personality Theory, and Clinical Research: The Kentucky Symposium. New York: John Wiley & Sons, Inc., 1954.

LEEDY, PAUL D. *Reading Improvement for Adults*. New York: McGraw-Hill Book Co., Inc., 1956.

LESTER, D. B., and OWEN, MARJORIE L. "How to Conduct a Manpower Audit," *Personnel*, Vol. XXXVI, No. 3 (May–June, 1959).

LINDAHL, LAWRENCE G. "How to Build a Training Program," *Personnel Journal*, Vol. XXVII, No. 11 (April, 1949).

LIPPETT, GORDON L., and THIS, LESLIE. "Is Training a Profession?" *Journal of the American Society of Training Directors*, Vol. XIV, No. 4 (April, 1960).

LOVEJOY, LAWRENCE C. *Wage and Salary Administration*. New York: Ronald Press Co., Inc., 1959.

LUNDBERG, G. A. *Social Research: A Study in Methods of Gathering Data*. New York: Longmans, Green & Co., 1929.

MCGREGOR, DOUGLAS. *The Human Side of Enterprise*. New York: McGraw-Hill Book Co., Inc., 1960.

MCLARNEY, WILLIAM J. *Management Training: Cases and Principles*. 3d ed. Homewood, Ill.: Richard D. Irwin, Inc., 1959.

MACRORIE, KEN. *The Perceptive Writer, Reader, and Speaker*. New York: Harper & Bros., Inc., 1959.

MAHLER, WALTER, and MONROE, W. H. *How Industry Determines the Need for and Effectiveness of Training*. P.R.S. Report No. 929. New York: Psychological Corp., 1952.

MAIER, NORMAN R. F. *Principles of Human Relations*. New York: John Wiley & Sons, Inc., 1952.

"Management Development Today," *Management Record*, Vol. XXII, No. 4 (April, 1960).

MARTING, ELIZABETH (ed.). *Top Management Decision Simulation: The AMA Approach*. New York: American Management Association, Inc., 1957.

MAYO, ELTON. *The Human Problems of an Industrial Civilization*. New York: Macmillan Co., 1933.

———. *The Social Problems of an Industrial Civilization*. Boston: Harvard

University, Graduate School of Business Administration, Division of Research, 1945.

MEE, JOHN F. (ed.). *Personnel Handbook.* New York: Ronald Press Co., Inc., 1952.

MERRILL, HORWOOD F., and MARTING, ELIZABETH (eds.). *Developing Executive Skills.* New York: American Management Association, 1958.

METCALF, H. C., and URWICK, L. (eds.). *Dynamic Administration: The Collected Papers of Mary Parker Follet.* New York: Harper & Bros., 1941.

MILES, JOHN R., and SPAIN, CHARLES R. *Audio-Visual Aids in the Armed Services.* Washington, D.C.: American Council on Education, 1947.

MILLER, NORMAN R. "Personnel Problems of Automation," *Personnel Journal,* Vol. XXXVIII, No. 6 (November, 1959).

MURSELL, JAMES L. *Using Your Mind Effectively.* New York: McGraw-Hill Book Co., Inc., 1951.

NEWCOMER, MABEL. *The Big Business Executive.* New York: Columbia University Press, 1955.

NEWMAN, WILLIAM H. *Administrative Action.* New York: Prentice-Hall, Inc., 1951.

NOEL, FRANCIS W. "Principles of Administering Audio-Visual Programs," *Forty-Eighth Yearbook, National Society for the Study of Education.* Chicago: National Society for the Study of Education, 1949.

Organization of Personnel Administration. Studies in Personnel Policy No. 73. New York: National Industrial Conference Board, 1946.

Organization of Staff Functions. Studies in Personnel Policy No. 165. New York: National Industrial Conference Board, 1958.

OSTERBERG, WESLEY, and LINDBOM, THEODORE. "Evaluating Human Relations Training for Supervisors," *Advanced Management,* Vol. XVIII, No. 9 (September, 1953).

PFIFFNER, JOHN M. *The Supervision of Personnel.* 2d ed. New York: Prentice-Hall, Inc., 1958.

PIERSON, FRANK C., and OTHERS. *The Education of American Businessmen.* New York: McGraw-Hill Book Co., Inc., 1959.

PLANTY, EARL G., and FREESTON, J. THOMAS. *Developing Management Ability.* New York: Ronald Press Co., Inc., 1954.

PLANTY, EARL G.; McCORD, W. S.; and EFFERSON, C. A. *Training Employees and Managers for Production and Teamwork.* New York: Ronald Press Co., Inc., 1948.

POLLOCK, ROSS. "A Philosophy of Training," *Journal of the American Society of Training Directors,* Vol. XIII, No. 11 (November, 1959).

POLYA, G. *How to Solve It.* Princeton, N.J.: Princeton University Press, 1946.

RICH, JOSEPH M. "Measuring Supervisory Training through the Sociometric Approach," *Personnel,* Vol. XXIX, No. 1 (July, 1952).

RIEGEL, JOHN W. *Executive Development.* Ann Arbor, Mich.: University of Michigan Press, 1952.

ROETHLISBERGER, F. J. *Management and Morale.* Cambridge: Harvard University Press, 1941.

RUSSELL, BERTRAND. *Authority and the Individual.* New York: Simon and Schuster, Inc., 1949.

SALTONSTALL, ROBERT. *Human Relations in Administration.* New York: McGraw-Hill Book Co., Inc., 1959.

SANDS, LESTER B. *Audio-Visual Procedures in Teaching.* New York: Ronald Press Co., Inc., 1956.

SARTORIOUS, HARVEY A. "The Rise and Fall of the Training Director," *Journal of the American Society of Training Directors,* Vol. XIII, No. 4.

SAVITT, MORRIS A. "The Retention of Management Training," *Journal of the American Society of Training Directors,* Vol. XIII, No. 2 (February, 1959).

SCHELL, ERWIN HASKALL. *The Technique of Executive Control.* 7th ed. New York: McGraw-Hill Book Co., Inc., 1950.

SCHNEIDER, ARNOLD E. "The Function of Education in a Growing Organization," *Journal of the American Society of Training Directors,* Vol. XIV, No. 2 (February, 1960).

SCHULTER, W. C. *How to Do Research.* Englewood Cliffs, N.J.: Prentice-Hall, Inc., 1926.

SCOTT, W. G. "Training Middle Management in Human Relations," *Journal of the American Society of Training Directors,* Vol. XII, No. 4 (April, 1958).

SHAW, PHILLIP B. *Effective Reading and Learning.* New York: Thomas Y. Crowell Co., 1955.

SIMON, HERBERT A. *Administrative Behavior.* 2d ed. New York: Macmillan Co., 1957.

SKINNER, CHARLES E. (ed.). *Educational Psychology.* 3d ed. Englewood Cliffs, N.J.: Prentice-Hall, Inc., 1951.

SOCONY MOBIL OIL CO., INC. *The Supervisor's Key to Employee Job Development,* New York, 1954.

SOCONY MOBIL OIL CO., INC., INDUSTRIAL RELATIONS TRAINING SECTION. *About Conference Leadership.* New York, 1955.

SPRIEGEL, WILLIAM R., and JAMES, VIRGIL A. "Trends in Training and Development, 1930–1957," *Personnel,* Vol. XXXVI, No. 1 (January–February, 1959).

Statements of Personnel Policy. Studies in Personnel Policy No. 169. New York: National Industrial Conference Board, Inc., 1959.

STRYKER, PERRIN. "The Growing Pains of Executive Development," *Advanced Management,* Vol. XIX, No. 8 (August, 1954).

"Study of Learning and Retention, A," *Training by Television,* SDC Report, 476–02–3. Port Washington, Long Island, N.Y.: Special Devices Center, U.S. Navy. Also, "The Comparative Effectiveness of Instruction by Television, Television Recordings, and Conventional Classroom Procedures," SDC Report, 476–02–2.

STUIT, DEWEY B. (ed.). *Personnel Research and Test Development in the Bureau of Naval Personnel.* Princeton, N.J.: Princeton University Press, 1947.

SUBCOMMITTEE ON ECONOMIC STABILIZATION OF THE JOINT COMMITTEE ON THE ECONOMIC REPORT, CONGRESS OF THE UNITED STATES, EIGHTY-FOURTH CONGRESS. *Automation and Technological Change*. Washington, D.C.: Government Printing Office, 1955.

SYMONDS, PERCIVAL M. *What Education Has to Learn from Psychology*. New York: Bureau of Publications, Teachers College, Columbia University, 1958.

Teaching with Radio, Audio, Recording, and Television Equipment. St. Charles, Ill.: DuKane Corp., Joint Committee of the U.S. Office of Education and the Radio-Television Manufacturers Association, 1952–53.

TEAD, ORDWAY. *Administration: Its Purpose and Performance*. New York: Harper & Bros., 1959.

————. *The Art of Leadership*. New York: McGraw-Hill Book Co., 1935.

TENNYSON, W. "Playback of Interviews," *Journal of Personnel and Guidance*, Vol. XXXII (January, 1954).

TERRY, GEORGE R. *Principles of Management*. 3d ed. Homewood, Ill.: Richard D. Irwin, Inc., 1960.

THISDELL, ROBERT A. "Why Not Measure Training Results?" *Journal of the American Society of Training Directors*, Vol. XIII, No. 10 (October, 1959).

THOMAS, V. L. "Let's Use the Flannelboard," *United Business Education Association Forum*, Vol. VII (April, 1953).

THORNDIKE, ROBERT L. *Personnel Selection*. New York: John Wiley & Sons, Inc., 1949.

THORNDIKE, ROBERT L., and HAGEN, ELIZABETH P. *Measurement and Evaluation in Psychology and Education*. New York: John Wiley & Sons, Inc., 1955.

TRICKETT, JOSEPH M. *A Survey of Management Development*. New York: American Management Association, 1954.

U.S. DEPARTMENT OF HEALTH, EDUCATION, AND WELFARE. *Vocational-Technical Education for American Industry*. Circular No. 530. Washington, D.C., 1958.

U.S. DEPARTMENT OF LABOR, BUREAU OF APPRENTICESHIP. *Apprenticeship Pays Dividends*. Washington, D.C., 1957.

U.S. NAVY, BUREAU OF NAVAL PERSONNEL, TRAINING DIVISION. *More Learning in Less Time*. Washington, D.C.: Department of the Navy, 1943.

UNITED WORLD FILMS. *Using Visual Aids in Training*. 16 mm., 14 min., b & w, sound.

URWICK, L. *Management Education in American Business*. New York: American Management Association, 1954.

————. *Notes on The Theory of Organization*. New York: American Management Association, 1952.

————. *The Elements of Administration*. New York: Harper & Bros., 1943.

VISUAL INSTRUCTION BUREAU. *Bulletin Boards for Teaching*. Austin, Tex.: University of Texas, 1954; also, *The Feltboard in Teaching*. 1955.

"A Vital Topic—Business Vitality," *Business Week*, No. 1602 (May 14, 1960).

WEBER, CHRISTIAN. *Reading and Vocabulary Development.* Englewood Cliffs, N.J.: Prentice-Hall, Inc., 1953.

WEINLAND, JAMES D., and GROSS, MARGARET V. *Personnel Interviewing.* New York: Ronald Press Co., Inc., 1952.

WHITNEY, FREDERICK L. *The Elements of Research.* Englewood Cliffs, N.J.: Prentice-Hall, Inc., 1942.

WHYTE, WILLIAM FOOTE. *Man and Organization.* Homewood, Ill.: Richard D. Irwin, Inc., 1959.

WHYTE, WILLIAM H. *Is Anybody Listening?* New York: Simon and Schuster, Inc., 1952.

INDEX

INDEX

Transfer—*Cont.*
  of training
    and attitude of learner, 120
    and instructor and method, 119
    law of, 404
    and mental ability of learner, 119–20
    and situation, 119
TWI; *see* Training Within Industry

U

Unconscious competence, 69
Unconscious incompetence, 69
Understudying, 354
Unexpectedness, as a stimulus, 111
Union co-operation with management in training, 296
United States, industrial growth in, 27–28
United States Department of Commerce, 237
United States Department of Education, 34
United States Department of Labor, 302, 304
United States Office of Education, 304
Unity and simplicity, principle of, 214
Use, law of, 92
USSR, production plans of, 3–4

V

Vestibule school
  example of, 252–53
  overcoming disadvantages of, 306
Vestibule training, 304–9
  advantages of, 305
  disadvantages of, 306

Vestibule training—*Cont.*
  examples of, 306–8
    in commercial bank, 308
    in insurance company, 307
    in restaurant and retail food-store chain, 307–8
Vocational and technical education programs, 302–4

W

Wartime training programs, 36–38
Watson, J. B., 82–83
What Went Wrong (case study), 14–15
White-collar and service organization, 297
Whitney, Frederick L., 430
Wholes, in Gestalt theory, 87–88
Whyte, William Foote, 5
Wilde, Oscar, 78
Wire recorders, as training aids, 208–13
Women workers, generalization on, 73–74
Work force
  analyzing, 152–53
  enlisting in planning, 294–95
Worker; *see* Employee
World War I, and employee training, 32–33
World War II
  as an accelerator for industrial training, 33
  normative survey research during, 392–93
  training during, 34, 391
  training need after, 35
Written materials, as training aids, 216–18

YZ

YMCA, 238
Zalkind, S. S., 221–22

This book has been set on the Linotype in 12 and 10 point Bodoni Book, leaded 1 point. Chapter numbers and titles are in 18 point Lydian Bold. The size of the type page is 27 by 45½ picas.

DATE DUE

SEP 27 '76			
GAYLORD			PRINTED IN U.S A.